Erskine Caldwell

Erskine Caldwell

A Biography

Harvey L. Klevar

The University
of Tennessee Press
Knoxville

Library of Congress Cataloging-in-Publication Data

Klevar, Harvey L., 1934–
    Erskine Caldwell: a biography / Harvey L. Klevar.
        p.   cm.
    Includes bibliographical references and index.
    ISBN 0-87049-774-X (cloth.: alk. paper)
    ISBN 0-87049-775-8 (pbk.: alk. paper)
    1. Caldwell, Erskine, 1903–   —Biography.
    2. Novelists,
American—20th century—Biography.   I. Title.
PS3505.A322Z69   1993
813'.52—dc20
    [B]   92-28494
                        CIP

To my family
Georgie and Leah and Rachel
who endured the making

Contents

Part 5. "Outcast among the Literary Guys"

Illustrations

Acknowledgments

To Virginia Caldwell Hibbs, without whose tireless support and fact the biographical story would have had no beginning or ending.

To James O. Brown, whose encouragement, resources, and work otherwise have gone unrewarded.

To the anonymous Texas foundation whose trust granted a year's living during the writing.

To Marjorie Currey, a gracious expediter who became a valued friend.

To Caldwell people who spent time and life, facts and impressions to help tell the story:

Family: Janet and Guy Gooding, Dabney Caldwell, Erskine P. Caldwell, Jay and Diana Caldwell, Drew and Sandy Fletcher, Rebecca Gooding, Mary Maner and once—Caldwell wife, June Caldwell Martin.

Special friends and associates: Corrie Wren, Mrs. Dorothy Barrow Atwell, Ben Farley, Guy Owen, Betty Pustarfi, Roger Straus, Mrs. Anne Lewis, Mrs. Bessie Jones, C. Waller Barrett, Ray McIvor, Ed Butler, Eddie Schwartz, Elizabeth Crotty, Vicki Goldberg, Zeb Connelly, and Dr. Bradley Gordon.

Dartmouth College, Baker Library and Special Collections people: Walter W. Wright, Edward C. Lathem, and Phillip Cronenwett; Suzy Schwoerke, Pat Fisken, Janice Ouellette, and Ken Kramer.

To readers and editors, whose careful regard helped shape the story's telling: Edwin T. Arnold, Sylvia Cook, Stan Ivester, Carol Orr, and Alexa Selph.

Introduction

I wanted to keep my private life in
isolation and at the same time felt a
compelling need to express myself
in some manner without prying
curiosity by another person.

       —Erskine Caldwell, 1987

Ever since my rural Texas childhood back in the early forties, Erskine
Caldwell has stirred a variety of wonders within me. The first resulted
from my surreptitious introduction to one of his writings during that
long-ago time.

Even then guilty of prying into other people's private lives, I discovered one day a copy of *Tobacco Road* hidden beneath some clothes in my
mother's dresser. Because books of any kind were unusual in our post-
Depression home, I guessed that one so carefully cached must be de-
lightfully sinful. Thereafter, whenever my parents were away, I read as
much as I could in stolen installments.

Ultimately, I discovered nothing in *Tobacco Road* either to fuel my excitement or to stimulate my interest. As one who hated turnips, raw or
cooked, I could not understand why Jeeter Lester, no matter how hungry, would try to steal them while others cavorted in the sand. And as for
Lov and Ellie May, Dude and the rest of the clan, they were too much
like our country neighbors up the road for their antics to hold my interest. So my first Caldwell-wonder: why had my mother chosen to read the
book, and why had she felt she should hide it from me?

The next wonder was not provoked until a couple of decades later. By
then armed with a professional excuse for peering into other people's
lives, I became involved in a study of cultural patterns within southern
writing. More specifically, I was curious about how personal experience
combined with sociocultural influences to inform fiction. How might a
writer's religious background blend with folk-spiritual expressions to
shape fictional translations of that experience? Within that context I
read all of Caldwell's works and was caught by dual wonders: why did his
early fiction seem so vital, and his later, so sterile?

Caldwell's early writings were especially perplexing. What literary al-
chemy had he concocted to make his early books—*Tobacco Road, God's
Little Acre, Journeyman*—and their characters—Jeeter Lester, Ty Ty
Walden and Griselda, Semon Dye—so memorable? His folk were grotesquely distorted, antically outrageous beings who almost instinctively
defied social conventions. His landscapes were eroded and pock-
marked, withered and made desolate by a combination of greed and
cosmic disdain. What was it about the lives of Caldwell's godforsaken
creatures that would appeal to millions of readers?

For those seeking clues to Caldwell's literary intentions, for those
looking for thematic coherence within his writings, he publicly offered
little direction. He volunteered no tell-tale beliefs, values, or intentions
to guide them; he was only a story teller. Neither did those stories yield
easy clues—of persistent themes or motifs, symbols or images—to direct the confused through his fictional mazes. Seekers—readers, reviewers, critics, all—were caught within the webs of those ambiguities
spun by Caldwell's stories.

With Depression experiences still recent in memory, most Caldwell
readers recognized his most obvious concern. Capitalism had failed;
once-landed freeholders now barely survived as sharecroppers. Ab-
sentee landlords lived in city seclusion. Bankers ran to greedy profit.
And striking, frustrated workers fought to find meaning through work.
Ultimately an economic system aimed at profiting from land and the labor of men had impoverished them both. That much about Caldwell's
writings seemed clear. That message, however, was a common one of
the times, not unique enough to explain the fascination with his uncommon stories.

Just as commonly, those Caldwell readers who weren't bemused either guffawed or snickered at the comic antics of those characters and
situations he created. While Lov Bensey clutches his turnips and resists
the "horsing" seduction tactics of the harelipped Ellie May Lester, her
mother, Ada, clubs him into groggy submission. Or Sister Bessie naively
accepts the "changing of the beds" regimen in a whorehouse that the
Lesters have mistaken for a hotel with more men than beds. In a short
story a newlywed farmer is proud of the intimate "pink things" his wife

wears. Wishing to impress his friends with her sophisticated tastes, he hoists her dress above her head. The boys whistle and rub their eyes. Her nakedness reveals no pink things like those found in fancy mail-order catalogs. The canon of Caldwell's early writings was rife with characters and situations whose antic behaviors defied both convention and good taste.

But between Caldwell's social protest and his comic vision delicately balanced a more ineffable—what? Paradox? Ambiguity? Religiosity? Or some other quality that eluded those who sought definition? Some early critics like Joseph Warren Beach rhetorically danced around it. Though Caldwell's characters represented "degraded types" defying "the manner of civilized beings," they also represented "strange flowers of humanity" emerging from their "dunghill soil of cultural degradation."[1] Another scholar, W. M. Frohock, after searching long in the forties, threw up his critical hands: "Caldwell's novels suffer from a multiplicity of meanings which are incompatible with one another."[2] Both before and during that time, other critics and professionals had placed him within the ranks of Faulkner and Hemingway, Steinbeck and Anderson. Faulkner magnanimously included Caldwell, along with himself, among America's literary Olympians, and in a final tribute, reckoned that *God's Little Acre* and his many fine short stories should be enough for any man. Despite the acclaim, attempts to unravel the mystery in Caldwell's early fiction defied even the most earnest. Until recently most critics remained puzzled about what combination of factors gave his writings their motive force.

James Korges, in his *Erskine Caldwell* pamphlet, argued persuasively for a critical reappraisal of this much-slighted serious writer.[3] At least his early works and nonfiction merited such attention. Scott MacDonald responded with the observation that Caldwell's use of repetition as technique in his short fiction transformed what seemed inane simplicity into the complexity of conscious craft.[4] Yet readers seeking a coherent interpretation of his fiction were confounded because his writings explored "the mystifying incoherence of real life."[5]

The first to succeed at least partially in deciphering the integers of Caldwell's mystifying equation was James Devlin.[6] He recognized that central to Caldwell's vision was the duality of human nature, the conflict between reason and feeling. His folk, Devlin observed, were creatures biologically determined to follow instinct in a loveless universe, because only those survival forces—hunger, sex, movement—gave meaning to their otherwise futile lives.

Sylvia Cook, a recent Caldwell critic, acknowledges the difficulty of categorizing his writing. His thirties works were obviously more compelling than his later ones, yet she sees within them all evidence of a conscientious practitioner of his craft. That critical blank between social criticism and antic humor in his best stories is filled by a static dynamic that transfixes his characters as they squirm "between the antics *and* motivations of a depraved and deprived human nature" (my emphasis).[7] In short, Cook estimates that Caldwell's "central concern with poverty in all its material, moral, social, and spiritual manifestations" lends his fiction a seriousness that too many critics have failed to acknowledge.[8]

Such careful reappraisals of Caldwell's writings are past due. They argue for him a literary respectability long denied by that establishment responsible for canonizing significant writers, those whose artistry offers unique insights into the human predicament. Certainly Caldwell's writings were not as inclusive or as tantalizingly complex as Faulkner's. Neither were they as starkly original or as carefully crafted as those of Hemingway. Comparatively, however—as recent criticism reveals—at least Caldwell's early writings should have granted him a portion of that respectability heaped upon Steinbeck, Faulkner, and Hemingway, all Nobel Prize recipients.

Before Steinbeck, Caldwell had condemned that system whose practices and neglect had impoverished the land and its people. He, too, had used biological determinism as the motivating force for his characters. His striking Will Thompson, before Steinbeck's Tom Joad, had challenged an industrial system that denied men the dignity and security of work. Yet a critical reappraisal of Steinbeck's early works had earned him the honor of a belated Nobel award. Why, I questioned, had not Caldwell also been granted a similar grace?

Before recent critics had cast about to seek Caldwell's larger meanings and strengths, I had remained bemused by my own private wonder.

What was that variable, that crucial essence, that made his pre-1940s fiction so much more arresting, more vital to me than almost all of his subsequent writings? I strained to find the difference.

Caldwell's universe did not vibrate with a hum of sacred forces and meanings. Within his still-lifescapes little moved—blacks moved quietly in the background, and automobiles were manic and noisy. Almost all other activity, however, was not so cosmically benign. Whenever people otherwise moved, they had been quickened by instincts, those needs that had always propelled creation from one generation to the next. They both searched for, and stole, food; they mated wherever their urgings gripped them. What marked them as different from animals, however, were their spiritual yearnings, their movements toward the still dance of transcendence.

Through his longer fiction at least, Caldwell celebrated eating and sexual coupling as forms of sacred communion, as transfigurations provoking awed public observance. But more than that, his otherwise comic beings stretched toward hope and occasionally longed for cosmic epiphanies. Some stared through a crack in a wall to see "clear to the back side of heaven." Others attended bogus revivals, "came through for the Lord," and then, emptied, lay transfixed, "staring at the heavens."

Caldwell's post-thirties writings, however, marked some changes. They included no characters motivated by cosmic inclinations, no outrageous grotesques moved by spiritual longings. Increasingly thereafter his figures became only social deviants. No longer unconscious and distorted victims of life forces urging generation, they instead were more respectable people seeking love, sexual gratification, and security within an otherwise meaningless, modern world.

Why had Caldwell's writings changed so dramatically within that short span between 1935 and 1940? Many before had asked similar questions but discovered no obvious answers. Caldwell's own reckoning, that the career-life of a writer was only a decade, seemed contrived. True, other writers of his generation—Faulkner and Hemingway, Steinbeck and Fitzgerald—had likewise experienced declines after periods of significant creativity. But unlike their writings, Caldwell's traced no gradual descent. Though various critics granted him the transitional

grace of his 1940 *Trouble in July* work or selected later writings, my
reading of that and his subsequent fiction noted an essential and precipitous difference between that ever-expansive body of writings and his
thirties canon.

I puzzled. Nothing in Caldwell's public life or literary record offered
adequate explanation. True, the Depression with its various exactions
had gradually wound down. Electricity, radios, and improved roads had
relieved the parochial isolation of even people like the Lesters and the
Waldens. Yet in the early forties and long thereafter, the dispossessed
still haunted the South; witness, they still lived up the road from me.

Caldwell's publishing record indicated a change of focus in the late
thirties. For a period of three years he had written almost exclusively
nonfiction, mostly photojournalistic accounts to accompany Margaret
Bourke-White's work. But I believed that such experiences, such redi-
rections, should not have affected Caldwell's fiction-writing ability as
profoundly as something else—perhaps personal—apparently had.

So I pondered and mused for a few years until the spring of 1977. I had
written to Caldwell. Hesitant about announcing my true biographical
hopes, I veiled them behind a credible agenda. As one long fascinated by
the coincidence of southern violence with religion, I wished to gain his
impressions through conversation. He congenially agreed.

My initial meeting with Caldwell provided impressions that later associations confirmed. He was a painfully diffident man, caring, but so
taciturn that conversation did not flow easily. He graciously and economically answered all questions but initiated no topics or queries of his
own. Shortly I followed his lead. We allowed long silences to hang between us as we sat in the April shade of the patio fronting Caldwell's
Dunedin, Florida, pool.

After some two hours of desultory talk, I dared the big question.
Would he mind if I attempted to write his biography? His immediate response, "Go ahead, I can't stop you," I explained, was not enough. I
would need his cooperation, his support, and access to all correspondence, records, and files. Because I realized how stressful that would be
for him and Virginia, his wife, and because I had no credentials as a biographer except a long-standing interest in his writings, I assured him

that I expected no immediate answer. I would forward a copy of my Caldwell-O'Connor dissertation and other writings for his evaluation. Then he could decide.

Virginia had been an interested but silent participant in this portion of our exchange. She then verbalized their initial apprehensions. A few years before, someone else had researched and written a biography, without the benefit of access to Caldwell's files. The Caldwells had been unhappy with some of his assumptions presented as fact. If Caldwell eventually agreed to my request, I was neither to read that person's study nor contact him for information. They did not want his interpretations to bias my own. As uneasy as I was with what that biographer could only perceive as a personal and professional slight, I recognized the condition as a necessity I accepted.

That day with the Caldwells also fed other impressions that later contacts reconfirmed. Caldwell was himself very much a self-determined individual. At the same time he obviously loved Ginny very deeply and depended much upon her guidance on issues that he himself had not yet firmly resolved. Because Virginia seemed to like me—and I certainly liked her very much—I felt that she could tip the final decision in my favor. It also was obvious that she, more than Caldwell, would welcome a biography; it could, she felt, help recall him to that respect that had been too long denied him. And so I left the Caldwells to mull what I only much later came to realize must have been an anguished decision. For a person always as anxiously private as Caldwell had been, the prospect of having someone pry so purposefully into his life must have been a dire one indeed.

A month or so later, nonetheless, Caldwell graciously responded positively to my request. He and Virginia would help me in every way possible. With his written permission I could have access to all correspondence and other materials secured at the four libraries that held various portions of his collection. By the summer of 1977, therefore, I began the process of trying to resolve my wonder about the origins of those changes reflected in Caldwell's post-thirties fiction.

Reconstructing Caldwell's life story proved to be a greater challenge than I had anticipated. Almost no correspondence or written records existed to provide insight into that period between his birth and his late adolescence—and not much more to chart the next few years as well. Most who had known him during that time either had died or had only vague and generalized recollections of him. That portion of his life, then, is necessarily shaped and informed by stories, those told about him and by him.

Among those stories told by him, *The Sacrilege of Alan Kent* is seminal. Though he often cautioned against using that work for biographical purposes, the evidence for legitimately doing so is persuasive. Places lived and injuries remembered, experiences marked and situations described consistently are either confirmed or elaborated upon in writings as admittedly factual as *Deep South*, *In Search of Bisco*, and *With All My Might*. A bee sting to the eye, hot grease down the collar, lonely wanderings in urban tenement districts—such events and occasions plus many more evocatively sketched what Caldwell elsewhere claimed as biographical fact. And finally, Virginia, who knew him so well, has noted: "Oh, yes. Alan Kent is definitely Erskine remembering."[9]

Essences from *The Sacrilege*, combined with clues from a variety of other sources, thus inform my story about the first twenty years of Caldwell's life. My reconstructions of his life and career subsequent to those years I offer with more assurance. They have been selectively shaped but are supported as faithfully as possible with a blend of evidence drawn from written materials, personal testimonies, and Caldwell's own public accounts.

Because Caldwell was first and foremost a storyteller, he could seldom resist embroidering fact with fantasy for the sake of story, that of his own life included. In many instances, I believe, he consciously used "creative license" for the sake of his readers and listeners; he wished to avoid boring them with pedestrian details. In other instances he both consciously and unconsciously used hyperbole, exaggeration, and emended elaborations to justify both his writing career and the events of his personal life. Many times, I am convinced, he did not intentionally try to mislead. Rather, what he publicly claimed or wrote was what he himself had come to believe—about his career, his former wives, and others.

Especially in situations where Caldwell's actions or behavior might have violated his own basic values or sense of responsibilities was he prone to revising his history. On one occasion, for instance, I had sent him a manuscript section that cast aspersions on his behavior toward one of his children. He became very upset and responded with a denial of all I had claimed. Fortunately I had written documentation—some in his own hand from that other time—to support my version of the events. Along with copies of that, I forwarded a copy of an assurance he had once offered to ease my early concerns. At one point I had worried about hurting him by recording painful events he might have forgotten. He had countered: "As for my feelings I suggest that you keep this in mind: The surest and most effective way to hurt my feelings—and Virginia's feelings, too—is for you to write a dull book about me. Everything goes, and that means the license to be lively and unrestrained."[10] Caldwell answered my defense with silence. Subsequently he apparently read only a very brief portion of the final manuscript that I sent for his information and comment. Based upon that, he had wished me well in placing it with a publisher.

My attempts to write a lively yet faithful account of his life were dogged by more than the challenge of collecting sufficient facts to weave into his biography and then balancing those facts against Caldwell's own versions of that story. Because he had lived such a long life, much had to be condensed, paraphrased, or omitted totally for brevity's sake. Accordingly, the chronicle of his later years is especially abbreviated. But he had cautioned against my writing a dull book, and his life became increasingly unremarkable, both literarily and personally.

Caldwell's lifelong tendency toward seclusion, his removal from the larger world except as a distanced figure in the crowd, likewise has shaped my telling of his story. The span of his life encompassed events and discoveries and attitudes more compelling than in any comparable period of time before. During his childhood rural people traveled in mule-drawn wagons, read—if at all—by kerosene lamps, and came together to entertain each other with stories about families, the antic neighbors up the road, or the shadowy idiosyncrasies of people black and white. Later, automobiles and rural electrification, radios and black-and-white movies with companion newsreels, changed people's travel habits, their nighttime home activities, and the types and scope of stories they listened to and watched, rather than told. Later yet supersonic airplanes zoomed them from place to place, and television beamed stories about Mayberry, R.F.D., and world events directly into their homes. White-robed lynchings gave way to candlelit civil-rights vigils; Father Coughlin lost his radio listeners. Eventually viewers watched as televised sketches of Judge Julius Hoffman and the Chicago Seven stirred their political sensitivities.

Beyond the obvious, so much more defined the nation and the world in which Caldwell so long lived and wrote. Weaving the threads of his story into the cultural tapestry of the times would have enriched it, given it a contextual focus. Finally, however, I allowed Caldwell's life itself to define the parameters of its story. He had always celebrated experience selectively, only as it had marked and defined him. I, therefore, followed those chartings that he—through correspondence, writings, and public speaking—had noted. The topics of his concern, I estimated, mirrored more essentially what was defining him than any social or cultural constructions I might impose upon them or him.

The consequence of that choice is that Caldwell's biography is selectively circumscribed, contextually self-defined. That seems appropriate since neither social nor public externals made his life remarkable. Rather, what makes his story arresting is the life he lived privately and through his fiction.

Because Caldwell's fiction always emerged from that private self, that synthesizer of self-perception and experience, Sylvia Cook's insight into his earlier writings is provocative on both the fictional and personal levels. Through his fiction, she believes, he sought "to explore . . . the connection between the comic futility of the human predicament, reaching for the spirit but mocked by the flesh."[11] And so did Caldwell's life also trace the outlines of his own unique human predicament.

Like so many others, Caldwell carefully balanced the comic and the tragic. He smiled wryly at his foibles. He endured stoically the pain of those outrages that he, rightly or wrongly, perceived either others or fate unkindly had hurled against him. And throughout it all he wrote—as if his essential identity, his personal fate, demanded it.

The wonder of it all is Erskine Caldwell's story.

# Part 1
The Web the Story Spins

Chapter 1

The circumstances of Erskine Caldwell's birth on December 17, 1903, scarcely hinted at a life more auspicious than his immediate surroundings. The house was unpainted inside and out.[1] Its bare, pine-board floors, walls, and ceilings appeared especially bleak during that winter-dreary season when he was born. A barren landscape stretched across hills to the horizon. Only tattered cotton-shreds drooped from shriveled stalks to break the monotony of fields surrounding the house.

None but the most dutiful could have transformed such hustings into the bountiful fields and vineyards of the Lord. But the father's pastoral charge demanded no less. The Associate Reformed Presbyterian church that Reverend Ira Sylvester Caldwell tended in the Coweta County settlement of White Oak, Georgia, was small. Its congregation numbered fewer than a hundred, and its accompanying Moreland mission-congregation was even smaller. Both were some ten horse-and-buggy miles from the larger town of Newnan. None of these considerations, however, dimmed the enthusiasm of either the young pastor or Caroline, his wife.

Erskine Preston Caldwell's christening service itself became a matter for story. His first name honored the memory of Ebenezer Erskine, the European founder of his father's church; the Preston name united him with his mother's respected patriarchal ancestors. The ceremony itself threw into light relief the dimensions of his parents' respective characters.

As Caroline Preston Bell told the story, Erskine was dressed in his white ceremonial finery.[2] She was to hold him until Ira took the child to complete the ritual. All proceeded well until she looked down and saw that Erskine had wet her dress. Fearing that the telltale stain would cause congregational tittering, Caroline clutched the child to her bosom when Ira reached for him to perform the service. What followed was a

Caroline Preston Bell, 1901. From *With All My Might* by Erskine Caldwell, published by Peachtree Publishers, Atlanta. Reprinted by permission of the publisher and the Estate of Erskine Caldwell.

comic scene of wife's grasping and pastor-husband's pulling. Finally he recognized the problem and proceeded with an adapted ritual. The incident nonetheless provided some humorous diversion for the congregation.

Other stories from Caldwell's few White Oak years also became a portion of his shaping legend. In prosaic terms he would one day acknowledge the commonplace: "How you behave has to do with your training. What your education was. The inheritance. The influences."[3]

As Caldwell's personal life and career would increasingly reveal, the effects of those influences, those inheritances, were to be profoundly lasting. And his mother's heritage, even more than his father's, would be translated to him. Caroline Preston Bell, more informally called Carrie or even Tarrie by her son, had her beginnings in the genteel environment of Staunton, Virginia. Although but one of six daughters and two sons of a C&O Railroad officer, her lineage had once been more aristocratic. English and Scottish ancestors from both sides of the family had

Ira Sylvester Caldwell, 1895. From *With All My Might* by Erskine Caldwell, published by Peachtree Publishers, Atlanta. Reprinted by permission of the publisher and the Estate of Erskine Caldwell.

Caroline and Erskine Caldwell, Prosperity, S.C., 1908. From *With All My Might* by Erskine Caldwell, published by Peachtree Publishers, Atlanta. Reprinted by permission of the publisher and the Estate of Erskine Caldwell.

fought honorably in the Revolution, a fact that earned her entry into the Daughters of the American Revolution. Strains of the gentried South Carolina Carters and Henrys had mixed heavily with the Bells' sense of propriety.

The Bells' impeccability extended beyond blood to religion. Their Presbyterian heritage hummed true since their Calvinist conversion generations ago. And Caroline was not one to deny her religious charge. In her generation she had often reminded Caldwell that his "forefathers exiled themselves and came to this country rather than come under the heel of totalitarianism."[4] Such orthodoxy she valued as a pearl of great price.

Schooled in proper comportment and self-assured charm, Caroline rounded off her education at the esteemed Mary Baldwin College in her hometown. There she earned an A.B. in English and classical languages. After completing her studies, she taught briefly at Agnes Scott College in Georgia before assuming a position at Due West Female College, a Presbyterian institution in South Carolina. Distraught after attending a relative's funeral, she had returned there via an evening train. Her obvious distress caught the sympathy of a young ministerial student traveling to Erskine College, an Associate Reformed Presbyterian institution in the same town. Family story tells that Ira Sylvester Caldwell vowed "then and there" that one day he would marry the young woman.[5]

Ira Sylvester, variously called I. S., Ira, or Bud, scarcely seemed the type Caroline would have found appealing. Although rangily handsome, he generally appeared disheveled or rumpled and hid his occasional stuttering behind a tobacco-chewing taciturnity. His background, moreover, was as unpretentious as hers was genteel. His ancestors, driven from Scotland for their religious convictions, became freeholding settlers in South Carolina regions. No aristocrats among them, his folk had remained generally unschooled landsmen and farmers.

Still, superficially, Ira Sylvester's religious credentials perhaps appeared as more doctrinaire than Caroline's. The American generations of the Associate Reformed Presbyterians carefully nurtured a rigorous, Puritan-like orthodoxy that Ebenezer Erskine built into the foundations of his purified church of reform. Within Bud's family, nonetheless, only his mother remained a staunch heir to Calvin and the ARP Church. Neither the father nor any of the six Caldwell children regularly attended religious services.[6] Because the mother "lived for it six days of the week and counted the days to Sunday," Ira sometimes accompanied her to church services. All acknowledged, however, that he preferred to "read books all Sunday long."

Bud's quiet decision to begin studying for the ministry at age twenty-three, therefore, mystified those who knew him well. When questioned he would say no more than that his mother had requested it. After that, moreover, she stopped bothering the other family members "about going to church or praying or Bible reading." More than a divine calling apparently had pushed Ira into accepting his ministerial charge.

At the time Ira began his ministerial studies, the seminary associated with Erskine College stressed the documents of the Westminster Confession of Faith and the teachings of the Larger and Shorter Catechisms. Puritan-like refrains—predestination, an individual's solitary and vertical relationship with God, reality as a form of sacred metaphor, the signing graces of duty, work, and frugality—all were incorporated into each day's living hymn. Ira, nonetheless, reduced them to a more comfortable rendition. He always "thought the Christian should be more concerned about bringing heaven to earth than about 'going to heaven.'"

Carrie and Ira's relationship mellowed through long association after their meeting on the train. Regardless of their romantic impulses, practicality and economic realities demanded that they defer marriage until after he was ordained. Throughout that seven-year wait, Ira's actions were exemplary. When he interrupted his studies to fight in the Spanish-American War, he wrote daily letters to Carrie, who had continued her Due West teaching career. In all matters he had proved himself both conscientiously dutiful and honorably responsible.

Consequently, on October 16, 1901, seven months after Ira's ordination, he and Carrie were married. He was thirty-one, and she, twenty-eight, and finally they stood ready to go wherever the Presbytery Board of the ARP Church sent them. That first assignment had been to White Oak, where the Erskine Caldwell family story properly began. Both spouses confronted individually taxing situations.

Facing a traditional, rurally undereducated congregation, Ira immediately began preaching and acting upon the tenets of his modified doctrine: education is not a prerequisite for salvation, but assuredly enlightens blind faith. He, therefore, first promoted relocation of the schoolhouse from "across the creek, nearer to the center of the community."[7] Afterwards he secured a teacher from Due West to help him teach in the school. From the pulpit, he urged parents to live frugally and, if necessary, to borrow money to support further education for their sons and daughters. For all of this and more, Ira was fondly remembered, but essentially he always lived and preached the same message—faith might merit heavenly reward but education represented its earthly foundation.

Carrie's situation, however, was not so satisfying. She had traded her semi-independent and self-defining teacher's role for that of being a pastor's wife and helpmate. White Oak's limited and rude environment was certainly not as genteel as that of Staunton or as satisfying as that of Due West. Community attitudes frowned upon her teaching in the revitalized school. She, however, could teach—was expected to teach—Sunday School, cater to the "country-spread dinners," and otherwise respectfully contribute to church and community.

Such narrow public definitions exacted costs that Carrie reckoned with almost a modern woman's measure: "I went with Father wherever he felt called to go, and suffered, bled, and worse than died backing him while he preached and practiced in life and works, peace on earth, good will to men."[8] Her sacrifice of self she could justify only with the trusting faith of Calvinist martyrs. Her identity, her rewards would flow from her husband's work in the fields of the Lord, in this instance the cotton-bearing fields of the White Oak vicinity.

The Caldwells had thus lived in White Oak some two years before Erskine's birth. A Dr. Levi Young delivered the child while various White Oak people claimed attendance. Although each cited differing years for the event, two other community couples marked their weddings and anniversaries by the December 17 date.[9]

Yet that same community concern that elevated a minister and his family likewise allowed nothing to escape its scrutiny. According to the local Miss Eunice Chesnut, Caroline Caldwell "didn't know how to manage" the child.[10] Such oblique criticism, however, did not keep the lady's mother from making "Erskine his first pair of pants," or the White Oak Carmichaels from naming their son Ira Caldwell. And finally, the community allowed that Erskine "certainly had a faithful father and good mother." What seems obvious though is that first in White Oak and later wherever the Caldwells served, a similar small-town vigilance was a constant and straining presence. Nothing any of them might do would escape notice and judgment of the community and the congregation.

Erskine's childhood incidents, some humorous and others traumatic, thus captured the community's interest even as they generated those stories that would shape his consciousness and mold his identity.[11] Once crawling free on the floor during a congregational meeting, Erskine randomly bit ladies' legs. Another time his mischief was not so cute. As a child who would "drink everything," he swallowed a slug of kerosene from the lamp supply. The fortunate resolution of that incident perhaps confirmed for Carrie, and ultimately Caldwell, the moral that she always drew from another more frightening story.

One day, bustling about the kitchen preparing a meal, Carrie had turned her back upon the toddler, who was in the room. Meanwhile he had wandered to the stove and tipped a pan of hot grease onto his chest and arms. The burns were serious and potentially fatal. When the doctor finally arrived, he could prescribe little more than the almost hourly application of unguents and clean bandages. Months of uninterrupted care from a loving mother had saved Erskine's life. But equally as compelling for the purposes of moral was an observation the doctor allegedly had made: "Considering the close calls this child has had, the good Lord must be saving him for something special."[12] His casual statement of wonder was one Carrie would tell time and again with perhaps a dual purpose. For her son its repetition could speak almost with the urgency of prophecy; for herself it could serve as a guilty reminder that a responsible mother must always be vigilant.

Though Caldwell himself did not recall the incident, Carrie's recitations seared the details of the event into his consciousness. In *The Sacrilege of Alan Kent,* a thinly veiled rhapsody-dirge of his early life, he relived the horror: "The grease flowed down my open collar and ate into

my navel. I yelled. The buttons on my underclothes became hot suddenly like the grease, and burned deep red holes in my tender flesh.
Only after seven months of pain could I sit upright in bed without
screaming in agony."[13] The experience was Erskine's, but the story was
Carrie's.

How special the child was really to be, at least for the Caldwells, was
reaffirmed in yet another way only a short while later. Caroline's recurring "woman's problems" urged a medically and socially more congenial location than White Oak offered. The family, therefore, relocated to
Prosperity, South Carolina, only a few miles distant from Due West with
its pleasant memories and associations. There doctors determined that
Carrie's condition called for a hysterectomy; Erskine would remain the
Caldwells' only child.

Caldwell's autobiographical accounts and his life experiences both argue the effects his being an only child "saved for something special"
were to have. Each parent helped shape the child and eventually mold
the man both through direction and example. Yet too little attention
from one and too much from the other created the person who would
one day spin into stories a mixture of both his mother's and father's concerns.

Because "I. S. was never around the house very much—he was always
out seeing about people, ministering"—Carrie most directly affected the
child during his most formative years.[14] Her values and concerns, her
priorities and directives were constants defining the scope of Erskine's
behavior and activities.

Raised as a southern lady, rigidly staunch in her Presbyterian orthodoxy, Carrie was neither a warm nor a flexible individual. "A very
strongly disciplined person, she always sat so that her posture was perfectly straight, her back not touching the chair while her ankles touched
each other but slightly." Always "very erect, very proper . . . she preferred tea to coffee because the English drank tea . . . and anything English
was proper."[15]

Even as Carrie's gentility required its proper decorum, time and work
likewise demanded her equal respect. Because not a moment was to be
wasted, she worked as if time were the measure of a person's merit. Well

into her eighties she would energetically dust with one hand while she patted her chin strap—a beauty aid to discourage sagging muscles— with the other. "Her life was so organized, it was like she was going to use every minute of her time," a niece observed.[16] But Carrie's obsessive bustling allegedly did not create tension: "Her home was disciplined and well-run, but it wasn't tense."

Carrie's behavior and strict sense of order were not the consequence of casually accepted practices and values. Rather, they flowed from a conscious effort to regulate and judge her daily life according to Puritan-like norms and statements of purpose. During an unspecified period of her later life, she outlined those principles that served as reminders to what otherwise might have become a lax conscience:

> An ideal for me. How to live for a day—
> (a) Early-Morning: hard labor of some kind.
> (b) Afternoon: busy hands, concentrated mind.
> (c) Evening: cultural pursuits! social recreation.

Elaborating upon these general goals, she applied the particulars to her own situation.

> (a) [mornings] - make the beds, clean floor or rugs, polish furniture; cook; wash dishes; market; write-translate.
> (b) [afternoons] - sew, knit, mend, paint, practice music, mold clay, work puzzle.
> (c) [evenings] - read, play games, theater, concert, lecture, conversation.[17]

No matter that she did not play a musical instrument or that concerts, lectures, and theater productions were not among the benefits Prosperity or the Caldwells' other out-of-the-way locations offered; these expressions represented aspirations, not actual accomplishments. They were but the practicalities of a Presbyterian orthodoxy that she observed for herself and as an example to others. As Caldwell one day acknowledged, "Now, if it's true that there is a universal Puritan tradition, possibly that influenced me a great deal in that I knew certain limits of conduct, training, or whatever there was in my environment. I knew certain concepts of morality."[18]

Carrie's attitudes and habits, combined with the contemporary definition of an acceptable role for a woman, proved to be telling in her interactions with the child. Limited in other expressions of self, she, like so
many other American mothers, devoted herself zealously to being a very
good mother and, in her case, one whose primary concern was that
Erskine live and act according to her values and dictates. Family story
affirms that Carrie "kept a very close watch" over him.[19] She was very
careful about where he went and whom he was with, because she didn't
want any influence "from the wrong kind." She "would brook no un-
couth word" or behavior. And though Erskine's "greatest interest in life
[at that stage] was going barefooted" like most other rural children of
that time, she had forbidden him that pleasure.[20]

Carrie's vigilance proved to have both immediate and lifelong effects.
Those writings that emerge from Caldwell's childhood memories suggest that her restrictions forced him into situations of poignant isolation,
longing, and escape. Writing *In Search of Bisco*—and later repeating the
telling in *With All My Might*—Caldwell harrowed his White Oak years
for a metaphor to capture the social and personal costs of separating
people on the basis of color. The account is just as compelling, however,
as a reminiscence that reveals both Carrie's character and her measure
of control over the child.

Through time Bisco, the son of nearby black sharecroppers, had become Erskine's only playmate.[21] Bisco often came to play at the Caldwells', and Erskine likewise visited his home. Sometimes his playmate's
mother, "a huge, soft fleshed woman," allowed both children to sit together on her lap while she sang mournful songs to them. One evening
Erskine followed his playmate home, where he found the cabin warmed
by a pungent pitch-pine fire and permeated by the odor of frying pork
chops. The mother welcomed and fed him and later prepared Bisco for
bed. Erskine also undressed so he could sleep over with his friend.
Bisco's mother, however, gently redressed Erskine and started leading
him home through the darkness. She knew his mother would want him
to come home and sleep in his own bed. Pleading, begging, and crying
had no softening effect.

The black mother and Erskine met Ira, lantern in hand, coming to meet them. Not only did that pale of light cast the warmth of the shadowy mother into the background; it likewise figured into relief those essential qualities and concerns of his respective parents. "In the dim light" his father appeared to be neither surprised nor angry. Yet he shook his head to Erskine's begging that he "spend the night with Bisco under the thick, warm quilts." The child began to cry when he had had to release the woman's warm hand. When Ira picked him up, however, Erskine stopped crying and put his arms around his father's neck to keep warm in the cold night. As they walked home, Ira told him that Tarrie wanted him to sleep in his own bed so she would know where he was.

By contrast, Caldwell's description of Tarrie is starkly factual: "Just before reaching our house, I saw my mother waiting for us in the lighted doorway. . . . When I begged her to let me spend the next night with Bisco, she said it was time to put a stop to anything like that and that I was never to go to his house again." Her reasoning—"that I was white and he was black"— delineated boundaries of southern custom and maternal expectations. Both haunted Caldwell long past puzzled innocence: "All that took place a long time ago in years. Nevertheless in time and implication the recollection of it has continued to remain clear and meaningful and unchanging." A yearning for friendship and a mother's warm lap, a father's cradling care and his own mother's careful expectations: all were to remain meaningful and unchanging.

Caldwell's characterization of his parents—the mother exactingly inflexible and the father sympathetically accepting—is a varying constant throughout those writings that rely upon memory and experience. In Prosperity a parishioner wanted to take the six-year-old Erskine to a circus that had come to town.[22] Concerned about respectability, Carrie vacillated. Ira finally decided the issue by declaring that the entire family should go; his decision did not ease Carrie's continuing concerns about what people might think.

Despite local customs, Carrie's sense of propriety came to mark her son as different in other, more telling, ways. Disdaining common dress for boys, she designed for him clothes that "could best be called a Russian blouse with short pants."[23] And though Ira did not outwardly counter his wife on this issue, on another, his arguments and patience exhausted, he challenged her through action.

Caldwell noted that Ira "was perturbed not only by my unmanly clothing but also was concerned about the fact that my long reddish hair had not been cut in several years and hung in curls to my shoulders."[24] When Carrie's also disapproving older sister came to visit, she and Ira conspired to spirit Erskine out of the house to have his hair shorn at the local barbershop. Caldwell recalled his response to that act of defiance: "On my way home from the barbershop, I had a glimpse of my strange-looking self in a store window and I wondered what my mother would say when she saw that I no longer had the long curls she had so often combed and brushed with expressions of pleasure. As for myself, I felt like a different person—so different that I wondered if I had mysteriously passed from one life and had entered another."[25]

Before the trio's return, Ira also purchased for his son "a pair of blue overalls and a yellow shirt" to replace the Russian blouse and short pants. Carrie's distraction was tearfully overwhelming; she allegedly told her son: "Don't come near!" thrusting her hands out to keep him away.

On another issue that was to mark Erskine even more essentially as different and under his mother's control, Carrie would not bend:

> In keeping with my mother's inflexible plan for my early training and educa-
> tion, she continued to instruct me at home in studies for my age instead of
> letting me attend the local school a quarter of a mile in walking distance
> from where we lived. As I had done before in South Carolina, I begged to no
> avail to go to public school in Virginia as all the other children of my age
> were permitted to do.[26]

The consequences of her rigidity Caldwell was to cite time and again both in his early semiautobiographical *Sacrilege of Alan Kent* and in *With All My Might*, an account written when he was eighty-three. In the early account he emphasized a single paragraph: "I had no playmates." In the latter work he repeats that lament three times within the space of two pages. The last mention acknowledges the anguish that his mother's staunchness had provoked: "Being kept out of public school and having no playmates had enough of a limitation of normal activity to bring about a personal calamity in the judgement of a young boy."[27]

How Caldwell responded to his mother's careful restrictiveness in ei-

ther fact or fantasy can only be guessed. In *With All My Might* he introduces an alleged childhood playmate—never previously mentioned in
any of his works—who, in a mirror image of Erskine, was dressed at all
times according to his mother's "strict dictates." That boy, one S. J.
Black, threatened several times to run away from home; Caldwell himself claims never to have had such thoughts. On the other hand his much
earlier *Sacrilege* account cites two occasions when that work's persona
takes long excursions from home. Once he spent a day and part of the
night with a drayman before his father located him. On another occasion in Charlotte, North Carolina, he boarded a train bound for Cincinnati. That time the conductor discovered him, stopped the train and
placed him on another bound for return. As in the Bisco episode, it was
Ira who found the boy and then took him home without censure.

In all of Caldwell's writings that incorporate reminiscence, Ira
emerges as a warm and companionable father. Whenever he came
home smelling of coal-smoke from his various train journeys, he would
play a guessing game with Erskine. Taking the train timetables, the boy
would try to match the respective coal-smoke odors with the lines his
father had traveled, thereby charting the routes of Ira's assignments.
Later, when the family lived near Atoka, Tennessee, Ira took the youth
for camping trips on a Mississippi River landing. One such outing war-
rants summary, not only for its picture of idyllic companionship but also
for the insight it offers into the dynamics of family life in the Caldwell
home.[28]

Father and son were camped on a tree-shrouded site where wildflowers and curling ferns grew in the shelter of tall willows, where night-
cries of bobcats and river-sounds of blue-stacked towboats pushing coal-
barges merged with the dawn-sounds of nightbirds and the smell of
woodsmoke. In such surroundings, the father would "slowly and hesitantly . . . as if he were alone in the green shade," gaze across the river-
distance and speculate about the Midwest with its undaunted and substantial spirit: "This was when I heard him say for the first time that he
wanted to go there and travel throughout the region and find out how
true to life his conception would be in reality." Several times thereafter
when Erskine and Ira were together "somewhere away from home," the
father repeated his dream.

Caldwell concludes the story by positing the cause for the end of both the dreaming and the camping trips. "Sadly, the time came when there would be no more camping trips" because Carrie's "anguished desire to go back and live among friends and relatives in familiar places" had taken them away from the river. Ira resolutely gave up all hope of their moving westward. He afterwards neither tried to dissuade Carrie nor "did he speak out in such a way that might have revealed his disappointment." Instead, he moved the family east to Wrens, Georgia, a place where they settled permanently.

Away from home, yearning to move westward but finally reconciling himself to Carrie's needs, Ira apparently intuited his son's yearnings to free himself from his mother's attempts to "sivilize" him, as Huck Finn put it. Perhaps he too longed to "light out for the territory." For one so casually accepting as he, Carrie's exacting proprieties and inflexibility were, no doubt, taxing. Though the two of them, according to most accounts, shared a reasonably happy marriage, their differing attitudes toward child-rearing practices, social proprieties, the socially dispossessed, and a host of other issues must have provoked conflicts.

Though one witness claimed to have heard Mrs. Caldwell "screaming like a banshee at her husband," such outbursts were not the norm.[29] Rather, for some years Carrie gained her ends through less vocal forms of coercion. By her own admission she used periods of frozen silence, lasting sometimes for days on end, to signal her displeasure, to coerce her husband (and child?) to meet her demands.[30] Finally one day Ira had had enough. He announced that if she continued to use such tactics, he would take his hat off the hatstand, leave the house, and never return. Apparently that threat served to change Carrie's behavior thereafter.

Chapter 2

A combination of factors distinguished Erskine Caldwell's childhood. The idiosyncrasies of rural Georgia separated him somewhat from mainstream American children. More essentially however, his parents' respective expectations and habits marked him as different ever after.

Perhaps the most critical variable in that equation was Carrie's determination to keep Caldwell out of the rural schools, to teach him herself. Her reasons for tutoring him privately until almost his twelfth year are obscure. One person who knew her well claimed that as a proud member of the First Families of Virginia, Carrie did not want him to associate with ruder schoolmates. Caldwell believed that she wished to "counteract the influence of poor grammar that people then were using—even the school teachers."[1]

Whatever Carrie's motives, her decision served to exclude him from the ordinary socialization experience even as it emphasized that he was special and different. It further affirmed for him that knowledge, first and foremost, did not come from mentors and books but from individual experiences gained by roaming free and observing.

Reinforcing that perception were both Ira's example and encouragement. Because he was away from home so much, Ira's returns would become occasions for telling stories about his experiences. His influence-through-example was further supported by his attitudes toward his son's childhood wandering and adolescent explorations. Whatever Ira's attitudes toward home education, seldom in Caldwell's accountings of that period did he ever set limits to the boy's excursions or to the varieties of experience he sought. In fact in their occasional excursions together he would use the varieties of behavior they observed as lessons about the human condition.

Circumstances encouraged Caldwell's meanderings; example and at least oblique approval lent them legitimacy. The consequences were that he became the solitary child, observing, listening, assimilating. Speaking once more from behind his *Sacrilege* mask, he charted the dimensions of some of his observations. Sometimes he "ran off to the woods and stayed there all day alone in the trees," or he stopped at the cemetery to watch old gravediggers at work. As they tended their fire behind a yellowed headstone, the boy observed that "two or three of the newer graves sank into the earth a foot or more."[2] On another occasion he recorded seeing a quarry-workman "blasted hundreds of feet into the air" and watched the man's wife and child come to retrieve him.[3] It is no surprise, therefore, that Carrie characterized Erskine as an "imaginative child who asked searching questions" about cruelty, suffering, and poverty instead of the usual innocent questions of childhood.[4] While most children his age were in sheltering schoolrooms, he was outside becoming a student of the human condition.

The painful recognitions that confounded Caldwell's experiences were probably no more traumatic than those of any other child who had chanced to look behind the veil. The difference, however, was that ordinary children glanced but briefly into the heart of mystery before being diverted either by siblings or friends. Erskine's situation did not offer such relief. Except for his mother and father, he had no one with whom to escape or share.

To imply that Caldwell's childhood was one of constant introspection and questioning would represent a distortion of reality. As he grew older and more independent, he casually occupied himself by walking, swimming, or hunting for rabbits. He undoubtedly found security in a sense of family, for when not traveling, his father "was always lively, happy," and the Caldwells "always looked like two people in love who enjoyed each other."[5] As a family, they enjoyed rare trips and family vacations that Caldwell acknowledged, as usual, through his *Sacrilege* child.[6]

They rode through miles of orange groves, but his father frequently would stop, purchase some oranges and peel them with his pocketknife. Or, in an instance of mutual respect and compromise on the part of his parents, the boy remembered when the family lived in a large hotel on the shore of a blue bay; they went "each morning to old cathedrals and each afternoon to the water." The mother loved old churches, and the father, blue water.

More often than enjoying family vacations, however, the Caldwells visited Carrie's mother and relatives in Staunton. One of her favorite travel stories, which Caldwell later borrowed as his own, involved Blue Ridge complications. Because the boy had become thirsty during a trip, Ira stopped to ask a black-bearded mountaineer where he could get a drink. The two shortly walked into the woods. After a long while they returned, the rustic stepping behind him with a rifle to his back. Without explanation, Ira cranked the car, stepped in, and drove the family away. Laughingly, he then responded to their curiosity. Thinking the traveler had wanted a real drink, the mountaineer took him to the still. When Ira refused his "corn likker," the man became suspicious and marched him back to send him on the family's way—with Erskine thirstier than ever.

Usually Carrie and Erskine remained in Staunton for extended visits while Ira returned to his work, some weeks later coming back to drive them home.[7] The stories from that Staunton grandmother's household trace a familiar pattern. Through practice and example, Erskine was reconfirmed in those exceptions Carrie encouraged almost as habit. One of the occasions generally involved breakfasts. Grandmother Bell always had been unswerving in her rituals:

> She used two bells to announce breakfast—one at 7:45 called the "getting ready bell" and the other at 8:00, meaning "you'd better be here" bell. Everyone was expected to be together for breakfast. Erskine would hear the first bell but fool around. When the second bell would ring, he'd lean over the bannister and say, "Mum-mum, was that the first or second bell?" He'd always be given a little more time to get ready.[8]

Caldwell also remembered other practices and exceptions observed in his grandmother's Staunton home.[9] One of his most vivid memories from those visits caused him to look with awe and envy upon a bachelor uncle. After coming home at about two in the morning, he seldom awoke before eleven. Erskine would be somewhat amazed as the usually rigid grandmother always fixed her laggard son "a big, fancy breakfast."

Visits to Caldwell's maternal grandmother's house no doubt reinforced his personal attitudes and colored his perceptions. More important to the spirit of his future writings and religious values, however, were to be his father's example and counsel, for as Erskine matured, he observed more closely Ira's faith in practice. That laconic man's humane sensitivity spoke more forcefully through his behavior than through words.

Although the Caldwells were always somewhat poor, they were not impoverished. Pounding, a congregation's food gifts, supplemented Ira's fifty- to one-hundred-dollar monthly salary, a less-than-princely sum even then. On the other hand, hungry people surrounded them. Whites and blacks seeking food timidly knocked on the porch of the Caldwell house. Sometimes exasperated, Carrie would protest to her husband, "We need it worse than they do," or "There's going to be a limit to how kindhearted we can be at this house."[10] But the Caldwells shared nonetheless, whether the poor came to them or the pastor went to the poor. To those who might have been too proud to request help, Ira delivered sacks of flour, bags of grits, or black-eyed peas whenever he drove into the country. More often than not, Carrie added a small bag of candy for the children or old people.

Other examples punctuated by Ira's laconic comments also impressed the son. Because he allowed Erskine to form his own opinions about God and traditional Protestant practices, the boy came to conclusions inferred from his father's behavior. He could never determine the extent of Ira's belief nor the degree of his orthodoxy from what he said; rather, Caldwell gathered clues from what he did not say. Ira never mentioned God or Christ to his son in private, and "in the pulpit his direct references to God and Christ were expressed symbolically for the purpose of inspiring ethical conduct."[11] Such theological circumlocutions may have satisfied the congregation, but they were not lost upon Erskine. Their consequences left him precariously balanced between his father's Christian humanism and the dictates of his mother's Puritan orthodoxy.

In 1911, before the boy was to turn eight, Ira accepted a call from the Home Mission Board of the ARP Church. They assigned him to Timber Ridge, Virginia, an assignment that affected both Carrie and Erskine in different ways.[12] As a type of home missionary, he was to act either as a roving peacemaker adjudicating congregational disputes or as an interim pastor. During periods lasting weeks, months, or sometimes a year or more, the family, therefore, had to move from church to church, community to community. Always but temporarily settled, the Caldwells, moreover, would feel the effects of being thrust into the emotionally charged situations Ira was expected to resolve.

The challenges no doubt appealed to Ira, whose judicious humanism often resolved the conflicts that either dogma or local traditions had stirred. For Carrie and Erskine, however, that mobile ministry demanded more essential accommodations. Her feelings can be inferred only from the numerous letter-articles she wrote for the Mission Board's *Monthly Bulletin* during that period.

Employing the biblical rhetoric of her traditional faith, Carrie argued that a Home Missionary was an apostle. Like Paul, he would have to "begin at least at Jerusalem—that is, home," because "the little patches encroaching on the garden and growing right up to the doorstep . . . are [also] fields white to the harvest."[13] As a co-worker in that harvest, Carrie used terms of militancy and faithful patience to justify those dislocations and disassociations forced upon her and Erskine by the demands of Ira's work: "When did woman, when her men folk had gone to war, sit idly by until the struggle was over? . . . We must have patience, we must have faith; we must 'do the work that lies nearest our hands and leave the rest to God.'"[14] No sacrifice could be too great, she implied, because faith and the justifying efficacy of the work would merit their own reward, no matter the human costs.

A portion of those costs associated with Bud and Carrie's movable faith were levied against Erskine. His memories of that period were associated with packing the family belongings "in two barrels [to] cart them to the train." Driving through nights to save lodging costs, eating Vienna sausages to avoid expensive meals, and settling into boarding houses or unpainted dwellings became a way of life. Denied the ordinary friendships and associations of a stable environment, Caldwell still found compensations. "The experience of living for six months or a year or sometimes longer in one Southern state or another," he felt, proved more valuable to him than any other type of education he might have received.[15] Against "circumstances that otherwise might have been tragic," he balanced the combined forces of a "fortunate destiny of birth" and his "wise and tolerant" parents.

Other acknowledgments, however, chart the deeper consequences of the Caldwells' transience: "When I was a boy, we moved so often I never had my roots down very deep," is simple enough.[16] Or, "I think that, for the most part, my life was conditioned by the fact that I did not consider anything as stable or stationary or unmovable. And by that I mean that life was fluid, I was fluid, I was moving all the time."[17] The larger accounting, though, tallies the psychological costs through admissions such as "I never had a home," or "I was always a long way from home and it seemed as if I could never get there."[18] A similar sense of randomness marks those memories Caldwell was to have of the places where the family had lived after they left Prosperity in 1911 and before they moved to Atoka, Tennessee, in 1915.

Timber Ridge, Virginia, he remembered because there, "disappointed and depressed, for the first time in life [he] had no playmates."[19] From the Cuban-populated town of Ybor City, near Tampa, Caldwell culled images of dingy streets where "brown, oily-faced children fought one another . . . with dirty sticks and stones" and recalled walks "through a large number of cigar factories amid a vomiting odor."[20] Although he was eight years old when the family moved to Charlotte, North Carolina, Caldwell's memories were just as vivid but less solitary. There they all lived in one room of a downtown boarding house where "streetcars crashed through the boulevard." In Charlotte also, he played in an apartment being built across the street, and once allegedly followed a girl's lead when she suggested they play "doctor and patient." Most unusual of all, however, he practiced for a minstrel show with an older group of boys and girls. But before the performance began, his father came to take him home, at whose urging one is left to guess. The show went on without Erskine. Allowed more solitary activities, Erskine there earned money by selling newspapers on corners or collecting tin foil for a ball to be sold to a junk dealer. While other children were in school, he eventually worked five afternoons per week for two dollars, delivering shoes for a local shopkeeper.

After the Caldwells' move from Charlotte to Bradley, South Carolina, Erskine initially "became restless and depressed by the lack of activity. All the other children in town were in school."[21] And on rainy days when he was housebound, his parents claimed that he became "an irrational and irritating chronic complainer." Eventually he began helping the postmaster sort the afternoon mail. So that he sometime might receive some himself, he sent away for free samples and catalogs. One day a young man astride a motorcycle rode into the village seeking one Erskine P. Caldwell. When he found the boy, he asked if he were the one who had sent the request for motorcycle information. After Erskine had gulped and nodded yes, the motorcyclist looked at him with annoyance before speeding noisily away in a cloud of dust.

There also Erskine collected scrap iron and rubber to make "a livelihood, a living" for himself. When asked, years later, if the *Sacrilege* embellishment of the story—about cutting rubber airline connections from standing freight cars to include among his scrap—was accurate, Caldwell could not remember. He did recall, however, ordering "blueing" for five cents a package wholesale and selling the envelopes for ten cents to black washerwomen in the area.

Erskine was almost twelve, large for his years, and fast approaching puberty when Ira received his next assignment to the Salem community church near Atoka, Tennessee. Except for its situation near the Mississippi, Salem was like many of those other southern enclaves with which Erskine had become already familiar.

Most significant for Erskine, perhaps, was Carrie's decision to allow him to attend school. What prompted her reversal is almost certainly not that sequence of events Caldwell described in *With All My Might.* There he claims to have labored long over a novel that told "the story of a young boy who ran away [to the city] from his home in the country to escape from the harsh tyranny of cruel parents."[22] When his parents allegedly read his "first work of fiction . . . their reaction was swift and uncompromising." Because his "spelling, punctuation and handwriting" were so bad, they decided he should "begin attending public school without delay."

Caldwell's version of the events is most likely apocryphal. *With All My Might* is essentially the celebration of a man who had spent a lifetime slavishly devoted to his calling. Consequently the "first novel" story revises his history to establish that effort as his initiation into fiction writing. Never before, however, had he cited that event. He once admitted to Carvel Collins that his impulse to write came only after he had "been in college awhile."[23] The boy's story, moreover, sounds suspiciously like a blending of elements sketchily borrowed from Caldwell's future writing experiences.

And finally, Caldwell stated that the story's shortcomings acted as the catalyst that moved his parents to enroll him in the "public school." The local Robison School however was not a public institution; it was an academy founded in the 1890s by two Robison brothers. Most likely its reputation and respectability convinced Carrie that it was an acceptable environment for Caldwell's first extended association with formal education.

Whatever Carrie's hopes, Caldwell's academic memories of the school were to be dim. Placed with his age group in the sixth grade, he recalled only one academic incident from his three years there. In a geography contest sponsored by the woman instructor, he had won a copy of Gibbon's *Decline and Fall of the Roman Empire*, long his most treasured possession.

Possibly the social interaction that attending school demanded was more painful and illuminating than anything Caldwell might have experienced in the classrooms. A half-century later in a vignette called "The Trouble with Knickerbockers" he humorously recounted a portion of that adjustment.[24] Despite Carrie's sense of style and propriety, no self-respecting rural youth in the school wore knickers. When circumstances, therefore, forced Erskine to wear them, the calf-length pants must have emphasized his differentness—his large size, reserved attitude, and social awkwardness. Against the predictable ridicule and disdain, Caldwell claims to have fought his way to school each morning.

Possibly to encourage healthy male associations for his son, Ira served as scoutmaster for the local troop. Apparently "Erskine was much interested in these activities and the boys liked his father very much as scoutmaster."[25]

During this period Caldwell experienced the onset of puberty and the awakening of those sexual impulses that would thereafter be central to his life and to many of his best stories. That is not to say he had not previously been a participant in that sexual curiosity common to children. When he and S. J. Black—the playmate who was switched by his mother for dirtying his clothes—were given a photo of five older boys masturbating, S. J. allegedly talked his eight-year-old playmate into trying to do the same. In the midst of their furtive explorations S. J.'s mother threw open the privy door. She proceeded to drag them out and called Erskine a nasty boy as she slapped him and forbade him to see her son again.[26]

On another occasion a female playmate initiated some "doctor-nurse examinations."[27] This time the two also were discovered by a mother, the girl's, and again Erskine was perceived as the villain. She yelled, swatted his bare rump with a board, and then glared angrily at him while she lovingly stroked her daughter's hair.

The third instance cited by Caldwell was darker yet.[28] While he was visiting in Staunton, a local deviant lured him into an old shed and tried to force him into a homosexual encounter. Wrenching himself free, the frightened boy ran home, where he told his questioning grandmother that he had been scared in the dark.

With such painful associations a part of his memory, Erskine entered the world of sexual awakening. He took girls for short drives in his father's flivver but was too bashful even to hold hands with a girl on the porch swing. How this new and mysterious force affected him must be gleaned from stories with their genesis in that period.

A male teacher in *The Sacrilege* gruffly cautioned: "Play games. Don't look through the fence at girls."[29] When Caldwell's fictional self, Alan Kent, follows a girl he long has admired, she runs away to hide behind a church organ. In another instance, a fence also separates the boy and a neighboring girl as they hang across it to talk "to each other until bed time."

Some of what were to be among Caldwell's most evocative stories—all written during his first four published years—appear to have been inspired by experiences harvested during his years in Atoka. Resonating with sexual wonder and awe, they yet convey the dark and forbidden—especially by mothers—dimensions of that life force Caldwell explored during that period.

In "Indian Summer," the narrator and his budding adolescent friend go swimming naked in their private creek-place.[30] After discovering a girl their age watching them, they decide to catch and punish her. As they strip her naked and coat her struggling body with bottom mud, Jenny becomes strangely quiet while the narrator smears her undeveloped breasts. Momentarily arrested, he looks into her eyes to make a discovery that halts the roguish play: "She's a girl." Bidding the less sensitive companion to stop, the narrator helps Jenny clean herself and dress. Initially threatening to tell her parents about what the boys had done, Jenny is subdued by the time the narrator leaves her at her gate. With hesitant reassurance, he says over and over again, "Jenny won't tell."

In a variation upon that theme of adolescent discovery, Caldwell's "Walnut Hunt" presents a narrator and his male companion who are wandering the countryside in autumn, this time ostensibly in search of walnuts. Instead, they find a girl they know, blood-and-dirt streaked, writhing in a ditch. They are puzzled about her behavior, but when the pair threaten to tell her parents, she pleads their secrecy; she is having a baby. Both boys run away, the companion stumbling and crying. The young narrator does not stop to look back until he reaches his front porch.

Other shadows may have darkened the morning-brightness of Caldwell's Atoka years.[31] One afternoon—again in autumn—Erskine saw a circle of grim farmers and timber cutters gathered in front of a crossroads grocery store. He hovered in hearing range and was horrified by the details surrounding the death of a black youth with whom he had once fished. Accused of raping a white woman, he was hanged from a tree and blasted with shotguns. Variations on this haunting awakening of southern adolescence would come to shape his stories in different ways.

In other instances, Ira's ministry both indirectly and directly provided occasions for Caldwell's coming of age. As the two of them once visited with a shop-keeping member of the congregation, the man whirled a black whip and announced that with it he could put the "fear of God into any Negro, living or yet to be born." Observing that his ministry had not accomplished as much as he had hoped, Ira took Erskine's hand and walked sadly away.

Ira's sympathies and convictions in other ways more publicly fomented antagonisms and ill will among the congregations he attempted to shape. Yet never did they become as heated as those within the Salem church. Although the "congregation was a rather close-knit group of 'good' people," they failed to appreciate their pastor's concerns with "the needs of sharecroppers and Negroes."[32] Consequently "considerable antagonism to him grew up in the Salem congregation. Some criticized him for not devoting much time to sermons and not being concerned about theological doctrine."

Neither did Caroline cultivate devotion from the parishioners. They judged her as "a rather intellectual woman," one "who did not take much part in church activities such as Sunday School and women's missionary activities." By simply stating "She had a great influence on Erskine," one congregational member seemed to cast blame more upon her than Ira for providing the son with poor example.[33]

Yet the hostility toward Ira did not openly manifest itself until Ira delivered a series of patriotic sermons accompanying the outbreak of World War I. Critics accused him of encouraging their sons to enlist, a tactic, they believed, aimed at sparing black and Jewish youths from service. The controversy became so heated that on at least one occasion night riders came by the Caldwell house, advising them to leave Tennessee immediately.

Not one so easily swayed by threats, Ira nonetheless used the situation to create an opportunity for Erskine. Perceived by the community as different before the fracas, Erskine was now even more of an outcast. The fear that was in the air, more than Carrie's "anguished desire to go back and live among friends and relatives in familiar places," most likely moved Ira to acquiesce to her urging. In the meantime, however, he realized that removing Erskine from the situation could only work to the youth's advantage.

Through friends, Ira finagled for Erskine a YMCA driver's job at a military camp near Memphis. Though only fourteen, but large for his age, the youth had picked up driving and mechanical skills from his father, whose fascination with cars had earned him the nickname of Auto. Consequently, for the first time in his life, Caldwell lived away from home, had a regular paying job, and possibly enjoyed his first sexual encounter.[34] All were to be counted among those experiences that eventually found their way into his stories.

Chapter 3

By the time Erskine had finished his summer's work, the Caldwells had moved for the last time—away from Atoka with those river camping trips he had celebrated. To satisfy Carrie's desire to be among friends and familiar faces, Ira had accepted a more congenial congregational call. The year was 1918, Erskine was almost fifteen, and the wars—both congregational and European—were concluded. Wrens, Georgia, a sleepy town some fifty miles southeast of Augusta, was like hundreds of other southern communities with populations of a thousand, more or less. Bordered by the scrub blackjack barrens to the north and east, the immediate environment consisted of cotton fields and hardscrabble farms.

The town itself appeared hardly more promising. A cotton gin, a cottonseed mill, stores, and other businesses were owned by whatever elite the town could muster. Well-to-do and poor, blacks and whites, lived in a ritualized acceptance of privilege and habit, security and poverty. A few automobiles, but more mules and wagons, straddled the red, sandy streets. Pecan trees, a scattering of pines, and various evergreens shaded alike the prosperous-looking white houses and weather-beaten dwellings.

Farmers and sharecroppers, mill hands and idlers, storytellers and spitters, all lounged and squatted in front of the general stores, meat markets, and barbershops sharing observations and stories. Thus, the Caldwells settled not in an old town with aristocratic memories and mansions but in a half-century-old community struggling to maintain its vitality and respectability.

The Associate Reformed Presbyterian Church in Wrens, a properly steepled, white-boarded structure with a congregation of some hundred members, stood southeast of downtown. Across the street was the tin-roofed and porch-fronted manse where the Caldwells lived—a five-room, single-story, long and narrow house. Although the church numbered among its parishioners the Wrens, second-generation children of the town's founders, it offered neither a remunerative nor strenuous assignment to Ira Caldwell. However, the community enjoyed rail service and was situated only sixty miles from Prosperity, where his brothers had settled during his second pastorate, and not much farther from Due West, South Carolina, and Erskine College. Thus, in a sense the move did mean a return to friends, relatives, and familiar places.

Caldwell recalled that "it was a lively place for me. Wrens was a boom-town [then]—lumber mills going twenty-four hours per day with their sounds permeating the town, cotton riding high, intense [inter-town] rivalries between baseball teams."[1] This sense of vitality, perhaps, helped establish Wrens as that locality whose figures and landscapes were to populate, define, and dominate much of his early acclaimed fiction:

> I was not a writer to begin with; I was a listener. . . . Oral storytelling was the basis of fiction. You learned by listening around the store, around the gin, the icehouse, the woodyard, or wherever people congregated and had nothing to do. You would listen for the extraordinary, the unusual; the people knew how to tell stories orally in such a way that they could make the smallest incident, the most farfetched idea, into something extraordinarily interesting. Many Southern writers must have learned the art of storytelling from listening to oral tales.[2]

That September Erskine enrolled in Wrens High School, not a pleasant transition. Two grade-years behind his age-mates, he entered as a freshman: "I was six feet tall, and when you fit into a class of first-year schoolers and you're six feet tall, you feel a bit awkward."[3] Because of this difference, he was placed among his third-year peers, but there, academically unprepared, he "floundered . . . wasn't really interested in the studies."

Outside of school, Caldwell maintained a participant-observer's reserve.[4] Those age-mates who remember him at all recall a youth who was often alone, who usually hung around Harris's general store and the barbershop, unobtrusively watching and listening.

Caldwell's solitary wanderings were even more remarkable on Sundays. While his father was conducting services at the ARP Church and people of other faiths wended their respective church-ways, he could be seen heading toward the resident chain-gang compound. There he and two or three other white people would visit some of the black friends they had made in less-fettered times. Sometimes Caldwell would bring or go buy extra food for the prisoners, but of perhaps greater interest was a black "man who would shine your shoes for a nickel and tell stories all day."[5]

Despite the superficial differences between their religious observances, Erskine and his father continued to share a comfortable companionship. In fact, Ira encouraged Erskine to examine all religious practices with a rational skepticism. He took him to all-night camp meetings and snake handlings, to watch "Holy Roller exhibitions on splintery wooden floors," and congregations caught up in tongues. They also attended Catholic and Jewish rituals and "philosophical lectures in Unitarian churches." Ira allowed the educational field course to speak for itself, but occasionally he did add comment: "I. S. said he did not think it was harmful for a person to have a belief in God or anything else worthy of veneration as long as he was rational about it and able to recognize and admit the limitations of a belief."[6] As had always been his custom, he neither coerced nor directed Erskine in his religious practices.

Freed from the demands of bickering congregational factions and more secure in a church of his own choice, Ira increasingly pursued his activities among the downtrodden and poor of the Wrens area. Dr. Amplus Howard, a fellow minister, observed that "sometimes he seemed more a social worker than a pastor."[7] Through both example and urging, he encouraged his parishioners to share his concerns. The congregation contributed Christmas offerings of food which he, Will Wren, and Erskine delivered to the poor, both black and white.

Wrens and its surrounding settlements had large numbers of both. By the early 1900s, first, tobacco raising and, later, cotton cropping had impoverished the land. The people remained—among the eroded clay ridges, barren sand hills, and scrub blackjack growths. Balancing between instinctive survival and starvation, they underscored the relevance of a gospel Ira took literally—to feed the hungry and clothe the poor. Stopping to look back at a dilapidated tenant house he and Erskine had just left, Ira would murmur what for him was almost a refrain, "That poor chap back there hasn't got a chance in the world to get out of the rut he's in as long as he lives. . . . And all those children. What's to become of them when they grow up?"[8] After a while the pair would drive through the afternoon's heat in silence, down some gully-washed dirt road to the next tenant family they were going to visit. The father helplessly bemoaned the conditions of the impoverished while the son filed them away in his store of experience.

Like others in the community, Ira and Erskine faithfully followed and cheered the town baseball team in its Sunday contests with other communities. Additionally, Ira developed a lifelong interest in the history and culture of the earliest inhabitants of Georgia. As a result, he began collecting around Wrens, and "paid school children a penny apiece for artifacts," until he consequently had barrels of them.

Not all of Erskine's forays among the people of the area were in the company of his father. One summer—during which is not clear—he drove the local physician, Dr. Pilcher, on his country calls. "Interested only in seeing how people lived in the country," he was glad to observe a doctor who made no distinction "between those who were able to pay for his services and those who were not."[9] Sometimes, in fact, Caldwell saw him leave "a dollar or two on a table or chair" before the two of them departed. On other occasions, Erskine rode along with the county tax assessor as "he nimbly combined political fence-mending with adjustment of assessments." If the adjustments were favorable to the farmer, the assessor and his young observer were rewarded with a meal. If they were not, the two munched on dairy cheese and soda crackers purchased from some crossroads store.

The people, their conditions, and their stories mesmerized the young Caldwell: "I used to hang around all the stores—the butcher shop, the barber shop, the drug store; I used to hang around all of them. That's what interested me. I was always meeting people, hearing them talk. . . . I had nothing else to do."[10] In Wrens, a community chronically depressed to subsistence levels, it is understandable that Caldwell could find little else to do. Neither could many others, even though there, as elsewhere, work defined the man.

Seeking the validation that work would provide, Caldwell took a job, without his parents' knowledge, as a seed shoveler at the local cotton-seed mill.[11] He recognized that his mother—"Caroline Preston Bell who had taught Latin and French at Chatham Hall," an elite Virginia school—would never have approved. Working the night shift, Caldwell sneaked out of the house after his parents had retired, to return before they awoke, have breakfast with them, and leave for school. Although his term of employment proved short, he learned much about human nature during that period. The ten or twelve fellow workers, black and white, were all socially and economically marginal people, and, as usual, Caldwell listened to their talk, since "nothing of the smallest consequence in the surrounding area escaped their discussion." "Family feuds, secreted births, mysterious deaths, violent quarrels, desertions, infidelities, and scandalous love-makings," were all part of their graphically detailed stories.

After a few weeks this exhaustive schedule took its toll; he fell asleep at the breakfast table. Though his mother understandably became upset, his father seemed "secretly proud or even envious" of what the youth had done. Both parents concurred, nonetheless, that he should seek less taxing and more respectable work.

By this time, Carrie's own writing activity served to focus Erskine's adolescent interest: "I think she was sort of an example. . . . She wanted to write."[12] In fact, Caldwell recalled that she once wrote articles, short stories, and possibly novels that she may have submitted to contests. Although he did not remember reading any of them, "in those days it rubbed off." "Maybe" he got the idea that he "could write some" from Carrie. And if a rural youth felt stirred to write, the logical place to see his words in print was the town newspaper.

Although Caldwell's rendering of his approach to, and subsequent agreement with, the *Jefferson Reporter* editor, Charles W. Stephens, Sr., is both long and certainly embellished, he much later boasted the experience as seminal to his eventual career.[13] The writing he was to do—allegedly without pay because of a misunderstanding—gained him the satisfaction of seeing his words in print. Claiming to have invested his mill earnings in a used typewriter, he aimed toward what could become a career. Caldwell's eventual disillusionment with his *Jefferson Reporter* situation left him still without a paying job but with a typewriter.[14]

Lacking other job opportunities but always interested in baseball, Caldwell then allegedly wrote to the sports editor of the *Augusta Chronicle*. Might he need a string correspondent to report the games of the Wrens community team? A batch of self-addressed stamped envelopes came as reply. Caldwell claimed soon to be publishing almost daily accounts under his own byline at the rate of two dollars per column. With such compensation, he could not afford brevity. Possibly the Augusta editor and his readers were equally intrigued by what Caldwell had written: "a blow-by-blow, bite-by-bite account of a savage fight between a visiting catcher and one of the local fans."[15] The fan was carried home unconscious, the player lost a part of his ear, and the naive young sportswriter lost some of the color that added to his daily column space and earnings. The team manager forbade for the future such detailed reporting. Caldwell claimed in *Call It Experience* that the sports-reporting stint had left him wanting "to write more than do anything else in the world."

Caldwell returned to high school that fall, but he remained an indifferent student who often skipped classes. As Caldwell related years later, he continued string-reporting with varying success for other Georgia papers throughout the school year. The following spring Ira took him to see Mark Ethridge of the *Macon Telegraph*. Sympathetically, the editor explained that Wrens was outside the *Telegraph*'s circulation area, but he offered whatever encouragement he could by way of advice. Caldwell should "go back to Wrens and write about things" he saw. If he wrote them interestingly enough, the stories would get printed: "It's all in the way you see it and write it that's going to count."[16]

Though Caldwell's account of his first writing lesson may have been apocryphal, he used it to confirm his storyteller's truth: "It's all in the way you see it and write it that's going to count." Caldwell enhanced the credibility of the event with by saying, "I remember the day very clearly": his father had bought them their usual dozen "sugar babies" to eat during the long, dusty trip home.

During the summer of 1919, Caldwell was again unable to find suitable work. He apparently, therefore, spent much of those three months doing what he had done throughout his life—experiencing and observing. When people from Matthews, a settlement some five miles east of

Wrens, came to town, he watched them with renewed interest. He looked closely at Sister Rouse, a widow evangelist untruly rumored to be lacking a nose. Local stories said she had married and preached with the teenager who followed her around.

Others from the Matthews-Keysville vicinity, generally called tobacco road people, wandered the town. Various members of the sharecropping-and-day-laboring Amerson and Prickett clans stood before the stores or lounged about the streets. Erskine recognized them as the same people whose decaying houses he had visited with his father or who once had knocked hesitantly on the Caldwell porch. They and dozens like them were the people and "things he saw happening in Wrens."

What the Wrens experiences contributed to Caldwell's personal and emotional growth must be inferred. His autobiographical claims rely on humor to skim the surface of what he must have felt at the time. Because of clumsiness and circumstance, he supposedly failed to make love to two willing girls, one a schoolmate and the other his mother's mulatto housemaid.[17] His parents wordlessly placed a series of What-a-Young-Man-Ought-to-Know books in his room. His avid reading of them sent him to the local druggist to buy his first pack of condoms for "a friend."

What lay hidden beneath Caldwell's public accounts of his Wrens years must be filtered from some of the stories with their roots in that time. The details of both "Strawberry Season" and "Picking Cotton" suggest that the process of personal and sexual discovery that began with the Atoka and YMCA summer experiences continued to shape his perceptions.

In "Strawberry Season" the youthful workers share a camaraderie that devolves to a sport they called "strawberry slapping."[18] One day the Erskine-character slaps a berry that has slipped down a girl's front. Hugging her pain, Fanny sits down to retrieve a berry crushed between "milk-white" breasts, themselves with centers "stained like a crushed strawberry." The couple kiss and sink to the ground. Finally at sunset they return to the barn, collect their pay, and take opposite directions down the road, for "it was the end of the strawberry season."

Caldwell's "Picking Cotton" story is a variation on a similar situation.[19] This time, however, his fictional youth, Harry, is tested by a riddle-telling tease called Gertie. Her riddles, gibes, and taunts frustrate him. They hint strongly that she has bargained her sexuality to advantage with a black picker. To avoid confrontation with both racial and sexual confusion, Harry throws Gertie down, stuffs her mouth with cotton, and jumps on her before he is forced to face the truth.

Neither casual gratification, miscegenation, nor sexual barter were to muddle one of Caldwell's most evocative stories about sexual mystery burning through desire. Caldwell had admitted to dating a few girls in Wrens, one whose half-brother reputedly "ran a gambling house just over the county line." Local story had it that Caldwell and the girl were engaged—most likely a few years later—but that her father threatened her with disinheritance if she married him. Besides the local suspicion that fed upon Caldwell's solitary nature, rumor claimed that he "had flunked out of two or three schools and was considered no good."[20]

A collating of local memory with the details of Caldwell's "Crownfire" story suggests that he and the girl were forbidden their youthful love. If they were, she might have seemed all the more desirable to him, and his story an even more evocative expression of longing. Sidney, a young man, had been "waiting all summer, ever since school was out in June, [to] walk with her along the road in the evening," but always she had avoided him.

Crouching one evening in the shadows, Sidney surprises Irene as she walks with her attention riveted upon the crown-fire glows. He hugs her, pleads his love, and touches her breast. Threatening to tell his father, she breaks free, runs a short distance and stops in a churchyard, her hesitance signaling encouragement. Once again, holding her tightly, Sidney places his hands upon her breasts, this time without her running away.

The couple enjoys their silent communion until she observes a "crown-fire" on the horizon—"the pine tops are burning." Breathing rapidly, Irene confesses that crown-fires frighten her; they cannot be stopped before burning themselves out. That recognition prevents her participation in their answering fire's mutual consumption. Running away once more, Irene does not respond to Sidney's request that he walk with her another evening. Yet he preserves a hope. He recognizes that "someday, possibly that year or years following," crown-fires again will burn through their lives: "New pines would spring up to take the places of burned ones, and someone would drop lighted matches in the underbrush."

Whether or not the Wrens girlfriend actually inspired Caldwell's story is immaterial. What is important is its captured wonder of a shared youthful awakening. As a mature writer playing upon memory for a recreation of adolescent desire, he placed into coherent focus what must have confounded him at the time. Youthful yearnings and passion will flower in another time when crown-fires again burn anew.

At the time Caldwell felt "it was depressing to be isolated in a small town such as Wrens was in those days."[21] His writings, nonetheless, argue that his almost three or more years there were truly seminal. Confined and restricted, neither emotionally nor intellectually refined, he could do little else besides collect and store in memory experiences and shadings, people and behaviors that would inform his best fiction when maturity and creative vision eventually merged.

Experienced beyond his years and possibly feeling more socially mature than he was, Caldwell was anxious to leave Wrens and home, even before graduating from high school. By that summer's end in 1920, he was more than ready to go. Although he had finished the twelfth grade, he had not completed his graduation requirements, because some sophomore credits had been lost in his transfer from Atoka. But he could imagine no advantage in fulfilling those: "I couldn't waste my time like that, so I just walked out like all the graduates did. I was through."[22]

Chapter 4

Motivated by their own values and experiences, Caldwell's parents encouraged him to seek more education and more life experience before settling upon a career. But circumstances limited his options.

The Caldwells urged him to attend college. Though he preferred a more congenial environment, his parents could not afford to send him anywhere other than to Erskine College: "They wanted me to go, and so out of deference to their wishes and the fact I knew they had no money for anything else . . . I went . . . even though I didn't want to."[1]

Superficially, Erskine College seemed ideal for a rural youth whose formal education had been abbreviated. Since Caldwell was one of but thirty-nine entering freshmen with backgrounds similar to his, he should have felt at ease among peers. The campus itself was peaceful with shading trees, a large brick main building, and accompanying structures. And Due West would not offer the distracting temptations of larger university and college towns. In fact, Erskine College had changed little since Ira Caldwell had enrolled there some three decades earlier. And therein was to lie the rub.

The college catalog outlined the institution's expectations for its students: intoxicating liquors, cards, dice, and other games of chance were forbidden. Further, students could not "bet on drafts, chess or any other games." Such restrictions were not to impose unduly upon Caldwell. However, another regulation governing personal behavior he either regularly subverted or covertly broke: "No student may leave Due West without the permission of the president of the college or some member of the faculty."[2]

Other expectations were equally as confining and uncongenial. "Every student [was] required to attend the religious exercises in the Chapel [at 8:45] every morning, and on the Sabbath to attend a Bible recitation in the college and services in the village church." Attendance at the other religious exercises and a Sabbath recitation class was compulsory. Additionally, "morning and evening at breakfast and supper" a student-body member conducted a prayer service.

Such an environment must have galled Caldwell's sensibilities beyond relief. Advised by Ira that church attendance was a privilege he could either accept or reject, he had already chosen the latter. Religion was fine for those who wished to engage in it; they were in fact "welcome to it." How the hallowed expectations and practices of Erskine College, therefore, helped confirm Caldwell's agnostic tendencies only can be guessed.

The college curriculum must have excited Caldwell little more than the school's regulations. Freshmen were to take three hours of mathematics, three hours of English, and two hours of Bible. The other nine hours were to be chosen from among Latin, Greek, German, biology, physics, and history. Correspondingly, Caldwell spent most of his time trying to determine how he "could get out of it and go somewhere else."[3]

Somehow Caldwell adapted to survival in that college whose name he shared. Academically he worked just hard enough to maintain the seventy-percentile grade average required for sports participation. According to Caldwell's version of events, he was an innocent accomplice both in his introduction to breaking college rules and to playing football. Habitually offering naïveté as excuse, Caldwell's story about his football beginnings presents him as but a pawn obliging to forces and pressures beyond his will and control.

The upperclassmen, who played poker almost without interruption during the school year, prevailed upon Caldwell "to smuggle complete meals three times a day from the dining hall" to the rooms where they studied the rules of chance.[4] Others likewise forced him to join the football team and to produce "a comely out-of-town young woman for every scheduled event on campus." Caldwell meant, no doubt, for his wry sense of humor to underscore the forced aspect of this coercion. In the process, he nonetheless portrays himself as a blameless innocent overwhelmed by those who used him to their own ends.

Caldwell's later fame encouraged others to tell perhaps apocryphal stories about his activities at Erskine College. A "regular" from the "fa-

mous Erskine College team of 1921" recalled that, to the team's cha-
grin, the "long-legged, shut-mouth freshman" came into one game to
replace the injured center.[5] As the team proceeded to beat Clemson 13–
0, Caldwell "made tackles from end to end—threw 'em for losses
dam[n] near every play." Another football-related story suggests that he
and another team member rifled the visiting team's trouser-pockets
while others were on the field. Supposedly both culprits were either severely reprimanded or expelled for their theft. Caldwell's own defense
carries within it a more convincing version.[6] He and the other youth had
merely played a prank by creeping into the visiting team's locker room
and randomly transferring the pocket contents from one pair of pants to
those of another.

A local resident was to recount a more plausible story. On an evening
before a scheduled midterm exam, Caldwell and one Andrew Murphy
"decided to take a trip," which lasted through the night. Walking and
riding trains to various stops in the area, they ambled around the Ab-
beville, South Carolina, square and then walked a twelve-mile return for
breakfast at Erskine College. Legend maintains that Caldwell's exam
results included personal comment: "Very fine as to diction. As to subject matter—fiction."[7]

Caldwell's confining circumstances may have forced him, for the first
time in his life, to accept and form some friendships. Caldwell apparently had company in some of his misadventures. He and a Joe Mose
had joined forces in the pocket-rifling episode, while another college-
mate was to remember Caldwell as "one of the boys." Through his *Sacrilege* chronicle, Caldwell cites visiting "a new friend," the two sitting up
all night drinking two bottles of Coca-Cola and smoking three cigarettes
between them. His Erskine College experience may thus have been
more valuable than he was ever to acknowledge.

In another sense that pre-exam train excursion both captures and dis-
torts aspects of Caldwell's behavior. Without a doubt, it represented but
one of many trips that took him away from the college campus. The opportunity for free rides on freights and other trains that ran regularly in
and out of Due West made such escapes easy. Such excursions, which
Caldwell casually attributed to a restless spirit, then and thereafter were

always inspired by a combination of more basic psychological impulses. Travel meant escape from repressing expectations as well as a reaffirmation of his essential privacy. Its anonymity granted him "breathing space," provided him with environments where family, teachers, or townspeople could not scrutinize and judge his every move.

At the conservative Presbyterian college, however, Caldwell confronted an intensified extension of his home situation. Its confining regulations were like parental expectations that had become increasingly exasperating.[8] Talking about youth in general a half-century later, Caldwell admitted that he had rebelled against his parents. Like other adolescents, he did not like anything they said or did, and he did not want to be around them; he "wanted to leave, get away." It was not that he disliked them, but as he was to recognize, "it was just that I had come to the point where it was time for me to get away, to do something different that I wanted to do, and not what they wanted me to do."[9] What they wanted him to do is vague, and how they expressed their wishes is a matter for conjecture.

But what Erskine College expected and demanded was neither vague nor conjectural. It sought, parentlike, to restrict Caldwell's behavior and mold his values. More than that, the college experience likewise involved almost constant social interaction and involvement. All such factors conspired to threaten the sanctity of his privacy and his sense of self.

If Caldwell then indeed felt unduly restricted and psychologically oppressed—as a child, a student, or an adult—his random wanderings and various trips might have served a dual purpose. On one level they offered freedom from repression; on another, they precluded all but superficial personal and social involvements. Traveling, with its public places and unquestioning faces, allowed a solitary retreat by then as comfortable as habit.

If such speculations seem forced, Caldwell's defensiveness appears almost obversely to feed them: "I've never been lonely—never! I like solitude because I like to be around where people are, but I don't like to get involved too much or obligated or anything . . . but solitude is a great thing—for me."[10] His pride in self-sufficiency not withstanding, Caldwell's habit of solitude had become like a turtle's shell. Though it initially offered essential protection and survival, it also became a burden he dragged throughout his lifetime.

His periodic excursions allowed Caldwell to complete his freshman year with a sense of relief and a barely acceptable academic record; but free for the summer, he confronted a dilemma. Though he did not want to hurt his parents, he did not wish to spend three months at home in Wrens. As a way out of his conundrum, he argued legitimately that work opportunities there were scarce, a line of reasoning with implications that Ira probably understood. Again through his associations Ira found Erskine a job in Calhoun, Georgia. Its Piedmont location seemed perfect for the seventeen-year-old youth; it was situated a distant 250 miles northwest of Wrens and home.

Although Caldwell's job as a stonemason's helper on a synagogue project was a good one, Carrie, herself escaping Wrens for a summer in Staunton, apparently required some convincing. His letters scarcely hid his pragmatic arguments. His first stressed that he was earning $3.50 per day; three weeks later he announced a fifty-cents-per-day increase with a questioning justification: "If I save $100 this summer, do you think my summer will be well spent?"[11] Yet Carrie may have been secretly pleased with another letter that revealed a degree of his dependency: "Send me some underwear post-hast[e], pronto, quick, am out, totaly [sic]."[12] Further, during one of Ira's trips to Tennessee, he slept over with Erskine, possibly as much to appease Carrie's worries as to enjoy his son's company.

Caldwell's return to the Due West college in the fall of 1921 represented but an elaboration upon his first year's experience. He enjoyed playing center on the football team; he also apparently enjoyed the sexual favors offered him by a blind date arranged by a companion.[13] Though he claimed initially to enjoy his classes, his interest in them began to flag by the end of the football season. By Christmas break he was downright miserable at Erskine College, with its various "religious impositions."

Increasingly, Caldwell continued to reach beyond its campus boundaries for the release and relief that overnight and weekend trips allowed. Beyond those parochial horizons, a larger world waited, and because he was "interested in life, wanted to go out and do things, college seemed to be a waste of time."[14]

Doing things meant leaving Erskine College, and with the beginning of the second term in January of 1922, Caldwell had had enough.[15] Taking the little money he had, he caught a train to New Orleans, where he must have looked like the urban initiate he was.[16] This "belle of the South" was a larger and more diverse city than he had ever before confronted. He nonetheless followed instinct and observation. Judging the flow of people and traffic, sensitive to sights and smells, Caldwell angled toward those poorer sections mixed with warehouses, decaying tenements, or houses whose windows advertised rooms for rent. There he found lodgings: "You have no money, you don't go to a Hilton hotel. You go someplace where you can find a room for three dollars a week. . . . You're going to find them in a tenement district."[17] In such areas, he could be independent, alone, and observing.

New Orleans's coastal location offered an almost ideal situation for both observing the unusual and seeking work. There Caldwell could lounge about unobtrusively listening to longshoremen. But what work he may have found remains obscure. Later promotional materials claimed that he once had been a gunrunner on a South American tramp steamer. Other accounts suggested that he had worked as a deckhand on a banana-freighter bound for Honduras and return. His New Orleans visit was so brief that such boasts were almost surely self-serving fabrications. Whatever the reality, he remained there no more than two or three weeks, until jobless, eating less and less each day, he departed.

During the interim, however, Caldwell may have enjoyed an association that would be incorporated into his future writings. In both *Poor Fool* and *The Sacrilege of Alan Kent*, Caldwell celebrated "a brown-limbed girl," one who, on the top floor of a warehouse, fed him every day and warmed him every night. Reduced to living in a grungy waterfront district and giving, rather than selling, her favors to a repressed rustic, she apparently provided Caldwell with an almost mystical experience. Unlike the more respectable Irene in Wrens, she did not run away from his hands on her breasts. Acquiescing, she unleashed forces that would allow him to see beyond oceans, to lift hills of earth.

Through his *Sacrilege* persona, Caldwell's wanderer later returns to New Orleans, seeking the girl and all she has come to symbolize. In a fantasy presented as reality, he sees her hiding naked behind a hill. Lifting it, he tosses the hill over the edge of the world so he can pick her up to whisper tenderly, "I have been looking all my life for a girl like you, with brown legs and white breasts and hair like gold in sunshine."[18] While she kissed his lips, he "laid her on a cloud," but when he had opened his eyes, the cloud and she had floated away.

Variations of this idyllic woman-figure drift in and out of the pages of *Sacrilege*. For Caldwell and his character, both loyal sons and honorable gentlemen of the chivalric South, the ideal woman was more than a figure on a pedestal. She floated ephemerally on a cloud—a cloud that could cast a shadow on a southern gentleman's life.

Not even the reality of a brown-legged New Orleans girl could feed Caldwell forever. Finding no work there, he followed the promise of a logging job in Bogalusa, some seventy-five miles north of New Orleans. During the last week of January 1922, Bogalusa however did not radiate southern warmth and hospitality. Its newspapers regularly touted warnings of Bolshevik-menaces and served up stories of Negroes raping white women. The week that Caldwell arrived, the town was waging a "National Pay-up" campaign recalling people to fiscal responsibility, certainly no advantage for a young stranger who found no job except a brief one selling Bibles house-to-house.

Without regular work, Caldwell's habit of wandering and solitary observation must have made him a suspicious figure in the town. According to local records of February 2, 1922, the police arrested and jailed him on that day.[19] Helplessly innocent by reason of circumstances, he nonetheless had been guilty throughout his lifetime of the complaints lodged in his affidavit of arrest. It charged that Erskine Caldwell willfully did "loiter around suspicious places without being able to give a satisfactory explanation therefore."[20]

How long Caldwell remained in jail and how he secured his release is uncertain. Facts strained from his various accounts indicate that by working through the local YMCA, he reached Ira, who after four days both secured his release and forwarded money for his return to Wrens.

Upon the prodigal son's arrival, Ira allegedly shook Erskine's hand and "smiled without a trace of displeasure." His only comment about the difficulty lodged in his two questions: "What did you think of Louisiana, son? It's nothing like this part of the country, is it?"[21] Ira's observation about Louisiana's people being different was valid. What homefolks excused and accepted as Caldwell's peculiarity, strangers suspiciously condemned in the name of law.

After Caldwell's Bogalusa venture he returned to Wrens and the comforts—and restrictions—of home, a fact he acknowledged in each of his autobiographical works. In both accounts, however, he curiously claimed to have remained there only some six months, until he gained admission into the University of Virginia in the fall of 1922. As a matter of record, Caldwell did not matriculate there until the autumn of 1923. He, in fact, remained in Wrens a full year and a half before finally leaving for Virginia.

Why Caldwell so reconstructed his past is not clear. His revision demanded that he subsequently contrive the dating of future significant life events to maintain that fabrication. His later sojourns in Pennsylvania and Maine, the sequence of his summer activities and academic courses, experiences central to his initial writing impulses, all had to be carefully realigned to account for that Wrens-year he attempted to erase from his public record. Caldwell always insisted that he had been singularly independent and directed toward a writing career. Perhaps his pride, therefore, would not allow him to admit that he had been confused and undirected for a year and a half after leaving Erskine College. Likewise he might have been loathe to admit his dependence upon the dual securities of family and whatever jobs and activities Wrens then provided.

During that time Caldwell admitted to writing string accounts for various regional papers. Most likely some of those other experiences that he attributed to his earlier adolescent years were accumulated during his eighteen months of "depressing" isolation in Wrens. Then he perhaps worked in the mill. Then he most likely accompanied Dr. Pilcher and the county tax assessor on their rounds and otherwise lounged about town inviting speculation from townspeople.

Rumor most likely whispered of his romantic interlude with the local gambler's half-sister. Local stories claiming that marriage between the two had been forbidden because Caldwell "was no good" and "had flunked out of two or three schools" then become more credible. There would have been no substance for such accusations during his earlier teenage years. Later, however, had a nineteen-year-old college dropout been seen loafing around town without gainful employment, such gossip would have had some suspicions to gnaw upon.

Whatever Caldwell's activities during that eighteen-month-period, he did cast about for options more congenial than those offered by the church college. He requested catalogs from state universities; the University of Virginia looked most appealing, but its costs were prohibitive. Then he happened upon a happy discovery. The Georgia United Daughters of the Confederacy supported an all-but-forgotten tuition scholarship for descendants of Confederate army veterans. Apparently genealogically qualified, Caldwell applied for and received the award. With the help of his parents, the support of respectable southern ladies, and income from part-time work, he could enroll at the University of Virginia.

That fortuitous coalition granted Caldwell the release he had sought. Almost twenty years old by then, he could finally begin to loosen the ties with family, church, and his parochial, Deep South environment.

# Part 2

"That's Why God Made Words"

Chapter 5

Caldwell left Wrens in September of 1923 with a sense of anticipation. He yearned to be "out of the rut of life and into the stream of life."[1] The University of Virginia, he felt, represented but the first step toward more exciting goals: "Washington, Philadelphia, Wilkes-Barre, Atlantic City, New York." He wanted to experience "the dynamics" of life as he had not previously known it.

Neither Charlottesville nor its university seemed dynamic enough to live up to Caldwell's expectations. Both were venerably respectable and small. Nestled in the Appalachian foothills, the town numbered only 11,000 residents. Yet like much of America at that time, it hummed with seductive promise. An expanding young population, giddy with the spirit of the twenties, chafed at the bonds of the town's propriety. The university, Thomas Jefferson's institution, had grown to 130 faculty members and 1,700 students. Both the town and its university were a world away from Due West and Erskine College.

Caldwell first registered for offerings as diverse as English literature, geology, psychology, Spanish, and physical training. Assigned to a university-approved boarding house with a roommate, Louis Ballou of Virginia, he was but a short distance from campus, at 110 Fourteenth Street. He next found work at Johnny LaRue's pool hall, a student hangout adjacent to the campus. For six dollars a week, he was to function as night clerk, cashier, and janitor. He was set for the year.

Academically, that year did little more to establish Caldwell's scholarly credentials than had his three semesters at Erskine College. He marginally passed all his courses except psychology and physical training. In the latter, the former football player scored thirty-one. His second- and third-quarter performances were almost duplicates of the first, except that he dropped Spanish during the spring term.

His work at Johnny LaRue's necessarily cut down on Caldwell's study

Erskine Caldwell, 1931.
Printed by permission of
Rebecca Gooding, Caldwell
family conservator.

time; however, more indirectly, his experiences in the pool hall perhaps
subverted his best academic intentions. In that essentially masculine environment, he was privy to information about secret stills and rumors of
sexual conquest, both imagined and real. Not all such stories were to be
believed, he discovered.

Acting on a tip from some local student nurses, Caldwell and Ballou
stealthily made their way one night to the rural home of a rumored boot-
legger, where they boldly knocked at the door. Eventually, it was opened
by a man they soon discovered to be a deputy sheriff. Hastening an apologetic retreat, the duo muttered threats of revenge against the conniving
girls who had tricked them into their brush with the law.

Not all of their expeditions were so futile. Ballou remembered that he
and Caldwell sometimes returned tipsy to their room. Lying there, each
trying to steady his own revolving bed, Ballou would hear his roommate's subdued giggling. When questioned, Caldwell would patiently
explain that he was composing jokes to be submitted to the *Virginia Reel*,

Erskine Caldwell, Burbank, Calif., 1934. Printed by permission of Rebecca Gooding, Caldwell family conservator.

a student publication. At a dollar per published joke, he supplemented his income with submissions to this and other publications.

Beyond such diversions, what else? Caldwell no longer played football, but according to Ballou, he did date occasionally. And as he became more disenchanted with the formalities of attending classes, he launched into a pattern of travel that had become his habitual escape at the Presbyterian school. During this year, Caldwell explored unfamiliar urban environments in both Washington, D.C., and Baltimore. This time he ventured out not so much to rebel against confinement as to observe the dynamics of life in motion. Temporary work supporting these stints—as dishwasher, milkman, theater usher—he subsequently embellished in autobiographical sketches as evidence of his once having lived life at the bottom. For Caldwell, living life, listening to its marginal voices—however briefly—was sufficient to satisfy his curiosity and, ultimately, to validate his fiction. Every incident and detail he would record mentally and later "call it experience."

But after a year of such freedom, how could Caldwell return to family, to Wrens, for more than a brief summer visit? He could not, though that is exactly what he claims in *With All My Might.*[2] Neither did he return that fall, as he there also claimed, to complete his second year of work at the university, nor to do that writing that supposedly only increased his "desire to become a writer of fiction depicting the reality of life."[3] All of that would come a year later.

With the completion of the academic year in the summer of 1924, Caldwell returned to Wrens only long enough to present his plans for the immediate future. He wanted to gravitate northward. Appealing to Ira's prejudice—that an economic and social system had conspired to enslave the poor—he must have convinced himself and his parents that a knowledge of economics would help him understand those dual forces. The famous Wharton School of Economics in Philadelphia seemed the best place to study a system that had manipulated the southern poor to its own advantage.

By this time, apparently resigned to Caldwell's desire to wander, the parents cautioned that they could support only the travel portion of his quest. They would drive him as far as Staunton and pay his railway fare from there to Philadelphia. Beyond that, he would be on his own.

After arriving in Philadelphia, Caldwell apparently drifted once more—like a modern-day version of Ben Franklin—to the city's boardinghouse-tenement district. He found jobs through help-wanted signs in windows or want-ad listings in the newspaper. Unskilled and anticipating summer-school enrollment at the University of Pennsylvania, Caldwell first took a night job at an orange-juice stand, tending customers, cleaning, and closing for the night. None of his letters to his parents mention the Shanghai merchant's son—introduced in *With All My Might*—who allegedly paid him handsomely to act as his guide.[4] Rather, by living frugally, he earned just enough to subsist and pay his summer school expenses.

But again, Caldwell achieved only mixed academic success, noting cryptically in a letter to his parents: "Passed two hours and failed one at S.[ummer] S.[chool]. That gives me two units for the summer. So it wasn't wasted entirely."[5]

Late that summer, Caldwell tried something that would feed some versions—and some exaggerations—of his life story. Pennsylvania had an Anthracite Football League, so called because of the coal miners' town teams it included. Its semiprofessional players practiced sporadically and were paid by the number of games played. Caldwell decided to add to his income by trying out for a regular place on a team. He was ruefully honest about the results: "I never made it through the regular season's training camp. . . . I received a busted nose."[6]

As the summer of 1924 waned, Caldwell had to make a decision. Should he return to the University of Virginia for the fall quarter? Letters to his parents show the level of his concern for them. He could not return to the university without financial help from them, a favor he could not ask. Although Ira by this time was supplementing his church salary by teaching and coaching in the local high school, Caldwell realized that the family finances remained strained. If he were to impose upon them further, he reasoned, "that would show [him] up as unmindful of [their] health and peace of mind."

Consequently, Caldwell proposed a worthier option. He would perhaps take a few more classes at Penn or Drexel University or move to Wilkes-Barre to seek a job and continue his studies. That should reassure them that he was not choosing that alternative "to have a good time or to keep from going to school." He truly wanted to finish college because his usual teachers had provided the lesson: "I have found out by experience and observation this summer what education means."[7]

If that approach had not been enough to convince Ira and Carrie, Caldwell bolstered its weakness with logic. Comparing his salary with that of others, he deduced that his two years of college had earned him a five-to-twelve-dollar weekly advantage over high school and business school graduates. Accordingly, he meant to apply for an assistant manager's job with Kresge's in Wilkes-Barre. To demonstrate the wisdom of his decision, Caldwell gave the example of a student he had known at Erskine College. He had "stopt [sic] school for a year" to work for Kresge's: "At the end of six months [he] was promoted to manager at fifty a week, married, and went back to get his degree. I would like to do the same, except for the marrying part, of course."[8]

A week later the "assistant manager" was on the job.[9] Earning twenty dollars per week, Caldwell was in charge of Kresge's glassware, woodenware and candy departments in the basement stockroom in Wilkes-Barre. His work—that of filling and packaging orders requested by the clerks above—was hard: "But I don't mind it so long as I can live without taking your money when you need it so bad."[10] He lived alone in a tenth-floor, five-dollar-per-week room in an apartment a half block from the center of town—at 40 North Main Street. That portion of his salary not paid in rent, he estimated, would go for meals in restaurants and other essentials. He pacified his parents by assuring them that they were not to worry about him: "That's why I came here, so I could pay my own expenses. . . . if I go broke or hungry it won't matter because I'm used to it by now."[11]

Possibly as much to justify his decision as to mollify his parents, Caldwell claimed to have "registered at Lehigh U.," in Bethlehem, over an hour away by train. He mentioned neither the tuition nor the distance, only later that he had "passed the tests O.K." Whether he earned any credit there is unconfirmable, and what else he might have done in Wilkes-Barre must be gleaned from hints in his *Sacrilege*.

In that fictional accounting, the body of a woman falling from eleven stories up flashes past his window. As one of those lifting her into the ambulance, he notices that her body feels like a "sack half full of potatoes."[12] At night, he lies in bed to think "of my own self in the everlasting silence of darkness."[13] Intimations of mortality stir the young man's thoughts as he wonders what earth's living people will be doing after his death.

On Sunday evenings, Caldwell's reclusive character goes early to his room, to sit by the window watching a man put a girl to bed: "She stood like a piece of unfinished sculpture while he took off her clothes."[14] Such scenes conjure visions. Opening his eyes, he sees a girl looking at him "with all the eagerness" he had ever hoped to find in her face.[15] Like the New Orleans girl, her body throbs with a fervor equal to his own. Women's beauty and promise continue to haunt Caldwell's solitary youth.

Glimpsing an eager girl's face in a crowd, Kent is taunted thereafter by her vision, one always leading him through the streets "in an endless circle." No one was to know "how lonely [he] felt without her."[16] Caldwell's Wilkes-Barre experience, screened through the imagined Alan Kent, forced him to recognitions he could admit only through fiction: "I had no place to go and nothing now to do. Almost everybody else I saw had someone who loved him and they were happy together."[17]

By November of 1924, Caldwell, soon to be twenty-one, had wearied of that solitary harvest he had once so avidly desired. Writing to his mother and father, he confessed, "I've found out what it means not to have a home you can go to at night."[18] Lest he too openly reveal a loneliness that others might readily admit, Caldwell cited his real reasons for wishing to leave Wilkes-Barre. Within that environment, he could not shake a persistent cold. Room rent and laundry costs, carfare and meals decimated his earnings. The quality of education at both Pennsylvania and Lehigh was inferior to that at Virginia. And with an uncharacteristic twist, Caldwell added, "It's the boys that made the school and *the* boys are at Virginia."

Again blaming others for his own questionable decisions, Caldwell contended that his extended self-exile had not been his fault: "I wanted to go back in Sept[ember] but couldn't as it ment [*sic*] you [*sic*] going into debt, so now if it's possible, I would rather be there than here."[19] By economizing, he would try to save enough to pay part of his thirty-five-dollar return train fare.

Caldwell's later autobiographical claims in *With All My Might* were fabrications. He had not motored directly back to Charlottesville in an "engine-knocking . . . fourth hand Ford roadster . . . bought with savings from his employment"—a car he later used to embellish another event.[20] Rather, he had returned directly to Wrens by rail. Because he had wanted to "come home [for] Christmas," his parents had purchased the thirty-five-dollar ticket. He had accumulated little or no money toward that, the purchase of a car, or even a new suit.[21] In fact, he had saved almost nothing from his Wilkes-Barre period except memories.

And thus, Christmas of 1924 found Caldwell home, and two weeks later, back at the University of Virginia for the 1925 winter term. His registration materials reflected some puzzling differences from those of the previous year. Listing 1903 as his birth year and Atlanta as his birthplace, he inserted "business" as his intended occupation. By the next term, he had changed his father's occupation to that of "newspaper editor." Such changes might be causes for bemusement were they not to be followed by Caldwell's even more puzzling behavior during those winter and spring terms of 1925.

Prior to that time, little in Caldwell's record indicated that he had intended to pursue a career in either business or fiction writing. He had recently worked as a stock clerk for Kresge's, and he had allegedly done some writing as a string reporter. He had taken some economics and English courses during his various stints at Erskine College, the University of Virginia, and in Pennsylvania, but his grades—and his letters dating from that time—reflected a barely superficial acquaintance with both disciplines. All evidence, therefore, for Caldwell's lifelong desire to be a writer of fiction has come from his own after-the-fact revisions, from stories told to establish an identity that in early 1925 seemed to have been only an inclination.

Caldwell's next two semesters at Virginia offer little to demonstrate his promise as either a businessman or a writer. During those two academic periods, Caldwell enrolled in four courses, all extending through both semesters. Accordingly, he should have earned a total of eight grades by the end of that academic year. Instead, he received only a first term grade of sixty-one in an economics course and a sixty in English C–1. Except for a zero in the second-period English offering, all other reports read "absent" or "dropped." Although Caldwell's scholastic performance had always been below average, never before had it been so poor.

In early 1925 Caldwell's interests flowed from deep and more immediate psychological needs wrung from his emotionally taxing Wilkes-Barre hiatus. Those revolved around finding the elusively idyllic woman and, with her, establishing "a home to go to at night." Early that spring he found that person.

While attending a concert, Caldwell spied her. She was Helen Lannigan, an attractive young woman accompanied by a student Caldwell knew. Margaret Armentrout introduced them.

Helen too had been an almost lifelong resident of the South, and she knew how to tell an arresting story. "I was seduced by Rachmaninov," she always began.[22] Caldwell's alleged opening comment to her was neither so romantic nor elevated. With the most common of terms he announced his sexual needs. Why had he approached her so degradingly? she asked. Because she had been asking for it by ignoring him in an English class they had shared more that a year earlier, was his reply.

Helen's story captures some of her characteristic directness, for she claimed to have told Caldwell, "Well, I'm sorry. I can't sleep with you now. I'm too busy." As a graduate student in French at the University of Virginia, she at that time had the lead in a French play. But when that was over, she "started sleeping with him," because they shared an overwhelming physical attraction and because "he was great in bed." What other qualities and differences united or separated them are a blend of Helen's earlier and later stories.

Helen's initial amazement at Caldwell's introductory comments would not have been insincere. She was no casual New Orleans or Wilkes-Barre girl. Although no longer a virgin, she was certainly not one whose background or reputation would have invited an approach allegedly as blatant as Caldwell's. Her Welsh-descended father was "Pop"

Helen Caldwell, Burbank, Calif., 1934. Printed by permission of Rebecca Gooding, Caldwell family conservator.

Lannigan, respected track coach at the University of Virginia. The family, moreover, owned over three hundred acres of wooded land with a 1777 rambling home on a lake near Mount Vernon, Maine. There she had spent her summers, but otherwise she was a respected southern belle.

A bright child, Helen had begun high school when she was eleven and graduated three years later. Staunch Episcopalians, her parents subsequently sent her to William and Mary. There she had majored in English, acquired minors in French and German, and graduated with honors shortly after her eighteenth birthday.

A Virginia graduate student when she met Caldwell, Helen was already well liked and recognized as a good student by most of the faculty there. Thus, her precipitous response to Caldwell's expression of sexual need seems to have been as uncharacteristic for her as his bold statement had been for him. Both Helen's and Caldwell's initial and subsequent actions invite speculation about why they might have departed so radically from their usual patterns of behavior.

The two seemed well matched only by virtue of their contrasts. Helen's full figure might have distinguished her from Charlottesville's would-be flappers. Otherwise, with hair bobbed to emphasize her oval face, her modest height and social ease would have made her appear almost indistinguishable from the university's smart set. On the other hand, Caldwell's more-than-six-foot bulk might have made Helen feel protected when they were together. A freckled face, red hair, and laconic manner spoke for his Scotch-Irish ancestry. But more intriguing than these qualities was an aura that Caldwell projected. A smoldering intensity, a sense of mystery emanated from behind the iron will he wore like a mask.

Caldwell's facade of self-reliant independence, his singular self-containment—all could have intrigued a young woman whose literary bent would have found appeal in such an unorthodox figure. Perhaps she believed she could encourage Caldwell to reveal his private self through his writings. Obviously Helen's effervescent loquaciousness served as a counterpoint to his shyness.

In hindsight, both Helen and Caldwell acknowledged that more than physical and psychological attributes drew them to each other. He recognized her abilities and interests; as a student of literature, she shared his "attitude towards reading and writing."[23] Helen was memorably impressed by his fierce determination to succeed as a writer.

Despite Helen's impressions, a puzzle: only a month earlier Caldwell had listed business as his anticipated career. His grades in English had always been lackluster at best. Except for possible newspaper stringer accounts and some *Virginia Reel* jokes, he had written nothing. He had no portfolio or secret trove of fiction or poetry to share with this attractive and accomplished woman with obvious literary interests.

In truth, what litany of accomplishments and achievements could Caldwell have recited to impress this young woman? His father was not a newspaper writer—except as a sporadic hobby—but an ARP pastor. His mother was an educated woman but functioned essentially as a self-sacrificing wife and mother. He had not completed his high school graduation requirements and had, in fits and starts, enrolled in and dropped out of four colleges or universities. Beyond that, what? He had traveled some within a limited world; he was a seeker and collector of experiences, but toward what end?

What could Caldwell have told Helen to explain, to justify his undirected ramblings? What could he have said to persuade her that he was a young man of purpose, of promise, to convince her that her love would not be misplaced because he would build upon his experiences to earn it?

Social psychologists have developed scenarios for the evolution of individual selves, theories especially appropriate for people as insecurely self-defined as Caldwell then seemed to be. George Herbert Mead hypothesized that first as children and later as adults, individuals seeking acceptance, approval, and love will shape themselves to meet the expectations of the "significant other." He used a baseball-game metaphor to elaborate upon that hypothesis. To be accepted as a credible player on a team, a person must learn the rules of the game, must then act and play in accordance with the other players' expectations. Failing that would encourage their rejection, risk their inclusion within the social construct.

C. Wright Mills has written persuasively about a vocabulary of motives. Motives are "the terms which persons typically use in their interpersonal relations."[24] If past behaviors seem incoherent or undirected, challenged individuals "construct accounts" of excuses, of justifications, or a combination of the two. In that process they adopt a vocabulary of motives whose rationale and values give legitimacy and coherence to behaviors that would otherwise be neither understandable or acceptable.

Confronted with the challenge of gaining the respect and love of a "significant other," of a young woman with academic and literary interests, what personal account, what vocabulary of motives might Caldwell have constructed to gain her respect, to earn her love? His mother had written randomly; his father also had written occasionally for newspapers, and he himself had allegedly done some casual writing. If he were to be perceived as a person of worth, of sufficient promise to merit Helen's love, his past academic wanderings, his many escapes and experiences demanded some justification. What would explain his previously unfocused personal history better than a desire to write? Writing fed upon experience; its cloak of creative respectability would have impressed Helen more than Caldwell's recently declared business aspirations.

And so Caldwell defined himself for Helen. And because she "was sympathetic and understanding and did not hesitate to urge [him] to follow whatever guiding light that came into [his] vision," because she encouraged him "to strive to perfect [his] writing," his past experiences became justified and his future course defined; he would be a writer.[25] That would identify him, satisfy his parents, and earn Helen's respect and love. All that remained to fulfill Caldwell's longings was to convince her that they could be "happy together," that together they could create "that home . . . [to] go to at night." How successful he was in becoming both the writer and the securely beloved man he imagined himself to be, the couple's future together would tell. How conscious he might have been of the invention that then had motivated him, he hinted only a year before his death. Asked to describe his accomplishments without praising himself, Caldwell had replied, "Well, it's one man's individual expression of an invented, created existence of life."[26]

It is small wonder then that Caldwell's general academic performance declined in those months of that winter's term. His energies were undoubtedly consumed in maintaining that delicate balance between his newly discovered obsessions—writing and Helen. Was the campus aware? Was Louis Ballou—again his roommate—aware of the essential intimacy of Caldwell's and Helen's involvement? Nothing directly had been said, but the fact was somewhat assumed.[27] Nonetheless, the assumption did not prepare Ballou for the contents of a note Caldwell hurriedly wrote to explain his borrowing of Ballou's white shirt. He and Helen, only weeks after their meeting, had eloped to Washington, D.C.

Behind the act hid the enigma. Six months earlier, relishing his independence, Caldwell had denied to his parents any interest in marriage. Yet according to Helen, it was he who insisted upon their elopement: "I didn't want to get married. Christ almighty, I didn't want to get married at all."[28] He would threaten, "Well if you don't, you are going to get pregnant because I'm not going to do a damn thing [to prevent it]." Forgotten are the additional supporting arguments he had used. Whatever their expression, they appear to have cloaked deeper needs that perhaps not even Caldwell could have verbalized.

Helen speculated at various motives, all mirrored in Caldwell's earlier experiences. Wistfully she mused, "I believe he was seeking a home, a sense of security," a perception echoing Caldwell's Wilkes-Barre confession.[29] Otherwise, Helen recalled his often-repeated claim that "he had to make an honest woman" of her. She was not the casual brown-limbed girl or one who gave her sexual favors as a gift to a raw-boned country boy. Rather, he seemed to perceive Helen as a lady compromised by a southern youth who was no gentleman unless he honorably redeemed his fault.

What other motives may have lurked behind Caldwell's conscious urging remain only elusive hints. Did Helen wear orange ribbons in her hair? Sixty years later he, like his Alan Kent persona, recalled their times together, riding in the "still somewhat serviceable"—and fictitious— roadster through "the honeysuckle-perfumed Virginia nights." And no matter that at the time Helen had bobbed ash-brown hair. Caldwell idealized it as "long and silky blond."[30] Was Helen, then, reluctant but with "the soft magic of her arms and legs," that idyllic woman whose promise haunts *The Sacrilege?* Most likely not even Caldwell knew what forces conspired to urge his marriage to a woman whose reality his later prose-poem would merge with the dream.

Chapter 6

The events of the young couple's elopement-honeymoon almost mocked those idyllic visions associated with genteel Southern romance. In Washington, D.C. frayed buntings still drooped from buildings consequent to Calvin Coolidge's inauguration a few weeks earlier. Tourists crowded the city's streets. Erskine and Helen were only two more people among many. But there on March 20, 1925 a justice of the peace married the couple who had defied conventions and parents to formalize their romantic union. Shortly thereafter the Caldwells caught a train for Baltimore.

Since Caldwell's only postceremony account is sketchy—an exceptional night spent on the return train to Charlottesville[1]— that story necessarily must be Helen's: "My wedding night . . . Erskine took me to five burlesque shows."[2] As unusual as such wedding night activities might have seemed, Helen was not shocked by Caldwell's behavior. Possibly similar motives had caused him, during their courtship, to show her his collection of "filthy French postcards." Likewise, Caldwell had been "well aware of what he was doing" during the burlesque tour. In her more mature years, Helen came to believe that he was only reacting against his Staunton grandmother, his mother's First-Family-of-Virginia postures, and the propriety of Carrie's sisters.

An answer he was to offer a half-century later, in response to a query about his fictional treatment of women, sheds some insight. Almost meditatively, Caldwell reflected, "I've never set out to debase woman in any way. My attitude probably originated back in my youth when women were living in a different era. . . . I could recognize the fact that in my early life there were two kinds of women, good and bad."[3]

The morning after their wedding, Helen claimed to have arisen from her bridal bed before daybreak while Caldwell still slept. She went to the window to see dawn lighting the city of Baltimore as well as the new days of her life. In that story, she lamented her situation: "My God, Helen, what have you done?"[4]

The news of Helen and Erskine's marriage preceded their subdued return to Charlottesville; hometown people visiting in Washington had noted the marriage record in one of the papers. Helen's mother "was being consoled by all the Episcopal clergy" and a bevy of sympathetic friends when the couple returned home. Helen and Erskine would have to inform her father, then hospitalized in Atlanta, as well as his parents. One may imagine what the newlyweds must have felt as they journeyed first to Atlanta and then on to Wrens. Helen's father was understandably upset, but eventually reconciled; Erskine's family "naturally was not pleased." Nonetheless all—the parents as well as the couple—had to accept and be reconciled to the marriage as an accomplished fact.

The couple had no apartment, no money, and no means of support. As students, they had no alternative but to rely upon parents, whose trust and hopes they had confounded. They did not, as Caldwell later claimed, immediately withdraw from the university, sell his car—he had yet to own a car—or move to a job in Atlanta.[5] Rather, upon their return to Charlottesville, the Caldwells moved in and lived with the Lannigans.

The individual adjustments were mutually trying. At least Helen was in a familiar environment, but Caldwell must have felt like an intruder and an outsider—almost certainly a strained situation for one long accustomed to privacy. A scant three months before he had been independent and self-supporting in Wilkes-Barre; now he found himself confined by marriage and dependent upon people who were little more than strangers. It was small wonder that his spring grade report marked only a zero and three "drops."

Parents and children realized that their arrangement was tenuous at best. The elder Caldwells had already helped as much as their means allowed. By extending their resources, nonetheless, both families scraped together enough to send Erskine and Helen to her parents' summer home near Mount Vernon, Maine. There they finally could enjoy some privacy, and Caldwell could, with Helen's encouragement, pursue his writing career.[6]

The Maine retreat was idyllic in most respects. Some two miles from the village of Mount Vernon, the venerable house sprawled across a tree-studded yard, with an expanse of lake beyond its fronting road and a backdrop of trees climbing the hills behind. Rustically furnished, its accommodations offered a cavernous long room with benches lining one side and a mammoth stone fireplace on the other. Some twenty rooms provided warrens of privacy and escape where Caldwell could write undisturbed. If he needed to be with Helen, she was downstairs. Only one verifiable consequence followed from the Caldwells' activities that summer. Helen became pregnant. She was to have a child some eleven months after their marriage.

Caldwell must have accepted this reality with his usual quiet resolve and a recognition that he who dances must pay the piper, but with what? His writing remained unpublished. A return to Virginia and the Lannigan household would likely have strained relationships as well as familial resources. A regular, paying job seemed to offer the only solution, but what could he, twenty-one years old, unskilled, and without a degree, do? Again, Ira reached out to help his son. He knew one of the editors of the *Atlanta Journal.* When Caldwell and Helen returned in the fall of 1925, first to Charlottesville and then on to Wrens, Ira encouraged his son to approach Hunter Bell, the city editor.

Caldwell's published accounts of his newspaper beginnings center around two different versions of the same story. His lighthearted *Call It Experience* —wherein he never mentioned Helen or their children— does not betray the anxiety that accompanied his job search. Thirty-five years later, in *With All My Might*—this time admitting Helen and the family—he hints at what he had felt: "Gripping my hands and shoving my clenched fists out of sight in my pockets, I told him in haste that I wanted to work as a reporter, that I had been a student at the University of Virginia, and that I had to leave to find a job."[7]

Once hired, Caldwell soon discovered that a cub reporter could not use his storytelling instincts to embellish reality. He had to reduce a "blue-Monday" suicide story about an itinerant worker to a "half-a-stick" column. It would be a dark Tuesday if the paper missed its deadline waiting for Caldwell to reconstruct the human drama buried beneath the facts. The editors squashed his wryly honest account of the inaugural run of Atlanta's gasoline-powered train. They failed to appreciate Caldwell's emphasis upon its conductor, who, after completing his elaborate departure rituals, reached back to board a train that had abruptly left without him.

Caldwell's literary inclinations also began to shape his judgments. Because Frank Daniel, a fellow reporter who was to remain a lifetime acquaintance, was aware of the Caldwells' strained financial circumstances, he surreptitiously urged the *Journal* book editor to direct some books for review to Caldwell. He could use the extra money. She complied, but two days later Caldwell returned a volume to her desk: "I don't think you'd want to review this book; there's nothing to it."[8] The book was Anita Loos's *Gentlemen Prefer Blondes*, and the person who had told Daniel about Caldwell's review was Margaret Mitchell, subsequently the author of *Gone with the Wind*.

Working with Frank Daniel, Margaret Mitchell, and Caldwell on the *Journal* staff was Frances Newman, another aspiring writer. Caldwell knew of Mitchell's southern panorama-in-progress. With Daniel's encouragement, he had read some of Newman's novel in progress, *Hard-Boiled Virgin*, each page "a final result of a full day's writing." Such efforts must have renewed Caldwell's fiction-writing aspirations, because he allegedly "would go home in the evening and write short stories [to] mail to magazine editors in New York."[9] They were always promptly returned, usually without comment.

Yet newspaper duties and financial concerns must have distracted Caldwell beyond measure. In addition to his regular *Journal* work, he reviewed books, often with Helen's help. Reviews printed in the 1925–26 *Journal* credited both Erskine and Helen. Additionally, the two of them collaborated on reviews for Cora Harris, who then published them in the *Charlotte Observer* and *Houston Post*. That work earned them nothing but the free review books Caldwell would sell or trade in Atlanta's used book stores to supplement his salary. Just as important, perhaps, he must have learned much about good and bad writing from these numerous volumes.

Money became an increasing concern with the approaching birth of the child. Helen could not work, so her time was spent mostly alone—housekeeping, reading, writing—in the apartment. Their small place, furnished only with books and basic necessities, was located in a marginal area surrounding downtown Atlanta, but Helen's travels were limited by public transportation and their precarious finances. Her sense of isolation during this period was underscored in her memories of the February 2, 1926, birth of their son: "I knew nobody. We didn't even have a telephone. [When my water broke], I went next door and the woman called Erskine."[10] For Helen, that day proved memorable for another reason. As Caldwell looked at Erskine Preston Caldwell, Jr., he took the baby's hand and for the first and only time she remembered, he looked tenderly moved. That day he seemed unusually gentle with Helen as well.

The baby's birth emphasized for the Caldwells the financial and psychological sacrifices they would have to endure if Caldwell remained with the *Journal*. The bill from the Catholic hospital had had to be paid jointly by the elder Caldwells and the Lannigans. Consequently, they weighed the security of a reporter's future against the promise of a successful writing career. Their combined confidence tipped the scale. Thus in May of 1926—at a time of year that is pleasant even in Maine—Caldwell resigned from the paper. Abandoning the security of his twenty-five-dollar-per-week salary, he mortgaged his future on a faith that burning desire and hard work would reap their own rewards. He, Helen, and the child, later to be nicknamed Pix, returned to Mount Vernon.

The place called Greentrees again provided the isolation and physical distance that Caldwell felt he needed in order to write his southern stories. Mount Vernon in May was idyllic: "The everlasting countryside was serene and unhurried, and the aches and pains of civilization were distantly remote. One could surely write in such a place, it seemed to say, if writing was ever to be done."[11] But the essentials of everyday living crept, serpentlike, even into this literary Eden. Just reopening a house the size and age of Greentrees was demanding. The well had to be primed, its pump greased, and the gasoline engine coaxed to life. Winter's residue had to be removed from porch and yard. Chilled rooms required opening during the warm days and heating in the evenings. If the Caldwells were to live marginally supported only by their parents, they had to plant and tend a garden and could not pay to have wood cut and hauled. Helen could, and did, perform many of the chores, but some remained for Caldwell to do.

Possibly more burdensome to the twenty-two-year-old new father was the pride he had to overcome for the sake of his stories. Without any income, the young family was almost wholly dependent upon both sets of parents. This was probably more painful than the poverty, hard work, and sacrifice both Helen and Caldwell offered in their quest for his success.

Helen's faith in Caldwell's promise must have been as strong as his own, because when he retreated into the solitude of his room, struggling to write, she washed diapers on a washboard, did household chores, and kept Pix quiet lest his crying disturb his father. This she accepted because she recognized Caldwell's "overwhelming obsession to write; that was the one thing that mattered to him. The only thing that mattered really. It mattered more than human beings, by far. I always respected this. It was the one thing he hoped to do in life."[12] Helen's respect for his compulsion to create apparently allowed her to excuse—like his grandmother, mother, and aunts before—Caldwell's moods and demands because "when he was in the throes of creation, . . . he was completely unapproachable, and nobody was allowed to make any noise in this house."[13]

Almost fifty years later, when Helen would have had reason to examine Caldwell's behavior more critically, she still almost meditatively justified him: "I don't think you can judge him by the same standards you'd judge an ordinary human being. . . . I think the very thing that made him a good writer was [the same] thing that removed him from the human equation. In other words he was removed from ordinary behavior by his genius, if such it was."[14] Ultimately, however, she also had come to reckon the costs: "He sacrificed everybody upon the altar of his muse."[15]

Helen provided more than companionship, a compatible home environment, and encouragement during Caldwell's fledgling writing years.

Intelligent, literarily astute, and direct, she was to be his lone reader and critic there in the rural isolation of Maine. Helen maintained that she "was a natural for Erskine" because she not only "corrected everything he wrote" but also "even used to type his damn stuff."[16]

In truth, Helen was "a natural." Not only had her training in English and foreign languages sharpened her grammatical skills, but she too was then a southerner in her observation and perceptions. True, genteel Charlottesville was a long way from rural Georgia, but Helen could tell whether or not a story rang true. And later, when Caldwell looked around Mount Vernon for some of his fiction, she could again judge the integrity of his down-easterner characterizations, because she had summered in Maine throughout her life.

Without question, the stories Caldwell was to write were his and his alone. Their settings, their themes, and their characters were expressions of his unique experience as cultivated by his fertile imagination, but Helen's critical appraisals emphasized the stories' strengths and underlined their weaknesses long before editors and readers would judge them. The success and acclaim that Caldwell's earliest writing earned, without a doubt, properly belonged to him. Yet justice demands that Helen's contributions be neither slighted nor underestimated. Without her support, direction, and editing, Caldwell's early writings and his subsequent career might have been different indeed.

A writer's success and acclaim depend upon publication, and that summer Caldwell felt driven as never before. Publication would mean not only recognition but also a release from the couple's dependence upon the Lannigans and the elder Caldwells. What they had felt about his abandoning the security of a paying job for the promise of a writing career can only be guessed. Therefore, Caldwell's failure to publish anything that summer must have been more than just a storyteller's disappointment; it injured the pride that otherwise might have validated the wisdom of his decision to work as a writer.

As September approached, Caldwell was confronted by another decision. Should he and Helen hazard the isolation and rigors of a Maine winter, or should they return as southern prodigals? Caldwell estimated that the strains of living once again with the Virginia in-laws would be less rigorous than bone-chilling cold. Yet they apparently became more taxing than he had remembered.

During that early fall of 1926, Caldwell decided he couldn't write at home—that is, in Charlottesville. He wanted to write in New York. With money from his parents, he bought a train ticket and rented a three-dollar-per-week room in one of New York's brownstone tenements. Helen did not accompany him because she already knew, but had not revealed, that she was pregnant again. Their financial situation and his writing aspirations made her fear that he might force abortion to resolve the issue.

But Caldwell soon recognized the tenuousness of his New York situation. Because he could not support himself there, and therefore found he could not write, he went back to the University of Virginia. This decision was not an admission of total defeat. Rather, it marked what for Caldwell must have been a humbling admission. Defining himself as a writer had not made him one. No matter his range of experiences, his hard work, and Helen's unflagging faith and support; he realized that raw experience and desire were not enough. What was lacking in his formula for success Caldwell sought by returning to the university, this time with a sense of purpose.

It was almost certainly during this period of focused seeking that Caldwell discovered the little magazines and the writers he always claimed to have found four years earlier, during his first experience at the university. It was also during this time that he became acquainted with Atcheson Hench, a professor whose class was to affect him so essentially. And perhaps for the first time Caldwell enrolled at Virginia, not merely to gain experience, but to learn what he needed to know if he was going to succeed as a writer.

This time Caldwell's choice of courses was more than casual; he registered only for those that he judged might prepare him for a writing career—a writing seminar, Old English, a course in the novel, and a sociology offering. The first two were taught by Atcheson Hench, a nononsense, demanding, and inspiring professor. His writing course proved to be particularly seminal. Caldwell later observed that it was then, in that seminar that met "upstairs at a round table in a building near the rotunda"— that he was put on the road to writing. Fourteen years after the fact Caldwell offered an unusually emotional tribute to Hench:

> The one thing that left an impression upon me, which I'd not take anything for, was the experience of being in one of your classes. . . . I still don't know what you did to me, and I doubt I'll ever know, but whatever it was, was the best thing that ever happened to me. Nothing that has happened to me since then has given me the feeling I used to have when I walked out of your classroom. I think I must have been a haystack on the verge of bursting into flames. That's the only way I can describe the feeling.[17]

His old professor attributed Caldwell's effusiveness to a feeling falsely burnished through "the golden glow of memory."

What had so ignited Caldwell's enthusiasm in Hench's classes is difficult to determine. Seminar participants were instructed to read broadly by choice, write something weekly, and then exchange impressions and critiques with the others. Hench himself would read and evaluate each piece of writing. What then might have excited Caldwell?

Hench's demands perhaps directed and forced Caldwell to read with a budding practicioner's eye contemporary writings in then-obscure journals such as the *New Republic, Dial, Forum, New Masses,* and the *Yale Review.* Their pages introduced Caldwell to writers as diverse as Virginia Woolf, Upton Sinclair, Langston Hughes, Ernest Hemingway, Henry James, and numerous others. Through their example, he realized that a life's reservoir of feeling could be channeled safely through story, that one's most private self could be shared yet hidden behind the veil of the written word. And finally, in that environment, the almost habitual "shut-mouth" could talk freely. He could write and discuss stories with classmates such as James Aswell, himself an aspiring writer, and Charles Wertenbaker, a would-be novelist.

Most likely, Caldwell's readings and associations led him to Gordon Lewis's bookstore, a gathering place for students with writing interests. Always short on money but generous with encouragement, Lewis promised to help publish any book Caldwell wrote if it had "extraordinary merit and promising sales prospects."

Caldwell's new associations, his writing vows to himself and Helen, and his increasing responsibilities gave him the identity and sense of purpose that had been missing in his earlier academic efforts. He suddenly became a serious student. For Hench's writing class he read voraciously among articles, essays, short stories, and pieces of literary criticism. Within each biweekly reading period, Caldwell charted anywhere between a minimum of 325 and a maximum of 650 pages. One of his log entries incorporates a revealing annotation for D. H. Lawrence's "Glad Ghosts": "One of Lawrence's best tales[,] privately issued. It is an example of the author at his best. (Don't tell the censors.)"[18]

Hench's grading of Caldwell's biweekly writing assignments ranged from C— to A. One story carried a C with the cryptic comment, "Sex too crude it seems to me." On a later work he wrote, "Staccato style forces too much attention." Caldwell's essay "Georgia Cracker" Hench marked with a B+, although that work had already become more significant to Caldwell than Hench's casual grade indicated. Discounting his news articles and book reviews, "Georgia Cracker" was Caldwell's first published career effort.

Printed in an obscure Girard, Kansas, publication called the *Haldeman-Julius Monthly,* "Georgia Cracker" is important as more than Caldwell's first published work.[19] With an uneven style and strident voice, it foreshadows some of those concerns that would shape many of his future stories. "A number of years ago, when I was in my teens, I visited in Georgia," it begins.[20] Caldwell presents a number of details condemning his native state's self-serving and parochial pride. His various indictments culminate in a more damning anathema: "So this is Georgia—whose inhabitants do cruel and uncivilized things; whose land is overrun with bogus religionists, boosters, and demagogues; whose politics are in the hands of Klan-spirited Baptists; and yet, whose largest city boasts of being the 'greatest city in the greatest state in the world.'"

This time Caldwell's grade report proved more respectable. With his lowest grade a C in sociology, he ranked among the top three in both Hench's writing seminar and his Old English course. That he did not receive higher marks must have frustrated Caldwell, for in 1965 he signed a copy of *In Search of Bisco* with a memory: "Inscribed by the author for Atch Hench. Because you were Dr. Hench in the days when I was bucking for grades and always had to be satisfied with a B− or C+."[21] Yet Hench's rigid expectations did not diminish Caldwell's respect for his teacher. Asked in 1949 by the alumni office for his recollections of the university, he claimed that without the professor's influence, he would not "have found [his profession] in the presence of anyone else.[22] Caldwell consequently was "grateful to Dr. Hench for being [his] U. of Virginia."

Midway through that academic year, the March 26, 1927, birth of Dabney, the Caldwells' second son, only could have confirmed the desperation of Caldwell's situation. Twenty-three years old and jobless, Caldwell and his family were so dependent upon relatives that again the grandparents had to pay the costs of the baby's delivery.

Having identified himself as a writer to gain Helen's love and support, Caldwell came to believe that he was consumed by "the urge—or speaking more realistically, this perverse dictate of fate—which decrees that . . . a person is to become a writer whether he wants to be one or not."[23] It was as "ruthless in its demand as the stomach is for daily food." Torn between responsibilities to family and what he increasingly came to believe was his writer's destiny, he chose fidelity to calling.

Despite Caldwell's "invented, created" career-self, his perception of himself as a victim of a perverse fate demanding that he write was also credible to a certain extent. Because his mother had believed that God had saved him for something special, because she had tried to protect him from harmful outside influences, from usual social interaction, he then and throughout the rest of his life was to feel awkward and to flounder in social situations. For such a socially insecure person, writing was the perfect calling. If social intrusions, if family confusions, if personal relationships became too taxing, too intrusive, Caldwell could always withdraw into a private world. There he could work as if fate rather than his personal choice had demanded it. His mother had encouraged his social isolation, and his father had introduced him to a variety of experiences; writing provided a congenial career to one as observant and solitary as he had come to be.

Thus, no matter the costs either to himself or to others, Caldwell felt bound to succeed. If that demanded swallowing his pride through financial dependence upon others, so he was forced to do. With determined resolve the Caldwells again departed for Mount Vernon shortly after Dabney's birth.

Maine in spring breathes renewed hope and promise. Ice leaves the lakes. Budding trees transform the landscape. The Caldwells thus returned during what is always an auspicious season. But Greentrees again imposed the many duties associated with opening and heating the house. Caldwell's chores became litanies he recited to celebrate the measure of his dedication: "Food meant potatoes, and I planted potatoes. Fuel meant wood, and I cut wood. Woodcutting soon became my daytime occupation. Writing short stories became a nighttime occupation, as did reviewing book after book for Cora Harris. And sleep, for a few months at least, became an almost unattainable luxury."[24] Although Helen claimed that "Erskine did not hoe as many potatoes or chop as much wood as he leads readers to believe," and that she continued to write some of the reviews, the fact remains that during this time, Caldwell could not singlemindedly pursue his writing.[25]

Attempting to appease dual hungers, Caldwell continued to write with a determination bordering on desperation. Story after story rolled from his typewriter. Yet translating life into story did not come effortlessly for him. Helen testified that "he didn't write easily; it was difficult for him. It was conceiving—the conception of a child when he wrote."[26] After she had cut through with a blue pencil and corrected his spelling and grammatical errors, Caldwell revised extensively. Because "he was possessed to write, . . . had this internal compulsion to write," Helen accepted the compulsion along with the exhausting demands it imposed upon them all.

In early August, Helen wrote to Carrie with a tiredness that had become almost habit.[27] Because Caldwell did not "like to have anyone around him at all," he had moved to a little cottage on the property near the lake. And although he did not feel well, he remained there day after day writing. He needed fresh air and exercise, Helen guessed, but he would not "stay outside." On pleasant nights, she would carry Dabney and his belongings the nearly half-mile distance to sleep over with him. In the morning she would return to the big house, where her grandfather had cared for Pix during her absence.

Caldwell's writing offered more than just a retreat from the distractions and obligations of family. It excused him from those social interactions that had always intruded upon his sense of privacy. Thus Helen had anticipated with mixed feelings the arrival of her old college friend, Margaret Armentrout, who had introduced Helen to Caldwell. Because Erskine had never been "sociable," he declared he would not leave the cottage "even for meals," during the period of Margaret's visit. There was little Helen could do since the friend was coming at Mrs. Lannigan's invitation. Beyond that, of course, the young Caldwells had no money. Less than a dollar remained in their funds.

And throughout all such distractions, Caldwell worked, most often alone in the cottage where he wrote unflaggingly throughout that summer and fall and into the winter. The results were less than auspicious. For as many stories as he submitted to little magazines or well-known journals, he received rejection slips. Yet Helen could not recall that he ever "experienced depression; he accepted whatever came his way." But as the year progressed, his and Helen's situations became increasingly trying. Maine's autumn nip became November's and December's chill. Caldwell moved back to the house where in the upstairs, unheated room he wore a sweater, leather jerkin, and overcoat as he typed.

Helen's difficulties also multiplied. Pix and Dabney—soon called Dee—were in diapers. To wash them, as well as everything else, she first had to heat water in boilers on a wood-burning stove, then rub the clothing on a washboard in a kitchen tub, and finally hang it inside, where the smell of drying diapers and kerosene permeated the winter-sealed house. Lacking electricity, the rooms had to be lighted with lamps during the long winter nights. Neighbors, such as the Clayton Dolloffs, dropped by occasionally to visit, but the couple had no close friends with whom they could share their isolation. Because Caldwell "had very little to do with [Maine] people," or with anyone else for that matter, their lives were socially confined.

The couple's exclusive companionship had opposing effects. On the one hand, it enforced a mutual dependence and love. At night when the children were finally asleep and Caldwell was not writing, they sat by kerosene lamps in front of the big-room fireplace and read—poetry, stories by Sherwood Anderson and Theodore Dreiser, novels by Morely Callahan, a then-contemporary Canadian writer much admired by the Caldwells. They also made love—almost "every night during the first five years" of their marriage, Helen came to believe.

Yet Erskine and Helen's constant togetherness may have exaggerated their personal idiosyncrasies and trying living conditions almost beyond endurance. Perhaps the children became too noisy or Helen's chatter too annoying. For unfathomable reasons, Caldwell adopted his mother's habit of retreating into stone-cutting silences. Sometimes a few days, sometimes a week, would pass before he would speak again. Since he would not break his silence either to accuse or explain, Helen would be puzzled and hurt. Such behavior made him seem psychologically brutal, yet she realized that "it would not occur to Erskine . . . that he was unkind to someone." Nonetheless, he always used his pain like a two-edged sword, punishing others as well as himself.

Just as Caldwell countered Helen's imagined or real affronts through retreat, so too did he finally cope with Maine's winter assaults. By February of 1928, with the wood supply gone and the family's circumstances emotionally taxing, Caldwell loaded the family, Borzoi the Collie, and his typewriter into their old Stutz car and headed south.[28] Since the previous summer, Ira had been seeking an isolated cabin in the Georgia–South Carolina border area where Caldwell could withdraw to write. He eventually found one, along with enough money to finance the younger Caldwells' trip.

After visiting with the Lannigans for only a few days, the family shortly arrived, via old U.S. Highway 1, in Wrens. After spending a few more days with the elder Caldwells, Erskine drove the fifty miles to a fishing shack on the Savannah River in Edgefield County, South Carolina. Except for occasional trips back to Wrens, he wrote sixteen hours per day in the piney woods location. He continued to perfect his short stories, but additionally, Helen recalled that part of his first published novel, *The Bastard*, was written during this period. Eventually, however,

that same wanderlust—or perhaps the need to escape—that had characterized his earlier life, returned. He left for Baltimore later that spring,
rented a room on Charles Street, and again wrote without interruption.
By late May, however, Caldwell once more looked toward Mount Vernon, the only real home he and his young family had ever had.

Helen's initial sojourn with the Caldwells had been congenial enough.
She and the children enjoyed the climate. Every day she pushed Dee in a
carriage as Pix ambled alongside. Unlike her reserved husband, the
Wrens people enjoyed Helen's friendliness.[29] Moreover, after her long
period of isolation in Maine and unrelieved child-care responsibilities,
Helen appreciated both the company and help the elder Caldwells offered. Although she enjoyed a comfortable association with both Ira and
Carrie, she especially respected her father-in-law. Generous and kind,
he would "give anybody the shirt off his back," and became for Helen "as
near a saint" as any man she had known.[30]

Unlike other family members, who respectfully were to call Carrie
"Mère," Helen could not grant her a similar regard; she had observed
Mrs. Caldwell in too many situations that belied the gentility most saw
in her. Carrie's heritage spoke as surely through her public behavior as
through her words: "Mrs. Caldwell was an FFV [First Family of Vir-
ginia] and never let anyone forget it."[31]

Yet increasingly through the years Helen was to see beyond that facade
to a woman whose private behavior called that grace into question. The
daughter-in-law came to pity Ira, because if she ever "saw a man berated by a shrew, [Caldwell's] father was by Mrs. Caldwell."[32] Once
Helen heard Carrie screech at Ira because she thought he had given too
much attention to a young woman with whom he shared his basketball
coaching responsibilities. On other occasions as well, Carrie would
scream with jealousy or "hit the ceiling" because "she was like that."

What Carrie may have felt toward Helen must be inferred, because
her letters to the daughter-in-law were always carefully polite and sympathetic. At times, she would express a genuine concern about Helen's
overwork and her health, but that solicitude may have had underlying
motives. Helen's functions made "her life too valuable to [them] all for
any risks to be taken."[33] Years later, nonetheless, Carrie was to offer

more obliquely judgmental impressions. She did not question that Helen had "meant to do well by her children," but like the biblical Jesse, "'false impressions grew into obsessions.'"[34] What Carrie estimated these obsessions to be is unclear, but "uprooting" them from the children's lives would "take time." Possibly both mother and daughter-in-law participated in long-sustained psychological jousts both to maintain and establish their respective rights to Caldwell as son and husband.

The Caldwells' return to Mount Vernon that summer was little different from earlier occasions. Helen managed the boys, tended the house and garden, and generally assumed the other responsibilities of daily living. Caldwell mostly continued to write, revising according to Helen's suggestions, and sending story manuscripts to magazines.

The rejection slips returned with their usual regularity. He came to accept them as part of his due: "Waiting, ever waiting, was an ordeal I probably imposed upon myself so as to generate enough fortitude and stamina to be able to endure the consequences of trying to become a published writer."[35] And thus, he had labored and told his stories without reward for more than three years.

Caldwell's stiff-necked pride, secured by a sustaining belief in "perverse fate" would not allow him to accept defeat. Admittedly, Caldwell received little encouragement from editors or readers, but otherwise he enjoyed significant support. Apparently without question, his parents helped him financially as much as possible. Psychologically, Helen daily granted him those dispensations not allowed to "ordinary human beings." She defended her choice by drawing comparisons with other writers: "Look at Hemingway, Fitzgerald, Thomas Wolfe, and D. H. Lawrence."[36]

Because such blind trust no doubt generated even greater pressure to succeed, Caldwell labored faithfully in his literary vineyard during those apprentice years. "In storytelling, what [he] wanted to portray was a revelation of the human spirit in the agony of stress or the throb of ecstasy."[37] Eventually, he began to see that his stories were beginning to assume "a shape and form," that their "imaginary incidents and events" would affect the reader. Ultimately he became convinced that "a writer himself must be pleased with a story before others could be"—that

weighing a story's emotional effect depended upon "some inner balance" within the writing itself.[38]

Less abstractly, Caldwell likewise came to believe that a story's content was more important than its style. Real people, captured through a
writer's personal observations and experience, would have to live again
within his stories. Because one could not create "out of a vacuum," everything he wrote would necessarily be "partly autobiographical."[39]
Thus Caldwell's continuing struggle was that of translating experience
into words, of transforming his private observations into stories whose
truths hinted at mystery and awe. But in the process, another summer
passed without a published work to acknowledge Caldwell's success as a
writer.

As another winter approached, the Caldwells once again abandoned
Maine so that Helen and the children could winter in Wrens. Caldwell
returned to writing in the Savannah River cabin. On the most obvious
level, the shifts between Maine and Georgia represented emotional and
physical necessities. Yet the moves may have been even more vitally important for Caldwell's writing; they forced from him a clarification of regional perspectives. While in Maine he had written about the South. He
could later test his fiction against reality in the Wrens area. Stories written in the South about laconic down-easterners could be judged against
their prototypes when he returned to Maine. Further, the respective sojourns encouraged Caldwell to reexamine his own beginnings and identity.

In addition to poetry composed during these periods, Caldwell sporadically wrote at least the first portion of *The Sacrilege of Alan Kent,* his
autobiography thinly disguised as fiction. Appropriately, the chapter
that sketched those epiphanies punctuating childhood and youth he entitled, "Tracing Life with a Finger."[40]

Chapter 7

The Caldwells left Georgia earlier than usual in the spring of 1929. Erskine planned a business venture to support the family while he worked and waited to have his writing accepted. He had "pieces" circulating in New York, and a young editor, Alfred Kreymborg, liked his work, but Caldwell's literary prospects continued to look dim. At one point he weakened enough to share his frustration with Ira: "If I could get only one piece accepted by an important magazine or published it would be easier to have hopes. Just now the one thing I do need is that kind of encouragement. I have been trying to write for a long time and it is becoming discouraging."[1] The encouragement he needed was then but a few weeks away.

During the spring and summer of 1929, Caldwell received acceptance notices for no less than three of his short works and an apprentice novel. *Blues* accepted "Joe Craddock's Old Woman" for its fall issue. Alfred Kreymborg, Lewis Mumford, and Paul Rosenfeld accepted another Maine story, "Midsummer Passion," and "Tracing Life with a Finger" for their 1929 collection *The New American Caravan*. Caldwell's literary cornucopia overflowed. Further, Erich Posselt offered to publish Caldwell's novelette *The Bastard* under the imprint of his fledgling Heron Press.

After so many rejections, why was Caldwell's writing so suddenly successful? We can only guess. Most likely his writing had improved, had achieved a better balance. Both accepted short stories incorporated themes and styles that would characterize most of his subsequent fiction. "Joe Craddock's Old Woman," in particular, provides an uneven but moving account of a pathetic woman whose husband does not recognize her work-worn body in death.[2] J. H. Wheelock, a Scribner's editor, was later to feel that a "certain grotesque over-realism" marred "the beauty and pathos of an excellent story." Less-sensitive Caldwell critics would repeatedly level similar charges against his writings for years to come.

"Midsummer Passion" balanced the other story's darkness with a wry, almost simplistic, humor. Employing a blend of repetition, comic humor, and sympathy, Caldwell spun his piece around a New England bachelor's sexual fetishes, its comic resolution stirring empathy for the character even as it underscored the isolation and repression that had warped him. A refined blend of the same techniques was to characterize most of his later successful stories and novels. Like a rustic Molière, Caldwell would mix the comic with the tragic, and in the process expose the foibles of human behavior both confounded by hungers and forces beyond understanding.

And "Tracing Life with a Finger"? Why might it have been published? Neither fiction nor autobiography, its voice and imagery suggest a poetry contradicted by its form; nonetheless, its power flows through a series of vignettes evoking a sympathetic response. The reader yearns to comfort, to communicate with, that solitary figure who shares his realizations and their pain from behind a mask. But what comfort is there, as critic Sylvia Cook was to observe, when "life itself is a desecration of any ideal or holiness or dignity," when "the sacrilege is . . . but a condition of existence?"[3]

Only a few years earlier, a reactionary group of young southerners based in Nashville, soon labeled the Fugitive-Agrarians, had challenged H. L. Mencken's characterization of the South as a literary "desert of the Bozarts." They proclaimed that new voices would shortly arise to declare their regional legitimacy. By title alone, Caldwell's novel *The Bastard* denied any claim to Agrarian respectability. Yet perhaps Erich Posselt's reading of the manuscript led him to believe he had heard one of the prophesied voices. The work certainly departed from any southern or American tradition except possibly that hinted much earlier in Herman Melville's *Pierre*, a work that also explored the psychological intertwinings of incest.

Caldwell's first long work unfolds like an existential, surrealistic nightmare. The protagonist, Gene Morgan, works the night shift in a cottonseed mill. There he observes his co-workers gang-rape and murder a prostitute. In a disassociated manner, he succumbs to the seductions of his foreman's young wife. Discovered, Gene shoots the husband

and throws his body down the stairs. A chance meeting with an enigmatic girl on a darkened street drives him into an abrupt marriage whose deformed, hairy issue suggests earlier hints of an incestuous mating. Because the wife sacrifices her life to the care of the child, Gene one day takes it to the park, where he drowns it. The wife stares out the darkened window expecting momentarily her husband's and child's appearance, but he never returns.

Although *The Bastard* most likely owed its inspiration to some of Caldwell's mill-work observations and experiences, its sexual adventures and promiscuous violence seem to have been but projections of imaginative fancy unleashed. They surface as existential horrors boiling up from primeval forces and fears reaching beyond rationality. That sparse, sensitive handling of Caldwell's short-story characters is absent in this novel; its gaps in plot coherence and rationality are filled with the murky darkness of random, amoral chance. That comic sense and human sympathy that were to balance blind human gropings in his later novels did not redeem this work. *The Bastard* was obviously an experimental, apprentice piece, one that incorporated some of Caldwell's later themes but which scarcely hinted at his future promise.

Although Posselt's decision to publish the book proved not to enhance Caldwell's literary reputation, it undoubtedly gave the young writer a psychological boost. Within a short span of months, he was to enjoy publication of works embracing three different genres—the short story, a form of cathartic poetry, and the novel.

But the Caldwells learned that success does not necessarily go hand in hand with wealth. *Blues* and *transition* gave recognition in lieu of pay, while *The New American Caravan* could afford little more. And *The Bastard*, when it was finally published, sold less than half its five hundred copies. The Caldwells' financial situation remained desperate.

Selling review books as he necessarily had, inspired a plan Caldwell hoped might support the family. With money borrowed from a small Lannigan inheritance, combined with a bank loan, the Caldwells would open a bookshop. Thus, in that early spring of 1929, they departed Wrens, not for Mount Vernon this time, but bound for Portland, Maine.

Having left the children in Charlottesville, both Caldwell and Helen devoted their full attention to establishing and stocking the Longfellow Square Bookshop at 668 Congress Street in Portland. Combining the remaining review copies with new books, they would sell to the public. But more than that, Caldwell planned to visit Bowdoin College and libraries in the area, hoping to "bring them around to buying" from a local business. Since Helen would shortly have to assume care of the boys, and Caldwell would resume his writing, they hired one of Helen's Boston friends to serve as assistant manager and salesperson.

The Portland bookshop experience did more than offer hope for financial self-sufficiency to the Caldwells. Freeing them from Mount Vernon's isolation, it encouraged them to meet and socialize with people whose literary interests and ages matched their own. One such couple, Dorothy and Alfred Morang, like the Caldwells were young and impoverished, but childless. Dorothy gave private piano lessons while Alfred painted, much as Caldwell wrote, without much critical success or monetary reward. But beyond their similar circumstances, the two young men shared even more.

Morang, a person of eccentric habits and eclectic interests, was the son of a marriage in which the dominant mother was publicly taunted for her evangelical beliefs and preaching. As a child, he soon became a victim by association of the harassment and rejection directed at her. He eventually retaliated in kind, variously scorning and at least privately vilifying the people of Maine. As resident critic, he had assumed a social outcast's guise, emphasizing his difference by wearing an old overcoat and shabby clothing with the defiance of a scarlet letter. Lest the people close their eyes to the obvious, he further offended their other sensibilities by bathing only as often as he judged necessary.

As ministers' sons, they likewise shared a common agnosticism. Beyond that, moreover, Morang's cynical humor balanced Caldwell's wry wit, a combination they would direct against the social and political systems that both scorned. Yet beyond these similarities lay more vital interests that fed their compatibility. Morang painted well, played the violin with skillful feeling, and held a vicarious appreciation for writing. Whatever their mutual appeals, Caldwell and Morang came to enjoy what was for both perhaps the first, and certainly the deepest and most lasting, friendship of their respective lives.

The year of 1929 was hardly the most propitious time to begin a bookstore venture. Yet Helen and Erskine's optimism, allied with their Boston friend's help, carried them and their business beyond that November's Black Monday and almost a year into the Depression. While Helen and her friend managed the store, Caldwell continued to write. His recent successes fueled a zeal to add to them. To Richard Johns, who had begun a new magazine called *Pagany*, he sent two stories with a letter of introduction honestly stating his situation: "You don't know me and neither does anybody else."[4] With what was to become a habit of exaggeration, he claimed to have been "working seven or eight years unsuccessfully" with only the year's three stories and the novel as measures of his reward. While Caldwell hoped that *The Bastard* didn't shock Johns, his overall appeal must have been successful. Johns was to publish four Caldwell works in the next three successive issues of *Pagany*.

"The Strawberry Season," a story of youthful desire and fulfillment, and "Inspiration for Greatness," the middle portion of what would eventually be issued as *The Sacrilege*, appeared in the first issue of the magazine. "A Swell-Looking Girl" and "John the Indian and George Hopkins" kept Erskine Caldwell's name before *Pagany* readers in the spring and summer issues of 1930. Except for his later southern stories, with their more darkly disturbing themes, the four offerings among them revealed the direction of his emerging writing style and strengths.

The "Inspiration" piece played Caldwell's sensitivity and poetic attention to detail against a romantic's values in an engagingly provocative quest. The other stories, however, traded upon those same strengths that "Midsummer Passion" had revealed; laconic directness combined with understatement and repetition to create tensions resolved through the stories' conclusions. And as before, those paradoxical blends of comic humor and empathy seemed as natural as life, because for Caldwell they were inseparable from life: "To me there is comedy in tragedy and tragedy in comedy."[5] Early readers of Caldwell's *Pagany* pieces were among the first ones caught within the deceptively intricate webs his stories spun. Common people, antic figures through their idiosyncrasies, provoked pity as their obsessions starkly revealed the irrationality of human motives and behavior.

A bare summary of "A Swell-Looking Girl" merely hints at the complexity hidden behind the simplicity in Caldwell's short stories. Lem, an innocent country bumpkin, obsessively and hurriedly marries a swell-looking girl named Ozzie. The "flimsy pink little things" she always wore had fascinated him beyond telling. Wishing to share his wonder with the local boys, Lem cajoles his new and properly bashful wife to hike her dress, to astound them with the glory of her undies. She does. The boys hoot and whistle; they rub their eyes "to make sure they were seeing right. Ozzie had on nothing at all under her dress."[6] Lem ignores the ribald joshing, lost in "trying to figure out why Ozzie wore those things one day and took them off the next."

This story, like so many of Caldwell's future ones, revealed more than a simplicity of style and theme masquerading behind "rib-poking" bawdy humor. Its "tall tale" charade allied Caldwell securely with those traditions established by writers whom literary historians were to call old southwest humorists. Sut Lovingood, another southerner's antic creation, would have been right at home with Lem and the boys.

During the next two years, Richard Johns and *Pagany* were to accept four more of Caldwell's stories for publication, a happy circumstance that provoked almost sycophantic appreciation. He praised the editor and *Pagany* as damn good, "at the head of the list by all methods of count and recount."[7] He likewise hoped that Johns never would be seduced into publishing "rotten pieces" by the likes of Dreiser, Anderson, and Joyce. Meanwhile, *Nativity*, another nonpaying "little magazine," accepted Caldwell's "Saturday Afternoon" for its winter 1930 issue. Unlike his previous stories, this told of that abiding horror Caldwell must have felt when, as a child, he heard casual stories of black victims butchered upon the block of southern prejudice.

Caldwell's sudden publishing success did not lull him into a false sense of security. Rather it seems to have stimulated him with renewed vigor; he continued to write and post a succession of short stories even as he worked to complete a second short novel called *The Bogus Ones*. Although he had always written with urgent fervor, in the early spring of 1930 Caldwell wrote with an energy born of almost brash confidence.

No doubt an unsolicited letter from Scribner's Max Perkins helped stoke Caldwell's enthusiasm afresh. He who had promoted Hemingway,

Fitzgerald, and Thomas Wolfe wrote with complimentary brevity: "I was much impressed by your stories in the Caravan, and thought it possible you might be willing to send something to Scribner's Magazine."[8] Seeking fresh talent, he and another young editor, John Hall Wheelock, allegedly had first discovered Caldwell through his stories in the little magazines. That claim was not entirely accurate.

Almost a year before, and without invitation, Caldwell had submitted a selection of writings to the *Scribner's Monthly*. Failing to hear from them, he made inquiry through an acquaintance, one Hurd Whitney; Fritz (Alfred) Dashiel responded immediately.[9] A careful reading of the manuscripts had not impressed the editors. Despite their occasional "flashes of character," the pieces, mostly from *The Bastard*, were sketches rather than short stories. Nonetheless, Dashiel advised that Caldwell was to stop by the Scribner's offices "if he comes to town."

As discouraging as Scribner's appraisal seemed, Caldwell had acted upon the general invitation. In fact, he visited with Perkins himself. Thus Perkins's letter a year later was not the result of fortuitous discovery. Rather it implied that, on the evidence of the *Caravan* story, Scribner's was ready to consider seriously whatever new material Caldwell submitted.

There are two versions of what happened subsequent to Perkins's letter of request. Because the facts themselves tell one story and Caldwell's later embroidering of them another, a comparison between the two is revealing. It suggests as much about Caldwell's storytelling methods as it does about his own self-perceptions.

Receiving Perkins's invitation, Caldwell immediately posted a story in response. Perkins rejected it as too anecdotal but indicated that he would like to see more. Within a few days, Caldwell forwarded "The Mating of Marjorie" and "A Very Late Spring," both newly written New England pieces. Anxious about their reception, he caught an overnight bus for New York two days after mailing them. Unable for some reason to see Perkins, Caldwell left a message with the secretary. He would stay overnight, until Saturday, at a local hotel where Perkins could reach him.

Perkins called Saturday morning, March 1. *Scribner's Monthly* had already accepted "The Mating of Marjorie." He would write Caldwell

later about the disposition of the second story. Five days later, he wrote
to confirm acceptance also of "A Very Late Spring." Dashiel, as manag-
ing editor, would forward the details of payment and publication dates.
Thus within the two-week period subsequent to Perkins's letter of invitation, Scribner's received three Caldwell stories and accepted two.

Two decades after the fact, Caldwell told a similar but provocatively
different story.[10] In his version, the initial letter from Perkins arrived on
a "gray autumn day" during that season of hopelessness. Thereafter,
Caldwell wrote and posted two stories per week, stories written throughout a long winter, first in Maine and then in a Georgia rooming house.
This literary courtship involving Caldwell's proposals and Perkins's rejections continued for some five months, with the editor rejecting all of
the implied total of some thirty stories. Finally in early March, the season of hope, Perkins wrote to confirm that Scribner's had accepted one
story.

That single acceptance touched off a frenzy. Caldwell allegedly wrote
for two nights and a day to complete those stories complementing the
eleven he delivered personally to the editor. After catching an overnight
bus to New York, he went to the Scribner's office, was thoroughly
"unnerved" by Max Perkins's secretary, left a telephone number, and
returned to his room to wait for a call. It came the next day. Although
Caldwell's dating of the call was accurate, his reconstructions of the conversation are apocryphal.

Much of that delightful account revolves around an alleged misunderstanding. Perkins supposedly told Caldwell that Scribner's had decided to accept two of his stories for publication, offering him payment of
two-fifty for the pair. Perkins interpreted Caldwell's long, noncommittal
pause as one of disappointment, whereupon he upped the ante to three-
fifty. Caldwell's tone conveyed resignation; he had hoped for more than
three dollars and fifty cents. The editor was confounded; he had meant
three hundred and fifty dollars.

The story, like so many Caldwell told in publicly creating his persona,
is an artful blend of fact and fiction. The factual two-week period of anxious anticipation he extends to a five-month stretch of frenzied work and
hope. The two rapidly accepted stories, he reduces to a laggard one. No

matter the actual financial details of Dashiel's letter. Caldwell uses his telephone conversation with Perkins as the basis for an elaborate conceit, one that establishes him as an innocent rustic so impoverished that even his dreams are properly humble.

During their actual telephone exchange, Caldwell and Perkins did discuss the content as well as the style of his writings. In a subsequent letter, Caldwell expanded upon both subjects.[11] As he always would, he then insisted that he did not "write for the sake of obscenity any more than [he] would write for a cause like Communism—or propaganda for Single-Tax, the Pope, more sewers, bigger Buicks and few[er] babies."

And as for his writing style, Caldwell claimed to write from the first-person perspective because he believed "that an idea can sometimes be more richly expressed from the personal point of view." But Perkins should not confuse him as a person with that "I" who had been inspired by a method: "As a matter of fact if there is any autobiographical experience in my work it will be found to a greater extent in those stories which are written objectively." Caldwell wanted to convince Perkins that as a conscious artist, his imagination rather than a hidden self shaped his writings.

The $350 *Scribner's Monthly* check could not have arrived at a more opportune time for the Caldwells. In that first year of the Depression, the bookshop had earned them only a minimal subsistence. Otherwise, however, it provoked a local notoriety for Caldwell and provided him with opportunities that tested his and Helen's marriage.

The 1929 publication of *The Bastard* had generally earned little either critical or public attention, but on the local level it had stirred both. When Caldwell stocked and attempted to sell copies of the book, a municipal judge, acting upon public complaint, had, with threat of arrest, forbidden future sales of the work. Caldwell and Morang privately seethed and railed at such myopic provincialism masquerading as justice. Caldwell wrote a statement of defense to be printed in the Portland paper.

In other ways, the bookshop indirectly promoted situations Caldwell accepted as more compromising. Returning via boat from one of his Boston book-buying trips, he and a young woman schoolteacher had enjoyed an overnight tryst.[12] Later during a weekend retreat to Mount Vernon, Helen had caught him and their strikingly attractive Danish store clerk "flagrante delicto" on the dock.[13] Shortly thereafter, Caldwell and Helen's bookshop friend managed to hide an intermittent affair for months before Helen discovered it. Naturally enough, each of the transgressions upset and hurt her, but "adultery pure and simple" she could cope with, "learn to accept after awhile." His longer affair with her friend, and Caldwell's subsequent relationships, those with "deep feeling," she could not.

Caldwell himself reacted to them all in some ways predictably and in others, not so predictably. In those instances when he was discovered, he offered various justifications and excuses, often shifting the blame to Helen. But more mysteriously, after his transgression with the schoolteacher, and some of his later ones as well, he had confessed to Helen. Even that was not unusual, but his vivid replay of the details she found both painfully cruel and strange. Finally she merely filed this idiosyncrasy into the same category with the honeymoon burlesque shows and the filthy postcards. All, Helen managed to intuit, somehow were reactions against the strong and proper women of his childhood.

Discounting its romantic distractions, the bookshop venture had proved costly in other respects as well. Its obligations and details too often pulled Caldwell away from that sense of writing as destiny that both his *Scribner's* success and Perkins's continuing encouragement seemed to augur. Consequently, before summer's end in 1930, the Caldwells left Portland, the Morangs, and an indebted bookshop that the friend would manage, to return to Mount Vernon.

The importance of the Scribner's acceptance in renewing Caldwell's determination to succeed as a writer cannot be stressed too much. A few weeks after his telephone conversation with Perkins, he uncharacteristically shared his dreams with his parents: "I've got this far, and I've got to go further. . . . I am working for the Pulitzer Prize, so help me God!"[14] With the endorsement of a number of prominent people, he would apply for a Guggenheim Fellowship whose support would enable him to write a novel that would "win the . . . Prize."

Apparently recognizing that his few published stories and an uneven novel would grant him scant consideration in the strenuous Guggenhiem competition, Caldwell had proceeded immediately to try to fatten his portfolio. Less than a month after the initial Scribner's acceptance, he asked if they would consider the manuscripts for *The Bogus Ones*, a novel, and a yet-untitled collection of short stories. Acting upon their subsequent agreement, he forwarded, in addition to the novel, his previously accepted stories plus fourteen new ones to round out the collection. His covering letter stressed both their importance and their costs: "And after many long years of disappointment, I'll still have enough enthusiasm left in me to await with eagerness your final decision."[15] But Caldwell also cautioned that without signs of continuing success, he feared his present pace "some of these years" might extinguish those fires of encouragement.

A month passed without any response from either Perkins or Scribner's. Perhaps as a gentle reminder, Caldwell posted two new stories that he had not yet completed when he had forwarded the first batch. Another month had elapsed before he heard anything from Perkins about either the novel, the collection, or the two additional stories.

Perkins finally responded with both promise and reserve. Scribner's would publish Caldwell's short-story collection in the spring of 1931. The two belated stories, the *Monthly* reluctantly returned. And as for *The Bogus Ones*, while every part taken alone "was striking," the whole did not seem successful. Perkins issued a caution.[16] Usual publishing practice precluded issuing a short-story collection without first publishing a writer's novel. Considering Caldwell's larger promise, Scribner's had made an exception in his case. If he wished, however, he could offer the novel to other publishers, with the understanding that, should they accept it, they should also have the short stories. Obliquely, Perkins was telling his young writer that as far as Scribner's was concerned, it was the book of short stories or nothing at all; the novel—a pedestrian piece veiling some of Caldwell's own Maine experiences—should not be published.

Caldwell responded to the mixed offer almost immediately. Though the decision about the novel was disappointing, he was reconciled: "I know there is one [editor] I shall always respect. . . . You see, I love the truth with all the passion that makes me hate a lie."[17] He therefore accepted Scribner's proposal to publish the book of short stories as well as the request for a few more stories to complete the book. He would attempt to provide that addition as soon as possible, but he needed their opinion: "Should the novel be shelved as a curiosity or could it be reworked 'to make it of any value'?" And the stories? Which did they think better? Those with the Maine or the Georgia settings? "I can't make up my mind over the problem of which place I should dig in, and concentrate," Caldwell confessed. In his response, Perkins tellingly avoided any mention of the novel. As for the stories, he favored those of the South because the material seemed fresher, went deeper, and seemed to have more meaning.

Despite Perkins's silence about the novel, Caldwell could not allow the subject to rest. Further inquiries about it brought no response from Perkins. After a month and a half, Caldwell attempted to force the editor's hand. A new publishing house had offered to publish *The Bogus Ones* as well as his next two novels. Although he wanted to stay with Scribner's if at all "humanly possible to do so," *The Bogus Ones* represented a year's work. Would they publish it if he revised the work? Citing a family to support through income from his writing, he pleaded for their understanding: "Just now my job is trying to live and write, but in order to write, I've got to live."[18] Perkins had confronted a stubbornness that Caldwell would always use—whether with publishers, wives, or others—to try to gain his advantage.

Perkins's response was neither compromising nor unduly sympathetic.[19] If another firm had agreed to publish *The Bogus Ones,* Caldwell should accept its offer. However, that would preclude Scribner's plan to issue his book of short stories, and with that he inserted an aggrieved note: "A publisher wishes to publish all that is to be published of the work of an author he takes up,—particularly as he bargains more upon the author's promise for the future than upon prospect of immediate returns." But Scribner's left him free to do as he wished.

Given that choice, Caldwell apologetically replied that he wanted to stay with Scribner's if they wanted him. At the same time, he reminded them that remaining with the firm meant losing the income the novel would have brought. Could he therefore have an advance against the projected book of short stories? Maine winters, Caldwell justified, were harsh, and he wanted to leave before another came.

His patience strained by Caldwell's five-month campaign to have his way, Perkins finally wrote with a directness he earlier had tried to avoid.[20] The novel they did not think a success, and short-story collections generally were unprofitable. But, he repeated, publishers make mistakes, and Caldwell was free, if he wished, to seek another firm to publish both the novel and short stories. As to an advance, Scribner's would allow $250 or $300. That in addition to the $350 for two more short stories—"The Corduroy Pants" and "Dorothy"—that the *Monthly* had just accepted was the best they could offer to aid his escape from Maine. Caldwell cast his lot with Scribner's.

Perkins apparently was justified in his rejection of the novel. Guy Owen, a much later Caldwell critic, estimated that rejection to have been a fortunate one.[21] As an apprentice work, it lacked coherence and contained spelling and structural shortcomings in abundance, but he otherwise noted its virtues. With a Maine setting, it attacked that region's puritanism with a doggedness that Caldwell would later apply to the South's version of that restrictive belief system. Since its story thinly veiled Caldwell's other experiences of the artist as a young man, Owen judged that it offered other autobiographical hints. The writer-protagonist is in a tense relationship—as Caldwell at least then was with Helen—with his live-in companion, to whom he is unfaithful. He and an artist friend equally find the novel's Portland setting restrictive both artistically and personally. And finally, as Caldwell himself did at the time, the writer enthusiastically reads and defends D. H. Lawrence with his celebration of human sexuality as an almost sacred impulse.

Scribner's rejection of *The Bogus Ones* did not interrupt Caldwell's impetus to write. After his parents' departure from what was to become their annual summer visit, he again moved from the family's big house down to the Parker Lake guest cottage. Leaving Helen and the two young boys to their own concerns, he used that privacy to write story after story. Each one he submitted to Helen for revision and editing before forwarding to Max Perkins.[22] Those not accepted by the editor he forwarded to other journals for consideration until, if any story was declined by six journals, he usually abandoned it.

Before 1930 ended, therefore, *Pagany* had published "John the Indian and George Hopkins," while *Nativity* had printed "Saturday Afternoon," a story Morris Renek was later to judge as one that "belongs with the best of American fiction." The year had been a good one for Caldwell's writing career. Discounting the rejected novel, a count of eight published stories plus twelve more to be included in the book represented an auspicious beginning for a new writer not quite twenty-seven years old.

Yet already rumblings of that storm of controversy—which thereafter would sweep Caldwell's literary reputation to-and-fro—could be heard faintly in the distance. The editor of the *Bookman*, after seeing the first story Caldwell submitted there, wanted to read nothing more: "We are not bathed in sweetness and light, but we positively hate the way you see."[23] A *Hound and Horn* editor cabled the other editors from Europe: "Under no circumstances print Caldwell."[24] Although such judgments may have smarted, Caldwell shared them lightly with Perkins.

Against such criticism, the young writer could counter his own integrity, his publishing success, and the confidence of Max Perkins. Beyond that, J. H. Wheelock, Caldwell's editor for the short-story collection, left no doubt of his opinion. Caldwell had an uncommon talent whose "understanding [of] people and the inner relation of events coupled with a talent for writing" promised to make him "one of the really outstanding writers of our time."[25] If he were willing "to keep at it," to discipline himself rigorously, he seemed bound for success; yet the editor advised that Caldwell might leave more to the reader's imagination, make his stories less obvious. Wheelock's tempering caution, no doubt, paled in the light of his more glowing assessment.

Willingness and discipline had long been essential qualities of Caldwell's character. But in his cosmology, hard work merited reward—one of justified pleasure. And for him, pleasure meant escape from the ordinary through travel—seeing new places, observing new people, experiencing the world. Consequently the Scribner's advance granted him the luxury of what thereafter would become an almost undeviating pattern—an extended trip after the completion of each new book.

Never having traveled west of the Mississippi, Caldwell was drawn to Hollywood. There he could punctuate his daily writing by observing people as they translated America's dreams onto celluloid. Helen was not to accompany him. Neither their financial situation nor her maternal responsibilities, and possibly Caldwell's desire for escape, would allow her that pleasure. Instead, she and the boys would drive first to Charlottesville and then await his return in Wrens.

The details of Caldwell's trip west are revealing. Apparently because he wanted to convey that he, first, was artistically dedicated and, second, poor, Caldwell tells of climbing aboard a bus early in October with only his typewriter, a cigarette-making machine, and one suitcase.[26] Unable to sleep while traveling, he interrupted the cross-country trip for a night's rest in Kansas City. What followed was a misadventure worthy of a traveling salesman's fantasy.[27]

Assigned through error to a room not yet vacated by an attractive young woman, Caldwell's fatigue precluded his cooperation with her desires. Asked about his line of work, he barely responded; he sold "paper—with words on it." Then as Caldwell fell asleep, he felt a heavy weight upon him, experienced "a pleasant sensation of falling endlessly through space." Always presenting himself publicly as innocent or seduced, he remained blameless; the young woman had helped herself while he was on the edge of a dream.

After arriving in Hollywood, Caldwell could not find lodging in the hotels. Experienced clerks were suspicious of travelers carrying typewriters. Eventually a displaced Georgia woman, catching his accent, rented him a nice room in her hotel, where he promptly fell asleep only to awaken to crashing sounds. Firemen were chopping their way through the door. Caldwell had fallen asleep while smoking in bed but once again, a woman forgave him. She led him to another room to resume his rest.

That expectation of female sympathy was a pattern not only in his life but also in his writings. A mother always forgave the wandering Alan Kent. The YMCA official's wife supposedly granted the young Caldwell her overnight comfort. A Baltimore pawnbroker's wife encouraged his living in their house until her suspicious husband halted the arrangement. Thus the Hollywood hotel woman represented but another variation upon Caldwell's prototypical woman—always understanding and forgiving, often offering him her sexual favors as reassurance.

The change of scene to Hollywood did not corrupt Caldwell's habits; it merely provided him with a different environment in which to pursue them. Once settled at 1511 North Wilcox Avenue, he continued to write throughout the month he spent in California. Wheelock had approved, without reservations, twelve stories for the Scribner's book, but eleven others required incidental revision or correction. The editor believed that two, "Var-monters" and "The Artists," should not be included in a first work. To meet the projected February publication date, Caldwell thus had to tinker with a list of stories as well as write two more to substitute for those the editor hesitated to accept.

But before Christmas of 1930, Caldwell was dissatisfied with his writing progress in California, a restlessness he would later attribute to an increasing desire to write a novel.[28] Yet he had already written novels. *The Bastard* had been the first, *The Bogus Ones* second, and Heron Press only that summer of 1930 had agreed to publish his third, *Poor Fool*.[29]

Like *The Bastard*, *Poor Fool* presented an excursion into surrealistic nightmare and irrationality. Poorly developed and motivated grotesques—an ex-boxer and his New Orleans prostitute-mistress, a four-hundred-pound abortionist with her homosexual henchman, her strange daughter—all served to complicate a tenuous plot. Surviving kidnap by the abortionist, saved by her daughter from homosexual rape and castration, the ex-boxer eventually is machine-gunned by his ex-manager's men. When his body is dumped into a canal, his prostitute-love flings herself into the water to join him in death.

Unlike anything else Caldwell ever was to write, both *Poor Fool* and *The Bastard* represented apprentice works exploring the extremities of imaginative horror. Two recent Caldwell critics, nonetheless, have used the novels to identify themes and and techniques that Caldwell would later apply more successfully to other works. James E. Devlin recognized "the mother figure who looms so large in Caldwell's later fiction," as well as those strains of episodic and random violence that mark people victimized by forces beyond their control.[30] Sylvia Cook likewise cites Caldwell's deterministic view of human nature. She, however, more

sympathetically and incisively explores his use of imagery—sexual, mechanical, and violent—and the links between motherlessness and de-
structive relationships as themes consistent with his later writings.[31] For
the more casual reader, however, *Poor Fool* seems to be but a collection
of episodic distortions spawned from the germs of adolescent fears and
reinforced by forms of existential schizophrenia. Whatever their source,
Caldwell apparently had exorcised his haunting obsessions before writing his next novel—the one that allegedly inspired his return from California to Georgia.

Chapter 8

Caldwell's arrival in Wrens must have presented an almost surreal study in contrasts. Recent images of beautiful people in limousines and movie sets where fantasy was projected as reality were juxtaposed against the reality of Wrens. He characterized the difference as "like returning to another world which I had rather forgotten."[1] And so it was because during that third week in December, Wrens stood winter-bleak in its surroundings. The town's set included poverty-stricken country people, mule-drawn wagons, and Model T's. In its back lots, horses dozed and chickens scratched among the droppings. Caldwell's six weeks in Hollywood, no doubt, brought home the contrast between its opulence and celluloid promise and the South's poverty and social reality.

More dispiriting than the area's brown cotton fields and dormant dogwood hedges, Caldwell "could not become accustomed to the sight of children's stomachs bloated from hunger and seeing the ill and aged too weak to walk to the fields to search for something to eat."[2] He claimed to have walked the countryside day after day, becoming increasingly depressed through the process. So he might have done, but other evidence indicates that more than observation had pointed Caldwell toward the subject of his next novel, *Tobacco Road.*

In addition to his pastoral, teaching, and coaching interests, Ira also wrote weekly columns for the *Augusta Chronicle.* Almost always they focused upon the degradation that sharecropping tenants, black and white, suffered in the name of public denial. His indictments became so strenuously insistent that area residents discounted Reverend Caldwell's accusations as those of a "calamitous nay-sayer." Failing to rouse local people to action, he consequently employed a scholarly approach to direct his polemics to a broader audience.

During 1929 and early 1930, Ira had written a treatise on the causes and effects of intensive agriculture upon the land and some of its people. His work, *The Bunglers: A Narrative Study in Five Parts,* appeared serially, beginning with the June 1930 issue of *Eugenics*, a journal of the American Eugenics Society. Fictionalizing his case study of a "home town" clan, Ira used the situation of the Benjamin Bungler family to level indictments against the system which had victimized them.

Once descendants of hardy Anglo-Saxon landed proprietors, the Bunglers had over successive generations been reduced to landless poverty through a combination of poor agricultural practices and policies of "our bungling society." Well-intentioned, family-oriented, and willing to work, they nonetheless lived in filthy, teetering, sharecropping shanties. There they farmed the depleted sand, worked sporadically in cottonseed mills and fertilizer plants, and generally existed as they could. Sometimes they begged for food and clothes or dipped snuff to minimize their hunger pangs. Through the years they had experienced a physical and intellectual decline exceeded only by their increasing numbers— spread through thirty Georgia counties and four adjacent states—a phenomenon for which one Bungler blamed his wife: "She breeds too fast."

Ira's concern was genuinely sympathetic as he cast about for the causes of Bunglers' victimization. He questioned whether their situations were a consequence of social inheritance or economic determinism. Ira saw "this strange, unhappy creature as he was buffeted about by the ruthless forces of life as a feather is buffeted by a hurricane. . . . [But] Benjamin Bungler was not an accident nor was he a freak of nature. He was the result of social, economic, and biological forces."[3]

Beyond impoverishment, the consequences were various. Physically and intellectually deprived, the Bunglers became willing victims of emotional excesses. In worship services, they would handle poisonous snakes, speak in tongues, "come through" for the Lord, or "dance the holy dance," a performance less reverent locals called the "Sunday hootchie-kootchie."

Just as Caldwell would use his father's interpretive focus for the theme of *Tobacco Road*, so his Sister Bessie and Dude characters would be but elaborations upon two people Ira first sketched into his study.

One of the principle [*sic*] workers in this particular meeting was the woman pastor of the church. She was the widow of the Methodist minister who was a member of a small Georgia conference. Some weeks after his death, she was missed from her home. Several days later she was found on her husband's grave. She said she was going to raise him from the dead. It was reported that she had to be taken forcibly from his grave. Subsequently she began to preach and was the pastor of the Church of Rattlesnake fame for a number of years. At the age of fifty odd years she married a school boy about sixteen years old. Although the boy had not finished the fourth grade in school, he alternated with his bride in preaching.[4]

For all its passioned conviction, Ira's narrative study received little recognition from the few who read it. Not until Caldwell translated Ira's Bunglers into fictional story did their concerns reach an audience broader than anyone might have dreamed. How Ira directly influenced his son's choice of subject at that time is unclear. Caldwell much later acknowledged, without saying when, that "he introduced me to the people he knew, who make up the characters of *Tobacco Road*."[5] Possibly Ira also had urged the different telling, because Caldwell had been back in Wrens for less than a month when he wrote cryptically to Perkins, "I am trying to get a new novel started."[6]

Distractions frustrated Caldwell's attempts to give full attention to the novel. Shortly after Christmas in 1930, Helen's father died, and the two of them had to go to Charlottesville for the funeral. After their return, Caldwell posted two new stories and a revised one for the *American Earth* collection. And even as he attempted to write his version of the Bungler story, other stories intruded. Writing to Perkins, he apologized for the compulsion that drove him to such amazing levels of creativity:

> I honestly hate to bother you and make a pest of myself, and I even tried to keep from writing anything awhile so I wouldn't be tempted to submit it to you, but regardless of what I wanted to do, this story ["Grassfire"] worked into me and I just had to write it. Sometimes when a story comes it won't let you read a book or go hunting or even sit in the sun and let crazy fools talk, until you write it.[7]

Thoughts of the novel would not allow Caldwell to sit in the sun either. We may infer from his lack of correspondence with Scribner's for the next six weeks that *Tobacco Road* consumed all his creative energies.

Where he worked during that initial period—whether in an Augusta boardinghouse or the Savannah River cabin—is unknown. Wherever, claiming the need for distance, he departed Wrens for New York City on March 9. There he rented a room at 72 West Fifty-first Street, where he immersed himself in completing the book.

Caldwell's later accounts in *Call It Experience* and *With All My Might*—with their detailed rendering of his poverty and frugality—seem accurately to reconstruct the single-minded determination with which he wrote. He did not even call Perkins, who by this time had become a respected mentor as well as editor. He did, however, accept an invitation from Mike Gold, editor of *New Masses*, to attend a party. There he met people who were already gaining reputations which were to grow—Lewis Mumford, Edmund Wilson, Laurence Stallings, Robert Cantwell, Georgia O'Keeffe. Even more impressive was his much-relished meeting with Mae West. And hovering on the periphery of the luminaries' glow was one Maxim Lieber, a new young literary agent who stalked Caldwell with enthusiastic promises. Hesitant, perhaps suspicious, Caldwell deferred Lieber's invitation to represent him.

Back in his room, Caldwell must have written as one possessed. During the three-week burst of writing in New York, he finished *Tobacco Road* in rough draft—less than three months after he had told Perkins, "I am trying to get a new book started." Amazing as that feat was, Caldwell characteristically used exaggeration to justify whatever rewards the work might merit. After completing the rough draft, he tallied the costs in a letter to Dick Johns: "Me, I have finished the book I've been doing these long, sometimes hungry, most of the time painful months. Ten of them. I got to page The End by working 22 days, from 12 P.M. [*sic*] to 12 A.M. That last month was hard, but the other nine were unbearable."[8] The unbearable months? Possibly Ira's June 1930 publication had planted a seed whose growth had pained Caldwell until he could write it away. Yet the more incredible reality remains. Caldwell seems to have written the first of his two most celebrated novels within a period of less than ninety days.

Like most writers, Caldwell could not immediately judge *Tobacco Road*'s worth. After revising it for a month, he felt confident that

Scribner's would "want to publish it." "It's not sensational, experimental, nor important; it is just human. Maybe it's not so good; but I have a sympathy for the people in it, and I have become attached to it. Enough," Caldwell concluded.[9] That sympathy declared him his father's son as surely as his storytelling showed Carrie's influence. Together their respective gifts were to fuel a future success that would be more than enough.

Whatever revisions Caldwell made—as usual, with Helen's editorial suggestions and intuitive sense—must not have been extensive; Scribner's received the completed manuscript on May 4, scarcely more than two weeks after he had finished the book in first draft. Then came what must have been an interminable period of anxiety as Caldwell awaited the editorial consensus.

That decision would have to evolve through repeated meetings in which editors weighed *Tobacco Road*'s assets against its liabilities. Compelling as its people and their story were, the book was certainly unorthodox in the raw honesty of its setting and theme, its primitive characters and their behavior. If they agreed, its publication would represent a radical departure from anything the reputable Scribner house ever before had offered to its public. Works by Wolfe, Hemingway, and Fitzgerald no doubt appeared respectable by comparison.

Tobacco Road's first sentence imposed a hitherto unacknowledged bleak landscape on the reader: "Lov Bensey trudged homeward through the deep white sand of the gully-washed tobacco road with a sack of winter turnips on his back."[10] The setting seemed scarcely to have been one offering possibilities for either pathos or comedy, yet the novel resonated with both. Impoverished beyond hope, Jeeter Lester, the ragged family patriarch, nonetheless maintained an essential faith. Someday, "God will treat us right."

The Lesters had been so "buffeted by the ruthless forces of life" that they emerge as scarcely recognizable human figures. They nonetheless express those primeval life forces—hungers for food, sex, and transcendental hope—that both ensure survival and betray their sacred instincts. The grandmother scavenges for grass, leaves, and roots that keep her alive. Jeeter steals turnips from his son-in-law. After devouring them, however, he hears his son's accusations "like the voice of God calling him to punishment." Not until decades later did Caldwell try to explain what moved him to present his people as he did: among people's motivations "physical survival is the first. . . . Then nature takes over after that and you have this impulse . . . or sexual proclivity."[11]

That proclivity, no matter how grotesquely or humorously expressed is, in and of itself, not laughable. Rather, "it was the actions of the Lesters that appeared funny to them." Flowing from nature as they do, mating rituals, antic though they may be, are sacred expressions inviting communal appreciation and awe because "sex is to me the same thing as . . . religion," Caldwell much later allowed.[12] And how sophisticatedly he had entwined the two most basic and sacred hungers into a single arresting scene only Sylvia Cook recognized decades later: "Both speech and action are meticulously choreographed to culminate in Ellie May and Lov's lovemaking and Jeeter's theft of the turnips."[13]

Comedy was as integral as pathos to the stories Caldwell told through *Tobacco Road*. Ellie May, a harelipped Lester daughter, seduces her brother-in-law by dragging herself bare-bottomed across the sand. Lov Bensey responds to her "horsing" "like an old stud-horse." He is seduced only after Ada Lester, the mother, stuns him into submission with a club to the head. Ellie May and Lov then "roll over and over . . . like tumble bugs."

Much later, Ira's widowed pastor of the Rattlesnake Church appears in Caldwell's story as Sister Bessie, a grotesquely noseless evangelist who takes a shine to sixteen-year-old Dude Lester. Praying over and rubbing against the youth, she bribes him with the promise of a new Model T into a marriage she perceives as God's will. The car purchased, the marriage finally accomplished, Sister Bessie and Dude drive into the Lester yard with horn honking. In a variation upon the traditional wedding exuberance and shivaree, the Lesters peer through windows and doors as the mismatched couple consummate their marriage. Laughable though the scene superficially seemed to appear, for the Lesters it was hierophanous. They stood transfixed with awe at the sacred forces of life expressing themselves.

But Caldwell's humor could not obscure *Tobacco Road*'s more compelling story, one which argued that the Lesters were neither freaks nor accidents of nature. Rather, in James Devlin's estimation, "the Lester tragedy is played out before the sagging cabin like a Greek drama before the facade of a temple."[14] In Caldwell's versions of tragedy they represented blameless victims of social, economic, and biological forces they could neither comprehend nor overcome. Through the circumstance of Jeeter's and Ada's deaths, however—they are consumed during their sleep by a sedge-fire Jeeter had lit to prepare the earth for planting—Caldwell assigned a blame more comprehensive than Ira's beliefs would have admitted. The Lesters, and thousands of others like them, were pitiable victims of a misdirected faith whose God-hope promised life but gave death.

Even a brief summary of *Tobacco Road* reflects the facets of the conundrum that the Scribner's editors confronted in deciding whether or not to publish Caldwell's novel. Issuing it would represent, at best, a calculated risk. The Depression economy and literary good taste militated against it. On the other hand, they already had rejected *The Bogus Ones*. Should they likewise refuse to publish this novel, there seemed little doubt that Caldwell would place it elsewhere and thereby permanently be lost to them. How could they resolve their dilemma?

As passing days became interminable weeks, Caldwell's anxiety about his novel was not his lone concern. Financial worries plagued him, because he had earned nothing in the six months since he had begun the work. As early as April he had written to Dick Johns at *Pagany* asking if he could offer any payment for a story to be offered in that journal's winter issue. Caldwell apologized for his request: "I wouldn't ask, but I'm down at the bottom and can't see anything coming my way."[15] The first week in June he invited the Morangs for a weekend visit if they could stand "simple fare, simple quarters and simple manners. Potatoes and cornbread most of the time, with cheese for dessert." Allowing even for exaggeration, the Caldwells once more were scraping the bottom of their financial barrel.

Throughout the early thirties, the Morangs often shared more with the Caldwells than poverty and the anxiety of awaiting Scribner's decision about the novel. During their casual visits, Alfred would play his violin to satisfy himself and entertain the children. Later, he and Caldwell discussed Morang's painting and Caldwell's writing. Politics was another subject they appear to have discussed and agreed upon.

While in New York, Caldwell had become friendly with Mike Gold, who only recently had returned from Russia and was still "full of it."[16] Nonetheless, Caldwell thought him to be "a damn fine man" even though their political views were not always wholly compatible. He allowed that Gold "doesn't think so much of my Communism . . . and he devoted most of our conversations to harangue. I tried to argue my special brand of communism with him, but I had little success." What Caldwell's "brand" was, is not clear. Malcolm Cowley recollected that during those early Depression years most young writers passionately embraced political examination and revision, many to the detriment of their careers.[17] Possibly Caldwell's Maine isolation and single-minded dedication to writing saved his life from similar fragmentation.

Almost five weeks had passed before Caldwell heard anything from Scribner's and then the response was less than satisfying. Always circumspectly sensitive, Perkins prefaced the broader subject by stating that "I'll tell you plainly that I think myself [*Tobacco Road*] is well nigh perfect within its limits. The difficulties on the sales account, however, are very great."[18] He cited the effects of the Depression. But beneath that overt concern, hid a more essential reservation: "All the people in the book are of such a nature that although they arouse your sympathy in a curious way (the humor that pervades the whole book is magnificent), they do not interest the reader in ways usual in a novel." He softened his impressions with the solace that later he hoped to write more favorably.

But that was not all. That same letter also rejected a story Caldwell had written since finishing *Tobacco Road*, one which was subsequently to gain for him award-winning recognition. Perkins explained their decision: "As for 'Country Full of Swedes' I think your idea is grand, and that the completion of the situation is, but I think it is one of those stories you have very much overdone, so it has become burlesque." The blows were not softened by Perkins's placebo that the *New Republic* was to issue a type of double review of *American Earth*, a clue to Scribner's estimation of that collection.

Caldwell posted his response immediately. The ultimate decision was
Scribner's, but his disappointment was keen. With both hyperbole and
truth, he first argued his personal situation: "After having spent something more than a year on the book, one can not lay a thing like that aside
lightly." He then proceeded with what amounted to a literary credo in
defense of his work:

> If you had said the book were rotten, it would be a different matter; but since
> I know *whatof* [*sic;* emphasis Caldwell's] it was written, and the trueness of
> its people and story, I cannot bring myself to believe that it should be thrown
> away unread with the published trash of yesterday. I should hate to be dis-
> barred from writings because I had made myself aloof to the 'tricks' of hacks;
> the sympathy of a reader—in my mind—is won and held by the intense re-
> ality of a story, not by its pleasure-pain.[19]

Caldwell wound down with a practical concern; he could not afford to
lose a year's labor without something to show for it. That he did not
blame Perkins personally for Scribner's reluctance to issue *Tobacco
Road* is evident from the letter's concluding paragraphs. He was sending
another story since "they come out on paper and it seems there is only
one thing to do—send them to you." Further, Caldwell sought his mentor's opinion. Would it be advisable for him to apply for a Guggenheim
Fellowship?

Caldwell's desperate honesty brought immediate reaction. As a consequence of what must have been a priority editorial item, Perkins
mailed news of the decision the day after Caldwell had sent his letter:
"This is just to tell you that we are for *Tobacco Road* and we shall publish
it in the spring of 1932."[20] Because the fall publication deadline had
passed, Scribner's would provide an immediate three-hundred-dollar
advance. Nonetheless, questions about sales still remained, issues they
would like to discuss with Caldwell; in the interim, yes, he should apply
for the Guggenheim. But somehow that all-important letter had been
misdirected. Not until five days after Caldwell had written did he receive
the news, telegraphed: "Accepted *Tobacco Road* on the 12th."

Throughout his *Tobacco Road* anxieties, Caldwell's published works
continued to accumulate. Various journals issued five of his works

during that year. Edmund O'Brien gave roll-of-honor recognition to three more Caldwell stories and reprinted "Dorothy"—a Scribner's original—in his *Best Short Stories of 1931*. Expectedly, the sales of *American Earth* had been weak as the reviews had been mixed, but proletarian journals universally praised it. Although Malcolm Cowley recognized Caldwell's promise on the evidence of that first collection, another critic claimed, to Caldwell's bemusement, that his stories were derivative. He rightly wondered from whom.

Because Caldwell's writings earned so little, economic necessity as well as hopes for a comfortable writing period pushed him to apply for a prestigious Guggenheim Fellowship. Strong in rhetoric but weak in specifics, his application statements would reveal more about the person than they would about his "plans for study." Mixing proletarian ideals with righteousness, he passionately but vaguely argued his credentials for writing what was to be *God's Little Acre*.

Generally, Caldwell aimed "to write a full-length novel of proletarian life in the South." While both *Tobacco Road* and *American Earth* presented studies of "a group of people existing under an outmoded system of agriculture and economics," he intended to explore theoretical alternatives in his next long work. He had "in mind something of the direction in which the masses must turn in order to live under the present and forthcoming condition of life . . . a sort of union of agrarian and industrial societies." Projecting his characters as those of the tenant-farmer and mill-operative classes, Caldwell lapsed into a type of polemic more congenial to readers of the *New Masses* than to a group representing establishment values and support.

Being "a Southerner by birth, by inheritance, and by residence," Caldwell explained, his sympathies lay with the millions who did not know what to do.[21] Should they live always "hand to mouth" in debt, uneducated, and awaiting a better day? always "undernourished, uneducated, and without a spokesman"? Southern writing too long had been obsessed with romance, magnolia blossoms, and Negro dialect. It was "time someone really wrote about 'life.'" He asked only for the time and the funds to present a different picture of the "lint-heads" and "poor white trash"; his past work and his seriousness of purpose indicated that he was qualified to write their stories. His statement included no claims, as his later reconstructions would argue, that this work was to be but an installment in that panorama of southern life which had shaped his writing intentions from their beginnings.

The recommendations of two who knew Caldwell's work best did little to enhance his chances for Guggenheim support. Citing his strengths, they nonetheless conveyed a suspect ambivalence. Atcheson Hench counted among Caldwell's strengths his good class record and his concern for the soil and people of humble origins, all expressed with a clear writing style that swept swiftly to what he had to say. Yet Hench tempered his praise with concern.[22] Caldwell's deliberate staccato style combined with a rhetorical drabness that so cramped his expression that they might stand as stumbling blocks to his development as a powerful writer.

Max Perkins's letter likewise praised Caldwell's ability and promise even while it conveyed a sense of bemusement.[23] Written with artistic integrity, Caldwell's stories gained their power from the author's unusual blend of human sympathy and humor—like Mark Twain in some respects, he yet differed. More than humor, a concern for sympathetically portraying his characters' degradation marked his work. *Tobacco Road*'s sensitivity and grim humor made that evident. Moreover, the twenty-six-year-old [*sic*] Caldwell, consistently had "refused to compromise his writing, or to endanger his position by any sort of an alliance." What Caldwell's development might be "rather perplexed" Perkins. He felt that his possibilities were great, that his future writing would be "of a very high order within its limits, . . . even if it [did] not transcend them." Thus, Perkins, Hench, and Caldwell all preserved their respective integrities in complying with the Guggenheim procedures. The selection committee would have to render final judgment.

His duties to the Guggenheim finished, Caldwell returned to his creative writing. Within the next few months, he submitted five more stories to *Scribner's Monthly,* all except "Bum" later to be printed by nonpaying magazines. Except for the three-hundred-dollar *Tobacco Road* advance, Caldwell had earned nothing in 1931. Anxious to write another novel that might warrant an advance, he sought Perkins's advice about doing *God's Little Acre* as projected in the Guggenheim proposal.

Probably as a consequence of the *Tobacco Road* unpleasantness, Perkins waffled. Scribner's preferred a novel with a down-east setting as its next Caldwell issue. Never one to allow others to direct either his writings or his life, Caldwell, nonetheless that October obediently tried to honor the request. First in Maine, then in New York, and finally in Wrens, he labored throughout the winter on *Autumn Hill.*

Caldwell's good fortune seemed to have been exhausted with the acceptance of *Tobacco Road.* Scribner's had been rejecting his stories with regularity. Legal entanglements followed Harcourt Brace's acquisition of Heron Press. By publishing *The Bastard* that firm, without Caldwell's understanding, had secured the rights to his subsequent two novels. Those transferred to Harcourt, which refused release of their rights to *Tobacco Road* for less than a $150 payment. Caldwell seethed, but eventually Scribner's paid the price, debiting the amount from his future earnings.

With that recent record, Caldwell pessimistically prepared himself for yet another disappointment. By January 26, 1932, he wrote to Morang with intuitive accuracy.[24] Although he had finished the novel "about the Mount Vernon country of Maine," shortly to send it off, he "half-way expected it to be turned down." Perhaps his lack of confidence in the novel was a consequence of the circumstances which had forced both its writing and its character.

In *Autumn Hill*, Caldwell expanded into novel an approach that had served him well in his previous Maine stories. The characters were as rigidly and penuriously warped by their culture and environment as had been the respectively suspicious natives of "A Country Full of Swedes" and "Corduroy Pants." But Caldwell failed to sustain the satirical humor of those deft character pieces through an extended work. In *Autumn Hill*, revealing idiosyncrasies of character and setting, language and attitudes became "a tale too long told."

After sending the manuscript, Caldwell began to experience ominous premonitions. A month later, he could contain his anxiety no longer: "For God's sake tell me about 'Autumn Hill' the moment you can. But forgive me for saying that—."[25] Perkins's reply was kind but obliquely foreboding: "I wish we could talk to you about [it]. In a good many ways it seems to me magnificent, but in other ways we feel doubtful about it."[26]

He fended Caldwell's impatience by advising that the publication of two novels within the same year would be injudicious. If Caldwell wished, he could stop in on his way north to discuss the issue further. The matter was too important to defer that long. Leaving the family in Wrens, Caldwell departed immediately for New York.

During their consequent visit, Perkins demurred, advising that Scribner's wanted *"Autumn Hill* to be big enough and complete enough to warrent [*sic*] complete promotion."[27] Against such warnings Caldwell hoisted hopes, foreseeing no problem in expanding it—with Helen's support and aid: "It can be done, and if you help me, it shall be. . . . I am depending on you . . . to tell me if the new part is fine enough. Without your help I couldn't do anything with it. I never know until you tell me."[28]

Caldwell had to believe that *Autumn Hill* was salvageable because they needed money so badly. Writing from New York, he urged Helen to approach his parents: "When you get ready to leave, ask them to give you what they can, including the twenty for the suit if possible. Some day we'll get out of this mess."[29] Within three weeks, he had expanded *Autumn Hill* and returned the manuscript to Scribner's with a cryptic "Here is *Autumn Hill."* And again he waited.

But fortune seemed entirely to have abandoned Caldwell. Although he had applied for foundation support to Yaddo as well as to the Guggenheim Foundation, he received apologetic rejections from both during that inauspicious year. Caldwell had every reason to feel dejected. With a novel in editorial limbo and no short-story sales in eight months, the dashed foundation hopes left him and the family with no foreseeable financial resources. No royalties had come from *Tobacco Road.* Although its reviews had been mixed, the sales in that early Depression period were slight.

With almost Job-like melancholy, Caldwell informed Perkins that O'Brien had chosen his "Warm River" for inclusion in his *Best Short Stories of 1932:* "After such a disasterous [*sic*] year, I am pleased, for I was certain they were not beyond merit."[30] His justifying complaint also served to remind Perkins and Scribner's that recently they had bought none of his short stories. Or perhaps he felt genuinely unappreciated, because two weeks later he commiserated with another writer: "I should like to get a story into almost anything now. They keep popping back like cold checks."[31]

As a matter of fact, those same works Scribner's had been regularly rejecting, other magazines published. Obviously no twenty-eight-year-old writer should have been dissatisfied with ten recently published stories. Yet recognition scarcely relieved other anxieties that plagued him in that disastrous year.

Not yet inured to critical reviewers, Caldwell suffered their carping criticisms. The reviewer for the *Portland Express* obviously had not understood *Tobacco Road*, Caldwell complained, because the critic had claimed it was obscene. Caldwell countered with what was to become his standard observation: "There is nothing obscene or dirty in the book, because the people in it did not live consciously obscene lives."[32] Meanwhile, European publishing houses, fearing the book's unusual honesty, were rejecting it with depressing unanimity. Before the end of November, ten had voted no, and one had misplaced its copy! His writing career appeared to be caught in a downward spiral; that steady patience of his long-unpublished years had eroded. Accordingly, for the first time, Caldwell decided to look outside himself for help in solving his problem.

Other factors may have contibuted to Caldwell's decision. A relatively unknown dramatist, Jack Kirkland, had sought permission to adapt *Tobacco Road* to dramatic form. About such matters Caldwell knew nothing. Possibly remembering his Heron Press–Harcourt lesson, he decided to turn to Max Lieber, the young agent he had met a year before at the New York party.

Acting with brisk assurance as Caldwell's dramatic agent, Lieber by May of 1932 had negotiated a contract for the rights to *Tobacco Road*. Although Caldwell would be paid no money immediately, he would receive 5 percent of the ticket revenues when the adaptation played before audiences. Allaying Caldwell's apprehensions, Perkins confirmed that he had acted both prudently and legally as far as Scribner's was concerned. And as for *Autumn Hill*, they still had not come to a decision.

Impatient with Scribner's four-month delay, Caldwell, without telling Perkins, gave "the book over to Lieber to handle." Because the agent had done "a good job" for Caldwell on the play, he had "confidence in him." Whether or not Lieber actually intervened finally to force Scribner's to action is unclear. Nonetheless, shortly thereafter Perkins's letter to Caldwell conveyed not only an apology but also a covert acknowledgment that the Scribner's decision might end their association with him: "I've got to write you now to say that we have decided against 'Autumn Hill' personally disappointing as it is to do so. I believed in it, I wish to say, and still more in you."[33] But six people had read the book and judged that the economic climate, along with the sparse sales of *American Earth* and *Tobacco Road*, militated against Scribner's issuing it. Perkins concluded with almost a note of farewell—"I can't tell you how sorry I am"—offering suggestions for improving the work if Caldwell decided to submit it elsewhere.

Caldwell's reply conveyed an almost consoling but noncommittal tone: "A rejection, even though it is a major one is not the end of the world. . . . Your suggestions are valued ones. I shall study them closely."[34] How he really felt at the time can be inferred only from Caldwell's recollections twenty years after the fact: "At first I was so discouraged and unhappy that I seriously considered giving up writing and turning to something else for a livelihood."[35] With Caldwell's full knowledge Lieber tried unsuccessfully for months to place the book with a number of presses, Viking first and foremost among them.

By rejecting *Autumn Hill*, Scribner's had relinquished its right to Caldwell's future works. Though Lieber assured him that he could place the book more favorably and lucratively with another publisher, Caldwell hesitated. More than a contract had bound him to Scribner's. They had taken stories and paid him handsomely as no others had. They were the first respectable publishers who had issued his books, thereby calling them to the attention of otherwise blasé reviewers. Possibly Caldwell felt a country-style allegiance more binding than the contracts Lieber recognized. But the agent, with Perkin's permission, argued with practicalities. Caldwell, with a family to support and a year's work invested in *Autumn Hill*, had to look out for himself. He owed it to himself to step away from Scribner's and Perkins.

Beyond all other considerations, Caldwell's indecision revolved around his respect and feelings for Perkins. His tribute to the man in *Experience* is one of the book's most movingly honest recollections— both a testimony to the editor and an essential revelation of the sensitive man who normally hid his feelings behind an impassive mask.

> After knowing Max Perkins as long as I had, it was disturbing to think that such a decision would mean I would no longer be in a position to call upon him for help and advice. I had come to look forward to receiving letters from him, and when I found one in the mail, it was always the first to be read.[36]

Lieber's arguments, nonetheless, were persuasive; money was dear, and reason rather than sentiment should direct his career. Accordingly, with stoical resolve, Caldwell forsook his three-year association with Perkins in favor of Lieber's monied promise. For all practical purposes, he bade a silent good-bye to his editor in a leave-taking that his future would argue had been more ominous than anyone could have guessed. His self-righteous belief that someone trusted—whether faithful editor, agent, or wife—did not fully appreciate his efforts thereafter would haunt his career and life.

Despite all of Max Lieber's confident assurances—and the 5 percent commissions he stood to earn—he was not successful in placing *Autumn Hill*. Most publishers read the manuscript only to respond with regrets. Viking Press seemed interested in Caldwell, but about *Autumn Hill* they waffled assurances to avoid promises. More than two months had passed since Caldwell had left Scribner's, yet he had neither earned any money nor been placed under contract with any publisher. To Morang he complained with mock-seriousness: "Money is getting more scarce each day with me. I'll rob a bank some day . . . and be rich for a change."[37]

Caldwell did not resort to that tactic, but he did adopt one almost as desperate. Helen had become pregnant some time before this.[38] He had become so painfully upset that, against her strenuous objections, he had forced her to submit to an abortion "by a butcher in Waterville." That experience he had transformed into his "true story," "Mamma's Little Girl," one wherein an unmarried youth takes his pregnant girlfriend to a doctor for an abortion. How Caldwell must have felt is economically expressed both through the story's style and its conclusion. Told from the first-person narrator's perspective, it mirrors Hemingway's style to express feeling through a sparse but careful narration of events. The story concludes when the young man has been expelled from the ether-reeking room to slide into a faint against the "rooms-for-rent" sign on the porch wall.

Shortly after the experience and the story it inspired, Caldwell and Morang collaborated in what they had hoped would be a money-making project. They offered a limited pamphlet-printing of "Mamma's Little Girl," with accompanying illustrations by Morang. That venture eventually earned them a total of twenty-four dollars.

As Caldwell confronted financial worries and the possibility of an arrested career, the year 1932 promised in every respect to be a nadir for Caldwell. Beyond that, moreover, increasingly his writing demands conspired with personal idiosyncrasies to foment domestic tensions. By way of example, Helen cited the time when she accompanied him for a scheduled visit to the Scribner's offices in New York. Before they had reached the elevators, Caldwell turned to her and said, "You wait for me here, Helen. You look too shabby to go up."[39] Hurt, she had remained below, until, her patience exhausted, she returned to their hotel. When Caldwell arrived, he greeted her with a cold-cutting silence which he maintained throughout the remainder of their trip. Increasingly he used such tactics to punish those who either thinkingly or unthinkingly disappointed him.

After all she had done as wife, mother, and faithful liege to support his writing career, Helen understandably came to question more and more Caldwell's love and appreciation. His emotional reserve, his suspected affairs, and his brooding retreats increasingly strained her love for him. Additionally, she judged, he was not a good father to Pix and Dee. Obsessed with writing, he seldom interacted with them. Their childish intrusions, noise, and mischief provoked an impatience that occasionally erupted into bursts of anger and unpredictable punishments.

One such instance indelibly impressed Dabney. Both boys very early recognized their father's almost puritanical aversion for the common words used to describe bodily functions. They consequently had evolved a repertoire of what they felt were acceptable euphemisms; feces, for in-

stance, became "hockey." One day Dee shared with Caldwell his drawing of a sheep in the meadow. "That's nice, Dee, but what's that dark
blob under the sheep's tail?" "That's sheep hockey, Papa." The boy was
never to forget or understand his father's response. Caldwell wordlessly
grabbed him, took him outside, and beat him with a razor strop.[40] Whatever other forces whipped Caldwell's response, he later revealed one di-
mension of them: "The kids are boys, both. The best I can say for them is
that they're both roughnecks. Now if they were girls, I'd more than likely
be praising them."[41]

In other ways also, Caldwell's confusing ambivalence spoke for a conflict of values, which, as Helen deduced, made him seem at times to have
been "two people." He could be "very sedate, grim, quiet," but on the
other hand be the type who would have enjoyed the *Kama-sutra* had he
read it. His writings, she believed, reflected "this fantastic interest in . . .
sexual variations on a main theme," themes that Caldwell always defended whether in excusing his own behavior or in justifying his writings. Such urges flowed from the "naturalness" of creation and human
behavior. There was nothing "dirty" in his books because their characters "did not live consciously obscene lives," yet Dabney remembered
being "switched" for sneaking into the family library to read *The Bastard.*

Possibly a similar conflict between values and behavior confounded
Caldwell in April of 1932. By then he and Helen had been married for
seven years, and a general sense of restlessness apparently affected them
both. With her usual candidness, Helen told him that she loved a man
she somehow had met in Charlottesville.[42] With him, she "spoke the
same language, enjoyed the same music . . . and poetry." Sensitive and
gentle, "he was perfect with the children." Claiming to have "lived with
him," Helen would have married the man had she been more selfish.
But saddling him "with a divorced woman and two children" would have
been unfair, destroying his legal career and political aspirations. And
again according to Helen, "Erskine knew this" because she had not tried
to hide it from him.

Caldwell may have known of Helen's situation, but that did not mean
he could accept it with equanimity. Writing to her from New York, where

he had gone to try to improve upon the *Autumn Hill* manuscript, his true feelings erupted:

> It's up to me to finish the thing, and I can if you will help me. But if you are going to keep that up like you did last winter, I may as well through [*sic*] the whole thing overboard now. I can't do a damn thing while I know that you [are] doing soming [*sic*] I wouldn't want you to do. If a person can't be honest, he can at least be fair and say he's not. There are too damn many deceitful women in the world now for me to perpetuate the lot. I'd rather not having anything to do that kind of thing [*sic*].
>
> If I can't trust a person behind my back, I shall certainly balk at trusting him in front of me. Capone attributed his success, you know, to the fact that he always put doublecrossers on the spot.
>
> If you want to get out, go ahead; I myself do not. If I had not loved you I wouldn't have married you. I wouldn't live with anyone else. It's either you, or nobody.[43]

Whether impelled by feelings of love or duty, Caldwell seemed determined to salvage the marriage, because when he returned from New York, he and Helen had a long talk. He said, "Helen, I'll tell you what. Let's shut both doors and not open them again."[44] Helen agreed. She would not write the lawyer again, and Caldwell would curb his infidelities. Believing that "maybe the way to cement things, to get back faith again, was to get pregnant," Helen did nothing to prevent the conception of the child who was to be Janet; Caldwell had not been pleased.

But before Helen settled comfortably into that pregnancy which she believed might pledge new beginnings, she was wracked by the discovery of a double betrayal. Erskine admitted that in 1931 he had spent the Thanksgiving holidays in New York with her friend from the Portland bookstore days, the friend whom he had promised to see no more. For husband and friend so to deceive her shook Helen as had none of his earlier infidelities: "it almost killed me. He had destroyed whatever love I had for him."[45] What justification he offered, Helen did not recall; possibly it was as ineffable as his lifelong psychological need to be assured by a woman—whether mother, wife, or lover—that he was indeed a good man who was unconditionally loved and appreciated.

Just as Helen tried to forgive Caldwell once more, she offered reconciliation to the friend through her following year's Christmas card. Accepting that graciousness immediately, the friend had responded with contrition and personal perplexity. What had caused her to violate a friend's trust, she could not explain, and perhaps she was a "preposterous person" for trying to continue a friendship which she had betrayed. It had been "shameful, indecent and immodest," but if Helen were willing to excuse, and Erskine did not mind, she wanted them to continue their old friendship.[46] Helen agreed, granting forgiveness to wayward friends with the same generosity she had extended to Caldwell throughout their marriage.

The maelstrom effects of his private and professional uncertainties Caldwell hinted in a September 1932 confidence to Morang: "I haven't been able to do a damn thing lately. If only we could get a settlement re: [*Autumn Hill*], I'd be alright. This thing has been up in the air since last January."[47] Reestablishing a correspondence with Gordon Lewis, a friend from their university days, he, nonetheless, assumed a nonchalant and jaunty bravado: "I'm out at Scribners; had some words in command I made good use of. Now I'm looking for another publisher . . . [and] sitting on eggs, waiting. God damn it. Lieber sold a story to The Yale Review (winter issue) and that's all between us and the wolf."[48] And perhaps seeking other diversions, Caldwell decided to journey via bus to New York for a September 28 Foster and Ford Committee meeting.[49]

Besides attending the rally-for-change in the dying days of the Hoover administration, Caldwell had other interests in New York. There he had "some meals and maybe a bed in the offing" during the time he planned to meet with Marshall Best, an editor at Viking Press. That firm had successfully avoided resolution of the *Autumn Hill* issue by dangling before Caldwell, through Lieber, a counterproposal. They would buy the options for his next two books for $100. The offer was one he could not refuse, since that would "be something to put fat in the soup." "God knows it's been lean long enough," he ruefully admitted.[50] Both Caldwell's anxiety and infatuation with Lieber combined to blind him to the fact that the terms did not improve upon those offered by Scribner's, an assurance Lieber had promised.

Concern about money alone did not force Caldwell to accept Viking as his publisher. Another consideration, just as impelling, moved him and swayed the publishers toward a contract. Despite the year's professional anxieties and domestic turmoil, his complaints about "not being able to do anything lately," Caldwell had another novel ready to offer some press.

At the end of April he yet toiled over *Autumn Hill*, but by the middle of October at the latest, the manuscript for *God's Little Acre* was in the Viking offices: "Seven editors and publisher's readers read the script, and there was not a single unfavorable report. And that, as Lieber wrote, is something in these days when publishers are so careful with their output."[51]

Caldwell can be forgiven the boasting he shared with Morang. Some twenty years later, Faulkner was to judge *"God's Little Acre* and the short stories, . . . enough for any man." Yet throughout the few months of the book's writing, Caldwell had mentioned nothing about it either to Morang or in his long "catch-up" letter to Lewis. Both were aspiring authors, and perhaps Caldwell deferred to their feelings or feared that giving words to hopes might have hexed its possibilities for success. Viking's ready acceptance of his latest work served to dispel the entire year's gloom. "I'm making final revisions on *God's Little Acre* before it goes to the printers . . . . I wish you could read it in script," he wrote to Morang. And then wondering where the money for the forthcoming southern migration would come from, Caldwell dreamed exuberantly and almost prophetically, "But what the hell, we only live once. There's a lot of the world I've got to cover in the next twenty years."[52]

Although Caldwell exaggerated the time required to write *Tobacco Road*, he made no such inflated estimates for *God's Little Acre*. Possibly sensing how good it was, he might have felt the time had come to shed his earlier modesty. Writing in *Experience* of the book's genesis and growth, Caldwell recalled the May beginning in the Mount Vernon upstairs room where windows overlooked the yard to the lake.[53]

He consequently maintained that the story and its characters were so close to the surface of his consciousness that as the pages rolled from his typewriter, he lay them unread, face-down, on the floor by his desk. Af-

"Greentrees," Mount Vernon, Maine, 1978. Photograph by the author.

ter only two months, two-thirds of the novel "had been put on paper," when guests arrived—his parents and the Morangs.[54]

By late August, Caldwell had completed his novel: "The writing of the final page, the final paragraph, the final sentence, and then the last word of *God's Little Acre* was the most satisfying experience I had had since I first began writing."[55] Juxtaposing the setting of a southern family farm against a milltown experience, the novel covered a broader scene, and therefore pleased him more than *Tobacco Road*. Now he felt that for the first time in his life, he could consider himself a professional writer. His self-assurance was justified. Worries, traumas, and distractions notwithstanding, he had completed *God's Little Acre* in less than four months!

That enthusiasm Caldwell had previously reserved for Scribner's and Perkins, he now transferred to Viking and Lieber. He generously credited them both for his change in fortunes. That confidence in a publisher

Erskine, Dabney (?), and Borzoi, at Mount Vernon, summer 1928. Printed by permission of Rebecca Gooding, Caldwell family conservator.

and agent had not been wholly misdirected. After *Tobacco Road*, Caldwell had wanted to write another southern novel—*God's Little Acre*—as his next project. Perkins instead had suggested a "down-East" work, and the ill-fated *Autumn Hill* was the result. During the four months between publishers, Caldwell had followed his instincts and written the second novel upon which his reputation and fortunes were to balance.

Erskine and Helen Caldwell with neighbor, Dabney, and Pix, ca. 1931. From *With All My Might* by Erskine Caldwell, published by Peachtree Publishers, Atlanta. Reprinted by permission of the publisher and the Estate of Erskine Caldwell.

Thus through both circumstances and their respective indecisiveness, agent and publishers provided a sense of freedom resulting in what was to be the most successful period of Caldwell's writing career.

After Viking's enthusiastic acceptance of *God's Little Acre*, and before the winter trip south, Caldwell settled back to take stock. He was still forwarding stories for consideration by *Scribner's Monthly*, and he mentioned to Perkins that he had enjoyed their recent talk and hoped to see him again. There and in a letter to Morang, Caldwell praised a book he had reviewed for *New Masses*. Edward Dahlberg's *From Flushing to Calvary* had been "one of the best books [he had] ever read," and with a deft stroke, he tried to boost Morang's confidence: "With your material you should be able to do a book just as good . . . the next step is to mold it."[56] On other occasions, perhaps tipsy from the elixir of his own formula for success, Caldwell almost pontificated through his friendly advice: "Hell, genius is 90% hard work. A man's native ability is pretty small, and only hard work brings it above the common, or garden variety of writing."[57] And Morang should feel proud of his work since Caldwell himself felt "damn good over it." "Don't cheat yourself of that pleasure," he advised.

As Caldwell's reputation grew, would-be authors sent him their writings to seek his advice. Exasperated by their "mish-mash," he burst forth with a rhapsody that captures that sense of sacred trust whose responsibility he believed the writer must bear:

> God what awful stuff. None of them knows how to tell a story. And that's what fiction is. Story-telling. What else is there to matter? The best story teller is he who tells his tale the most convincingly and beautifully. That's why God made words. Words are to tell stories with. They are delicate; we ought to handle them with the love and care a mother does her baby.[58]

With some of his six-hundred-dollar advance from Viking (less Lieber's 5 percent), he allegedly bought three dictionaries—one for the upstairs room, another for the living room, and the last for the kitchen. The remainder of the sum went toward other luxuries—meat, a new typewriter, and paying of debts.

The Caldwells remained at Mount Vernon longer than usual during the winter of 1932–33. With *God's Little Acre* scheduled for January 1933 release, Caldwell had promised Viking either another novel or a collection of short stories for fall publication. Whatever acclaim *God's Little Acre* received would benefit the new book. Thus working against that deadline, he postponed their southward trek until late in January.

As usual, they stopped first in Charlottesville before driving on to Wrens. This year, however, they interrupted their Wrens visit with a trip to Indian Rocks, Florida. Following their reacquaintance through correspondence, Caldwell wished to visit his old college acquaintance, Gordon Lewis, and his new wife, Ruth, at their island place. During "a week I'll talk about the rest of my life," Caldwell and Lewis reestablished a camaraderie supported through letters and visits until Lewis's death some twenty-five years later.[59]

Back in Wrens by February 6, Caldwell anxiously awaited each review of *God's Little Acre*. Naturally, proletarian publications and reviewers enthusiastically praised the book. More satisfyingly, establishment voices, with some reservations, likewise generally approved. Louis Kronenberger of the *New York Times* wrote that the whole situation on the Walden's farm read "like an elaborate off-color story skillfully combined with an enlarged comic strip."[60] He, nonetheless, granted the unusual book its original and lusty vitality, one wherein "melodramatic, tragic tones" betrayed "the comic muse" who seemed to have inspired the work. Horace Gregory, writing for *Books*, began, "As a novel *God's Little Acre* has its faults." He recognized the work, however, as one by a "gifted writer," whose effort represented "an important step in the development of an important young novelist."[61]

The day after these reviews appeared, Caldwell smarted from even their mildly disapproving stings. Writing to Lewis, he first accepted their criticisms but eventually fumed:

> I suppose you saw the review in the *Times;* not so much worse than *Books;* but still far from the mark according to how I see it. I realize now how imperfect the novel is, and it sets me a-burning to do the next one better. The next time I'll not make the theme as prominent as a wart on the end of your nose—I'll make it a boil under the seat of your pants. That'll make them stand up.[62]

Later reviews, however, indicate that some critics were already standing up. Robert Cantwell in the *New Republic* called Caldwell a satirist whose characters were akin to Don Quixote and Alice in Wonderland, with *God's Little Acre* "among the most powerful of recent novels."[63] *Saturday Review* predicted, on the basis of this work, that one day Caldwell would produce an outstanding novel. But the review that perhaps hurt the most was that offered by Dahlberg, whose own book Caldwell had so praised. His own work doing little to discredit the hypothesis, he felt that as a "proletarian" novel, *God's Little Acre* fed the suspicion "that it was a bourgeois fault to be able to write well." And more damningly, Dahlberg declared that "it has little to recommend it aside from a few highly amusing and picaresque touches and the deft portrait of Pluto Swint."[64]

Reviews as harsh as Dahlberg's would always—though publicly unadmitted—hurt Caldwell. Thus he had been "surprized and pleased" that Stan Salomon's congratulatory letter revealed that he, at least, had " 'got' the novel." "That's what the book is, of course; the story of digging for gold is merely the web the spider spun to snare the innocent. And how many were snared!"[65] What else the book was Caldwell would not reveal until many years later, and that to Carvel Collins, always a caring critic and acquaintance: "The novel's central theme . . . is the attempt by the leading character, Ty Ty Walden, to hold his family together under all circumstances. . . . He is attempting to arrange what a family is supposed to do, I think, which is to stay together."[66]

Recent critics such as James Devlin and Sylvia Cook identify some of those other themes and motifs that catch readers in the web Caldwell has spun: power, the generative forces of natural urges and machines and dreams, work and sex as expressions of those forces, and tensions between rural and urban values. The containment of any of those forces provokes explosive defiance, both Dionysian and violent.[67] Most critics during Caldwell's time were not so perceptive, and he steeled himself against the slings and arrows of those who failed to appreciate his intentions, whether in his writings or in his life.

Throughout his lifetime Caldwell cultivated a defensive pessimism that allowed him to survive the disappointments of both reviews and people: "If you'll believe the worst of everything every time, you will never be taken by surprise. That's the way I am. And by believing the worst all the time, when the worst proves false, you can rise up the scale; otherwise, you'll have to go the other way."[68] And thus then and always Caldwell carefully balanced against the dual fears of rejection and blame.

Chapter 9

Because Caldwell wanted to resume work on the novel that would eventually become *Journeyman,* the family abbreviated its winter's stay in Wrens. By February 26, 1933, they were back in Mount Vernon, in fourteen inches of snow, enduring the discomforts of a demanding and drafty old house. In the month since its release, *God's Little Acre* had sold its first printing, a phenomenon Caldwell had never before experienced. Although he would have preferred that Viking follow that success with a short-story collection, the editors were reluctant. Unlike the editors at Scribner's, they insisted upon a more commercially successful novel. With the promise of a small advance on that work, Caldwell, reluctant to formalize that restriction, nevertheless went to New York as soon as the banks opened after their Roosevelt-imposed holiday.

Still poor, Caldwell sought to economize wherever he could during his visit to the city. Within that group of young writer-intellectuals he had come to know in New York was Nathanael ("Pep") West. West was working at the time on *Miss Lonelyhearts* while he managed his uncle's exclusive residential Sutton Hotel in the East Fifties. Attempting to hide Depression vacancies from the general public, he encouraged struggling writers to lodge there for little or nothing. Staying there "gratis in a three room suite," Caldwell "read portions of [*Miss Lonelyhearts*] while it was in progress." What he thought of the work was reserved for later: "How he ever got away with *Miss Lonelyhearts* is beyond me. . . . I can only figure it out on the basis of luck."[1] During his four-day visit he met, among others, such figures as Alec Woollcott, Noel Coward, Leane Zugsmith, and Harry Hansen, a writer and reviewer who, for the next twenty years, would favorably review Caldwell's books. Additionally, he talked with Jack Kirkland, who was still struggling to adapt and produce *Tobacco Road.*

By mid-March, Caldwell learned that *God's Little Acre* was in its third printing. Still that meant "nothing because the total sales to date [had been] only 3,500." He was cheered by other events, however. Patrick Kearney, who had adapted Theodore Dreiser's *American Tragedy*, was "working like hell" to dramatize *God's Little Acre* also. *American Mercury* had actually paid for "The Man Who Looked Like Himself," which it was to print in its May issue. Otherwise both *Tobacco Road* and *God's Little Acre* had been accepted by the Cresset Press and Martin Secker, respectively, for British publication. Stan Salomon and others were predicting that *God's Little Acre* would earn the year's Pulitzer Prize for Caldwell, a rumor he, hope-against-hope, discounted.

Against such optimistic omens, Caldwell balanced reality. The fanfare about the book was both pleasing and discouraging, provoking him to a mood of resignation reinforced with defensiveness:

> There's nothing much I can do about the novel now. I did my damnedest in
> the writing of it. What peeves me right now is the way so many readers and
> reviewers went blah-blah about what they said was comedy, and not a word
> about the theme of the book. Christ! Can't they read? Or after reading are
> they afraid to report what the thing is readly [*sic*] concerned?[2]

Painfully baffled and frustrated when readers failed to see the themes of his writings, he nonetheless never gave any more substantive clues than those offered in his Guggenheim application. Eventually, Caldwell did prepare a public—and possibly a personally salving—response: "When I was asked to explain the meaning of a story or novel, I could only say that it meant what it said to the reader. I had no philosophical truths to dispense, no evangelistic urge to change the course of human destiny."[3]

Further, a recurring complaint—perhaps legitimate for the last time in Caldwell's life—continued to punctuate his correspondence during this period of early 1933. Realistically, he estimated that financially, "we're just about sunk." The royalty advance from *God's Little Acre* had long ago been spent, and book sales had not yet erased that debit. Living expenses had consumed the small *American Mercury* payment, while *Tobacco Road* was still Jack Kirkland's dream, one in which Caldwell placed little hope. The national bank holiday had locked the few dollars the Caldwells had in a Portland checking account. For all his literary acclaim, he was still abysmally poor. Winter's end in Mount Vernon only contributed further to the bleakness Caldwell felt throughout that "late, late Spring."

And then on Sunday, the last day of April, Caldwell rushed to a mysterious meeting with Lieber in New York City. When Helen met him at the bus upon his return, he handed her a sheet of paper. It charted a schedule of the times and places he was likely to be within the next three-and-a-half months. He had signed a contract with Metro-Goldwyn-Mayer films to work as a scriptwriter, first on location in Louisiana and then in Hollywood. Within forty-eight hours, Caldwell was to leave Mount Vernon and then depart from New York by air to arrive in New Orleans by Saturday, May 6, 1933.

Fortune had again come full circle. Caldwell would earn 250 Depression dollars per week for the duration of the contract. Throughout their married life, he and Helen had survived—with money given, earned, and borrowed—on considerably less than twenty dollars per week, so this bonanza, apparently negotiated through Lieber, seemed incredibly generous.

But the accompanying problems equally were confounding. What about domestic arrangements? Caldwell encouraged Helen to travel with the boys by train to Hollywood, find an apartment, and await his arrival there. Because she was then eight months pregnant, however, she felt that she could not cope with the details of this option. (In retrospect, she mused, perhaps that had been a poor decision.) Instead she decided to remain in Mount Vernon. Although the Caldwells' improved financial situation would cover hospital expenses, she had prepared in pre-Lamaze fashion for a home delivery and planned to proceed accordingly. By then, Caldwell's parents would be there for their annual visit, and his earnings would permit the luxury of a nurse during Helen's postnatal period. Accordingly, Caldwell departed for Hollywood via his Louisiana detour.

Separated from family and essentially alone for what would be more than three months, Caldwell was to endure a sense of desolation as profound as that of his Wilkes-Barre experience. The long letters that he wrote daily to Helen and at least biweekly to Morang provided more than a log of his experiences. They charted his concerns and exposed facets of his personality that had never before been so starkly revealed.[4]

Caldwell's first plane trip, at "5400 feet and at 120 miles an hour," had been something. But not until he arrived at New Orleans's Roosevelt Hotel—not the top floor of a waterfront warehouse this time—did he learn some of the details about his assignment. MGM director Tod Browning and his assistant, Chandler Sprague, had come to Louisiana to shoot exterior scenes for a picture about the Cajuns. Within a week or so, everyone was to move about sixty miles from New Orleans to "some god-forsaken bayou" where the property men were erecting the "exterior of a place to be known as Manilla Village, a sort of whorehouse on a Hollywood scale."[5] Caldwell was to work with Sprague on the dialogue—conditionally. As he understood the situation, they awaited final direction from Hollywood, because his assignment depended upon the resolution of a decision involving another writer:

> Faulkner was to write the dialogue, but he stays drunk most of the time and neither Browning or Sprague like him—They have to get rid of him before I can start, & so today I am doing nothing (except reading the script) and waiting for Faulkner to go back to Oxford.[6]

Allegedly, Browning and Sprague had requested Caldwell as their first choice, but Faulkner was already under contract, so the company had tried to save money by using him.

As long as the company kept paying him, Caldwell claimed indifference, but he regretted being away during Helen's confinement. Even though his parents were to be there, should she need him, money notwithstanding, he would return immediately. And he began offering some of that condescendingly sage advice that he heaped upon Helen whenever he was away. She was to keep matches away from the boys or they would burn the house down in five minutes, and she had better look after them closely or they would "go wild" in the couple of months he would be away. He acknowledged that Helen could "manage Dabney all right," and Ira, when he arrived, would "be able to handle Pixy." Instructions and directions, plus details about money, costs, and saving became refrains in almost every letter.

During that first week, Caldwell already sounded what was to become a recurrent theme: he could not wait to return home. Awaiting resolution of Faulkner's situation, he directed Helen about fertilizing the garden, not letting "the lawn grow out of Clifford's control," nor allowing the boys to go to the lake without her. Helen must have responded with her own lack of confidence in Caldwell, for he bristled defensively:

> Don't get foolish and think all kinds of silliness. . . . I'm trying to get some money for you & I don't give a damn about anything or anyone else. If I did, I'd tell you. But I don't and that's all there is to it. Just because I don't say a lot of things, don't think that I never feel them. . . . When you discover that I care a hell of a lot more for you than you do for me, you won't be questioning my faith any longer. Don't forget that. . . . Write and tell me how everything is and if you still love me.[7]

Four days after Caldwell's arrival, Faulkner departed, and he was finally permitted to write dialogue. He wrote to Helen, "If they don't like what I write, I'll also be going." Six days into his contract, he complained with what was to become a litany of disgust, "Picture business is pretty hokey and my stomach may turn any day." As Caldwell perceived it, his job was "to make people talk, and with a reason; motivate their action and direct so-and-so to raise a window, light a cigarette, and shoot his brother."[8]

Although Tod Browning seldom bothered Caldwell, his absolute authority nonetheless caused Caldwell to mutter that "a director should interpret the script, instead of trying to write the story or say how it should be written." Pleasing six people, observing "1000's of taboos," and sweating in ninety-six-degree heat that incubated cockroaches that looked "like Irving Thalberg" (MGM head), made Caldwell increasingly yearn for the coolness and freedom of Mount Vernon. In lieu of being there himself, he advised Helen to "hold the book (and work on it some more)," and to "keep the house in good repair" since he was coming back. He also confessed his emotional dependence upon her: "I'd be in a pretty fix without you. What could I do without you there all the time. There wouldn't be any use in going back."[9]

But if the situation was unsatisfying at the Hotel Roosevelt in New Orleans, Caldwell feared it would be worse on location. Eleven days after his arrival, he traveled there in a "forty-five mile per hour speedboat," after which he and others lived in a shrimp fishing village where everything was elevated on stilted platforms, since there was no solid ground. But after only five days on location, Caldwell and the rest of the crew went back to New Orleans, packed, and boarded the Monday-night Sunset Limited for Los Angeles. Arriving on Thursday, he found two telegrams from Helen awaiting him. The baby, Janet, had been born on Wednesday, May 24, 1933, and all was fine.

Caldwell's handwritten, five-page letter briefly expressed relief that Helen was all right and gladness about there finally being "a real Janet." Otherwise, he talked about the money he had forwarded, his efforts to wire his parents then en route to Mount Vernon, and a description of his assigned office. Whatever his true feelings about being away during the baby's birth, Caldwell could not openly admit to her. That same day, however, he did express them to Morang: "It was hell to have to be out here at such a time—but what in hell can a man do in this capitalistic society but try to earn a living?"[10] Yet the system would not swallow him because he had learned that the trick was for him to "do the bastards" before he got "done," then to get his and get out.

Renting a ten-dollar-per-week hotel room, Caldwell settled in six blocks from his MGM office. Because he did not want to spend "a lot of money," he practiced a frugality that had become habit. By refusing to buy a car, rent a four-room apartment or "keep a couple of girls," he attempted to hold "out tooth and nail against going Hollywood." Eventually, "once or twice a week," he had to confirm that he drank nothing stronger than beer. Like a stone tablet carved with essential virtues, Caldwell presented his self-righteous rigidity. That, combined with hard work, he offered as evidence of a character different from, and by implication superior to, the ordinary Hollywood types with their excesses: "But it is no joke—no more than my refusal to sit in overstuffed chairs in directors, supervisors, and Sam Marxes [sic] office. If there is no hardbottomed chair, I ask for one."[11] Like his mother Caldwell maintained certain observances that he later traced to their source: "Now, if it's true that there is a universal Puritan tradition, possibly that influenced me a great deal in that I knew certain limits of conduct, training, or whatever there was in my environment. I knew certain concepts of morality."[12]

Such a morally elevated vantage point allowed Caldwell to observe and pass judgment upon what appeared as a modern-day Babylon and its people. California itself was no fit place to live; there was no soil, "nothing to put your feet on." "God did not intend for people to live here on this desert—anyone can tell that."[13] More than the environment confounded this southerner whose indignation revealed itself as he repeated a story he had heard:

> You must have read a story or two by one Senora Babb in Story and other places. Anyway I found out the other day that she is a well-known Hollywood Boulevard character. The kind that is kept to the tune of a thousand a month by the Stetson hat money, and who in turn, keeps a friend to the tune of three-hundred a month. And to carry the damn cycle to its logical conclusion, they say that the last named friend keeps his girl to the tune of a hundred a month. That's far enough. But I am glad to hear that the Stetson money is giving so many boys and girls well-paid jobs—now turn me out a flaming screen script on that![14]

As much as the stories, the famous people whom Caldwell observed provoked his judgmental disdain.[15] Robert Montgomery he perceived as "an ass," and "that fellow, Gable, showing off in a yellow, turtleneck sweater," gave him a pain. Joan Crawford in a room next to Caldwell's practiced voice by running up and down the musical scale for three hours, while Frances Dunn wept and screamed in his office because "the producers had turned thumbs down on her rotten screen tests." If that combination would not "drive you crazy," a person "just didn't know nothing."

Through association and comparison, Hollywood writers attracted both Caldwell's interest and censure. Against Phil Stong, more than anyone else, he leveled his righteous indignation.[16] When Caldwell asked the native Iowan "about the revolution in Iowa," Stong discounted the unrest as a minor conflict stirred by a handful of communists "who did not amount to anything." Such a "completely capitalistic" myopia that refused to see " . . . that people in his own country were starving" stoked Caldwell's ire. As far as he was concerned, the man who had made a lot of money from his *State Fair* and more yet from script writing was nothing more than a "literary whore."

Just as righteously but less harshly, Caldwell committed others to his categories of "the rejected and elected." Anita Loos, whose *Gentlemen Prefer Blondes* had provoked his disdain in the *Atlanta Journal,* he equally dismissed as what "you might expect." Both Laurence Stallings and Paul Green, however, he judged to be writers with honor. With true integrity, each was returning to the sanity of North Carolina—Stallings after telling "everybody from Thalberg and Meyer on down to go to hell with their infantile pictures." Green similarly had told the producers "nothing doing" when they demanded that he write script for a "tripe picture." These and other writers, such as Nathanael West and S. J. Perelman, Caldwell had met when they gathered at Stan Rose's Bookshop to exchange literary camaraderie and Hollywood gossip.

Pep West, more than most, eluded Caldwell's easy classification. Although West and Perelman often called, inviting him to social gatherings, Caldwell avoided involvement with them. Beyond that isolation he wrapped mantlelike around his proud self-reliance, he maintained a cautious distance from West. Puzzled about why a studio would have purchased film rights to *Miss Lonelyhearts*, he additionally felt "there wouldn't be much lost in New York" if West decided to remain in Hollywood.[17] That estimate somewhat changed later. Given a story "called something like 'Blind Date,'" West claimed to have "struck a match to it, put the ashes in a match box and turned it in."

Those who refused to pander their talents in exchange for wealth only strengthened Caldwell's revulsion for the indignities he felt script writing heaped upon a writer of conscience and talent. When MGM suggested that dialogue for the bayou picture "be made sort of a dog-Spanish," he "refused to do a damn fool thing like that." Not even for $250 a week would he "write dog-Mexican dialogue when the people who do the speaking are French."[18] Consequently, the producers assigned him, with Harry Behn as continuity writer, to a Cascade timber picture that was to be directed by Howard Hawks.

The success of this combined effort was crucial to Behn, with whom

Caldwell already had developed a warm association. Unless Hawks liked the final product, Behn was through. Although the two of them wrote and rewrote the script, Hawks did not accept it because "the people were too realistic." The director wanted them "to take the plot of *Red Dust* and superimpose a Northwest background," which Behn and he had failed to do.

And so Caldwell stubbornly marked time as the days of his contract and Hollywood confinement passed. Handed two more scripts, he "promptly read and handed [them] back with a shake of his head." Assigned to adapt Rose Wilder Lane's *Let the Hurricane Roar* for King Vidor, whom he respected, he worked but two weeks before the director left for another studio. Then because Caldwell's August 5 contract deadline was only three weeks away, he was assigned to a two-reeler "piece of tripe called, naturally *A Wicked Woman*," a work he did not complete.

Throughout that time, Caldwell recorded complaints that varied only in their expression. "It's a hell of a way for a man to earn a living," captured their essence. He had "a craw full" of the entire business and would "have to disgorge two or three times before leaving."[19] The whole situation created a disgust so nauseous that he vowed not to remain there "after August fifth for a four figure salary even if it were offered."

Only the family's financial needs forced Caldwell to fulfill the full term of his contract. That was a concern he made clear almost daily to Helen but especially when she was questioning his fidelity or occasionally reminding him of her own Mount Vernon difficulties. When a technician's strike threatened the two remaining weeks of his salary, Caldwell was torn between his ideals and his own financial realities. That threatened five-hundred dollars, less Lieber's commission, was to be "living money," since everything else had gone toward paying debts and having Helen buy a new Ford. Yet he voiced his principles: "I'm siding with the strikers, of course; but I also realize that the individual in the present constituted society has to fight for existence. If he doesn't do it, there's no one just yet to do it for the individual collectively."[20] Such sympathies, perhaps, attracted him to occasional John Reed Club meetings in the Los Angeles area. Asked to speak there, however, Caldwell assuaged his conscience by donating ten dollars instead.

In other ways as well, Caldwell found himself caught between the slats of principle and practice. Advising Helen about securing a winter's wood supply, he dictated shrewd market tactics. If most of Mount Vernon was tied up with the local bank's closing, she "should be able to buy wood cheaper now, for cash, than later when people there have more money." Given a choice between abstract justice and dollar-reality, Caldwell declared his essential values: "The idea is to get hardwood . . . at a price to suit the times."[21] Not always blind to that contradictory aspect of his character, years later he perhaps provided the clue; he did not "care for individuals": "I'm interested only in groups . . . only in the masses."[22]

Against Hollywood's celluloid dream for the masses, Caldwell had to play his own real world, one whose needs involved interests and obligations more essential than those covered by his contract. Pornography charges brought against *God's Little Acre* in New York had been publicized and discussed both locally and nationally. In the case brought for trial before New York Magistrate Court Judge Benjamin E. Greenspan, John S. Sumner, representing the New York Society for the Suppression of Vice, argued the plaintiff's case. Viking Press called upon some sixty literary authorities to defend the novel's, and Caldwell's, integrity. People as diverse as Carl Van Doren, Malcolm Cowley, Henry S. Canby, Elmer Rice, and Sinclair Lewis spoke for the book's literary legitimacy. After hearing all arguments, Greenspan dismissed the case, deciding that Caldwell "had chosen to write what he believes to be the truth about a certain group in American life," and that "*truth* should always be accepted as a justification for literature."[23]

That memorable decision vindicated *God's Little Acre* and reinforced Caldwell's literary credibility. More than that, for good or ill, the publicity attending the trial fixed Erskine Caldwell's name and reputation firmly in the public mind. Reconciled to the reality that no novel would shortly be forthcoming from Caldwell, they nonetheless wished to capitalize on the "free" publicity. Consequently, Viking pressured Caldwell for stories to be included in the *We Are the Living* collection, a book Caldwell's and Lieber's combined insistence had urged.

Without Helen's guidance this time, Caldwell vacillated as he tried to choose the stories to be included. Always before, he had relied upon her help and direction in perfecting his works. From New Orleans, he had advised, "Do all you can with [the *Journeyman* manuscript] so it will be finished as far as you are concerned."[24] Two months later, Caldwell asked Helen to reread what he had written, to see if she "could find anything wrong with it." She was to tell him "what feeling" it gave her since he could not decide "whether it [was] any good or not."[25] Finally having selected the works for the Viking collection, he yet waffled, wishing she "could have read it at least once" before it went to press. No doubt she could have found much that would have improved the book.

Yet, in other ways, the couple's letters bristled with those respective insecurities and needs that even at continent's distance strained their marriage. Knowing Caldwell as she did, Helen questioned the monk-like denials offered in his daily letters. The few diversions he mentioned—a Russian movie followed by dinner, swims at Malibu Beach, a Fourth of July air show—too often included an inadvertent but suspicious "we." Beyond that, there was a studio secretary, Ruth Carnall, who, to spare him unwelcome intrusion, intercepted all his calls. Such circumstances fed Helen's suspicions about his fidelity.

In various ways Caldwell attempted to dodge the accusations in Helen's letters. She knew "damn well" that as long as he had her, "nobody else [had] ever been anything" to him; he would always be faithful to her "in the present or future" unless she let him down. To confirm his overwhelming desire for Helen, he offered a proposal. Upon his return, could she meet him in Chicago? Caldwell's need for her was so compelling, her lovemaking so satisfying, that he could not stand deferring its pleasure the extra two days it would take him to reach Mount Vernon.

Caldwell had sketched the scope of his desires so narrowly and vividly—as his letters often did—that he must have offended Helen as a person; he hurried to correct this mistake. For him, she represented a variety of women. When reading one of his stories, he knew her as a critic, but cooking dinner, she appeared to him as a housekeeper. While he was in California, however, Helen was "not being any of those," since, as he explained, "out here, I remember you as somebody getting naked when I want you."[26] Perhaps that would explain why she had misunderstood him. Above all, Caldwell appreciated Helen's gift of "being able to be as many women" as she wished because "one person becomes tiresome."

When such defensive tactics failed to appease Helen, Caldwell countered her thrusts with attacks of his own. When she inadvertently allowed some bills to go past due, he railed: "I wish to Christ you would pay them up instead of trying to cover them over."[27] Always believing that she had never "been born with much sense," if she would listen to him, he'd try to teach her some. When Helen defended some friends Caldwell thought had rotted "when they [got] to the top," he again berated her: "I tried to make it plain to you that you've been a damn fool, and that you ought to behave with sense."[28] After Janet's birth, he had told Helen how to feed and wean her, because like a puppy, a kid could be trained to do anything. And as for Helen's dieting intentions, she should weigh between 140 and 145, "not a pound more, not a pound less." Caldwell's instructions for purchasing their new car covered everything from trade-in negotiations to washing dust from its finish.

Caldwell's letters revealed a personal ambivalence that shaped his life even more than it did that of most other American men of his generation. Because he was the man, because he was the hard-working, self-sacrificing husband, he had the right to judge and direct, control and dominate, the woman, his wife. As a woman she was not to be trusted, was not competent enough to make common-sense judgments about anything. Conversely, he needed repeated reassurances of her love— "tell me . . . if you still love me"—and he would have been "in a pretty fix" without her. He desired her physically. A painful dissonance resounded between what his culture told Caldwell, the man, that he should be and what his own personal insecurities suggested that he was, a man in many ways dependent upon a woman, in this instance, Helen.

Without a doubt, their long separation strained Erskine and Helen's relationship, but more than that, his isolated situation had reduced him to an emotional state even more distraught than that revealed in his letters from Wilkes-Barre. Cultivating solitude in his hotel room, refusing to sit in overstuffed chairs, and otherwise "holding out tooth and nail against going Hollywood," overwhelmed even Caldwell's proud and puritan-like stoicism. With a sense of amazement, he admitted that he did not "know what in the hell [he was] doing all the time."[29]

Toward the end of his contract period, Caldwell appeared to have become a victim of a surrealistic nightmare much like that which Pep West would recreate in his *Day of the Locust.* Using imagery that *Locust* was to amplify, he shared with Helen the disassociation he felt. With the help of the scenery department, the whole thing could "easily turn out to be a dream." Every week his disorientation became worse: "This is more like a long sleep than anything else. The beginning of it was when I left Mount Vernon, and I probably won't wake up till I get back. Then I'll feel like a Rip Van Rinkle [sic]. I'll just have been dead for the summer, and get back to see it all gone."[30]

Several incidents would testify to the painful conflicts between Caldwell's rigid conscience and his more basic human needs. From his office across from the staging lot of an MGM musical, he could look out his window to see scantily clad girls going to and fro between the wardrobe department and set; Helen was not to think that he was making a try for them. It was not that they weren't good-looking enough or anything like that: "It's just that they remind me of you."[31] Helen might well have wondered whether Caldwell was expressing his love for her or alleviating a guilt provoked by his spying on attractive girls in chemises.

Because no priest stood between him and the powers of forgiveness, Caldwell could turn only to Helen with his guilt. Yet like the Old Testament figures who blamed first Eve and later Susanna for their lust, Caldwell likewise distorted facts to excuse himself from guilt. Woman was the temptress; in his instance, Helen was to blame:

You know damn well the reason I ever liked anybody else (momentarily) was because it was the contrast. It's just that I couldn't help being a fool about anybody (no matter whom) with what you lacked. Call it round breasts, firm legs, or mental or physical agility. It doesn't matter what you call it; the fact was that you were abnormal. And I can only stomach normality. . . . You will be normal when your mind and body reacts to my conception of naturalness, and I don't think my conception is warped. I like healthy people: men and women. I can't stand perversion in people, in writing, or in life: I won't have anything to do with any of it because I know it is more satisfying to be natural. That's come out of the earth, or whatever you call it, and it endures. If you are abnormal, then I wish none of it; if normal, then I'll have to take all or nothing.[32]

Within Caldwell's confused rhetoric lurked his saving justification. His masculine conceptions, urges, and desires were normal because they were natural and "of the earth."

Such psychological turmoil, however, forced even Caldwell to acknowledge his recent erratic behavior. He could not understand what made him "write all these damn fool letters." It must have been his dreamlike confusion and the fact that he hadn't "had [Helen] for nearly three months—or anybody—." But what else could he have done? Caldwell's outline of possible alternatives charted the parameters of his dilemma. His denials, as well as his mock-serious plea for understanding and singular exemption, exposed the dimensions of that struggle between the demands of nature and conscience.

Some persons would masterbate [sic] I suppose: I won't, because it isn't the real thing, and I would feel even worse (if that's possible). And I wouldn't take anybody unless I asked or told you first, and gave you a chance to forbid it. And the only kind of girl I would take—no matter if you did say I could have the other kind—would be a prostitute. She would have to be the kind of girl I'd never seen before and would never see again. I couldn't take any other kind of girl, because she would be too much like you—and I'd be dissatisfied. I could only feel that you were a hundred times better. I'd feel rotten. Maybe you'd better sign an order for one intercourse with professional prostitute, good only for one time, and void on and after August 5th![33]

No matter the sexual satisfactions provided by either the Wilkes-Barre girls or—his denials notwithstanding—Hollywood secretaries, Caldwell subsequently became guilt-ridden. He had shared with Helen details of his tryst with the Boston schoolteacher on the boat, an act of confession seeking perhaps both excuse and forgiveness. This time, little-boy-like, he sought her permission to satisfy his needs; without that for-giveness he would otherwise squirm with unconfessed guilt.

Caldwell relished the approach of August 5 and the end of his Holly-wood bondage. His earnings by then would have paid all the bookshop debts, and having squared himself with all the "Portland sons-of-bitches," they could "one and all, go straight to hell and roast there."[34] "Through with being in debt," and therefore somewhat thankful for Hollywood's contribution to his independence, he nonetheless vowed never again to return. In fact, given the opportunity just once, it would please him "like nothing else to tell them to go to hell," and that "in no mean language too."[35]

Chapter 10

Most of the summer had flown before Caldwell returned to Mount Vernon in mid-August of 1933. Feeling "like doing nothing for the next couple of weeks," he may have taken the boys to a wrestling match in Portland, as he had promised from California. Otherwise, his letters to Morang hinted that he sought a return to his identity as a writer: "A short story is a statement" wherein the writer tells "people what happened once-upon-a-time . . . to somebody, somewhere, sometime."[1] The artistry of the telling provoked the reader to empathize with what the writer had felt for his subject. And although "putting up with the Hollywood idiots for three months" had sort of wrung him dry, Caldwell soon returned to revising the novel he had written before departing.[2]

Journeyman provided a sense of satisfaction even as he hoped soon "to have it done and off his hands." When his Viking short-story collection, *We Are the Living*, appeared on September 25, he feared that half of the stories were punk and the book might get by only "by the skin of its teeth."[3] Caldwell's qualms proved unjustified, as reviewers almost universally acclaimed it. *We Are the Living* was "a rich book, full of honesty, humor and feeling" with stories as indigenous to American soil "as a corn cob pipe or a Ford car." Although some critics liked Caldwell's novels better, his stories about the "living" conveyed more "feeling," were more emotionally satisfying. Yet one reviewer tempered his praise with caution; Caldwell owed it to himself as a creative writer "to produce less rapidly." Events would soon conspire with Caldwell's increasing fame and evolving priorities to make that a reality.

Completing his revisions to *Journeyman* by early September, he and Helen delivered the manuscript to the Viking editor, Marshall Best, visited with New York friends, and attended to pending business.[4] While Caldwell conferred with Lieber, who through Kirkland had found a producer for *Tobacco Road*, Helen dined with Bennett Cerf, who had become a close friend. Back in Mount Vernon by midmonth, Caldwell once more offered a familiar refrain; they were financially "broke as well as flat" until somebody paid up.

Again he anxiously awaited editorial decisions, wondering whether or not Viking would take the novel. "But what the hell?" He had written rotten books before.[5] Finally Viking cautiously agreed to publish *Journeyman*. Their acceptance was so tenuous, however, that Caldwell submitted the manuscript to Carl Van Doren and William Soskin for their evaluations. He hated to publish it if it were bad, but likewise was reluctant "to leave a gap" in his work. To Morang he admitted his indecision: "So you see, I'm plainly up a tree. I made that mistake with *Autumn Hill*, I think now; and I'd hate to repeat a mistake. . . .What to do! What to do!"[6] What he apparently did was to invite distractions.

After his New York visit, he grumbled to Morang about getting "balled up in the goddam capitalist nra parade," an inconvenience making him "more sore than ever at the Hitlerized government." Someday, he guessed, he'd "probably join the party if for no other reason than to be able to say, and say proudly," that he was a Communist.[7] Subsequently, during the second week of October, Caldwell wedded principle with practice, agreeing to write an article for the *Daily Worker*. To research it, he made a hurried trip through the Ohio Valley to see firsthand worker conditions under capitalism's beleaguered system. At Lieber's urgent request, he returned to New York to discover himself caught up in a capitalistic joust of his own.

Publicity surrounding the *God's Little Acre* trial had made Erskine Caldwell a recognized name. Consequently, as rumors of Viking's reluctance to publish *Journeyman* seeped through the publishing network, Jack Harcourt of Harcourt Brace approached Lieber. He had offered two hundred dollars, manuscript unread, for both the rights to the novel and the unexpired portion of Caldwell's contract. Lieber negotiated his client's release from Viking, received a signed contingency contract from Harcourt, and anxiously awaited Caldwell's return to present him with the accomplished fact. With Lieber's assurances, Caldwell "politely told Viking to go to hell" justifying his decision as neither totally mercenary nor fickle.[8] Why should he allow Viking to publish a book the firm disliked? Beyond that, Helen, Morang, and Lieber had agreed that Caldwell should publish *Journeyman* regardless of Viking's reservations. He "hoped to Christ" the three were right.

The three may have been right, but their collective judgment was not to be confirmed by Harcourt's subsequent decisions. After having read the manuscript, Harcourt's lawyer advised the firm that it would be dangerous to publish it.[9] Additionally, with some justification it seems, both Viking and Harcourt felt that Lieber had mutually and unconscionably deceived them in the process of cutting the deal. When Jack Harcourt learned of this complication, "he became very indignant and washed his hands of the whole affair." Using the contract's contingency clause, he withdrew his offer and left Caldwell bound to Viking, whom he so recently had told to go to hell.

Since Viking editors judged that publication of *Journeyman* would be legally unwise and ultimately harmful to Caldwell's reputation, and because they questioned Lieber's tactics, they remained unenthusiastic about issuing the novel. Marshall Best urged Lieber to try to sell the book and the unexpired portion of Caldwell's contract elsewhere. He could not. Caldwell by this time may have concurred with Marshall Best's estimation; as a represented author, he had been "the victim of a very unfortunate set of circumstances."

With such distractions, Caldwell could not write at Greentrees. Hoping a change of scenery would help, he took a bus to New York, rented a basement room—its grilled door suggested it might have been once a speakeasy—at 163 West Seventy-sixth Street, and tried to retreat.[10] He directed Helen to keep his address secret because he wanted neither to have to see anyone nor to have "people bothering" him. But Caldwell could not escape distractions and found he couldn't "do a damn thing with all this hell going on."[11]

Two overriding concerns confounded Caldwell's intentions. First, he could not concentrate on his stories as long as the *Journeyman* situation remained in doubt, and second, Jack Kirkland had his adaptation of *Tobacco Road* in rehearsal. The book was "raising so much hell" with his nerves that he felt traumatized and "shaky all over"; if he "*knew* it was good" he would allow its publication. Although he thought it was, he wished Helen were there in New York "to tell [him] what to do." It was "hell to have to take the book on [his] head when there were so many yeses and noes."[12] And as much as Caldwell tried to divorce himself from the *Tobacco Road* dramatization, he did not wholly succeed. He "attended two rehearsals and made some suggestions," but anxieties about the novel, not about the play's public reception, exercised him.

Either despite or possibly because of the tensions, Caldwell worked that much harder during his ten New York days to complete the short story "Kneel to the Rising Sun." Upon his return to Mount Vernon, Helen recognized it as "the best story Erskine [had] ever done . . . or anyone else for that matter."[13] Yet when Lieber tried to sell the work, some editors, like Lee Harman of *Harper's*, rejected it because the story was "too cruel and sadistic and made him sick." Possibly Lieber's politics as much as the story's sympathies repulsed him, because he had blurted out, "You fellows who think life is just a dung heap make me sick. I know all about crop-sharers."[14] Finally Max Perkins once more came to Caldwell and Lieber's rescue, confirming Helen's judgment by accepting Caldwell's southern classic for *Scribner's Monthly*.

But before either the disposition of "Kneel to the Rising Sun" or *Journeyman* could be resolved, the Caldwells found themselves embroiled in the excitement attendant upon the opening night of *Tobacco Road*. The December 4, 1933, premiere at the Masque Theater shocked, moved, and confounded both audience and reviewers alike. Caldwell liked the adaptation, surmising that if he "had had much to do with it, it probably wouldn't [have been] much different" than it was. But he was disturbed by the audience's response. Most hid their discomfort behind tittering or else laughed outright, reactions that mystified and offended Caldwell. He believed the "audience never did need to find something to laugh about because to [him] it was sad."[15] Joseph Wood Krutch mulled the tragicomic strains of *Tobacco Road*, confessing that he found it funny, "though ambiguously so," as he believed its author intended it to be. Most other reviewers were not so perceptive, yet they too felt themselves confused and ambivalent.

Brooks Atkinson, writing for the *New York Times*, epitomized that general bemusement. Caldwell's *Tobacco Road*, he felt, was "one of the grossest episodes ever put on stage," with the theater never sheltering "a fouler or more degenerate parcel of folks" than the hardscrabble Lesters. Nonetheless, the play carried within it "moments of merciless power . . . and a malevolent glow of poetry" beyond the rudeness of its statement.[16] Walter Winchell of the *Daily Mirror* titillated his readers, and perhaps assured the play's success, with his caustic broadsides. The southerner Stark Young, reviewing for the *New Republic*, praised *Tobacco Road*'s faithful reproduction of its rhythmic Georgia language— "the writing itself can be listened to inch by inch." He believed, moreover, that Caldwell had given the audience a work of art, one whose realism had been "unified and transmuted into something . . . where something was not before."[17]

Erskine Caldwell, Jack Kirkland, and Henry Hull as Jeeter had combined to give audience and reviewers a play like none other then currently on Broadway. Yet for the first week and a half, *Tobacco Road* did not meet expenses. Then a combination of Caldwell's reputation, the hand-wringing sensibilities of some reviewers, and a positive endorsement from Captain Joseph M. Patterson of the *Daily News* gave it some hope. After much initial skepticism, Caldwell allowed the play a fighting chance. Two months after its opening, even when "the house was sold out to the roof . . . and customers were turned away by the dozen," he felt that the production might survive "another month—maybe two more."[18] But Caldwell had never been one to be seduced by optimism.

Leaving the play to its fortunes, the Caldwells loyally returned to Wrens in January of 1934. Again his trip home was just that—one to discharge family expectations, to reestablish regional ties, and as always, another experience-gathering opportunity. During one of those forays with Ira, he came "pretty close to getting [his] neck stretched in the state of Georgia," but got the story he was after anyway.[19] By this time at least the literate citizens of Caldwell's home state had read or heard about his characterization of the region. Some felt that he had distorted reality for his own fame and profit.

Stopping in New York on their way to Maine, the Caldwells again saw the play. This time Caldwell "was convinced" that it was good. But other prospects proved less promising. Meeting afterwards with Marshall Best at Viking, the two of them settled upon a compromise for *Journeyman*. The firm would grant him a thousand-dollar advance upon the book but publish it only after he had written, and they had issued, another of his novels. Further, as a precaution that *Journeyman* would neither involve them in another court case nor injure Caldwell's literary reputation, they would print it initially only in a limited, numbered edition.

During the trip home, Dee and Janet broke out with measles, and only a day later both Pix and Caldwell came down with the mumps. Five feet of snow and a cold house greeted the family when they arrived in Mount Vernon three days later than planned. Because Caldwell was so sick, the household responsibilities—stoking the stove, heating the water, cooking broth, washing clothes, and caring for four sick people—all fell upon Helen. After a few days of inactivity, Caldwell arose from bed to write, but suffered a relapse—a complication not without its benefits. He could in good conscience excuse himself from delivering talks promised that month at Bennington, Princeton, and the Universities of Georgia and Vermont. Possibly to hide his disappointment, he claimed relief since he'd "rather write a short story any day than make a talk."[20]

Thus for almost two weeks Caldwell kept to bed. He used the time to read his accumulation of little magazines, to wonder what effect Dean Jagger's leaving the role of Lov Bensey would have on the play, and to speculate whether or not E. J. Basshe's projected adaptation of *God's Little Acre* might be better than that of *Tobacco Road*, though that had proved to be good enough. Of the twenty-six plays that had opened in December, *Tobacco Road* alone remained by February 15. When Theodore Dreiser and Carl Van Doren recommended it to the Pulitzer Committee for the 1934 drama prize, Caldwell anticipated the possibility with some glee. "That play is going to give Walter Winchell piles yet. Remember his review of it?" he asked Morang.[21]

Tobacco Road did not then or ever win the Pulitzer Prize. Nonetheless, during its seven-and-a-half-year run, its earnings were to provide Caldwell with a measure of financial security and almost-freedom he never before had been able to enjoy. For the first time in almost a decade of marriage, he did not have to write and worry incessantly about providing for his family. When the *Daily Worker* requested that he go to Detroit to research and write a four-part series on auto industry working conditions, he could comply. After he departed on May 7, Helen received a message that Ira requested she relay: "Tell Erskine . . . to try to track the facts exactly."[22] The pocket memo in which Caldwell jotted his impressions preserves those facts as he perceived them.

Visits to Dodge, Briggs Manufacturing Company, Murray Body Corporation, Hudson Motor Company, and most dramatically, Ford, revealed the same pattern: exploitation of the workers for the system's gain. According to Caldwell's notes, speed-ups forced two hundred men to be carried out on stretchers during one eight-hour shift in August 1933, while Ford's hiring department forced applicants to pay fifty dollars down if they wished to be considered for a job. During those tenuous years, the same company paid four dollars per day, in accordance with NRA guidelines, but took it back "for rent, lights, groceries, etc."[23]

At the Dodge Corporation, the same guidelines allowed machines to run at such excessive speeds that during one night shift, two workers lost fingers and a falling motor killed another. Negroes could not live in Ford's Dearborn; they were run out by paid cops: " 'No niggs are allowed after dark—white man's town.' " Yet as odious as Henry Ford's methods and practices were, Caldwell did not exclusively blame the man. Partially excusing him, he perceived that "Ford himself is a victim of the capitalistic system." Caldwell sent Morang copies of his *Daily Worker* broadside, since his friend could not afford to subscribe even to a paper printed for the masses.

Shortly after Caldwell completed the Detroit assignment, he and Helen took a short trip to Nova Scotia. On the surface at least, their relationship seemed to have stabilized, since their letters no longer dwelled upon accusations and recriminations. Perhaps their release from the strains of poverty had eased some of the tensions of their nine-year marriage. In the six months since *Tobacco Road*'s opening, they had saved almost $2,000, a reserve allowing Caldwell to resist the offers that MGM once again had been making since mid-March of 1934.[24]

Caldwell did not tell the studios "to go to hell," but he did politely defer their increasing offers. He told himself and others that "it would be foolish to go out there" while his weekly drama royalties provided more

than the offered $500 weekly salary.[25] Setting aside principle for prag-
matic fact, however, he allowed that in his "old age that [salary would]
look pretty damn good."

Monday, June 18, found Caldwell in New York en route to Hollywood
with the promise of a six-hundred-dollar-a-week, two-month contract.
By Friday morning, he was in his Hollywood office, this time one luxu-
riously appointed with two desks, a silk-covered sofa, six soft chairs, and
carpeting, but still no typewriter. Caldwell did not complain about the
absence of a hard-backed chair.

The first Hollywood stint had apparently made an impression upon
both the Caldwells; this time Helen would join him there. Leaving Dee
and Janet at Greentrees with a hired nurse and Norman Cushman, a
friend of the family, she would take Pix with her on the Chicago Chief.
Until Helen departed on July 11, Caldwell's daily letters again became
epistles of instructions and advice, but hinted at nothing about his
deeper needs.

Meeting them at the railroad station "in a swank car without a top," he
showed them around Hollywood before taking them to their house near
the Playa del Rey beach. That location pleased Helen and Pix, and, as
Caldwell wished, separated him "from the Hollywood crowd." Ruth
Carnall, the MGM secretary who had fueled Helen's jealousy the previous summer, lived nearby. As neighbors, she and Helen came to a
comfortable understanding that would continue through the years.

Professionally, only a $350 weekly salary increase and a plush office
separated Caldwell's Hollywood summer of 1934 from that of 1933. Assigned to write dialogue for *A Wicked Woman*, he apparently did not recognize it as the same "piece of tripe" he had left unfinished the previous
summer. Almost casually, he noted that given a choice between a secretary and a typewriter, he had chosen the latter "in as much as the name
of the picture is *Wicked Woman.*"[26]

Within a week, Caldwell had written twenty pages of dialogue but
guessed he might be in the doghouse because he "took out all the rain,
rag-dolls, crooning, and other items of Hollywood trappings and wrote a
story about people."[27] MGM's more expensive screenwriter proved to be
no more tractable than had the cheaper one. Nonchalantly listening "to

them raise hell," he wrote as he wished.[28] Eventually Caldwell's stubbornness exceeded the script directors' patience. Less than a month after his arrival, he unremorsefully boasted of sticking to his principles: "I was kicked off . . . *A Wicked Woman* when I refused to write on the second one—*A Lady Comes to Town*—because I told the producer that even God himself couldn't write a screen play with any life in it when Joan Crawford was to play the lead."[29]

Before the eight weeks were over, Caldwell apparently had learned more than had the Hollywood directors. MGM wished to extend his current contract and salary by a month, and Paramount had made "a hell of a big offer." Once having thought never to see the day when he would refuse "a thousand-a-week offers," Caldwell nonetheless decided that no studio had enough money to get him on the lots again. Scriptwriting was "no job for a white man." Though he had compromised two months of honor for six hundred dollars per week, he vowed that no amount could seduce him permanently from his own story writing.

Thirty years old at the time and enjoying a degree of both fame and wealth, Caldwell must have reexamined the priorities that fate had imposed upon him. During the previous eight months, he had written only a few short stories. *Journeyman,* in the meantime, had remained in limbo until Caldwell could release it by first writing another book for publication. As had increasingly become his habit, he struggled to assert his own literary values through his written dialogues with Morang. Writing remained "a lone-wolf job in more ways than one." A person still had "to do his own writing . . . and say to hell with anybody" other than himself. Caldwell realized, however, that a writer "had to pay for getting mixed up" in the Hollywood business where writers and players passed through "like chips on a river," some going up, some going down, and some hanging on.[30]

He had learned that a person should not be deceived by the system, no matter what its rewards, because that system used people for its selfish profit. As evidence, Caldwell cited Hollywood's successful efforts to lure both Henry Hull and Dean Jagger—and eventually Jim Barton and others—from their Broadway leads in *Tobacco Road.* In their greed for big names to ensure bigger profits, film producers had threatened the play as well as the livelihoods of the hundred or so people dependent upon its continuing. But the Hollywood moguls remained purposely blind; they were "afraid to recognize poverty, or that there are people in America who don't have enough food to keep them alive."[31] As evidence of his ideological sympathies, Caldwell agreed to a request by Clarence Hathaway, editor of the *Daily Worker*. To gather impressions for a series "on the dried up Middle West," Caldwell would extend considerably his family's return in order that he might preserve both his political and writing integrity.

Thus, the third week in August, the Caldwells left Hollywood in their new Ford convertible so he could explore the reality of mid-America's crisis. Employing a practice that was to become custom, he episodically presented his impressions through stories told to him in casual encounters with people like a grocery store proprietor in Madras, Oregon; the filling-station operator in Spokane; and an auto camp owner in Montana. His storytellers, like "Cap" who shuffled, tugged at his coat, and scratched his head, became the characters in his stories. In a variation of the type made famous by Sinclair Lewis, a wealthy Iowa farmer rhapsodized about his state. A "dump-picker" near Omaha, a Grandpa Price who preempted the family's total water supply for the luxury of a bath— these and others fed Caldwell's version of deprivation in the Midwest.

During this trip and subsequent to it, Caldwell apparently perfected a method he long would practice in gathering and translating his materials.[32] Leaving the hotel or motel—dressed not as if he were "going to a 5 o'clock soiree," but comfortably casual with "some old clod-hoppers"—he would drive through the countryside, looking for a certain person or farmer. Studying the neighborhood, the type of house a farmer had, checking to see if he had "weeds in his pigpen or whether his wife [had] curtains on the windows," Caldwell would categorize his subject. If the machines were kept in a shed, he guessed the guy to be hardworking. Machines rusting in the rain told another story. Caldwell had no formula or ritual for introducing himself to such people; he merely had "to go out and do it."

Without the benefit of a recorder, taking only skeletal notes, including names, places, and reminders, Caldwell later would "reconstitute—not

recreate but reconstitute—the atmosphere, the tenor, the impression"
he got:

> A guy is embittered about something. He doesn't like what's going on in
> Washington, or what's happening to his son or daughter-in-law. It's one of
> those kind of things where you have to find the origin, the basis for com-
> plaint in life. . . . You get the essence of his life with one little incident, and
> he can go on and talk for an hour and make circles, like dropping a pebble in
> a pond. Once he says something, that means the core of the whole thing. You
> go on from there. [Later] you build up the periphery of it; you build up all
> the essence of his life . . . the real point of his existence. I call it reconstitut-
> ing his life, his conversation.[33]

Always with an eye to the human condition, with a carefully attuned ear
to the dialect, the cadence of a particular human's voice, Caldwell would
thus experience and later "reconstitute" essences. Mixing a reporter's
skill with the storyteller's art, he focused upon the "pebble in the pond,"
its circles rippling through his retelling.

After "covering 5,500 miles and God knows how many states," the
Caldwells arrived in Mount Vernon in early September, sunburned,
windblown, and exhausted. Yet even if the trip had "taken three months,
it was worth it," Caldwell concluded.[34] Nonetheless, he had less than
two weeks upon his return to write the twenty-four Midwest articles.
Once "the series [was] all done, signed, and sealed, and in the hands of
Monte Bourjaily," however, Caldwell questioned its reception.[35] Would
readers endure so many installments? He half-jokingly expressed a suspicion that people hated him "enough in person without taking the trouble to read what [he wrote]," an assessment given some credibility by the
events of the next few months.

By mid-October only one paper, and that a southern one, had run the
"Cross-America series." Apparently once more feeling he had little
published to show for a year's work, Caldwell urged Lieber to push Viking toward publication of *Journeyman.* Marshall Best and Harold
Guinzburg repeated their reservations. Because they believed *Journeyman* was not as good as either *Tobacco Road* or *God's Little Acre,* its publication would not advance Caldwell's reputation. Furthermore, if they

were asked to defend its censorship through the courts, they could do so only with embarrassment—not with the pride that had moved their defense of *God's Little Acre* as a fine and important contribution to literature.

If Best and Guinzburg hoped such arguments would erode Caldwell's persistence, they misjudged the strength of his self-will. Finally Guinzburg had to concede partial defeat if Viking hoped to keep Caldwell—and the augmented profits his name had come to earn. He agreed to publish *Journeyman* in a limited edition of 1,475 copies without the condition of printing another Caldwell novel first. Possibly he granted this concession either to compensate for Viking's refusal to publish in book format Caldwell's serialized midwestern sketches, or to encourage him in their hope that he would have a new novel "ready in the near future."[36] That expectation was not to be realized for another six years, long after the Viking hopes had died.

Various distractions had increasingly taken their toll from Caldwell's creative energies. He had written *Journeyman* before his first Hollywood experience, before the fame brought by the *Tobacco Road* production, before the money from both had freed him from a poverty demanding that he write as if life depended upon it. Furthermore, that circumstantial and essential privacy so crucial to his writing for the previous ten years appears to have been violated and interrupted beyond immediate retrieval. Throughout October he tried once more to fan the familiar creative fires, but finished only two or three stories.

As usual, Caldwell could not write while embroiled in those conflicts that his own pride would not allow him to abandon. Instead he fumed and complained about the "publishing bastards" who kept him "up in the air all the time."[37] Consequently, the reading public did not see much new from Caldwell's typewriter in 1934. Four short stories—"Back on the Road," "The Cold Winter," "Maud Island," and "The Sick Horse"—appeared. Only the last, however, could Lieber place in a reputable, paying magazine, *Esquire.*

With the increased earnings from both Hollywood and *Tobacco Road,* the Caldwells were no longer forced to undergo their extended winter migrations to Wrens. They could now afford "to pay Oscar" two dollars per cord for wood to carry them through the hard winters at Mount Vernon. Only once in the past two years had the family returned, and that for a short visit. By January of 1935, however, Caldwell returned alone for a ten-day busman's holiday. Possibly stimulated by the experiences of his Dust Bowl tour and encouraged by the curiosity that *Tobacco Road*'s characters piqued among eastern audiences, Caldwell both visited his parents and gathered fresh impressions for a series of articles on sharecropping for the *New York Post.*

With Ira as his companion and guide, Caldwell once more drove country roads through barren fields punctuated by sagging gray houses. According to Caldwell, nothing had changed; the region, and, in fact, the "whole country was the same." Those lives whose stories he had told through *Tobacco Road, God's Little Acre,* and the forthcoming *Journeyman,* would appear differently in his series. Long before John Steinbeck's *Grapes of Wrath* captured public attention and sympathy, Caldwell wrote about the impact of technology and change upon a bewildered people.

The *New York Post* series claimed that in the past, sharecroppers had earned a marginal security by clinging to their situations. More recently, government price-support systems and programs encouraging mechanization had displaced large numbers of sharecroppers, forcing them into a day-labor market during a period when there were no jobs. The dual effects of that process were grim.

During the time Caldwell and Ira had been surveying the area, a girl died of malnutrition, her body twisted and knotted from rickets and anemia—"all of this five miles from U.S. #1, twenty five miles from Augusta and twenty miles from the county seat." Other displaced people had no homes. A family Ira had pictured in his Bungler study became the tenant farmer who moved his family into an abandoned schoolhouse. Another displaced tenant, with eleven children and a wife who lay bedridden with anemia, tried to support them with what he could earn splitting "kindling splinters."

Such people were but victims of a collusion of regional forces, all conspiring to keep federal relief benefits from those who needed them. Then–Georgia governor Eugene Talmadge—he of the snapping red suspenders and everybody's friend—denied state relief appropriations to the poor. On the local level, officials refused to admit they had poor among them, denying the impoverished access to federal program benefits legitimately theirs. Though all the deprived suffered, the "Negroes were the chief victims of a system which distressed the poor of the entire region."[38] If his few readers had missed the points of Caldwell's novels and some stories or audiences had laughed in the wrong places during *Tobacco Road*, they could not misinterpret his intentions in the *New York Post* articles. Finally Ira's concerns would catch the attention of thousands.

After Caldwell and Ira completed their survey of the Wrens area's poor, they traveled to Fernandina, Florida. There on the northeast coast, Caldwell wanted to buy some property. Then if the Caldwells could "get some work done, and make enough money to save," they could return south when school was out.[39]

The Caldwells' improved circumstances further allowed Caldwell to offer Alfred Morang something more substantial than encouragement and writing advice. The Morangs had continued to subsist marginally on earnings from his paintings and Dorothy's piano lessons, but Morang's physical condition further complicated their situation. A heavy smoker, he coughed much, a symptom, doctors then believed, of tuberculosis.

Subsequent to that diagnosis, Caldwell responded as the friend and person he was. Pleased to be "in a position to be of a little help," he pledged monthly checks "for twenty-five bucks, to start off with March 1st," continuing thereafter as long as necessary.[40] Morang was not to let the matter of repayment bother him. While the checks were not gifts, they represented installments on "a loan without interest that [could] run for the next hundred years." Although the loans were to extend but twenty years, Morang never could repay them except through loyalty and friendship. Long past what would appear to be Morang's honest deserving, Caldwell dutifully continued to pay the price of personal allegiance and honor.

The tenant-farmers articles that had run serially in the *New York Post* beginning February 17, 1935, evoked incredulous sympathy from East

Coast readers. They wished the names and addresses of those people Caldwell had described so they could send clothing, food, and money directly to them. Georgia readers and newspapers likewise responded with incredulity—but without sympathy. "Prominent citizens" angrily wrote disclaimers. People and conditions such as he described existed nowhere in their state. Caldwell presumed that the general outcry would quieten "as soon as they could hush it up."

But the righteous citizens did not soon succeed in hushing it up. Subsequent reports by the *Augusta Chronicle* and other regional papers not only confirmed Caldwell's claims but also cited cases even more abysmal. With such publicity, the *Post* commissioned Caldwell to do a series with even broader regional scope than the earlier one. Accordingly, he hastily departed Mount Vernon in mid-March to board a train for Wrens. There he met Ira, where they cooperated on what might have been "Auto's" dream: father and son would travel and work together to report on poverty conditions in the South.

The two Caldwells traveled by automobile for about a week through parts of Mississippi, Alabama, and Georgia. Throughout the tour, Ira and Caldwell were to combine their individual talents and interests. Although his father had interspersed his Bungler study with supporting photos, Caldwell had not used this medium in either of his previous projects. On this trip, however, he took some fifty photographs, "at least a half dozen good ones." Their trip proved satisfying and uneventful except for two incidents. During one, they "got chased out of an Alabama county." Another time Caldwell "had to hold a fellow with a knife—sore because the Chronicle [had] printed that his sister was an idiot"—while Ira talked him down.[41] Despite Ira's contributions to the project, when the *New York Post* ran the series during the week of April 8, Erskine Caldwell's name alone appeared in the by-line.

Although both Ira and Caldwell acted with sincerity in their treatment of the South's dispossessed, the two *Post* features certainly did not harm *Tobacco Road*'s success. It continued to play to packed houses, earning royalties that Caldwell would estimate by 1936 to have been about a thousand dollars per week. Adding to its reputation, Henry Hull had formed a road company which gave its first performance of *Tobacco*

Road on March 17, 1935, in San Francisco. Thereafter it would wind its way throughout America's cities, where all who could read knew Erskine Caldwell by name and reputation. That fame alone assured newspapers and journals that his articles would be read with credibility.

Shortly, sales of *God's Little Acre, Tobacco Road,* and Caldwell's short stories were to boost his weekly writing income almost equal to that of the play. *Tobacco Road* had sold little more than five hundred copies in 1932, when Caldwell had had three concerns: the quality of his writing, money, and fame, in that order. Three years later, after he had risen from rags to riches, all had been erased. Any nagging doubts about what he or critics might have felt about his writing were shouted down by the many popular voices acclaiming his success.

Either that, or Caldwell would not even admit privately that he might have been wrong in pushing for the publication of *Journeyman.* This time the essentially negative reviews which the January 1935 offering of the novel collected did not provoke him to written complaint. One critic raised the spectral possibility that Caldwell already seemed to be repeating himself. Another felt that *Journeyman* presented only nightmarish characters caught in a warped situation devoid of hope. Even the usually positive and friendly critic Robert Cantwell responded lukewarmly. Unlike Faulkner, who involuted his meanings, Caldwell outdid himself through *Journeyman's* directness. Judging from reviews alone, Viking may have been wise indeed to have issued a limited edition of the novel. That tactic not only minimized their losses but also precluded obscenity trials.

Despite Caldwell's apparent disregard of the *Journeyman* reviews, five months later he did acknowledge those that greeted his collection of stories called *Kneel to the Rising Sun.* Although generally favorable, he acknowledged them all as of "the expected variety . . . half plus, half minus."[42] In fact, after he "had worked off steam" through some other writing, he came to think "they were of a great help." Ultimately, however, Caldwell offered what was to become his credo of solace: "The higher you go, the harder the whacks on the head."[43]

Through *Journeyman,* Caldwell caricatured a God-speaking rogue who seduces, gambles, pimps, and preaches in religion's guise. A Di-

onysus in another time and place, Semon Dye introduces those companion forces, sex and religion, into an impoverished and withered southern
enclave. Humorously tracing the amoral shenanigans of a man who selfishly gulls the God-hungry, the book underscores a transcendent awe
that gripped preacher and victims alike. In one instance, three men, including Semon Dye, peer through a crack in a cow-shed wall to look
"clear to the backside of heaven." In another, a girl, exhilarated by Dye's
sexually charged preaching, experiences an orgasmic conversion with
cosmic overtones. Afterwards, "she lay in the wagon bed staring at the
heavens through the waving branches of the pines." Avoiding those two
confounding examples of Caldwell's most powerful and religiously
charged writing, reviewers instead only belabored the grotesquely obvious. They failed to understand, as Caldwell implied, that any "religious" experience was better than the emotional stagnation and hopelessness with which isolation, poverty, and ignorance wrapped the
misbegotten.

Against reviewers of *Rising Sun*, those who balanced praise with
words like "horror," "violent," and "revolting," Caldwell privately offered a storehouse of experience and story. Many times he had heard of
young children and "old people, too," like Lonnie's father, who had
been eaten by hogs. The Arch Gunnard types who squirmed in religious
orgies on other occasions cropped dogs' tails for the fun of it. And the
violence? Years later he cited causes for those themes upon which his
stories spun.

> Blame it on the humid climate, on the physically and emotionally rousing
> tempo of its numerous primitive religions, on an innate conflict between
> white and Negro races, on inadequate educational advantages, on a smol-
> dering psychological complex about the Lost Cause of the War Between the
> States, blame it on the present-day descendants of British robbers, mur-
> derers, rapists, and other criminals who were among the early colonizers.
> But, regardless of a single cause or a combination of causes, the fact remains
> that strains of cruelty and violence were indigenous characteristics of the
> white Anglo-Saxon Protestant population of the Deep South.[44]

Man's inhumanity to man had been a persistent if muted theme in Caldwell's southern writings. *Kneel to the Rising Sun*, however, did not strain

through silence the blatant details of those horrors that had for so long been a part of his early experience. Memory and observation confirmed his beliefs that in desperate southern conditions, "the white man was taking out his anger," venting larger frustrations, upon the Negro as scapegoat.

"Candy-Man Beechum" and "Blue Boy" were among his strongest offerings upon that theme in *Rising Sun*. Other stories, such as "The End of Christy Tucker," "The People vs. Abe Lathan, Colored," and a much later novel, *Trouble in July*, were to extend the nightmarish circles of human violence. Yet the comic, with only hints of the contextual causes, likewise traded upon variations of the indignities racism had wrought. "The Fly in the Coffin," "The Negro in the Well," "Nine Dollars Worth of Mumble," and, peripherally, "August Afternoon" represented loose-jointed, thigh-slapping excursions into the happier light of southern black life and black-white charades. Not Stepin Fetchit caricatures, Caldwell's characters spoke with all the rhythmic beauty of black dialect. Yet their situations winked at human idiosyncrasies and foibles as revealed through people who just happened to be black.

But no matter the realities and sympathies caught through Caldwell's stories, certain critics had questioned their truth. After *Journeyman*, written in 1933, Caldwell did not write another novel for seven years. Some *Rising Sun* reviewers suspected that he had distorted reality through his exaggeration. Such assaults upon his personal and writing integrity urged him to defend his honor: "By that time, I had become determined to vindicate my writings about the South . . . to show that my fiction was as realistic as life itself."[45] Perhaps only coincidentally, Caldwell wrote no more fiction until after he had cooperated in a venture that used photos to corroborate the truth of his stories.

In the meantime, since there wasn't "much happening" in Mount Vernon, the Caldwells decided to spend a month traveling through Manitoba, Saskatchewan, and British Columbia. Helen's memories of that first extended time away from the children, alone with Caldwell, remain as pleasant as the occasion was unusual.[46] They traveled, before the time of transcontinental highways, from Mount Vernon to Montreal, and on to Vancouver. Despite the gravel roads and fourteen flat tires, Helen thought that Caldwell had remained relaxed, that they were happy as they visited Lake Louise and drove up the Caribou Trail. The vacation was a well-deserved luxury after a decade of shared hardship and work. Respectively but thirty-one and twenty-nine years of age, they had three children and, during the heart of the Depression, money in both savings and stocks. Looking ahead, they must have anticipated continuing success and happiness in that summer of 1935.

Having returned to Mount Vernon, however, Caldwell could not write his stories with the same ease and fervor as before. Perhaps freedom from anxiety, the effects of recent carping reviews, or the Hollywood distortions had taken their toll. Or it might have been as he claimed. Journalistic impulses were "fomenting" his blood, "reviving his spirits." Reviving them from what, Caldwell did not say, but he wanted to put those skills "to use" before writing his next novel. Neither did he admit that he wished to use them for gathering evidence that proved his fiction built upon truth rather than distortion. Whatever the causes, "this urge to return temporarily to journalism was important" to him.

Caldwell satisfied that desire soon after his and Helen's vacation trip. Little more than a week had passed before he was in New Bedford, Massachusetts, where he went to report on the conditions of the workers in the milling industry. But by mid-August, Caldwell waited restlessly while the editors took "their own good time . . . on the cotton mill piece."[47] During the interim, he could not write. He did, however, allow the *Atlantic Monthly* to have "The Negro in the Well" for a price since they had "put on a groveling act and said they'd be tickled pink to have a story."

But the satisfaction of being courted by a respectable journal was not enough. That familiar restlessness of youth, interrupted and confined by years of writing, marriage, and poverty, still sought fulfillment. Only two years earlier, Caldwell had forecast that there was "a lot of world" he had to cover. Little more than a month after returning from the Canadian trip, he began covering at least the American portion.

Traveling alone by car in a drifting odyssey, he meandered from Mount Vernon through West Virginia, Illinois, Missouri, and then via Route 66 to Los Angeles. Yet the reality of traveling alone, seemed to have lost some of its solitary allure. After three days on the road, he confessed to Helen that he "must be getting old," because every time he went away, he wished to get back sooner and sooner. He probably would "never go away for as long as a month again," cryptically admitting that "maybe this is what you were talking about."[48] In other ways also, his letters written during the trip revealed that some substantial changes had come over Caldwell. He no longer told Helen how to raise the children, how much to pay workers, nor directed her to work on one of his unfinished manuscripts. Instead he told her to check some stock certificates which should have arrived—"10 shares, Midland Steel; 10 shares, U.S. Steel; 30 shares, Mesta Machine."[49]

In addition to gathering impressions about the devastation wrought by both drought and the Depression, Caldwell had driven to California to seek a house for the family's escape from Maine's 1935–36 winter. But before he could accomplish that task, he received a telegram from Henry Hull and Sam Byrd, on tour with their *Tobacco Road* company. After seven successful months in San Francisco, the play had moved to Chicago. There a court-ordered injunction, apparently pressured by the Catholic Church, halted its first performance. Hull and Byrd requested that Caldwell come immediately to help defend his adapted work.

Leaving his car in California, Caldwell arrived in Chicago aboard the *Navajo* on Friday, September 27, 1935. Chicago was indeed in turmoil over *Tobacco Road.* Mayor Edward J. Kelly defended his city's inviolate honor against the production's imported immorality, while newspapers presented headlines and articles pro and con. Pastors issued condemnations and defenses from the pulpits. Every headline, each congregational sermon during the six-week struggle only enhanced the play's scandalous appeal. Newspapers in Minneapolis and Dubuque, Des Moines and Sheboygan, raised the hue and cry. In fact, a third road company playing *Tobacco Road* was scheduled to open October 7 back east in Buffalo.

Although Caldwell's "three-week junket to Chicago just about ordered" his coffin, and fighting the Catholic Church had been like sticking his head in a cannon, he did gain satisfaction.[50] Finally the Federal Court of Appeals ruled against Chicago and the forces of decency. *Tobacco Road* opened there to guaranteed financial success. And for Cald-

Erskine Caldwell at 1085 Verdugo Ave., winter–spring 1934–35. Printed by permission of Rebecca Gooding, Caldwell family conservator.

Erskine Caldwell at the beach, winter–spring 1934–35. Printed by permission of Rebecca Gooding, Caldwell family conservator.

well, this trial, like the earlier one challenging *God's Little Acre,* mixed his literary reputation with notoriety, a combination whose tangled strains would echo throughout his career and life.

That heightened profile almost immediately subjected Caldwell to those annoyances that usually plague public figures. He began receiving both letters of praise and personal defamation. Donation requests flooded in. More noisome yet, he worried about an extortion letter, and the following year sought federal help in halting threatening calls placed to Helen and the children.

Back in Mount Vernon by mid-November, Caldwell and the boys departed there a month later, bound by car for Burbank, California. After a swing through Charlottesville and Wrens to visit family, Helen, Janet, and a babysitter caught the Sunset Limited to join them. Caldwell had rented a house at 1085 North Verdugo Avenue, just about as far as he "could get from the movie crowd."[51] There they settled in for what

Dabney, Janet, and Pix Caldwell, winter–spring 1934–35. Printed by permission of Rebecca Gooding, Caldwell family conservator.

Helen and the children especially remember as among the family's most satisfying times together.

For the first time during their marriage no major books or projects detracted from the Caldwells' time with the family. He wrote some short stories and articles for journals, corresponded with Lieber about usual business affairs, and waited as the agent sought a photographer who could cooperate with Caldwell on his next anticipated project.[52] Otherwise he was as free as he was ever to be, and the four months in Burbank seemed almost idyllic.

Without the children, the Caldwells took occasional extended trips across the border, where he so enjoyed himself that he hated to leave. And the children, especially Dee, remembered that California period as a happy one when they all seemed "truly a family." Every weekend, it

Helen and Dabney Caldwell, winter–spring 1934–35. Printed by permission of Rebecca Gooding, Caldwell family conservator.

seemed, they did something, most often Caldwell taking them to baseball games, where they watched Joe DiMaggio play in the minor
leagues. On one occasion he even took the boys for an airplane ride,
while at other times everyone would go for picnics by the sea. Near the
end of April, the Caldwells reluctantly turned back toward Maine. On
the way, they stopped in Detroit, this time not for Caldwell to reevaluate
the impressions of the Ford factory he had reported on less than two
years earlier. Instead he sold their car and bought a 1936 turquoise Ford
convertible directly from the factory.[53] Before mid-May, the Caldwells
were back home in Mount Vernon.

Part 3

"Trapped and Double-Crossed"

Chapter 11

The dual comforts of being home combined with a sense of financial security would never be enough to satisfy Caldwell, as long as work remained to be done. Consequently he impatiently awaited that person who would complement his next project. He intended to silence his critics by showing that his fiction "was authentically based on contemporary life in the South." To accomplish that, however, Caldwell needed a photographer whose pictures would confirm the reality of those people who moved and spoke through his stories.

Such an accomplished person was not easy to locate. Berenice Abbott, a photographer of some renown, had initially agreed but ultimately declined in favor of some more pressing European obligations. Lieber then had approached Margaret Bourke-White about working on Caldwell's project. A free-lance photographer with her own small studio, she was at that time engaged in an assignment for Henry Luce. In fact, a photograph Bourke-White shot for the Montana federal dam project was to be featured on the front cover of the first November 25, 1936, issue of *Life*.

Bourke-White seemed an ideal choice as the other person in Caldwell's venture. Like him, she had not come casually to her career but had achieved it through experience, determination, and hard work. The daughter of a gentile mother and a Polish-Jewish father who had worked as an engineer, Bourke-White, like Caldwell also, drew upon her father's interests for a portion of her intangible legacy. His fascination with photography and techniques for improving camera design most directly were to shape her career. But more essentially, Bourke-White remembered him as "an abnormally silent man." He seldom talked except when they were outdoors, where his love for natural history and herpetology became the bond uniting father and daughter.

By the time Lieber approached Bourke-White about the Caldwell

Erskine Caldwell and Margaret Bourke-White, 1937. Printed by permission of the estates of Erskine Caldwell and Margaret Bourke-White.

project, she was an ostensibly independent young woman of thirty-one. Once married, she almost casually had begun taking pictures to help support her last year at Cornell University. Advised by a photo shop manager and a retired photo-supply salesman, she specialized in architectural, landscape, and factory shots for commercial brochures and advertisements.

After college, Bourke-White both figuratively and literally climbed in her career. She perched at dizzying heights to shoot cityscapes, scaled beams, turbines, and hydroelectric facilities to capture in detail the generators, gears, and designs that vitalized American technology and industry. Wading through slaughterhouse offal, she traced the journey of "Hogs" for the first issue of Henry R. Luce and Parker Lloyd-Smith's *Fortune* magazine. Bourke-White succeeded admirably because she soon found that "to be a woman in a man's world" proved to be a "distinct advantage."

"Horseplay Hill," Darien, Conn., house owned by Erskine Caldwell and Margaret Bourke-White, ca. 1978. Photograph by the author.

Darkly attractive, vivacious, and consciously well-dressed, Bourke-White appears always to have manipulated men to her advantage and use. Early in her career, she had wiled Luce into carrying her cameras as they photographed factories. Later she had charmed a ship's captain into stopping the vessel in midpassage so she could better photograph butterflies emerging from their chrysalides. The governor general of Canada, Lord Tweedsmuir, then held her reflectors and acted as Bourke-White's aide-de-camp as she worked.[1] During her World War II assignments for *Life*, she was to be accused of using her feminine advantages in gaining access to privileged battle-zone opportunities. Whether such sniping was vicious accusation or fact, Bourke-White's success in a male-dominated field could not be argued. In competitive engagements waged in defense of her art, she had learned shrewdly to turn what could have been feminine disadvantages into winning tactics.

But more relevant to the project Lieber offered, she too had reported the conditions of the drought-stricken Midwest only shortly before Caldwell had recorded his impressions. Her shots accompanied *For-*

tune's "Drought" feature. And just as Caldwell's experience apparently had redirected his interests, so Bourke-White's encounter had reshaped her vision.[2] Earlier, while "discovering the beauty of industrial shapes," people had been "only incidental" to her. On the plains, however, she saw "people caught helpless." Suddenly "it was the people who counted" as she "saw everything in a new light."[3] That conversion had sent her seeking a collaborative author with whom she could do a book enabling her better to understand her fellow Americans. Thus Bourke-White's and Caldwell's separate paths had converged in that early spring of 1936.

Almost immediately after Lieber's offer, Bourke-White assailed Caldwell with her professional enthusiasm and personal charm. She was "happier about this" than she could say. Among all living American writers, he would have been her first choice for such a cooperative book venture. To have had him "drop out of a clear sky" just when she had decided to take pictures that were closer to life seemed "almost too good to be true."[4] Bourke-White cautioned, however, that she could not begin the assignment immediately. She had other projects and obligations first to complete and meet.

After the family's early May return, therefore, Caldwell had no alternative except to bide his time while he waited for Bourke-White to complete her other work. First a month and then two months passed. Ready to begin the project immediately after the California break, he instead wasted time awaiting the pleasure of a woman who obviously placed her own interests ahead of his. He was impatient with such nonchalance. Other facts and some rumors, moreover, made the Caldwells respectively apprehensive about his assignment with Bourke-White—if she ever found time to begin it.

All those who knew Bourke-White's work confirmed that she was, without a doubt, an excellent photographer. Others, however, who otherwise knew of her cautioned that she was a forcefully strong and sometimes unscrupulous woman. Pinckney Flansburg Estes, Ira's old friend and a successful New York lawyer, raised what must have been warning flags for Helen. Her circles reported that Bourke-White was not to be trusted around married men. Forbidden as they were, their challenge

allegedly excited her; further, their marital status preserved that freedom essential to Margaret's career. And finally, rumor had it that she
had been the "other woman" in a tragic situation that finally destroyed a
fine Virginia gentleman's marriage.

For different reasons both Erskine and Helen thus sought to minimize
their respective concerns about Bourke-White. They settled upon a solution. Ruth Carnall would come from Hollywood to act as Caldwell's
secretary-aide during the trip. No doubt Helen trusted her as a less-
threatening rival than the unknown but glamorous photographer. Finally by July 12, 1936, four months after Bourke-White's enthusiastic
March agreement, everything had been arranged and scheduled.

On that Sunday, Caldwell was in New York City, where Bourke-White
and Ruth were to join him for the drive south. Already aware of Caldwell's inflexible regard for schedules and meeting times, Carnall was
there ready to leave. Bourke-White, however, called to plead an extension; she had not yet completed some necessary assignments. Reluctantly and stiffly, Caldwell compromised. He and Ruth would drive to
Augusta; Caldwell would visit Wrens, and then return Friday to meet
Bourke-White's plane when she arrived in Augusta.

In her confident ability to maneuver others, Bourke-White failed to
realize that her behavior might have seemed irresponsible. Yet she had
already strained Caldwell's limited tolerance for irresponsibility, both by
breaching an agreement and relegating him and his project to a position
of secondary importance. He fumed to Helen. If Margaret was not in
Augusta by Friday, he would call the deal off and tell her that he was
through. In fact, he already wished the "thing was over and done with."[5]

Thursday night Bourke-White trod upon even shakier ground. Calling him in Wrens, she requested yet another day's extension, promising
thereafter to be there "no matter what happens." But Caldwell's patience had been exhausted. He "had enough and called off the trip,"
spelling "the end of the fiasco." Immediately after talking with Bourke-
White, he sent Helen a message telling her he would return home the
following week. She herself could have told Bourke-White something
about the level of Caldwell's expectations.

Acting from a confidence in her persuasive skills and charms, Bourke-

White nonetheless flew to Augusta on Saturday. From there, she sent a message to Wrens, whereupon Caldwell did come to the hotel. Her subsequent public account, and his postcard report to Helen, represent different versions of the same truce. According to Bourke-White, she and Caldwell had shared a wordless communication as they had drunk their coffee. When the last drop was gone, Caldwell looked quietly at his hands before saying with a smile, "That was a big argument, wasn't it?"[6] His next question had been to ask when they might leave. Caldwell had written Helen a different story. During their Saturday meeting Bourke-White had so "begged and cried and promised to behave," that he reluctantly had agreed at least to start the trip.[7]

On one matter at least, all principals on the trip agreed publicly and privately. The first five days involved warfare among conflicting personalities, wills, and emotions. Bourke-White had gained an initial reconnoitering position by preempting the passenger side of the front seat. Ruth, as the "hired girl" had sat, supposedly by choice, in the back seat with all Margaret's photography equipment. Bourke-White had played her position's advantages, making a careful study of her author-partner, "trying to guess what was in his mind." Because her silent father had given her a lot of practice in such psychic ferreting, Bourke-White had felt relatively competent in reading Caldwell's silence.[8] Carnall's back-seat position had allowed her to see and guess what was in the minds of both the man and woman in the front. Literally and symbolically she saw herself as odd-person out.

Both Caldwell and Bourke-White in their later respective public accounts acknowledge that Ruth had been less than happy with her situation. But Caldwell's private report to Helen crackled with the dramatic fire that had sparked among the threesome. Aggravated by the heat, all had been getting on each other's nerves anyway when, two days out, he and Bourke-White engaged in a scrap "that could be heard for miles around" Montgomery. Bourke-White, "naturally" enough had cried, promising to follow his suggestions. But only a day had passed before the two of them "had another spasm near Meridian" and yet a "second big scrap that night in Jackson, Mississippi."[9] To add to "the cat-fights," Ruth and Margaret also had had a skirmish, and Caldwell had not known what would happen. He thought that if he could learn to get along with Bourke-White, he might let Ruth go home as she had asked to do.

Yet Caldwell had remained in a quandary. Since both were accustomed to getting their own ways, he had not known what might happen if he and Bourke-White were left alone. Only if the two of them could get along together would there be any possibility for a book, a shaky prospect since Caldwell had guessed he would "be doing well to get back with a sane mind." Lest Helen become too concerned, however, Caldwell had assured her: "Try not to get down because it is a lot worse for me than it is for you." Whether or not his lament moved her to sympathy was to be forgotten among situations demanding even greater understanding and excuse.

Within hours after Caldwell had assuaged his wounds by writing to Helen, the conflicts he had described were variously resolved. Bourke-White must have realized that in a battle of the wills with Caldwell, she had more than met her match. Whether wishing to salvage the project or to win their fiercely contested war, she had called upon the "distinct advantages" of her womanly reserves. In her autobiographical *Portrait of Myself*, Bourke-White gave her version of the victory.[10]

As usual, Caldwell had carried Bourke-White's equipment to her room, where he had suggested that they abandon the project; he felt like a tourist guide showing someone around. She had pleaded for its continuance, for "this opportunity to do something worth while." Failing to move him with this appeal, she had begun crying: "Then suddenly something very unexpected happened. He fell in love with me. From then onward, everything worked out beautifully."

Ruth Carnall later reported this moment of Bourke-White's victory less euphemistically to Helen. Increasingly incensed by her rear-guard assignment, she had observed more than battle engagements between Caldwell and Bourke-White. Amidst the verbal assaults, she had recognized the signs—flirtatious glances, accidental touches, an assumed dependence—that had hinted at Bourke-White's ultimate victory over her stoical rival. Ruth's eventual spat with *her* rival, no doubt, had had dual motives. She had sought to challenge her seating arrangements but also somewhat jealously to protect Caldwell from the other woman. She lost the afternoon argument and later that night observed that she and Caldwell both had lost the war.

Although Caldwell had carried Bourke-White's equipment to her lodgings, he had left shortly thereafter. Subsequently Ruth had seen him return to Bourke-White's room, where she, her nakedness scarcely concealed, had admitted him.[11] To Lieber Caldwell later privately had confided that "she raped him."[12] Whatever the preliminaries, the results were conclusive; Caldwell remained with her through the rest of the night. Ruth's reaction had been that both of a blatantly outmaneuvered chaperon and spurned woman. Without explanation, she immediately packed her bags and caught a train for California. The secretary-aide had abandoned her position.

Their private frustrations and tensions apparently satisfactorily resolved, Caldwell and Bourke-White continued their daily work as the complementary professionals they were, with her now watching this enigmatic man with heightened interest:

> Whether he was aware of it or not, Erskine Caldwell was introducing me to a whole new way of working. He had a very quiet, completely receptive approach. He was interested not only in the words a person spoke but in the mood in which they were spoken. He would wait patiently until the subject had revealed his personality, rather than impose his own personality on the subject.[13]

His approach to his subjects was little different from that he so often had watched Ira use, but to Bourke-White it appeared unique:

> Erskine would be hanging over the back fence, and the farmer leaning on his rake, the two engaged in what I suppose could be a conversation—that is, either Erskine or the farmer made one remark every fifteen minutes. Despite the frugal use of words, the process seemed productive on both sides. . . . Erskine had a gift . . . for picking up the shade and characteristic of the state in which we were working.[14]

From his perspective, Caldwell equally had marveled as the camera transmuted his emotionally volatile partner into a cool, precision-shuttered photographer. Once he had placed her bulky equipment properly, she catlike awaited that instant when Caldwell's probing exposed the vital expression whose moment she captured. That passion she brought to their romance was also applied to her art.

When Bourke-White's carefully treasured praying-mantis eggs had begun to hatch, they had stopped immediately so she could record their metamorphosis. Yet Kit—as Caldwell soon came affectionately to call her—likewise could shoot with reckless daring. Four days before the end of their trip they had invaded a road-gang group in Richmond County, Georgia. Against the guard's wishes, Bourke-White rapidly shot pictures before he could react to threaten them away. Two days later, with their official permits in hand, she more casually had taken those pictures later to become famous in *You Have Seen Their Faces.*

No matter the obstacles placed in their way, Caldwell and Bourke-White were both too strong-willed to be denied. On both the personal and professional levels that was part of the excitement that energized their relationship and their project. Locked out of the Holiness Church in South Carolina, they jumped through a window. While Caldwell changed her flash bulbs, Bourke-White switched between cameras to take pictures as quickly as she could. Her shots captured women in ecstasy, "coming through for the Lord," just as they had in Caldwell's *Journeyman* orgy.

Their daily log and working notes cryptically recorded such happenings next to each day's schedule of their travels.[15] Just as persuasively they also reflect the differences Ruth's departure had made.[16] The scenes shot during the first five days of their expedition—in Georgia, Alabama, Mississippi, and Arkansas—were elaborately identified. Those taken thereafter were but cryptically noted. August 4 found Caldwell and Bourke-White seventeen days into their trip and back in Georgia. How closely they retraced Caldwell's earlier trip with his father is uncertain. They did, nonetheless, spend the last nine days of their project-period in the Tobacco Road country of his adolescence. Keysville and Augusta, Georgia, Edgefield and Pee Dee, South Carolina, were all within thirty miles of Wrens.

In Keysville, members of a clan familiar to most area residents stood

Mr. and Mrs. Dude "Bungler," as they appeared in Ira Caldwell's "Bungler" study in *Eugenics* 3 (June 30, 1930): 207.

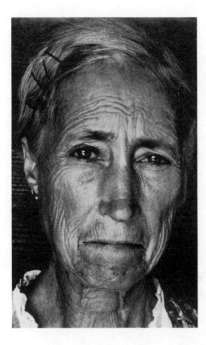

Mrs. Dude "Bungler" as she appeared in Caldwell and Bourke-White's *You Have Seen Their Faces*, 1937. Reprinted by permission of the Estate of Margaret Bourke-White.

John Willy "Bungler," son of Mr. and Mrs. Dude "Bungler," from *You Have Seen Their Faces*, 1937. Reprinted by permission of the Estate of Margaret Bourke-White.

Mr. and Mrs. John Willy "Bungler," from *You Have Seen Their Faces*, 1937.
Reprinted by permission of the Estate of Margaret Bourke-White.

for pictures that would comprise the last three plates of *Faces*.[17] Mrs.
Dude "Bungler" and her son appeared in the last two; the son and his
wife prefaced them both. Mrs. "Bungler's" face reflects the passing of
time; each of the studies of John Willy declares him to have been a "spit-
tin' image of his pa." Thus that local family, earlier subjects for Ira's
"The Bunglers," Erskine's *Tobacco Road*, as well as his *New York Post*
series, became anonymously yet more famous through Bourke-White's
photographs.

Whether captivated by their romance or intrigued with their assignment, Caldwell and Bourke-White extended their project beyond its
scheduled completion date. More suspiciously yet, Caldwell had not
been writing Helen his usual daily letters. When he finally touched base
at Wrens, Helen's five wrathful letters awaited him. Feigning innocence,

he offered excuses.[18] She should not jump "at hasty conclusions" but believe that the assignment "had been no easy chore." He "would have written oftener if it had not been for this weather, trip, and . . . the cat and dog fights for the past two weeks." Caldwell played for greater sympathy; such tensions, added to the pain from an injured shoulder made him feel as if he had "been through the wringer."

And as for the extended schedule, Caldwell had modified it because Bourke-White had wished to spend two or three more days in the Wrens area and two more in South Carolina. Consequently he would not return to Maine before Saturday, August 15. What happened to Ruth, Caldwell claimed not to know: "I've been too hot, tired, and generally disabled to even wonder what became of Ruth and why. All I can think is that maybe homesickness, heat, and cat-fighting set her off."[19] He wheedled for some sympathy and understanding. Instead of always expecting the worst of him, Helen should recognize the fix he had been in. After he and Margaret completed the trip, he hoped "to be able to close the book on the matter."

But that was not to be the satisfying conclusion. What Helen suspected, she indeed soon was to understand, and Caldwell's hopes were to be overwhelmed by forces greater than his guilt. He was not "able to close the book on the matter" of Kit.

By August 13, Caldwell had left Bourke-White and hurriedly driven the two days to Mount Vernon. Because the elder Caldwells had arrived earlier, Helen and Erskine could not immediately confront the issue of his relationship with Bourke-White. Ruth's accusations, combined with the new techniques he had introduced into their love rituals, convinced Helen that he and Bourke-White had enjoyed an affair. But at that time Caldwell would not confess the depth of his feelings for Margaret.

Those feelings became, nonetheless, the recurring theme of letters and telegrams Caldwell—affectionately called Skinny by all who knew him personally well—had begun sending to Kit within a week or two after his return. One of the first measured the scope of his passion. Using love combined with a flagellating pathos—often reinforced with sexual urgency—as his arguments, Caldwell repeatedly pleaded his dependence even as he reproached Bourke-White for her stubborn independence.[20]

Dear Kit:

As you may have guessed, I am pretty well down these days. One thing on top of another brings these things about. I have an awful feeling that I will not see you again; I have a terrified feeling of our drifting apart. Then when I do think I may see you again, the feeling is that I'll be merely another customer coming into your house on a schedule that may or may not conflict with the previous customer on the schedule. The whole thing amounts to this: I think of you as a part of us, never as you alone. It is a sort of need for you to make us one, and you have said in no uncertain terms that you are not interested. And so, I am at the point where I can't go down much further.

You know how I love you, and how so very much I want you, and how so completely I need you. There is nothing much I can say on top of that. If I don't suit you, if you do not care for me to that extent, if you are determined to keep me from crossing the line, I bow to your wishes. The last thing I would ever do would be to try to force you into something you have no desire for.

I am going up into Quebec for a while. This will be my only address. If you would a letter send, it will be forwarded, and I'll be the most delighted person in the world when it reaches me. I have no idea when I am coming back. Though, as a matter of truth, if you should send for me I'd come as fast as I could even if I had to make a couple of trips around the world to reach you. I still have that extraordinary feeling I had when I first came to know you: that I was waiting for you to say, come into my arms and stay as long as you wish to, and stay forever if you want to. And even now I still believe you will say it, either this time, or the next, or the next. It is that hope that makes me look forward to seeing you so eagerly the next time, the time after.

I have your pictures, your touch still resting on me, your kisses: I have all these things with me day and night, and they seem to be a sort of promise. If they were not that, I would not even be able to write letters to you, much less look forward to your asking me to come to see you, to come in a hurry.

But it is precisely that which I do look forward to. I have a feeling that this time you may feel differently, that you may let me come inside of you, that you may let me stay this time. What else is there to live for, if a person has an animal-like instinct to love someone as I do you? I am not in love with your knowledge, your style, your this and that—I am in love with you, your heart and your soul. Everything else about you, your skill, your dress, your education, is something I take delight in merely because you possess them.

This could go on and on. I would much rather talk to you about such things than to try to write to you about them. But you seem always so anxious to change the subject, that I never am able to tell you how and why I love you. As if you cared, I guess.

Anyway, it will take the heart out of me if you don't write and say you wish me to come down to see you. I can't come on any other basis, because I've got so now that I feel as if I am an intruder. If you do want me, you can think of some strictly businesslike matter that wants attention without delay. I am afraid if you said, simply, come and sleep with me, I would be at a loss to explain what's-this-all-about-and-what-s-it-leading-to [*sic*]. And no wonder, if it should lead to what I want most in the world.

I love you,
Skinny[21]

Possibly to help forget Kit, to resurrect his old writing impulses, and to reconfirm his relationship with Helen, the Caldwells relocated shortly thereafter to Quebec. Throughout September Caldwell remained faithfully in their Hotel Frontenac room trying to write while Helen explored the city and practiced her French. But he accomplished little; his obsession with Bourke-White thwarted his best intentions. By the end of the month, the Caldwells returned to Mount Vernon where he also chafed. He pleaded the necessity of returning to New York to work with Bourke-White on the book, a plausible subterfuge. The excuse failed to deceive Helen, since she claimed to have known "what was going on though Erskine wouldn't admit it."

In early October, therefore, Caldwell took a room at the Taft Hotel. There, he told himself and Helen, he could write; there he told Bourke-White she could come to help him work on their book. When the two were together, however, they worked precious little and resolved even less about their relationship. Malcolm Cowley, seeing them at a meeting advancing some left-wing cause, observed a love so radiant that "their presence transformed the room." Borrowing imagery from Wallace Stevens's "Anecdote of the Jar," Cowley analogously claimed that like the jar, the two of them together gave focus and form to an otherwise slovenly group. Comparatively, all others "had become the wilderness in which they gleamed."[22]

But Bourke-White's *Life* assignments, the necessary travel, made her presence as mercurial as the love she professed for Caldwell. Plead though he did, his demands could not compete with those of her career. Her "first loyalty was to *Life*. . . . [her] professional work came first."[23] All that she made clear. If he wished, he could accompany her, but she would not limit her photography assignments for him or any other man.

No woman—mother, wife, or lover—ever before so frustratingly and tantalizingly had denied Caldwell. Friendless except for Morang, he could admit his bafflement only to Helen, wife and confidante. He saw Bourke-White on Sunday, October 18, but refused to accompany her on a three-day trip. After her Wednesday return, she would depart for the West Coast on Thursday. Resolving, "that's that," Caldwell wrote Helen that she had nothing "to worry about." Characteristically, he shifted blame for the trouble to her. She had seen an "excuse and then played it to the limit, not taking into consideration the fact" that he liked her best of all—even when she had "beat [him] down as [she] did."[24]

From Wilkes-Barre, Caldwell had claimed his parents' situation had caused him to stay overlong. From Hollywood, he had blamed Helen for his temptations and aberrations. This time too she was at fault because she had "beat him down." Most likely, she had berated him—for his adulteries, silences, and condescending attitudes. Eleven years of marriage, no doubt, had made her criticisms of Caldwell the man as sure-handedly direct as her criticisms of his writings. Beyond that, Helen's personality had not easily allowed her to dote, to soothe. If his childhood experiences led him to expect emotional pampering from women, that kind of motherly comfort was more than her nature would permit under the circumstances.

On the other hand, neither did Bourke-White seem to be the type of woman to offer that psychological balance that Caldwell's emotional insecurity required. Enthusiastic, motivated, and striking in appearance, she projected an image of the self-assured career woman.[25] All of these she was, but that was camouflage. Beneath it all, she remained a woman who could charm the powerful—including Stalin—to her bidding, who cried to win her ends, who wept with grief when fumigators, misdirected to her office by a jealous peer, killed her whole lot of praying mantises.[26]

As one devoted to "capturing essences" throughout a lifetime, Caldwell, no doubt, sensed Bourke-White's essential nature. Though "there was no personal involvement when she was working at something," when Kit later redirected her attention to something else, to him, "suddenly everything would change."[27] She became relaxed and loving, a quality that made him feel she "had the contented expression of a kitten who has just swallowed a bowl of cream." For this reason, Bourke-White thought, he lovingly nicknamed her Kit.[28] But more than this, all those who were knowledgeable testified that she was as innovative in making love as she was in plying her photographic skills.

And Bourke-White's attraction to Caldwell? Their first meeting left her with the impression "of a large, shy man with enormous restless shoulders"—one whose "tight-locked face" suggested a man who rarely laughed.[29] Caldwell's obvious reserve also piqued a curiosity that was hers by both nature and profession. Speaking about photography, she used terms that might have applied to him. Nothing attracted her "like a closed door," her camera not at rest until she had "pried it open."

And emanating from behind Caldwell's "closed doors" were vital forces that even those who disliked him acknowledged. Peggy Smith, Bourke-White's secretary whom Caldwell all but abhorred, observed that she "could almost feel the male/female relationship" when he walked into a room. That chemistry, she noted, always had intrigued Bourke-White.[30] Such latent sexuality, enhanced by Caldwell's "married safety," perhaps became the current charging their initial relationship, but more subtle psychological impulses urged its continuation.

Through numerous comparisons and associations, Bourke-White tied Caldwell essentially to memories of her father, that "silent father" whose habits gave her practice in fathoming laconic men like Caldwell. Describing him during their southern trip, Bourke-White admitted to her brother that Caldwell "was more silent than father and more shy" than the brother himself.[31] As she came to know him better, other similarities reminded her of that "first man in her life." Like her father's opening for her the doors to the natural world, Caldwell's "very quiet, completely receptive approach" introduced Bourke-White "to a whole new way of thinking." With childlike enchantment recalled, she watched this other man open doors, not to nature this time, but to human beings. As a photographer, she marveled at the manner Caldwell used to expose the subject's inner self, an essence her complementary photographs captured.

More covert urgings must have drawn Bourke-White to Caldwell. Almost childlike, she used a variety of tactics against his fatherlike dominance. Charm, pleading, and tears moved him to excuse her tardy arrival for their scheduled trip. Later she experimented with argument, shouting, and pouting. Ineffectual against Caldwell's stronger will, she finally resorted to tears so he would take her into his arms and love her.

Through her surrender, Bourke-White perhaps played the last card within her stack of womanly tricks to assure completion of the project. At the same time, however, she submitted to the force of Caldwell's dominant will. Peggy Smith-Sargent, familiar with Bourke-White through a lifetime's association, affirmed that psychological probability. In all other relationships, she believed, Bourke-White always had been the stronger one, so exclusively so that being the dominant person had become habit. But Caldwell had proved the challenging exception, "the first dominant character she had run into."[32]

Whatever the conscious attractions or subconscious needs, within less than two months Bourke-White and Caldwell found themselves inextricably intertwined in a relationship affecting them and others. But in late October of 1936, he could admit that neither to Helen nor himself. Having resisted the temptation of traveling with Bourke-White, he requested that Helen come to New York for the weekend of October 23. They would stay at the luxurious Piccadilly at West Forty-fifth street, not at his Kit-tainted Taft lodgings. Putting his love for Bourke-White behind them, Caldwell offered the New York weekend as a pledge of his intentions to abide by his duties to Helen, marriage, and his writing.

Consequent to that shared experience, the Caldwells returned once more to Mount Vernon, but there his last state was worse than his first. Helen and the family pitted his guilty conscience and will against the temptations offered by Bourke-White. Abstracted and restless, he could not write with his accustomed dedication. With varying excuses, he traveled more and more frequently to Augusta, where he mailed impassioned letters to Bourke-White and received her answers addressed in care of General Delivery. With lovers' deceit, the two conspired to hide their love from Helen, who, this time as before, hoped that surreptitious trysts would exhaust the lovers' infatuation for each other.

But such was not to be the case. Caldwell continued to find excuses to travel to New York. When Bourke-White was in the city, they worked on the text for *You Have Seen Their Faces.* When she traveled, he attempted to write short stories. Caught in a state of agonized stasis, he squirmed throughout. Nothing could be completed or resolved until his relationship with Bourke-White became more clearly defined. His personal values and needs demanded that he "make an honest woman" of her. Bourke-White, however, rejected all his arguments, pleas, and tactics aimed toward marriage. She would not jeopardize her career to indulge the psychological idiosyncrasies of Caldwell's conscience. Against what he interpreted as personal rejection, he increasingly used his periods of silence both to mask his pain and to punish the offender. Neither an indulgent mother nor accepting wife, Bourke-White, nonetheless, could not break free from the man whose silences reminded her, in some respects, of both her father and her former husband.

At least two of Caldwell's letters during this period included clippings— accounts about hotel managers looking askance at obviously unmarried but registering couples. Bourke-White understood their oblique intent. By the beginning of 1937, therefore, she agreed to a compromise contingent upon a concession from Caldwell. She would share accommodations with him and masquerade as his wife, if he would agree to psychological counseling. No longer could she endure the emotional violence of his stone-cutting silences. Thus their joint appointment with Harry Stack Sullivan—and Caldwell's subsequent January 23 referral to Dr. Charles K. Friedburg—coincided with their move as Mr. and Mrs. Erskine Caldwell into a suite at the Beekman Towers.

How long Caldwell honored what must have been a condition of their

living together is not determinable from any records. In notes to herself
for her autobiography, Bourke-White claimed that he made "swift progress, so entrancing, so pleasant to be with. Even those tense muscles of
the face which I had noted the first day we met, slipped off like a melting
mask. At the end of one month he said he knew more than the psychiatrist knew and stopped his visits."[33] Vicki Goldberg, in her arresting biography of Bourke-White, provides the incisive conclusion: "While his
old life in Maine hounded him and his new life with Margaret balanced
precariously between bliss and disaster, Erskine briefly feared he was
going to pieces. He had more faith in a woman's ability to put him back
together than a doctor's."[34]

Although their charade of marriage somewhat placated Caldwell's
conscience, it was not without predictable complications. Peggy Smith
was to intercept and reroute Bourke-White's professional calls. When
she called, she was to "ask for Mrs. Caldwell."[35] Meanwhile, the real
Mrs. Caldwell endured the rigors of winter and approached the limits of
her patience in the old home at Mount Vernon.

Caldwell had claimed to Helen that his opening a separate New York
checking account was a matter of convenience. That deceit and the
Beekman Towers idyll, however, were uncovered in one stroke. Signing
the year's lease in the name of Mr. and Mrs. Erskine Caldwell, he had
listed their Augusta banker as a reference. With small town regard and
possibly some suspicious intentions, the banker one day asked Helen if
they planned to move their account and residence to New York. A letter
from the Beekman Towers management indicated that a Mr. and Mrs.
Caldwell had signed a lease with that establishment. Graciously, Helen
publicly covered for Caldwell's deception. Being often in and out of the
city, she explained, they had rented convenient lodgings there. Privately, however, Helen had acted with directness. Leaving the banker's
office, she stepped across the street and wired Caldwell to come home
immediately. He arrived the next day.

What did Erskine have to say for himself? she demanded.[36] Again he
asked for understanding, acceptance. Could they not go on the way they
always had? During the course of their confrontation, she realized that
this time Caldwell was not caught in just another casual affair. Stronger

forces had swept aside his habitual sense of duty, determination, and guilt.

Motivated both by love and her hopes of saving the marriage, Helen granted Caldwell a period of exception. Since he did not want a divorce, Helen gave him a year during which he was either to get Bourke-White out of his system or to marry her. During that period, furthermore, he was not to approach Helen sexually. So Caldwell agreed to that "more or less," although he "didn't keep [the second] part of the bargain." Granted such exceptional grace, Caldwell returned to New York with a sense of diminished guilt. He had received permission, as it were, not to engage a prostitute this time, but to test his love for Bourke-White against the greater security of his marriage.

In certain respects, Bourke-White held all the advantages in their relationship. Since she had no marriage to be threatened, because Caldwell's love ranked second to her career, he would have to make all the necessary concessions. If he wished to pursue his own career, if for either love's or principle's sake he had to preserve his marriage, he would have to make all the accommodations. He would be forced to shape his conscience accordingly.

With Helen—before Hollywood and wealth, without fame's distractions and love's abstractions—Caldwell always had written with dedication and a sense of dutiful determination. With their goading, he had completed each of his major novels in three months or less. Short stories had rolled from his typewriter almost without interruption. During that time his personal correspondence with friends and associates revolved about his concern for writing, the details of placing his works, and his resigned frustration with critics.

But by the fall of 1936, Caldwell had written no novel for three years. The short stories had been few. Moreover, he no longer corresponded with other struggling writers. His few letters to Morang became more sporadic, shorter, and expressed no concern about his writing or anyone else's. Truly, Caldwell's public newspaper accounts, his serialized surveys, and *You Have Seen Their Faces* still railed against injustices. But privately, he no longer wrote Morang letters seething with complaints about social and economic inequities.

Other evidence also hinted at changes in Caldwell. Letters to Helen, once laden with charges about editing his writings, raising the children, or paying workmen and bills, now directed her "to watch General Motors and sell when it shoots up to about eighty," or to buy Briggs Motor Company—a corporation three years earlier he had condemned for exploitation—and work on the income tax statement. Otherwise Caldwell expressed concern only about those conditions and personal turmoils associated with their mutual trauma. But even some of those he cloaked in market metaphors: "I'd like to tell you at this time that your stock has gone up a lot from its low," or "I owe you a lot, and God-speed the day when I can repay you—with interest plus a bonus."[37]

To blame Caldwell's departure from fiction, his changing values and interests entirely upon his relationship with Bourke-White would be simplistic. Then thirty-two, married eleven years with three children, and published for seven, he might have been ripe for change. Perhaps his claim that "journalism was still in his blood" was as honest as it was excusing. And possibly Hollywood, fame, and money had seduced him from writing fiction. Or it may have been as simple as a personal conviction he later offered to Bourke-White as excuse—"The life of a writer is just ten years."[38] Inferring from that and other clues in a combination of Bourke-White's statements and Caldwell's writings, Vicki Goldberg best summarized his change: "It looked almost as if an essential vitality had leached out of Caldwell's talent."[39] Whatever the cause, Caldwell's personal and professional transformations coincided so closely with his involvement with Bourke-White that a cause-and-effect relationship between them appears compelling.

The temporary resolution of what Caldwell should do about the two women in his life—about his basic conflicts between duty and desire, values and feelings—briefly freed him from his psychological traumas related to writing. In January 1937, he sat once more at his typewriter, in New York this time. During Kit's absences, he wrote to satisfy one more obligation—that of completing four more stories for a forthcoming Viking collection. His writing, combined with Bourke-White's absences, turned Caldwell's thoughts more frequently to Helen and all they once had shared. Whenever Bourke-White was out of the city, he wrote to

Helen, each time offering tidbits that she might add to a larger hope. Her "stock had gone up," he would have "some good news" for her soon, or he promised to see her shortly.

Indeed, Caldwell did see Helen soon. Throughout the first six months of 1937, he alternated between residence in New York and Maine. Each month—save March when he and Bourke-White had traveled once more through the South—he logged at least three trips between the two places and two women.[40] The frequency of the four-hundred-mile trips alone testifies to those feelings that must have driven Caldwell, a man love-obsessed and duty-torn.

Chapter 12

As much as his trips between Mount Vernon and New York, Caldwell's letters betrayed the dimensions of the conflict he delicately balanced. They attested to both his levels of guilt and dependence upon Helen. Because he anticipated another southern tour with Bourke-White that March, Caldwell completed four short stories by the end of February. On March 1, he forwarded them to Helen—with directions: "If you are satisfied with them, correct them and send them to Lieber right away."[1] Yet even as he referred to his coming trip with Kit, Caldwell reassured Helen of his love. "Unless the wires were down," he would call her on March 10 from wherever he was. To prepare for her separate visit South, he directed that she buy some clothes, so she would "look nicer than anybody else." He was glad she was "going to be down there" while he and Bourke-White traveled, so she wouldn't be "so far away." And so Caldwell embroidered ambivalence into a pattern to satisfy his essential needs.

Whenever Caldwell was alone, without Kit in New York, he wrote Helen, expressing his concerns, love, and pleas for understanding; when he was in Mount Vernon with Helen, however, he wrote Margaret with variations upon the same themes. From Mount Vernon late in January, he assured Kit that being there made him "realize that nobody else in the world," not even Helen, meant anything to him.[2] As evidence, Caldwell vowed that he had not, nor would he, touch her as long as he was there. Then in February—shortly before the time he mailed the stories and letter to Helen from New York—Caldwell wrote again from Mount Vernon, pleading for Kit to meet him back in the city on March 1. At that time, with Helen and the children downstairs in the house, he had written:

> I've never been happier than I am right now, not being here but being so deeply in love with you. To tell the truth this (here) is almost impossible. I

can only stay in order to get business items straightened out. . . . I love you and no one else can come between us. . . . I'll probably stay a bit unhappy whenever we are separated. I go to sleep every night holding you tight in my arms and when I wake up, you are still there.[3]

And repeating a message that was to become an insistent, two-year refrain, he concluded, "I can't be satisfied with a part of you. I need all of you all the time to be completely happy. And I want it to be as long as we live."

And yet only a week later, Caldwell assured Helen that he wanted her "down there," so she would not be so far away. Apparently excused from responsibility by both women—as always had become his habit—Caldwell nonetheless agonized on the horns of a dilemma. Later, placing that situation of divided loyalties into reflective context, he could say only, "One day a person feels one way, another day he feels another."[4]

The southern trip that Caldwell so encouraged Helen and the children to make perhaps helped to assuage his conscience and serve as a peace offering to her.[5] While he and Kit enjoyed their comfort at Beekman Towers, Helen struggled with the children and bone-chilling inconveniences in Mount Vernon. If he and Bourke-White were to travel the warm South while she sat Maine-bound, that inequity surely would exceed her limits. Therefore, he planned their mutual accommodation. Bourke-White and he would leave the Ford convertible in Augusta, purchasing another one there. When Helen arrived by train, she could pick it up at Lyon's Garage for her drive to visit the elder Caldwells in Wrens.

Pained by Caldwell's absence during a trip that once had been their annual ritual, Helen nonetheless spared the Caldwells from the truth about their son. She supported as the whole truth the professional charade the couple had offered during their earlier, brief visit with the parents; they were continuing their search for *Faces* materials.

Upon Caldwell's and Bourke-White's March 3 arrival in Richmond, he sent Helen an affirming wire, one which also conveyed his current concerns:

I have a good idea who wears best now [stop] If we got into Ballanca [stock] it will have to be watched and when it reaches twelve or better put a stop-loss

order on it one point under the top [stop] . . . This business not what you
might expect and will probably be very glad when over. Much love. Skinny[6]

Perhaps the trip was not what Helen might have imagined. Judging from
field notes more elaborately detailed than the sketchy ones hurriedly jotted during the first trip, Caldwell and Bourke-White, this time not so
freshly victims of love, worked as dedicated professionals. From Bonifay,
Florida, to Johns, Mississippi, from Clinton, Louisiana, to Marked Tree,
Arkansas, and finally into Georgia and Tennessee, they traveled, capturing most of the subjects that finally appeared in *Faces*. Though the
second trip proved less tempestuous than the first, it certainly provided
sounder artistic results.

With Caldwell and Bourke-White's return to New York, and Helen's
to Mount Vernon, their situation settled into its previous pattern. While
Bourke-White traveled, Caldwell generally returned to Helen and the
comforts of home. Yet his letters and love notes followed Kit wherever
she went, stressing his unremitting love; he missed her all the time,
couldn't sleep without her at night. If they were never to be day-and-
night together, life would have no meaning for him. But she was not to
worry about him; he would be grateful for whatever she gave him.[7]

And to Helen, Caldwell wrote from his and Bourke-White's New York
place because he felt "down and out about everything." Wonderful as
she was for sticking with him throughout the affair, she was to "keep a
stiff upper lip . . . until something happened." When that day arrived,
he'd be the most grateful person on earth and would repay her "for being
the finest person in the world." What he wanted most was for them to get
back where they belonged, though he admitted that couldn't be done "as
long as this girl [was] in the middle." Someday, however, when both
Caldwell and Helen knew "it" was over, they'd have plenty of time to
celebrate, a fact she could write in her book next to Skinny's vow: *"I do
love you."*[8]

What Caldwell was doing during this period besides writing lovelorn
notes and letters to Kit and expressions of fealty to Helen is not clear. On
a much later occasion he quoted his grandfather, who allegedly had
said, "The happy man is the one who has three women in his life—his

mother, wife, and mistress."[9] In the summer of 1937 Caldwell had all three—emphatically in that order. Yet if he was happy, the outward signs were not obvious. Whatever other writing he was doing was sporadic at best; little evidence exists to argue that he did any. Before much longer, his mother complained that the Caldwells had heard nothing from him; they did not know whether he was dead or alive.[10]

That sense of freedom that allowed Caldwell to write four short stories in the first two months following Helen's reprieve evaporated. By May, his moral dilemma became a solitary obsession with tragic undertones. Rejecting psychiatric help from secular priests such as Sullivan and Friedburg, he could gaze only within. And there Caldwell's conscience was caught, squirming but immobilized between an inflexible personal code of honor, duty, and love and his "animal-like instincts." A May 10 letter to Helen traced a desperate hope, that fate, a guiding hand, eventually might direct him.

> Needless to say, I miss us (you and me) more all the time. Maybe it will get so that the tide will turn the other way, and then there won't be any question at all anymore. Please do all you can for me—maybe just trying to give me a chance. It's something like being given a term on the chain gang, maybe. See what I mean? I don't think I'll be on the gang for life, so just try to give me a chance to escape, or serve out the sentence. . . . Anyway, I love you. And I miss what we should be having now.[11]

Helen apparently intuited the honesty of Caldwell's chain-gang analogy and sympathized to a degree with his misery. She allowed him to continue living first with Kit and then with her. And of course, his letters to each presented continuations of his usual pleas and complaints.

During Caldwell and Bourke-White's periods together, they collated pictures and texts, sometimes changed place names in their book, and moved toward the completion of *Faces*. But Caldwell's writing duties and Bourke-White's assignments, his and Helen's domestic confusion, exacted various tolls from them all. Although Janet was too young to respond consciously to the tensions, the boys were not. Perhaps seeking Caldwell's fatherly attentions, they rambunctiously fought, sometimes stretching his patience past reasonable anger. Then he would coldly

erupt. Years later Dee was to remind Caldwell that he still could not see a
razor strop without flinching.[12] And Pix, always more boisterous and ex-
troverted than his younger brother, seemed especially troubled during
that disruptive spring of 1937.

Without completing the 1937 school term, Pix had departed for New
York to live briefly with Skinny and Kit, as he familiarly called them
both. He and Margaret liked each other, but her assignments and the
hotel environment precluded his living there. Shortly after that he was
shunted back to Helen at Mount Vernon, and later when she became ill,
she sent him to her mother in Charlottesville. His impressions of feeling
"shuffled back and forth" perhaps suggest the deeper confusions each of
the Caldwells experienced as they respectively struggled with their domestic trauma.[13]

In midsummer, Caldwell allegedly requested that Helen come to his
and Bourke-White's place in New York to help edit *Faces*. There she
claimed to have glanced into the bedroom and seen, with some amuse-
ment, black silk sheets on the double bed. But no matter who contributed to the editing of *You Have Seen Their Faces*. It was completed and
given to Viking Press before Bourke-White's next extended assignment
scheduled for July—a trip aboard the *S.S. Distributor* to the Great Slave
Lake region of Canada.

Again abandoned by Kit, Caldwell returned to Mount Vernon, where
he unproductively bided time during her absence. Because the *Distributor* docked at only specific, far-distant ports, their radiograms were delayed in delivery, a reality neither recognized until later. From Augusta,
Caldwell sent Bourke-White three telegrams in one day—at a cost of
$11.40, he noted—but received no replies. For her part, Bourke-White
also agonized; Caldwell's letters and messages initially had not arrived.
Did he realize how alone and out of touch with him she felt? She had a
terrible feeling that she was "just pouring messages into a bottomless
sea," useless because Caldwell neither called for nor read them. Could
he not send her just "one small wire?"[14] And so their mutual laments
continued until finally their emotionally charged letters and wires
reached each other.

Somehow, as a consequence of either Bourke-White's—or an Augusta postal clerk's—accident or design, one of her letters was misdirected from Caldwell's General Delivery address to the Mount Vernon one, where Helen opened it. What she had known, but perhaps always avoided imagining, lay sprawled in words across the paper before her. She only then realized that even as Skinny had lived with her, he had written surreptitiously to Kit. Obviously, theirs was more than the passing fancy or short-lived affair she had hoped.

That recognition canceled the conditions of Helen's year of grace, her understanding, and her patience all in a single stroke. Caldwell in his next letter to Bourke-White confessed that he had "had the law read" to him, and that before long he'd "be called upon to do something." Yet he urged her to write as openly as before because, he promised, there would be no more opening of his letters. Skinny needed Kit "to live for and with"; could she not offer him any hope?[15]

Helen, who always had understood, who had relented to Caldwell's needs, finally had become relentless. The sympathy, therefore, that Caldwell had always expected, first from his mother and later from Helen, this time he sought from Kit: "I don't know what would happen to me if I couldn't find you when you come back. If I don't have you, I won't have anything in the world because you know what has happened."[16] Caldwell did not blame Helen for her attitude, but he hated "not having anything." Bourke-White's errant letter had forced Caldwell's dilemma to a resolution.

Before Bourke-White's return, Helen sent Caldwell back to his New York apartment. His presence only added to an emotional trauma further complicated by her physical pain. Treating the latter, a local doctor recommended a hysterectomy, a remedy she refused to accept before obtaining a second opinion from Dr. Isabel Knowlton, a New York specialist and friend. That physician also advised surgery, but of a type whose consequences would be corrective and not so permanent.

After the surgery had been scheduled but before it had been performed, Caldwell had received a concerned inquiry from his mother. Helen's last letter to the elder Caldwells discussed her forthcoming "major operation" but more fundamentally, it conveyed so little of "her usual cheerful outlook on life" that they were worried. Her attitude had seemed "almost despairing, or at best depressed."[17] Because Carrie was involved with summer school at the University of Georgia, Ira Caldwell—experiencing some teaching-related emotional anxieties of his own—nonetheless planned to come to New York to be with Helen. She urged Erskine also to give Helen all that emotional support she seemed so obviously to need during that difficult time.

Obedient to his mother, Caldwell came to be with Helen at the hospital prior to her surgery. As Helen told the story, his father was already there, when the three of them fell into a discussion of what was to be done with Pix during her hospital confinement and subsequent recuperative period. Though the boy already was on the train to Charlottesville, Caldwell complained; that was not a "fit place" for Pix to be since Mrs. Lannigan "allowed drinking in the house." Helen allegedly turned to him with his father standing by, and said, "Erskine, between drinking and adultery, what have you got to say?"[18]

Helen's story of the subsequent events is elaborately and dramatically embroidered. Under Isabel Knowlton's skilled hand, she emerged from the surgery without any complications until seriously stricken with edematous swelling. Her condition became so tenuous that Jim Barton, then playing the lead in *Tobacco Road*, and his wife offered daily Mass intentions for her recovery. Bennett Cerf came to visit each day, sometimes bringing champagne. Caldwell visited only occasionally, until the night of Margaret's return.

The next morning, Caldwell called, recounting with explicit detail "everything that had gone on" between the reunited lovers the night before. Helen's temperature consequently shot up to such a degree that Dr. Knowlton forbade her to accept any more calls or visits from Caldwell. During her gradual recovery, Helen slowly accepted that as far as the marriage was concerned, "that was the beginning of the end." Toward the end of August, 1937 she returned to the children and Mount Vernon, but not before Caldwell and Bourke-White had departed for a three-month trip to California and places west.

Somehow—perhaps either Erskine or Helen had offered the clues—the elder Caldwells learned that their son's marriage was staggering toward its conclusion. Carrie shared with Helen her foremost concerns.

Her letters to Erskine's New York address had gone unanswered. Was he still alive? And then pointing accusingly at Caldwell's seductress, his mother justified his recent behavior: "I feel that he had been trapped and double-crossed. No wonder he could not write anything worthwhile. He should have come down and stayed with us. If only we had known—."[19]

Six days later Carrie once more had written to Caldwell, this time a long eight-page letter. Offering a variety of explanations for his behavior and mildly suggesting dutiful reconsiderations, she, as always before, granted him understanding and sympathy:

> I am so distressed that I cannot think straight nor write very intelligently. I am so sorry for the trouble, and while I love Helen and the children it is only natural that you should be my first thought and concern. Living up there in Maine the year round has put you in an intolerable position. You need to have daily contact with *Men* [Mother's emphasis]—not women of whom I have a poor opinion—who, even if they are ignorant, have a heart and a brain, and who can think and talk. But I am hoping and praying that you and Helen will consider the children before anything else in the world. . . . It requires a great deal of sanity, strength of character and some sacrifices for people to live harmoniously under the same roof—keep Pixie with you if possible. . . . We had hoped to have you all down with us this winter. Erskine, if you need any money remember you can borrow on the farm or sell it. If you need any help that we have in our power to give, let us know.[20]

Those considerations disposed, she wrote of the elder Caldwells' other worries. Since father needed rest and could no longer teach, they would be financially strapped.[21] Then, either not knowing that Caldwell was with Bourke-White or obliquely urging his return to responsibility, she concluded, "Write me how H. is. With love to you all. Devotedly, Mother."

How Caldwell responded, how he felt as a consequence of his mother's letters, and how he reacted to Helen's all-but-final rejection is not known. Whatever his feelings, they were balanced by his being with Kit. She was doing a Hollywood assignment for *Life* and there, unlike Caldwell before and later, she spurned the temptations of moviedom: "Warner Brothers offered her fifteen hundred dollars a week, much more than she could earn on her own, but she didn't hesitate to refuse."[22] Otherwise based in Santa Monica, they enjoyed California and adjusted, for the first time during an extended period together, to their individual differences.

Publicly, Caldwell was as withdrawn as Bourke-White was gregarious, he as cautiously saving as she was recklessly extravagant. Whereas Bourke-White lavished dollars on clothing and hours on appearance, Caldwell always had been indifferent to both. The moralist who drank only beer if he drank at all, who supposedly objected to Pix's living in a house where liquor was served, found himself teamed with a sophisticated woman whose social rituals offered cocktails as a form of communion. But again, whatever accommodations their teaming demanded necessarily would be Caldwell's.

Yet his initiation into a life with Bourke-White did not wean him from what he felt for Helen, the children, and his old friend, Morang. Less than six weeks after last calling Helen, he wrote her from his and Bourke-White's rented house in Santa Monica.[23] The two of them had been traveling, with brief visits to Ensenada, Mexico, and San Diego, but if Helen wished to write, she could address her letters to 320 East Forty-second Street. Caldwell, furthermore, reminded her that should she become worried about anything, he was the person to see because he was "taking care" of her. And perhaps further hinting that all was not well between him and Bourke-White, he hoped to come back to Mount Vernon soon to see her and the children. Finally, as if to convince Helen of his past spellbound conditions, he repeated that oft-tendered vow: "I've got back on my feet again, and I'm going to stay on them from now on, or else." In the same letter he mentioned Morang, almost as if to remind himself as much as her that he had not abandoned all his personal responsibilities.

Ever since the *Tobacco Road* performance had assured Caldwell's financial ease in 1934, he periodically had sent checks for small amounts to Morang. Always long on hope and promise, Morang, nonetheless, never had been able to support either with reality. Indeed, his and Dorothy's situation waned even as Caldwell's waxed. Additionally Morang's physical health continued to complicate a precarious economic and emotional balance. A hacking cough, aggravated by smoking, had always bordered on the consumptive, but finally in the winter of 1936-37, Portland doctors concluded that he had a touch of tuberculosis. If he wished to regain his health, he would need an extended period in the drier, warmer Southwest.

Since the Morangs' resources would have taken them scarcely as far as Mount Vernon, much less financed a move to Santa Fe, the Caldwells had given them the money necessary for the relocation. Morang remained confident that he and Dorothy could subsist in Santa Fe as they had in Portland, he by offering painting lessons, and she, piano instruction. All of them covertly recognized that Caldwell's continuing loans would have to subsidize the Morangs for a long time to come. Thus in September of 1937, Caldwell wrote Helen that Alfred had decided to remain in Santa Fe for another year, a decision and situation Caldwell would continue to support.

By the time Caldwell and Bourke-White departed California in November, Viking issued *You Have Seen Their Faces* to almost universal critical acclaim. Reviewers praised both the photography and writing. One critic could not decide whether Caldwell's journalistic ability or Bourke-White's photographic skill had provided the study with its force.[24] Malcolm Cowley, always sympathetic to Caldwell's work, this time also included Bourke-White. Her photographs, a new form of art, were beyond praise.[25] A *New York Times* reviewer believed that Caldwell's finest writing had turned "the book into a sledgehammer to pound home an idea that the pictures somehow go beyond."[26] Although subsequently the book was to be judged more critically, at the time most critics recognized its innovative force.

Successful as their collaboration on the book had been, Caldwell and Bourke-White's partnership was proving less satisfying by that November. Departing Santa Monica, they swung through Santa Fe because Caldwell wished both to see Morang and to introduce Kit to him. Yet by this time their differences, combined with his anguished conscience, increasingly sent him brooding into those silences which Bourke-White neither could, nor would, tolerate.

During their three uninterrupted months together, she had come to recognize him as "a fine and very worthwhile man," but one "whose inner security was beginning to act as a blind against the world." The silences acceptable in her father, she could neither understand nor endure with Caldwell. His "frozen moods . . . seemed to have no traceable cause in a world of reality," and the unfathomable silences ended "only in violent tempests."[27] What form those tempests took Bourke-White never publicly stated. Peggy Smith-Sargent guessed that he sometimes had been physically abusive. Caldwell himself uncharacteristically admitted that the two of them engaged in face-slapping bouts which he had initiated.[28] Such encounters between these two fiercely self-determined and dominating individuals made at least Bourke-White realize that they were in an unhealthy relationship. Once she therefore "tried to leave him." Apparently either before or after the Morang visit she had told him of her decision. On that painful occasion, Caldwell had stopped the car to talk it out on "a sandswept road." According to her version, she gave up her intentions because he pleaded that she could not "leave us."

Because Helen made no association between that nuance of Bourke-White's public story and one of her own, her version of what happened after the confrontation is more convincing. During Caldwell's California tour with Bourke-White, Helen advised her lawyer to initiate divorce proceedings. Before any papers could be served, however, she received a telegram from Caldwell in Santa Fe. Kit had left him, and he was ill. Could Helen take a train there and then drive him back?

Whether from motives of love, sympathy, or those larger exceptions she always had felt Caldwell's great talent deserved, Helen complied with his request. Leaving the boys in school under a neighbor's care, she and Janet caught the *Chief* for Santa Fe, where they stayed at the La Fonda Inn until Caldwell—whose illness had remained undiagnosed—was well enough to travel. During their return and without knowledge of Helen's already formulated plans, Caldwell asked her to sue him for divorce, naming Bourke-White as the correspondent. That ploy, he hoped, might force Kit to marry him. Helen claimed, however, to have rejected a portion of his plea—"Erskine, I shall not wash your dirty linen in public," but she continued the divorce proceedings.[29]

Thanksgiving of 1937 found Caldwell back in New York, where he engaged a suite at the Mayflower Hotel with its exclusive 15 Central Park address. Once more he and Bourke-White exchanged love-filled telegrams as both tried to forget their rift as well as the causes that provoked it. Helen had returned to Mount Vernon, but upon Caldwell's insistence, she and the children planned to spend a portion of the winter in Florida. They had barely settled there before some misfiled divorce papers forced their return. Stopping to visit her sister in New York, Helen stayed over for a few days and there met Margaret for the first time; she liked her at once.

The three of them, Caldwell, Helen, and Margaret—husband-lover, wife, and mistress—went to a bistro. Margaret asked Helen if she wanted a drink. Yes, anything with scotch would be fine, she replied. At this point in Helen's story Caldwell became angry, banged his fist on the table and said, "Goddam you women! Helen, you never drank when I was home, and I'm trying to teach Margaret not to drink, and you both defy me."[30] Both the women supposedly drew back to howl with laughter while he glowered.

Afterwards, they talked about efforts to stage *Journeyman*. Already the producer of *Tobacco Road*, Sam Byrd, had talked Caldwell into dramatizing his later novel. Investing together five thousand dollars toward production costs, Caldwell and Bourke-White shared their first "thrilling and hectic" work interests since their cooperative *Faces* venture.

For the first time in the year and a half since meeting Bourke-White, Caldwell in that new year of 1938, worked with enthusiasm. The fact that both of them shared a vested interest in the results perhaps rekindled his former sense of urgency. He wrote to Morang with old familiarity: the play was scheduled to open on Saturday, January 29; he had been working fifteen hours per day; and with his usual refrain, Caldwell vowed that it would be a long time before he got "tangled up in show business again."[31] Almost his old self once more—he appeared fully alive and satisfied only when involved in his work.

Amidst Caldwell's preparations for the opening, he also rushed to complete revisions for a new edition of *Journeyman*. Viking wished to issue it simultaneously with the opening of the play. Additionally, he wrote a script for a workers' film group, and most significantly of all, reported to Helen that he had completed four short stories. She praised his accomplishment with all her former enthusiasm but expressed a regret. "More than anything else" she missed their working together on his stories.[32]

Although Helen intellectually had committed herself to divorce, her emotions occasionally betrayed her. While Caldwell remained in the familiar whirl that they had shared for so long, she adjusted to a life whose greatest excitement revolved around the children: while the boys participated in scouting activities, Janet studied tap, acrobatics, and ballet. But such diversions scarcely compensated for the excitement of being with Caldwell when lighted billboards spelled the Caldwell name—hers as well as his—for an expectant public.

The sense of loss was not Helen's alone. Ten-year-old Dabney had been reading some of his father's stories and liked "Candy Man Beechum" most of all. Didn't Erskine think that sometime he "should dedicate a book to the kids?"[33] Later that year, when Gramps—Helen's maternal grandfather—had nagged and criticized Pix incessantly, Helen wrote with a sympathy she had gained through her own experience. Since one could do little else, she had tried to teach Pix merely to accept criticisms and conditions as they had been "imposed by life." He nonetheless remained hurt and unhappy. Helen agonized helplessly about his painful confusion: "He goes off camping alone for days at a time—and it breaks my heart to see him brood so much."[34]

Otherwise Helen wrote about taking the children to Christian Endeavor meetings, about their grades, expenses, and the weather. Small wonder that she at least once weakened:

> Somehow your letter gave me a warm feeling . . . a feeling that somehow, someway, you were here with me, still. I had felt so alone for such a long time, and depended on you for so many years that the shock of being alone has left me wavering, I guess. You can never know how much I do miss you and all that we had together. I miss so much our trips, our long talks about work, our working over and over your stories.[35]

Helen signed the letter with "best wishes, always."

When Helen's letter arrived, Caldwell already stood amidst the swirl of activity and confusion that would sweep him farther and farther from Mount Vernon, Helen, and the children. Floundering, he could not stop to count his losses. The smaller ones became obvious with the Saturday, January 29, premier of *Journeyman*. Newspaper reviewers and critics immediately howled their choruses. Though they universally praised Will Geer in his lead performance as the rapscallion preacher, they heaped all their ire upon both the play and its subject. Brooks Atkinson of the *New York Times* vowed that *Journeyman* thereafter would make him think kindly of every play from then until doomsday.[36] Another reviewer pronounced it "duller than ditchwater and not quite as clean." Brooklyn papers judged the play "aimless, shoddy, and sickeningly childish," its characters "slow-moving, pointless freaks." Other critics used the by-now-familiar "dirty and obscene" labels to condemn the work.

Although the new owners tried various tactics to salvage what promised to be a disaster, only Joseph Wood Krutch, reviewing for *The Nation*, came to the play's defense, and then with mixed feelings.[37] Finally, whether incensed beyond patience, or in a vain attempt to save his five-thousand-dollar investment—apocryphally multiplying that amount many times over in *With All My Might*—Caldwell uncharacteristically defended *Journeyman* by publicly stating his motives for writing the book. Semon Dye, though come to life through Will Geer's performance, was not a realistic characterization of a living person. Neither was the work itself obscene or dirty. As a storyteller, he had merely created a character whose behavior reflected the foibles of some religions and their ministers. Ultimately *Journeyman* attempted "to show the effects of bogus religion and bogus preachers upon the characters of the Southern people."[38]

Coming to his son's defense, Ira's letter to the editor in a New York paper testified to the play's verisimilitude.[39] But neither new producers nor written explanations and defenses could save *Journeyman*. Whereas *Tobacco Road* was to run through the years and 3,182 New York performances, the second Caldwell adaptation limped through a few weeks, with 41 shows.

Even as Caldwell worked to help save the play, he pursued other arrangements. Despairing of that novel promised as surety for *Journey-man*'s publication, Viking would issue another collection of Caldwell's short stories. He, therefore, pulled together those pieces published during the previous three years, added "Runaway" and "Wildflowers," and gave that to the editors. He was too rushed to do more. He was making preparations for another cooperative venture he and Bourke-White had planned for the spring.

Together they wished to explore Czechoslovakia and some of the Balkan countries before browsing through Spain, France, England, and other European places. In the Slovenian regions they planned to collaborate on a project that would, in essence, duplicate what they had done in the South through *Faces*. In addition to attending to all those details demanded by a five-month trip abroad, Caldwell also made other arrangements.

Lacking a lawyer of his own, he secured Julius Weiss, Bourke-White's attorney, to represent him in the upcoming divorce proceedings. Together they worked out in broad detail those conditions of settlement acceptable to Caldwell. Mrs. Margaret Salter, his personal secretary of some three months, would answer correspondence, deposit checks, and issue payments to Helen, Morang, and his parents, either as required or needed. All such contingencies prescribed, Caldwell prepared to experience a new continent, and a new life.

Chapter 13

A heavy fog enveloped New York and its harbor on March 31, 1938, the day Caldwell and Bourke-White boarded the *S. S. Normandie* bound for Le Havre.[1] Settled into their separate but adjacent first-class cabins, they awaited departure. Tugs nosed the ship into the harbor, but the fog increased in density. By nightfall, the outward-bound *Normandie* was forced to drop anchor in Gravesend Bay until the following day. A ferry had gone aground in Totenville; another had been involved in a collision. Had Caldwell lived in an earlier time, he might have perceived the events as omens for pause: a fog-shrouded harbor, anchor in Gravesend Bay, and two ferries lost in the murk.

Surely the *Normandie*'s departure from the dock marked endings as well as beginnings. It carried Caldwell, for the first time in his thirty-four years, from his home country to foreign lands. Aboard ship, he pointed away from White Oak, Georgia, his parents, and wife of thirteen years. Each had contributed to his development and growth as a writer. Shortly a southern writer would pronounce that "you can't go home again," but Caldwell, no doubt, would have dismissed that caution also.

Yet even before Caldwell had steamed three days from home, another writer stood on Georgia soil citing Caldwell's past as promise for American literature's future. Speaking at Emory University, Louis Untermeyer looked toward an era of American cultural maturity. For evidence, he drew upon the examples of Faulkner, Hemingway, Caldwell, O'Hara, and Steinbeck. These few only had been true "to an author's first duty—that of keeping an eye on the material" of their time, of telling the truth as far as they could see it and "thus widening a native culture."[2]

Caldwell had long been true to his first duty, to his native culture. But by April of 1938, moved by forces stronger than duty, he had molded his interests to Bourke-White's, shaken off both domestic and career responsibilities to follow her to Europe. Wagering the familiarity of the old against the excitement of the new, he gambled that his future success would rival his past accomplishments.

By April 10, Caldwell and Bourke-White had arrived in Paris to be met by a press more than a little curious about a then-unorthodox couple. The two of them talked with reporters about their plans for the trip.[3] As they traveled through the respective countries, they hoped to get a feeling for Czechs and Hungarians, to capture their personalities, explore their lives, and to see where they worked. There, as in France, Caldwell would not be totally unknown, since translations of *God's Little Acre* had been issued in both countries only a year earlier.

The couple, however, encountered unanticipated difficulties. Though Bourke-White's photography transcended language barriers, Caldwell's ear did not. If he could not understand the Czech-Hungarian people, how could he tell their stories? In Bohemia and Moravia the two Americans managed to communicate with a combination of English, signs, and gestures. In Slovakia and Ruthenia, however, something as simple as ordering a meal became an exercise in confusing frustration. These were not the familiar Tobacco Road people whose language patterns and rhythms he could verify with a southern wife, one who understood the subjects as well as the man telling their stories.

But as of April 18, 1938, Caldwell no longer had a wife. While he traveled an ocean away in Czechoslovakia, Helen had met with lawyers and a presiding judge in a Kennebec County, Maine courthouse. On the Monday after Easter, he accepted her uncontested charges of cruel and abusive treatment as grounds for divorce.[4]

The terms of settlement were straightforward and sparsely defined.[5] Helen was to retain custody of the children; Caldwell could visit them at reasonable times and have custody of them together or separately for one month each summer. He was to pay $2,600 per year as wife and child support on a monthly schedule. In lieu of alimony, Helen was to receive $12,000, to be paid, after some initial adjustments, at the rate of $1,000 per year. If she were to remarry, her 25 percent portion of the support payments would cease, but as surety for the other entitlements, Caldwell had approximately eighteen months to establish a $25,000 trust account in a bank of his choice. Because Helen's mother still owned Greentrees, there were no additional conditions for property settlement, but Caldwell was to pay Helen's $500 legal fees. After so much, that was all. The Caldwell marriage had been terminated, and its accounts settled.

Released from women—mother and wife—for almost the first time in his life, Caldwell, on Easter Monday, April 18, was both legally and symbolically free to put off the old man and take on the new. But he could not so easily assume a new identity. In her autobiographical work, Bourke-White cites an instance from the Czechoslovakian trip during which Caldwell's behavior enigmatically and painfully changed.

Near the Hungarian border, a Czechoslovakian press officer and his wife accompanied the two Americans as hosts and translators. The day's excursion had been fruitful as Caldwell chatted openly and pleasantly with the host and hostess. That evening, however, "over coffee and liqueurs," when "a cool breeze began to blow," Bourke-White looked at him with puzzlement: "His face turned white and his skin was drawn."[6] Caldwell had retreated into one of his almost catatonic silences. Basically "sensitive and almost uncannily perceptive about others," he appeared "largely unaware of what was happening," of the ungracious tension and pain his behavior cast like a pall over the group. Neither she nor anyone else had understood his abrupt transformation.

Yet the clues to a clearer understanding lie buried in Bourke-White's account. She prefaced the incident by placing it within the context of an "Easter trip." If the day that Caldwell had slipped away into silent withdrawal was Easter Monday—in that year on April 18—he might have been suffering conscience-wracking realizations.

Never a drinker, then Caldwell drank liqueurs. Socialized by precept and example to be honorably faithful, he sipped them with a mistress in an alien land. Further, during that period, perhaps that very day, his wife had divorced him. That legal act publicly declared that Helen had not forgiven him, in fact, had rejected his love and him. Moreover, Bourke-White subsequently had confided to Helen that he had blamed Margaret for the breakup of the marriage: "If it weren't for you," he'd say, "I'd still have my family. . . . He felt guilty about it."[7] Such considerations well might have turned Caldwell's face white, drawn his skin, and caused him to retreat from Margaret into pained silence.

Bourke-White left no doubt that their Czechoslovakian project likewise suffered as a consequence of what she perceived as Caldwell's ungracious and moody behavior. Whatever its causes, she felt that it prevented their close association with each other and with their subjects. The cooperative spirit that had given depth to the *Faces* study failed to energize the European project.

Whatever Caldwell felt can be inferred only from hints and guesses. During this trip, he suddenly resumed writing biweekly letters to Morang. Throughout the eighteen months when he had vacillated between Helen and Kit, he had written his friend but a few cursory notes. Instead he shared his feelings with one or the other woman. But after Helen's divorce and Kit's criticism of his moody behavior, Caldwell was left only with Morang as his confidante. Unlike his brief notes of the recent past, the letters from Europe were long, revealing accounts that included observations and impressions about his European publications and Morang's art.[8] Significantly they almost never mentioned Kit. And despite Morang's obviously dependent, almost sycophantic responses, Caldwell told him to "be sure and write" via Mrs. Salter.

His recent divorce, the signs of European unrest, and the constant travel all, no doubt, had made Caldwell yearn for the comforts of the familiar. Hungary, he had observed, was "going nazi" like all of middle Europe. But "after dealing first with the German brown shirts, and then with the Hungarian green shirts," he had perfected the Nazi salute as well as the citizens. After their time in Eastern Europe, Caldwell and Bourke-White returned to France before departing for England where "she had some things to do." Then Franco's revolution in Spain caught her interest, so they traveled there.

Prague, Budapest, Paris, London, Madrid: all were a long way from *Tobacco Road* country. How far Caldwell's alliance with Bourke-White had removed him became evident through the reviews of *Southways*. It stood alone as his first published book of fiction since his involvement with her.

Viking's June publication of the collection inspired few critics either to praise the work or to prophesy his place among America's great writers. Some isolated reviewers, such as one for the San Francisco *Chronicle*, praised Caldwell's improved technique and his re-creation of the southern setting. Most of the reputable New York critics, however, expressed reservations. The usually sympathetic Harold Strauss of the *New York Times* labeled *Southways* as Caldwell's weakest volume of short fiction, one hovering within an "air of listlessness and casualness."[9] Jonathan Daniels, always one of Caldwell's most loyal southern enthusiasts, felt he had provoked no tears at all when he had turned deliberately heartrending.[10]

Disappointed reviewers had no way of knowing of Caldwell's personal turmoil during the period he had written the stories. Yet William Soskin groped perceptively close to the heart of Caldwell's darkness. It was silly to make literary judgments about him during an extraordinary period, one wherein artists' essential natures were being "hurled about and hammered and burned in a chaotic social era."[11] Yet during a time when Faulkner, Hemingway, Steinbeck, and Wolfe were to write some of their most powerful works, the quality of Caldwell's writing began declining. That decline suggested that conflicts and forces more personal than social had "hammered and burned" his essential nature, had redirected his literary vision and interests.

While Bourke-White pursued her photojournalistic tour through a Europe in turmoil, Caldwell wrote little. Increasingly he yearned for home, a sense of place. Only three months into the trip, he had told Morang that he'd "be pretty glad to get back to America" and "glad to stay there for a while."[12] Shortly thereafter, he instructed Mrs. Salter to seek a furnished house within sight of Long Island Sound. Additionally she was to complete arrangements toward the purchase of a gray convertible—a Ford like his father always had driven.

Whatever the strains of their recent relationship, when Caldwell and Bourke-White disembarked from the *Aquitania* on August 31, they appeared as a loving couple to the reporters who met them. Their two-cabin arrangement, however, fooled no one. One dubious reporter measured the distance separating their accommodations. While Bourke-White denied the possibility of marriage, Caldwell glumly said nothing.

Like Scott and Zelda Fitzgerald before them, they appeared as romantic celebrities to 1938 audiences struggling through an otherwise dreary decade.

And romantic they sometimes were, or could be, on those occasions when Caldwell's moods, when their respective joustings for dominance, did not prohibit their expressions of love. In New York, shortly after their return, Caldwell surprised her with a welcome-home party. Vicki Goldberg, working from Bourke-White's unpublished notes, tells the story:

> "I was told to close my eyes for ten minutes . . . and during that time I could feel soft surfaces touching me on the cheek and hands and forehead. Little mysterious swishes of sound. What could it be? I hadn't the remotest idea. Then when I was allowed to open my eyes I found that Skinny had filled the whole room with beautiful balloons in all sorts of lovely pastel shades. . . . and hanging to one of them was a lovely little gift. How could anyone resist a man like this?"[13]

Because Mrs. Salter had located no suitable house, Caldwell immediately had sought one while Bourke-White resumed her periodic national assignments. Between times he also worked on the text of their European book that was to be published as *North of the Danube*. Within two months, he had located a nearly finished house. Between them, Bourke-White and Caldwell divided the costs of the $22,000 lot upon which it was being built.

Located in Darien, Connecticut, fifty miles north of New York City, the place was idyllic. Somewhat secluded and surrounded by woods, the white clapboard house incorporated a large living-room fireplace and an expanse of French windows opening upon the back lawn. There upon a slablike rock outgrowth, Bourke-White could bask nude or Caldwell could write. After his first visit, Ira caught the spirit of the place: its quietness and seclusion served as a healing balm to frazzled nerves.[14]

The home, slyly called Horseplay Hill, was the first for each of them. With his unusual share of male pride—and perhaps for the sense of control it would have included—Caldwell wished to purchase the property in his name alone. But Bourke-White would not so easily barter her independence and freedom. Both shared equally in its costs, a type of expense-account sharing already established in their joint southern and European trips. But this time was different. Bourke-White obviously resisted the loss of control that this form of Caldwell's "caring for her" would have exacted.

Caldwell scarcely had time either to contemplate the mortgage or to enjoy the comforts of home before he and Bourke-White were off again. Assigned to a feature on Roosevelt at his Warm Springs, Georgia, retreat, she worked there while he visited his parents and attended two road performances of *Tobacco Road.* In Augusta, Ira brought some of the barefoot sharecroppers to the play. One reportedly wanted a part because he could "cuss better than that fellow that is Henry Peabody"; he had, to boot, a real Ada and Pearly at home. In Atlanta, censors "put the play on the fire and tried to cook it" but as a result, the production played to capacity crowds. After his week in Atlanta, Caldwell returned to Warm Springs to wait until Bourke-White "finished her job."

If Caldwell had looked homeward to Darien as a place to "sooth his frazzled nerves," he enjoyed but a brief peace. Letters and appeals from Helen began to arrive regularly. Even before the Warm Springs trip, seven-year-old Janet visited Skinny and Kit in their new home. She enjoyed a "swell time," and, like the two boys later, "fell in love with Kit," whom she considered beautiful. Helen expressed pleasure that Erskine had visited the elder Caldwells, because she knew how much they missed him. She herself missed him "so many times."[15]

Helen's admission might have seemed only more puzzling than gratifying to Caldwell. Nine days after their divorce, she had married Norman Cushman, both her and Caldwell's friend during their Mount Vernon days. "Cush," as everyone called him, allegedly married Helen to save her from herself, but more likely, having been much around the Caldwells, he had come to love both the children and Helen at least as much as they liked him. An unpretentious, caring man, Cush never earned much money either as a local builder, a wartime shipyard worker, or an Elizabeth Arden employee. He nonetheless earned the children's abiding respect.

Sometimes Helen's letters pleaded severe financial needs—to pay doctor bills or to replace the washing machine. Or she was "simply desperate" for a three-hundred-dollar advance on the next year's alimony payment.[16] When Caldwell either refused or advanced only a hundred because he claimed he could afford no more, she accepted it with resignation and sage advice: "It is a long life and a tough one, Skinny, but if you can keep your faith in people, and your sureness that you are doing the best you can, it need not be an unhappy one."[17]

Meanwhile, he rushed to complete the manuscript for *North of the Danube.* Though his editors were becoming increasingly impatient with him—just as he was dissatisfied with them—Viking wished to publish the book as soon as possible. With Caldwell's work completed shortly after the beginning of 1939, Viking rushed it into print by March. Already Europe rumbled with that conflict which primed readers for its reception.

Contrary to Bourke-White's belief that Caldwell's behavior flawed the work, critics praised *Danube* with a universal acclaim. Accolade followed accolade, with *Booklist*'s review summarizing the spirit of them all. Caldwell had "caught the land, its people and their problems."[18] His prose spoke with simplicity, dignity, and the artlessness of fine writing. And words could not capture the breathless beauty of Bourke-White's pictures. So finally in 1939, and at age thirty-five, Caldwell earned the praise he always had desired. Graciously, no one noted that it was not fiction which had claimed it.

Even before that, however, Caldwell's works had ranked him among the literary elite of the thirties and early forties. Following Untermeyer's lead, Lewis Gannet declared Caldwell to be the most distinguished living writer in America. Joseph Wood Krutch added to that praise. From the likes of Thoreau, James, and Howells, the literary torch had passed to Pearl Buck, Ernest Hemingway, and Erskine Caldwell, with Caldwell's seeming the most original and substantial talent of the period. Among luminaries such as Van Wyck Brooks and Malcolm Cowley, John Steinbeck and Ernest Hemingway, he had served as vice-president of the League of American Writers, a leftist group with membership by invitation only.

Because of such acclaim, only Caldwell and a few others perhaps realized how little fiction he recently had written. By 1939, he had not produced a novel in more than five years. The short stories he once forwarded to Max Perkins in weekly batches of twos and threes had dwindled to a few per year after his meeting Bourke-White. She, her interests, and her wishes displaced writing as Caldwell's obsession. Moreover, traveling, working, and living with her were not enough. His personal honor, rigid conscience, and emotional insecurity demanded more. Until Caldwell formally could appease these, his storytelling impulses—like those chain gang victims he used metaphorically in describing his bondage to Kit—would remain shackled.

With the *Danube* obligation satisfied, Caldwell directed the full force of his persistence toward breaking Bourke-White's resolutions against marriage. He referred to the many instances of public embarrassment, the *Aquitania* docking situation among them. When they moved into their Darien home, the local newspaper properly featured them as Mr. and Mrs. Caldwell. But reasons more compelling than public appearance caused Caldwell to try to overcome Bourke-White's resistance to marriage. As with Helen before, Caldwell argued that he had to "make an honest woman of her."[19]

Such private appeals Caldwell transmitted through telegrams when they were apart. Telegram after telegram followed her wherever she traveled. The first, Caldwell sent, addressed only to "Honeychile," as a disguised honeymoon invitation from the Honolulu Chamber of Commerce. In another, the county clerk of Reno asked for her autograph, the *S.S. Lurline*, her charm, and the island, her order for March sunsets. Skinny requested nothing for himself except "one prepaid word spelled YES."[20] One day later "Sugar-babe Bourke-White" received an offer she apparently could not refuse. That telegram advertised "a highly desirable position in life open for combination maid, wife, mistress."[21] "Skinny Hawaii or Bust Caldwell" advised "Toots" to apply for same without delay.

Bourke-White's rigid career responsibilities were as strong as ever. Beyond that, the emotional risks also were frightening. Again Goldberg's translation of Bourke-White's dilemma: "She tried to discount her constant longing to be with him and the pull of his love's wild urgency and wilder need. She was wary of heat—'Don't think these ferocious things burn too long'—and she had reason, but then too, she was predisposed to control everything."[22] She felt otherwise also increasingly "drawn" to this man with his insistent, little-boy appeals, one who often spoke of a loneliness unbroken by any close friends. Finally she reasoned that perhaps if she became his wife, such legal assurance "would lighten the burden of insecurity which he seemed unable to cast off."[23] If marriage would help, Bourke-White decided to yield to his insistence.

But neither was Bourke-White blind to the difficulties that marriage to Caldwell would involve. Seeking to avoid some of them, she allegedly made him sign a contract of conditions even as they flew to Nevada for the marriage ceremony. That agreement outlined her apprehensions. If some difficulty between them arose, they were to "talk it out before midnight"; he was to treat her friends as courteously as he would his own, "to attempt to realize and control his fluctuating moods." And finally, Caldwell was not to try to seduce her away from her photographic assignments. Thus Bourke-White used a signed personal agreement to allay her misgivings so that Caldwell might appease his conscience with a legal document. They obtained their license in Reno on February 28, 1939. Only the ceremony remained.

In Reno, the two cast about for an alternative to being married in that notorious marriage-mill town. The Nevada map marked Silver City, a name that caught their romantic imaginations. Engaging a taxi, they stopped en route so the driver could find someone in a Carson City hotel who might accompany and marry his passengers. During the delay, Caldwell, as usual, concocted a story whose association through imagery is amusingly pathetic. He worried because cattle-trading wasn't legal after sundown and he wanted "this marriage to be legal."[24] Levity hid whatever real concerns he had, but in a seldom-used Episcopal chapel, attended by the taxi driver and a tobacco shop proprietor, an empowered state representative married Caldwell and Kit before sundown. In a ceremony just as privately, personally, and legally absolving, he had married Helen some fourteen years before.

Dockside journalists crowded about the honeymooning couple as they boarded the *S.S. Lurline* from a San Francisco pier. This time Caldwell and Bourke-White occupied the same stateroom without raising eyebrows. In Honolulu, the chamber of commerce may have greeted them and they may have watched March sunsets, but honeymoons cannot last forever. Three weeks later they had departed the Royal Hawaiian Hotel bound by plane via San Francisco, to Darien. There finally they settled in legally as Mr. and Mrs. Erskine Caldwell.

Awaiting them was an unusual but appropriate wedding gift from Henry Luce—a lawn "bundle-bed," large enough "to ride around in, sleep in, or do nothing in."[25] Later the two of them used it occasionally to sleep out under the stars, but that last week in March, work awaited them. Bourke-White departed shortly on an assignment to the Savannah, Georgia, area, and again Caldwell followed her, but this time with different intentions. Almost too casually, he admitted to visiting "the old home to look around." He stayed there only long enough to encourage his parents to seek a new home in Augusta, one that he would purchase, and he then returned alone to the emptiness of the Darien house.

That return "to the old home" became but Caldwell's first step toward reestablishing those patterns that the traumas of the divorce had blocked, and that marriage to Kit had unlocked. From Darien he wrote at least two letters of reaffirmation, one to Morang and another to Atcheson Hench, his old professor. To Morang: "I wish you were closer so you could drop in once in awhile."[26] The letter to Hench, his first in seven years, was one of thanks as well as desire. Without that seminar where he felt "like a haystack about to burst into flame," he never would have been set on the road to his writing career.[27] In fact, he would like to sit in on it again. Hench attributed Caldwell's uncharacteristic effusiveness to the "golden glow of memory." And as for the seminar, another professor now taught it. His response implied that nothing—Caldwell's career included?—could be resurrected through memory or repetition alone.

In other ways as well, Caldwell tried to pick up the thread where he had dropped it somewhere among the labyrinthine confusions of Hollywood, wealth, and Kit. He wrote a blurb of praise for Nathanael West's own version of the Hollywood nightmare, *The Day of the Locust*. Caldwell, the writer, likewise began checking sales figures for his latest books; *Faces* had sold fewer than 20 copies during the first six months of 1939, and *North of the Danube*, for all its glowing reviews, was to limp to only 948 sales by the end of September. He directed his grumblings about Viking's poor promotion policies to Marshall Best, who reacted with a prickliness Caldwell could not have missed.[28] Sales for *Danube* were weak and slow; in fact, the firm would lose even more than it had expected. But more to the point, it had spent over six times as much for publicity of Caldwell's work as it had on Steinbeck's *Grapes of Wrath*.

Best's comparative thrust, no doubt, hit home. Only five weeks after its issue, critics universally praised Steinbeck's work, boosting it toward a Pulitzer Prize and the National Booksellers Award a year later. Early in his career, Caldwell himself had vowed to win a Pulitzer Prize. Now he may have realized that in the race between the turtle and the hare, he had been caught agonizing.

Certainly ahead of Steinbeck in 1936, Caldwell's emotional traumas of the intervening years had declared him the loser. While Steinbeck had published *In Dubious Battle*, *Of Mice and Men*, *The Long Valley*, and finally *Grapes of Wrath*, respectively, Caldwell's fiction had been limited to *Southways*. In fact, in January of 1939, two months before he married Bourke-White, he admitted to Morang that except for the Eastern European book, he had nothing "to show for a year's work, and that's that." Without much enthusiasm, he allowed that he might get around to writing some short stories soon.

No matter the praiseworthy accomplishments of *Faces* and *Danube*, their glowing appraisals and limited sales had not boosted Caldwell's literary reputation. After his marriage, therefore, and after his return to *Tobacco Road* country, he declared himself ready to resume his fiction writing. He would begin with a novel—one he, for the first time, announced was to be another part of the panoramic depiction of southern life.

Sometime during May, while sitting on the moss-covered rock at Horseplay Hill, Caldwell began writing the book that was to be *Trouble in July*. With Bourke-White often gone, he worked as he had in the past—with determination and dispatch, and while juggling various other interests and responsibilities. Long interested in regional differences, he had conceived an Americana-type project. Regional writers would "describe and interpret the indigenous quality of life" in their respective sections of America. Such accounts, he anticipated, would create a mosaic whose similarities and differences characterized the unique national experience. Wishing to edit such a folkway series, Caldwell approached and wrote to regionalists who could contribute to it.

Before that project could be pursued, however, Caldwell needed editorial assurance that the works would be published. Viking's Marshall Best and Harold Guinzburg were less than enthusiastic. His record during their six-year association did not justify granting him any favors. Even reassurance of the imminent completion of the long-delayed Caldwell novel could not placate their skepticism. Using Steinbeck's proven profitability as a lever, they refused Lieber's arguments for a larger royalty advance and sales percentage for *Trouble in July.* Because Lieber, as usual, had been talking behind the scenes with another firm, he refused Viking's offer to renew the terms of Caldwell's old contract.

The termination of Caldwell's association with his second reputable publisher relieved them all. Admittedly, he did not have "the same feeling about withdrawing from Viking" as he experienced in breaking with Max Perkins and Scribner's. By that time, Caldwell had accepted writing and publishing as companion business negotiations rather than creative associations.

The new firm, to be known as Duell, Sloan and Pearce, was a venture established by Charles Duell and Samuel Sloan, young editors breaking away from Doubleday, and Charles Pearce, an aspiring Harcourt Brace editor. They had already negotiated publishing rights with Martha Gellhorn, Rockwell Kent, Conrad Aiken, and Frank Lloyd Wright. Lacking an established luminary within their fold, they granted Caldwell the concession of his editing, and their publishing, the Folkways Series. Always financially provident, they perhaps hoped to compensate for what they guessed would be the series' losses through Caldwell's reputation and future works.[29] In Caldwell's memory, the agreement—one for which he could write his own contract terms—was concluded with a handshake during dinner with Charlie Duell.[30]

With a publishing guarantee for the Folkways project, Caldwell was free to complete and revise the manuscript for his forthcoming book. Not even new beginnings, however, could free him totally from the obligations of his past. Regular letters from Helen reported on the children's health, progress in school, and social activities. She passed along information about old neighbors and her garden plantings. But more pointedly, Helen cited the costs of raising three growing children, running a household, and covering unexpected illnesses and other emergencies. Too often, he felt, she requested advances on her payments from him.

Never very patient with Helen's financial management, Caldwell generally sent her only a portion of the requested amount. Although she knew that *Tobacco Road* royalties continued to earn him handsome figures, he always cited his own financial straits. But on one occasion at least, Helen refused to accept his self-serving excuses: "I *do* resent it sometimes fiercely. It was after all of your doing, not mine, Skinny. I worked hard for you for many years . . . and certainly asked for little enough. It's not my business . . . how much you spend, but I do question your figures."[31] She knew that he exaggerated when he claimed to live on only fifteen dollars per week, and apparently forgotten were those assurances that should she ever need help, she was to come to him. More demeaning and humiliating yet was his questioning the expenses associated with her lingering surgical complications.

In other ways also, Helen tried to force Caldwell to confront and accept responsibilities lingering from the past. Despite the visiting rights granted him by the divorce decree, Caldwell had never returned to Mount Vernon to see the children. Repeatedly Helen urged and pleaded that he come at least briefly for their sake: "Skinny, *why* won't you come see us before you go South? The kids all miss you so much—need you too. It's cold, but your room is warm and ready for you. Please."[32] And in her closing, Helen repeated *"Please* come, Skinny." Had she herself not visited him and Kit in Darien "without hurt or rancor in her heart"? After all, she was fonder of Kit than almost any other girl she knew, and as for Caldwell himself, she would always preserve "a deep and steady affection that remain[ed] unchanged by time or circumstance."

But Caldwell refused to return to Mount Vernon either for the children's or Helen's sake. And therein was forged what was to be a familiar pattern. If the children wanted to see their father, they had to go to him.

All three of them missed Caldwell and consequently looked forward to their Darien visits. Only Pix, however, reached out to seek a common ground by writing "Skinny" long, typed letters. "Talking man to man," he requested an electric casting set for his thirteenth birthday. He had been thinking of a scout uniform but rejected it in favor of his "kind of counting on" a promise Caldwell had made.[33] Because of Pix's unhappiness in the Mount Vernon school, Caldwell had told him he could go to Fishburne, a private military school in Virginia the coming fall term.

Otherwise Pix talked of the movies he had seen, about his brother and sister, and "Fluff," the seven-toed cat the family had taken to Skinny and Kit. Before concluding with a familiar "so long, Butch," the boy made one more request. Would Caldwell write sometimes—not books, because their "bad words" made them off-limits to him—"but a letter." And as a gentle reminder of another promise apparently made, Pix counted on going to the 1939 World Fair, where his father could go on the parachute with him.

Whether or not Caldwell took Pix to the World Fair with its parachute jump is not clear, but Helen made perfectly clear that she thought Caldwell had denied him and the other two children in different ways:

> Janet had a good time but was very disappointed not to go to the Fair, as was Dabney not to have seen it thoroughly. Skinny, I wonder if you realize what a serious thing it is to break a promise to a child? Nothing you have to do is as important as keeping a promise to one of them.
>
> I am afraid that what you have done to Pixy is irremediable. You had no right to promise him last fall that he could go to [Fishburne] school this fall if you couldn't keep that promise. You can certainly afford trips to Europe, Hawaii, or China—theatres, plays, expensive houses and deluxe entertaining— but any sacrifice of your personal comfort for the kids, you will not make. You owe all of them more—you owe me much more—than you can or will ever repay. For self-gratification, you wrecked their home, their life and

mine as well as your own creative genius. No adjustment that I can ever
make will take the place of what they and we should be having, building together. Therein you failed them, betrayed them and me—.[34]

No evidence remains that Caldwell ever replied to Helen's letter or her
charges, but without a doubt they verbalized a wrenching accusation.
What defenses could he have offered had his self-righteous stoicism allowed him to admit either to himself or Helen what he truly felt? But that
he could not do. Instead, like a Greek tragedian of old, he only could
hide behind a blind, skin-drawn mask, suffering in silence those painful
realizations that neither an accusing Helen, Margaret, nor anyone else
could ever know.

Except for a faltering career and a wife whose own ambitions placed
him second among her priorities, what else did he have left? That summer of 1939 provided few compensations to offset a lifetime's losses.
Personal reaffirmations were only beginning, and the new novel was still
in progress when suddenly the children arrived for their summer visits.
Because Bourke-White was sometimes gone, he alone was expected to
accompany Janet, Dee, and Pix on World's Fair excursions. Sometimes,
in fact, he sent them there accompanied by the maid. Moreover, his
promise that Pix could attend Fishburne Military Academy in Virginia
proved premature. Then he had not anticipated that summer's purchase
of a $6,800 house in Augusta for his parents, nor the $22,000 he and
Bourke-White would spend for a lot adjoining their Darien property.
Additionally, the children's $25,000 surety trust fund, stipulated by the
divorce terms, came due that summer. During that period, the bank returned one of his checks for insufficient funds.

Other expenses also drained his accounts—the $500 invested in Sam
Byrd's production of *John Henry*, biweekly purchases of $100 savings
bonds listing Bourke-White as beneficiary. Neither had Caldwell tallied
the costs of living up to Bourke-White's social expectations. That summer he paid a tailor $400 for three suits, selected under her careful su-
pervision. The bill for five dozen bottles of wine for one of her parties
likewise proved costly. Such by-then habitual expenditures explain why
Pix had to swallow his Fishburne hopes even as Caldwell had to accom-

modate Helen's irate gibes. The total annual costs of his attending the military school would have added $960 to Caldwell's expenses.

As Caldwell tried to juggle children's visits, financial obligations, and his writing responsibilities, he further had to adjust to Bourke-White's absences. From Poughkeepsie, she sent a six-month anniversary wire: "Your wife Kitty sends this ditty to tell you Heaven dates from Silver City";[35] his own message was less poetic—"I love you," repeated fifteen times. Both knew that within less than three months Kit's scheduled European assignment would separate them for six months. This time Caldwell would not accompany her. His career demanded that he complete the book and pursue the American Folkways project. His writing identity reassumed, he would not threaten its renewal even for love of Kit.

Finally October 17, the day of Bourke-White's departure arrived, a leave-taking described by the *New York City Post*. Carrying a bouquet of red roses, Skinny accompanied Kit to the dock, where they embraced with a "long, long" kiss. With that, Bourke-White left to pursue her career while Caldwell readjusted to being alone for months. One of his first acts had been to write Helen.[36] Six days after Kit's departure she responded sympathetically, reminding him also of how seldom he wrote. How long would Kit be gone and for what purpose? She knew he would be worried and "at loose ends," but she was so pleased about the book. And possibly as much for Caldwell's sake as for the children's, Helen pleaded once more that he visit them in Mount Vernon.

All who loved and knew Caldwell well expressed concern about the effects of Bourke-White's extended assignment. Even his father wrote one of his rare letters:

> It occurs to me that it is time you've undertaken a great Southern story. You can write about the South better than you can about any section. At the same time you are not well enough acquainted with the South. You will invariably make mistakes until you get better acquainted. I suggest you come down here while Margaret is away and make a careful study of things Southern. . . . I am going to your birthplace, White Oak, on the 16th of October. Make your plans to be here at that time. I've not been very well for a few weeks and I'd like to have you drive me. The trip would be worth a great deal to you.[37]

While Ira's letter empathized with his son's personal situation, it pointed more obviously to his reservations about the quality of Caldwell's writing. Two years earlier, Carrie claimed that his being "trapped and double-crossed" by Bourke-White had caused it to suffer. Now Ira judged that Caldwell had been away from the South too long. A decade later Atcheson Hench was to confirm Ira's apprehensions, but in October of 1939, Caldwell could not have been convinced of any of their concerns. He had been alone before; furthermore, his just-delivered *Trouble in July* manuscript would stand as a disclaimer to his father's fears.

And so Caldwell, who three years before had conceded to Helen that he disliked traveling alone, left Darien to wend his way alone across America for three months. Seeking Folkway writers along the way, he stopped in Wrens and accompanied Ira to White Oak.[38] A photo of Kit that she had promised to send via Margaret Smith did not arrive there before he left. It did not await him in New Orleans either. Daily his letters reaffirmed his love for Kit, but day by day he likewise tallied complaints against Miss Smith, the secretary responsible for mailing the photograph. Almost paranoically, he accused her of always so disliking him that either ineptly or purposely she had misdirected it.

Bourke-White's various responses—first from London and later from Italy, France, Romania, Switzerland, Istanbul, Bessarabia, Yugoslavia, Syria, Bulgaria, and Turkey—attempted to appease Caldwell's distrust of Peggy Smith. More importantly, she pledged a love that made her miss him more than she could express. And on October 31, a new name appeared in one of her letters. She advised Caldwell to "Tell Patricia I dream of her too."

Because *You Have Seen Their Faces* had been inscribed to a "Patricia," she might have been the child of their dream-future. But from Bourke-White's first allusion to this particular Patricia until the first of February three months later, her future correspondence especially—and Caldwell's occasionally—pulsed with excitement and new vitality. In early November, she wrote that Caldwell's "sketch of little Patricia" had been so darling that she placed it "next to the picture of her father."[39]

Thereafter Bourke-White dreamed, perhaps with fantasies of motherhood and family long deferred—of the picnics and trips the two of them would enjoy with Patricia. She bought matching Christmas caps for Patricia and Caldwell. Little babies reminded her of Patricia though something in her bones told her she would "turn out to be a Patrick."[40] On one occasion, Kit even included Patricia's name with those of Susie and Fluffy on a letter addressed to the household cats at Horseplay Hill. A mid-January telegram addressed to Patricia Caldwell alone stated, "Have bought embroidered leather jacket for your hope chest. Tell Papa leaving Thursday for Istanbul."[41] A combination of Kit's possible pregnancy-rapture and her long absence from Caldwell inspired her Thanksgiving 1939 message: "On Thanksgiving Day, I gave thanks for my husband who taught me what love is and for Skinny who teaches me what living is."[42] Such cables and the couple's numerous letters confirmed passions as emotionally charged as those which had flowed through their initial letters three years before.

Yet that love did not blind Bourke-White to the threat that Caldwell's extended and brooding silences continued to impose upon their marriage. Probably urged either by the reality or hope of her pregnancy, Bourke-White almost immediately resumed her insistence that Caldwell seek psychological counseling:

> I will send you pictures of Patricia as I find them. But you must do something to yourself first. You must do those important things about those sides of yourself you don't know about. You must, must, must. I love you so much, but I love the good sides of my husband. . . . Getting those things fixed and realizing they have to be fixed will make the difference in the kind of future life we want to have with Patricia and all those things.[43]

Throughout the next two months Bourke-White's letters presented variations upon the same urgent theme: if their marriage were to survive, Caldwell would have to seek treatment. Finally he acquiesced to the point of agreeing to meet with Dr. Clara Thompson for an early January 1940 appointment.[44] Recognizing Caldwell's rigid pride—his aversion to psychological probing of his private space—Bourke-White continued her barrage of forceful support.

Meanwhile Caldwell continued his westerly meetings with Folkway writers, eventually arriving in Santa Fe by November 10 for a visit with

Alfred Morang. Bourke-White's picture did not await him there either. He was convinced Miss Smith lost it purposely to hurt him, a scheme in which he confessed she had succeeded.[45] Bourke-White consequently so "bawled out" her secretary that Smith wrote him a letter of apology. Everything she tried to do for him always went wrong. Macy's even refused to reimburse her the one dollar Caldwell had spent on a toaster purchased from them but repaired elsewhere.[46] During that time also Caldwell checked with Mrs. Salter, who cared for his interests in Darien. He hoped money was piling up. He had dreamed one night of saving a hundred thousand dollars in 1939, which in the light of day still could "be close to that figure."[47]

In Los Angeles—where he and Kit had spent weeks together—Caldwell's overwhelming yearning for Bourke-White made him break their prenuptial agreement. Using arguments that revealed as much about his perceptions of a writer's destiny as they did about his values, he obliquely urged her return. First he cited that book on insects she always had wanted to do. If she did not do it, someone else would beat her to it. But more importantly:

> *Books* like objects of art, are not thrown away like the morning papers. . . . It hurts me to see others doing the things you by right should do. I want my wife to be the one to produce those things of permanency. . . . You have that God-given element of scientific inquiry—it is given to only a few—and this talent, combined with your other talent, is something that nobody [else] in the world possesses. Not to use it is a sacrilege and to let others not as talented as you preempt it is unholy. . . . The world is going to be here a long, long time. A person has only a few short years to contribute his talent to it. You must not waste any time because you must do these things for Patricia's sake—she'll expect it of you. Please think about it carefully. It is the only chance we have because when we die, we'll be dead millions and millions of years.
>
> Hurry.[48]

His letter pealed with the rhetoric of puritan salvation: "God-given to only a few," "talents," "sacrilege," "unholy," and the preciousness of time. With all the strength of his creed, with the force of his essential beliefs, Caldwell called Bourke-White back to him and his strain of personal salvation.

Then and thereafter he recited those other needs that called for her early return. Since he considered her his "best friend and severest critic," he anticipated her sending some "notes of changes" that would help make *Trouble in July* a better novel. Apparently he forgot that Bourke-White was no editorial Helen. Reminding her that she had been gone almost two months, he asked when she would return. Couldn't she give him "some little word . . . to live on?"[49] Wouldn't she tell him something like that to keep him from being so despondent? Caldwell's later appeals became plaintive litanies.

He could not sleep at night. He would stop breathing if he could, so that upon her return they could do even that together. He was "hanging on day after day" waiting for the time she would come back to their lovely Darien house to give it her touch and smell and look. Yet he feared the homecoming might "be the same ole story of a stranger" when she finally returned. What was he to do with her?

He seemed to feel that if Bourke-White would but trust him with her life, that dependency "would be a very good thing for them" because he knew "a little about how to live." Once she tried it, he was convinced she would be glad she had turned herself over to him. More than any words, Bourke-White's behavior provided her response. Six weeks were to pass before she ended her assignment and returned to Darien. Obviously she would not allow Caldwell to take charge of her.

Attempting to satisfy need through movement, Caldwell remained in Los Angeles only three days before leaving for Tucson. There he visited Harry Behn, his Hollywood script-writing associate, and somehow managed to meet Sherwood Anderson, that respected writer whose example had guided his own early works. Accompanied by Anderson's wife, the three of them had spent an afternoon in the Cactus Forest, planning later to do some digging in the mountains.[50] Before they could leave, however, Caldwell became so terribly sick, that, barely lucid, he drove himself to an El Paso hospital.

Admitted on December 11 with a dangerously high fever of 107 degrees, Caldwell's condition was soon diagnosed: Chicken pox! Like the mumps earlier, this childhood illness was critical for Caldwell the adult. Despite Carrie's good intentions, her careful sheltering during childhood only deferred those physical and psychological effects of his isolation from others. Writing from his hospital bed, Caldwell asked Mrs. Salter to buy something for the children's Christmas stockings. She was to pay from "$5 to $7" each for the presents and forward them in his name to Pix, Dee, and Janet.[51] He anticipated something for Bourke-White also. Columbia Pictures was interested in film rights to *Tobacco Road*. She was not to be surprised if some day he slipped $100,000 in her stocking.

The week's hospital confinement apparently caused Caldwell to reconsider his earthly estate. Julius Weiss was to draw up a document leaving everything to Bourke-White in case of his death. Otherwise, he feared Helen might claim it.

Departing El Paso for New Orleans, Caldwell yet did not find Bourke-White's lost picture awaiting him there. Neither was it in Miami, where he had gone "to escape from friends," and to mark the New Year, the beginning of his thirty-sixth. He did receive, nonetheless, some twenty cables from Kit celebrating almost a year of that marriage spent mostly apart. Her letters also professed a continuing love even as they urged him to keep his rescheduled February 1 appointment with Dr. Thompson. Caldwell's physical illness had forced cancellation of the first meeting with the analyst, but Patricia's and their future happiness depended upon his keeping the second.

Just as his long separation from Helen had made him seek satisfaction from a Hollywood secretary, so Caldwell's distance from Kit caused him to reach out to another woman during her absence. This time it was a young college newspaper reporter who came to his hotel to interview him. Before leaving Miami Beach, he convinced her and her parents that interrupting her studies for work experience in New York would be to her advantage. Caldwell would "play good samaritan and introduce her to New York." By January 8, she had begun writing "Dear Skinny" letters.

Departing Miami to make more arrangements for the Folkways Series along the way, Caldwell returned to Darien by mid-January to find two letters awaiting him. The Miami girl, indeed was coming, but she questioned the "advisability" of her living in the house while his wife was away. Though "everything would be legitimate, so to speak" she hated to have "people waggling their heads."[52] Instead, she would find a room and job in New York. The other letter contained a much belated invitation to attend *Juno and the Paycock* with a married and attractive New York socialite.

How Caldwell responded can be guessed only from her acknowledgment. Sorry about his chicken-pox episode, she otherwise found his note "so very sweet." And what he had said—"Incredible!" Though she hoped he would "stop being lonely—somewhat," she found herself in bed with the grippe where she "thought too much."[53]

Despite Caldwell's many public denials, the loneliness that had always been a constant in his life he admitted only to those women with whom he sought relationships. It was that admission of vulnerability, his "little boy-like" forlorn appeals for comfort, that initially attracted them to that otherwise stoical man. Or so his history and their testimonials invariably reflected.

The Miami coed did come to Darien. Much, much later Caldwell uncharacteristically and economically allowed: "She was pleasant company in my loneliness."[54] Her twelve-dollar-per-week clerking position in a publishing house, plus the small amounts Caldwell advanced covered her expenses. Until Bourke-White's return, she encouraged him to call whenever he felt in the mood for a "literary *tea.*" Then, and during Kit's later absences, she visited Caldwell in Darien until August when she returned to Miami and college. Her wistful departure note concluded with what must have been a mutually provocative memory: "P.P.S. 929 Michigan Ave. [in Chicago?] Do you remember?"

Throughout the period of Bourke-White's foreign assignment, Caldwell faithfully wrote her, even after the coed had come to ease his loneliness. Bourke-White's responses, beginning in February, became remarkable through two omissions. On January 31, she had written from Rumania to tell him of buying a cape for Patricia, and not coincidentally, to remind him of his February 1 appointment with Dr. Thompson. But thereafter neither her letters nor Caldwell's ever mentioned either Patricia or Dr. Thompson again.

Almost by mutual agreement it seems, both Patricia and the necessity of Caldwell's psychiatric appointment had been erased from, or buried within, their primary concerns. The compelling speculation is that if Bourke-White indeed had been pregnant, she somehow had lost or aborted the child in what would have been at least her fourth or fifth month of pregnancy.[55] Regardless of what may or may not have happened around February 1, 1940, Bourke-White's letters never again mentioned either Patricia or the necessity of Caldwell's keeping an appointment with Dr. Thompson. Thereafter the two of them immersed themselves in their respective and only sometimes congruent careers.

Chapter 14

Because Bourke-White was not scheduled to return until mid-March, Caldwell confronted the early February reviews of *Trouble in July* alone. Most southern reviewers seethed about Caldwell's story of racism played out to its violent conclusions. Walter White, then secretary of the NAACP, wrote to express his appreciation and hopes that the work would win the 1940 Pulitzer Prize.[1] More publicly, Richard Wright, speaking through the *New Republic*, praised Caldwell's honest treatment of the evils that racist xenophobia promoted in the land where cotton had been king and the black person a slave.[2]

Discounting *Trouble*'s sensitive theme, most mainstream reviewers focused upon the book as evidence of Caldwell's definite "falling off," his reshuffling of characters and themes from his earlier fiction. Clifton Fadiman feared that repetition hinted formula.[3] But a reviewer from England more directly expressed what other reviewers merely implied. *Trouble in July* apparently marked "the end of a stage in Mr. Caldwell's development."[4] A much later critic more specifically marked the difference: "*Trouble in July* [was] more concerned with social and ethical conduct than with spiritual cravings."[5] Such critiques appeared to confirm both Ira and Helen as common prophets speaking with different voices. Either Caldwell was no longer "well-enough acquainted with the South" or indeed his obsession with Bourke-White had wrecked "his creative genius." This time, however, Ira judged more gently. The new book "was good" but Caldwell should widen his field with a great book about the middle class.

The year 1940 was scarcely the time for an author to issue anything other than his or her best work. True enough, Steinbeck, with Pulitzer Prize visions dancing in his head, had written nothing, but Hemingway shortly published *For Whom the Bell Tolls;* Faulkner, *The Hamlet;* and Richard Wright, *Native Son.* Even the old master Sherwood Anderson had spun pleasantly nostalgic webs through his *Home Town*. Thus the critics might have expected and hoped for more from Caldwell's first novel in six years.

As the reviews for *Trouble in July* appeared, Caldwell struggled with other issues. Charlie Duell wanted to discontinue the Folkways project, since he felt it was unlikely to make money for anyone. Though paid precious little for his editing chores, Caldwell stubbornly argued for the importance of such regional works that he believed would make a lasting contribution to the body of American literature. Otherwise, he worked to compile a complete collection of seventy-six short stories for inclusion in Duell, Sloan and Pearce's *Jackpot* compendium. His almost-epigrammatic comments that prefaced each piece perhaps revealed more about Caldwell's attitudes toward recent *Trouble in July* critics than about the stories themselves.

Through a stock-pedant-figure, one Professor Horatio Perkins, Caldwell attacked those who made "a profession of tearing flesh from the bone." Critics became literary scavengers who gained reputations and livings by officiously misrepresenting simplicity as mystery. At one point he chided them through the professor: if "Perkins would relax, he might at least get a little fun out of some of these stories."[6] Though Caldwell seldom responded publicly to critics, his comments in *Jackpot* shot barbed darts at those whose reviews hurt him more than his pride otherwise allowed him to admit.

As Caldwell continued to work on the *Jackpot* preface-pieces, his letters to Bourke-White anticipated her arrival. About mid-April, when the day finally came, she had been gone almost six months. If Caldwell had hoped, however, that she might rest by remaining home for a while, he was disappointed. After only a few days, she left once more, this time speaking before groups and to radio audiences about those changes shaping Europe and the Balkans. It seemed that if Bourke-White were not shooting the event, she herself wished to be the event.

Eventually, however, throughout the remainder of 1940, she and Caldwell traveled throughout America. Ostensibly gathering materials for their *U.S.A.* project, they also used the opportunity to get reacquainted with each other and their land. Bourke-White had promised from the Balkans that upon her return, they would work together and be happy. And so Caldwell, always struggling to meet the needs of his wife, wordlessly yielded once again to Bourke-White's priorities, compromising his own storytelling instincts to satisfy more urgent personal needs.[7]

Rambling the continent for six months scarcely allowed either the security or creative solitude Caldwell's best writing always required. Once he had traveled with Bourke-White beyond the Danube, but in mid-1940, they journeyed westward without any apparent plan except gaining regional diversity through momentum. Much of June they spent in Monterey, California, July in Mexico, and September, back east in Darien, but shortly afterward they were on the move once more. The Kansas harvest called them into the heartland of America, to wheat farmers and grain elevators, Oddfellows Lodges and sewing circles, small towns and railroads. As they rode atop freight trains rattling from one stop to another, they also "sat on their heels in box-cars" listening to trainmen, watching the unloading of sheep and cows, the loading of furniture and pipes—movement, with Caldwell and Bourke-White a part of it. To Cedar Rapids, Iowa, by air, and then by car to the Hutterite country of South Dakota. Omaha, Chicago—places and people as impressionistically fleeting as the Burma Shave signs that marked their passing.

After a Santa Fe visit with the Morangs, mid-November found Caldwell and Bourke-White in the Southeast—in Columbia, South Carolina, and then at the Ringling Brothers' winter quarters in Sarasota. By November 22, they roamed places as diverse as Salt Lake City, Provo, and Elko, Nevada. December 2 they spent in Tucson. Bourke-White and Caldwell were in Texarkana by December 6, but home in Darien before Christmas.

By January 3, 1941, Caldwell appeared alone in Norfolk, Virginia, and before the end of that month he spoke to one of Morang's classes in Santa Fe. If the Caldwells' background plan had been—as Bourke-White afterward implied—to experience America's geographical diversity, they certainly fulfilled it in the second half of 1940 and the first month of 1941. The static serenity of *Say, Is This the USA* does not convey the frenetic unfolding of the experiences that informed it.

Only casual hints offer clues to the state of Bourke-White and Caldwell's relationship, and of his own personal situation, during that period. Judging from the work published from that trip, Goldberg—herself a photography critic as well as biographer—thought that the photographs and texts often were incongruous; it was "as if Margaret and Erskine had been on different trips."[8] More directly on September 5, 1940, Harry Stack Sullivan's office responded to an August 22 query from Caldwell's secretary. The psychiatrist to whom Mr. Caldwell previously had been referred was Dr. Charles K. Friedburg of 1088 Park Avenue.[9] Almost certainly Caldwell's brooding silences so pained Bourke-White that she had forced him to initiate an inquiry he alone never would have considered.

That assumption is reinforced by Goldberg's careful sifting of Bourke-White's autobiographical notes, which she then uses as reinforcement for her perceptive speculations and conclusion. Caldwell's "anger and withdrawal" made Margaret feel as if

> a new ice age had settled into her life for a time of ruin and devastation. "The frigid wave surged upward. . . . once begun there was no staying it. Until hard as I tried to stay aloof—as one can do with a stranger—when so close and in the same household there is no holding apart. In retrospect that seems to have been the goal. When I was ground down to fine dust then he magnificently, with spaciousness and good humor, would raise me up." Erskine's unpredictable moods were like a strategy unconsciously devised to subjugate her, to dominate her totally through the twin masters of fear and largesse.[10]

Why then did Bourke-White remain in a marriage so often stressed, so personally devastating? Goldberg's answer is that "it could not have been only the challenge; she must also have had a profound attraction to the idea of being mastered. She who sought control in everything had long feared that achieving it confirmed the loss of her femininity. In her marriage Margaret repeatedly endured being forced into a humiliating submissive role."[11] One of Margaret's fellow staff members offered her confirming impressions: " 'She was being kind of a frightened wife, very subservient to him. He was very bad tempered, and she was trying to be the sweet wife. You'd think she was the original faded lady department if you didn't know she was Margaret Bourke-White.' "[12] But the question no one asked: if her personal equilibrium was so ravaged by Caldwell's behavior, what must he himself have been experiencing? What forces caused him to inflict so much pain upon the woman he loved, upon the woman so essential to his sense of male identity?

Caldwell's published works from that chaotic time indicate that he had not abandoned totally his storytelling instincts. The August 1940 issue of the *Jackpot* collection drew almost universal accolades. The stories proved that Erskine Caldwell was a natural among storytellers. His "gusty [sic] tales of sub-human folk" and the black-white tragic episodes stood as examples of Caldwell at his best, "a best which was excellent." The *New Yorker*'s brief review pithily summarized almost universal consensus: "First rate reading." No one could know, of course, that only "The End of Christy Tucker," "Handy," "The Aggravating Goats," and "My Old-Man Hasn't Been the Same Since" represented new stories published during that year.[13] Otherwise almost all the stories in *Jackpot* were written in those fruitful years before Bourke-White "trapped and double-crossed" Caldwell the storyteller.

Other evidence suggests that even as Caldwell traveled hither and thither with Bourke-White, he could not escape the siren song of what he estimated as his special destiny. Lieber advised against his wishes to resurrect the old *Autumn Hill* novel. During that period also, he responded sympathetically to other writers, for the past three years ignored and all-but-forgotten. To Le Garde Doughty, an old Georgia writing acquaintance, he offered empathy. To Josephine Herbst he lent a sum of money so she could finish a novel.

Somehow during that hurried October, Caldwell found time to experiment with writing a "Mexican Musical play," which came to nought. But more psychologically rewarding, his *Jackpot* work provoked acknowledgments from other writing masters. Hemingway, whom he had never had met, sent Caldwell an inscribed copy of *For Whom the Bell Tolls*. Theodore Dreiser's unsolicited letter yet more openly bowed to Caldwell's large talents. *Jackpot* reminded Dreiser of *The Spoon River Anthology*, for him, an American classic. Caldwell's collection was another, one whose stories were "full of the stupidity and aspiration of man."[14] Caldwell thought enough of this heady praise to forward a copy of the Dreiser letter to Duell, Sloan and Pearce.

Thus one might wonder what troubled Caldwell that fall and winter of 1940–41 as he followed Bourke-White's whimsy whether in the United States or Mexico. Did she recognize the costs of his accommodations? If she did not, Caldwell could not tell her. He instead anguished behind the masks of those icy silences he used to punish both himself and those who defied his control, those who failed to appreciate the sacrifices he had made for their sakes. For Margaret he painfully had abandoned wife, family, and home. For her sake he had traveled and sacrificed his writing, his own "God-given talent granted to only a few."

But with the first month of 1941, Caldwell hurried to complete the *U.S.A.* manuscript—so that he might accompany Bourke-White on an even more far-flung venture. While yet involved in the *U.S.A.* travels, she had announced that she "would like" to collaborate with him on a fourth book—this time a Russia-scape.[15] Admittedly, Russia was a portion of that "lot of world" he once had wished to see. But more compellingly, if he had not joined her, he would have been forced to accept another lengthy separation. Whatever his compulsions to write about the known and familiar, he thus once again deferred them. For the sake of remaining with Bourke-White, he chose to experience and record the exotic.

With all obligations and official clearances satisfied by mid-March of 1941, the Caldwells flew to San Francisco for their West Coast departure. There, possibly hoping to recapture some of their romance of two years before, Bourke-White and Caldwell boarded their honeymoon ship, the *Lurline,* for the sea-portion of their journey. His by-then Hollywood agent Alvin Manuel, his wife, and numerous reporters stood at dockside to wish them farewell. Marion Manuel felt sorry for Caldwell. Even though by then Bourke-White "had Caldwell dressed up pretty well" and liked "to show him off," she had seemed more concerned about her cameras than him.[16] After reaching Hawaii, the couple enjoyed a few days together in Honolulu before flying out via the China Clipper.

The trip provided the type of excitement that was Bourke-White's habitual fare, but for a Georgia boy it spelled international adventure. In Hong Kong, the pair waited a week to catch a cargo plane to Chungking.[17] There, to escape Japanese bombings, they hid in caves as they waited the eight days it took the Soviet ambassador to stamp their visas. Then a Gobi desert sandstorm forced the plane down at a Mongolian military field. That extended delay forced them to miss a weekly flight from Hami to Alma Ata. Again they waited. Finally after two days of flight and an overnight stop, they reached Moscow the first week of May 1941.

The Russians welcomed the pair as respected guests. Bourke-White had traveled there before. And because Caldwell's translated novels already had earned both substantial rubles and readers, the couple enjoyed lavish Moscow treatment and accommodations.[18] Beyond that, government-approved writers like Caldwell enjoyed privileged status. Before the disruptions of war descended upon Moscow and Russia, therefore, Bourke-White and Caldwell enjoyed caviar, vodka, champagne, and all the other amenities Russian hospitality could then provide.

Initially that must have been all that Caldwell enjoyed. During that time Bourke-White had become exasperated with him. While she roamed the city looking for faces and events to shoot, he refused to leave their room. It seemed to her that " 'he was barricading himself against new experiences and tending to withdraw into the world of his earlier activity where he felt at home . . . making a retreat to Tobacco Road.' "[19] And so indeed he was. For four weeks Caldwell stayed in his "protective shell" and looked backwards to a more satisfyingly familiar time and place. There he began to write some of those wonderfully nostalgic pieces that later would become a part of *Georgia Boy*. In their Moscow hotel room Caldwell thus tried to appease the conflicting demands of both Margaret and his muse.

Most of May the two thus spent their time waiting for travel permits. When they were finally granted, they reduced an expected more extensive itinerary to a two-thousand-mile trip to Kharkov, Tbilisi, and the Black Sea. The eruption of the Russian-German war on June 22, 1941, found Bourke-White and Caldwell at a Georgian resort at Sukhumi. With all dispatch, they rushed back to their Moscow hotel. Awaiting them there on June 28 were stacks of radiograms. As two of only a few Americans on the new war front, they were to provide almost the only on-site record of what was happening in Russia during the first two months of the conflict.

The *U.S.A.* project had forced Caldwell to march to Bourke-White's photogenic drummer. Now, however, they both kept step with the frenzied drums of the war throughout their Russian assignment and even beyond. Bourke-White resumed her duties for *Life*. Caldwell worked both as a correspondent for the North American Newspaper Alliance and as a twice daily—3:00 A.M. and 3:00 P.M.—broadcast journalist for Columbia Broadcasting Company. He also agreed to write some articles for *Life* magazine.

Deadline pressures demanded that Caldwell write hastily and yet more hastily to revise censored materials. Each night Luftwaffe planes roared over Moscow to drop their bombs. Every day Russian-citizen volunteer crews emerged from shelters to repair the damage as much as possible. Caldwell's postmidnight trips from the National Hotel to the broadcast studio became tentative gropings with headlights shuttered through darkened and bomb-pocked streets. Two weeks into his broadcast assignment, the transmitting station was destroyed beyond repair. He then continued his broadcasting from the National Hotel, no secure haven itself.

Bomb blasts and tremors lit the nightscape outside the windows. As bombs fell dangerously close to the building, the windows themselves occasionally rained in. During the frequent raids, Caldwell remained too dignified to crawl under beds. Instead he took shelter behind a sofa, where he would sit with a bearskin rug over his head and shoulders, "staring from the corner like a big Russian bear."[20] Bourke-White hid under their bed, where the Lindberghs and Trotsky had allegedly once slept.

A partial listing of subjects Caldwell covered for the CBS "World Tonight" program shows the extent of his coverage: "Moscow under war described," "Description of German bombers shot down," "Disguised air fields near Moscow," and "Heavy fighting at Pskov, Smolensk."

Wartime tensions and strains placed additional burdens upon Caldwell and Bourke-White's relationship. His silent withdrawals continued to exasperate and embarrass her. In the midst of camaraderie and drinks with fellow journalists and reporters at the National Hotel, Caldwell suddenly fell into one of his silences. This time he abruptly retreated to his and Bourke-White's room. The woman who once naively believed she could understand silent men once again stood helplessly confounded and angry.

Early in October of 1941, Bourke-White and Caldwell finally left Moscow via train for Arkhangelsk. Boarding a convoy steamer, they carefully threaded their long, cold way through the White Sea, across the Barents into the Norwegian Sea and finally to the Firth of Clyde. Winter fogs protected the ships from all but a few attacks.

In London Caldwell set immediately to work, accepting a contract from the *Daily Mail* to write seven war articles based upon his Moscow and Smolensk experiences. A messenger came daily to the Savoy Hotel to collect the accounts. Before he completed these, moreover, Hutchinson and Company asked him to expand the series for a work to be collated with Bourke-White's photographs. Within a week he had *Russia at War* ready for publication. Four days before the Caldwells' scheduled London departure, the same company offered to publish Caldwell's wartime diary as *Moscow Under Fire*. Working with his usual speed, Caldwell edited and amplified hundreds of pages of notes to finish the manuscript before the scheduled departure.

The task completed, the Caldwells flew from England to Portugal, there boarding the Yankee Clipper for New York to arrive home in Darien by the first week in November. Within the past seventeen months, they had crisscrossed the U.S.A. and had hopped from place to place around the world. Yet even during that hectic period Caldwell somehow managed to publish eleven short stories he had written under circumstances that would have confounded all but the most obsessed storytelling writer.

Their return to the states earned little respite for either Bourke-White or Caldwell. With the nation little more than a month away from its own entry into the war, radio audiences and various groups hungered for the duo's firsthand impressions and accounts. In fact on December 30 of that year while visiting the elder Caldwells, they both spoke to Ira's congregation in the Wrens ARP Church. Usually, however, Bourke-White and Caldwell appeared separately on programs to present their respective interpretations.

To fragment further Caldwell's energies, Duell, Sloan and Pearce urged that he write a book based upon his Russian radio broadcasts and news accounts. He began that project in late November. By the end of December, he had mailed the manuscript to the publishers. Wishing to capitalize upon a receptive audience, they had *All-Out on the Road to Smolensk* off the presses in February of 1942.

Three months into the patriotic fervor that gripped Americans after Pearl Harbor, reviewers almost universally approved Caldwell's contribution, one that dispassionately accentuated air raids, tank battles and a people's heroic response to war. Even more, however, it presented "a convincing, and at times exciting portrait of a people resolute and undivided battling for independence behind a competent military leadership."[21] Caldwell basked once more in the warmth of approval. The one bad review he read, he interpreted as telling more about the reviewer than about the book.[22]

Always anxious to translate experience into fiction, Caldwell began work almost immediately on a novel "about Russia at war." The national mood, the times, and Caldwell's own personal situation combined to urge such a work even in the midst of other opportunities and commitments. On his way to Texas to do a magazine piece, he stopped to give a talk in Memphis on February 22. A March 2 newspaper interview in Atlanta headlined his concern: "Invasion of U.S. by Nazis and Japs envisioned by Caldwell." By March 11, Caldwell was speaking in Cleveland, and on the twelfth, in Detroit. Both on different lecture tours, Caldwell and Bourke-White met briefly in Milwaukee on March 16. He departed for Columbus, Buffalo, Philadelphia, and Schenectady to lecture, autograph copies of *All-Out,* and sign defense stamps. In the meantime, Bourke-White went her own way to complete her speaking commitments.

Bourke-White's assignments became ever more consuming and far-reaching. With American troops fighting on the battlefields of Europe, her career demanded that she document that action for *Life*. Both Bourke-White and Caldwell realized that a parting once more was inevitable. He, therefore, tried one more tactic to get her to stay. Because she so had enjoyed Tucson, he purchased a house for her in the city's Catalina Foothills area. But she perhaps rightly felt that jealous as he was of *Life* magazine, he offered it as a bribe to lure her from the East. Unwilling to accept "another set of golden chains," she consistently evaded his requests for its color and decorating schemes.[23]

Justifiably sound though Bourke-White's suspicions were, Caldwell's motives no doubt appeared just as defensible to him. As long as she followed *Life*'s priorities, she would never fulfill her "God-given element of scientific inquiry to produce things of permanency." Furthermore, as long as he traipsed along behind her, he never would fulfill his God-given sense of destiny either. By rejecting Caldwell's offer of caring for her, teaching her how to live, Bourke-White's behavior appeared selfish and uncaring. That must have been reconfirmed for him in that spring of 1942 when Bourke-White asked *Life* for an overseas assignment. And yet she puzzled: "Erskine's frozen moods were just as unaccountable and difficult as in the beginning."[24] Upon such dissonant notes Bourke-White departed by mid-March of 1942, this time to cover the battlefields of Europe.

Placing his faith once more in his trinity of work, motion, and frequent letters to Morang, Caldwell plunged into writing his next novel, another Russian experience story to be called *All Night Long*. Interrupting that work long enough to do another Texas magazine piece, he hurriedly swung westward to visit Morang in Santa Fe. Then he returned to the Darien house, empty of all except Bourke-White's beloved cats. He wrote through sheer determination, vowing to complete the book by July 1 unless he "dropped dead before then."[25]

Except for almost weekly letters to Morang, only two matters of moment interrupted Caldwell's writing efforts. Some months before, Rhoda Lynn, his secretary of two years, had abruptly left without leaving a trace.[26] Therefore he requested that the Florida coed who had assuaged his loneliness during Bourke-White's last absence, come again to act as his secretary and editorial assistant. That she loyally did, but a few months later he thought he'd have to let her go since she was "not worth much" to him anymore. He did not do so immediately, but she obviously did not satisfy all of his needs.

The other concern revolved around Pix. Only sixteen, he had misstated his age to enlist with the marines. Although Helen and Caldwell could have remedied that situation by exposing his deception, they decided against a tactic that would only antagonize him. The best they could do was allow him his choice and hope for his safety. With that reluctant acceptance, Caldwell wearily returned to the novel. Toward the end, his mind and emotions felt so numb he could not tell whether he was coming or going.[27] According to schedule, nonetheless, by July 1, he gave *All Night Long* to Lieber for delivery to the publisher.

After that Caldwell's plans were definite. He would rent the Darien house, release the Florida girl, and head West. After visiting Morang and attending to Los Angeles business for a week, he would go to Tucson to write until the following spring. By then he hoped Bourke-White would have received a furlough from *Life*.

But even Caldwell's best-laid plans sometimes came to naught. He could not rent the house. He could not hurt the young woman by telling her to go. Leaving everything behind except her, he did visit Morang and did reach Los Angeles where he lodged at the Knickerbocker Hotel. For his companion, he rented separate accommodations.

But the week in Los Angeles stretched into three months after Al Manuel, money-tongued as usual, snared a $1,250-per-week contract for Caldwell. He was to write the script for Warner Brothers' *Mission to Moscow*. A week after finishing his latest novel, he wrote again to please others rather than himself. Manuel, in the meantime, did not rest on his commissions. Less than a week later, he talked Metro-Goldwyn-Mayer into purchasing the rights to *All Night Long* for $50,000. Despite such earnings, Caldwell occasionally still muttered to Morang about how little money he had.

Although subsequent script revisers would not give him credit, Caldwell claimed to have finished the preliminary draft of *Mission to Moscow* before his craw once more became so full that he had to leave Hollywood. Convincing the coed that her future lay there, by late September he had resumed his interrupted stay in Tucson. Thus in that southwestern autumn of 1942, Erskine Caldwell, then almost thirty-nine years old, sat before a typewriter in an empty Foothills house trying to write himself home again through fiction.

Part 4

"Grunting and Groaning—
to Win an Existence"

Chapter 15

Early autumn in Tucson offered both a change of scenery and a change of pace, both of which Caldwell apparently sought. In the words of his acquaintance Woody Guthrie, Caldwell's life had been one of "hard traveling," in every sense. The years of struggle with Helen and his travels with Bourke-White had exacted their tolls. Tucson became the place where he could make both a literary and personal stand.

Isolating himself from familiar places and faces, Caldwell planned to concentrate on his writing until Bourke-White returned. As had been Caldwell's custom when separated from Margaret, he initially bombarded her with a flurry of letters and cables. He was lonely and needed her to help him write a good book, the one he had worked on in Moscow. He needed her direction in decorating her new house. "She was his only love and always would be."[1] He was despondent because he had received no letter since September 10, no cable since the twentieth. As the days passed, his vigil became increasingly anguished. He cautioned his parents that "if Margaret failed to return by the following July," he planned "to join the army"—despite his lack of vision in one eye.[2]

In selecting Tucson as a wintering place, Caldwell placed himself in a situation not unlike his time in Wilkes-Barre: everything and everyone was unfamiliar. He knew only Harry Behn, who with the help of students, produced radio programs for the university. Wishing to introduce his student-associates to a celebrity, Behn invited Caldwell to speak to his class on October 6, four days after Caldwell had vowed to join the army if Kit failed to return. June Johnson, "the prettiest and brightest of them all,"[3] remembered the day well. Her interest was not in radio but in literature, "and her ideal was Erskine Caldwell."[4] Consequently, Harry and Alice Behn invited June to their home to have dinner with Caldwell. Shortly thereafter he reciprocated, having the three of them to his house for an evening meal.

Erskine and June Caldwell, Tucson, Ariz., ca. 1951. Printed with permission of the Estate of Erskine Caldwell and Dartmouth College Library.

Outside those occasions, however, Caldwell and June Johnson met to explore mutual interests. They rode horseback through the greasewood, as he recounts in *Call It Experience*, and they probably discussed writing during "the daylight hours on the roof-top sun-deck" of the house he had bought for Bourke-White. No matter, somehow, somewhere, the famous but now-lonely writer and the awestruck college senior came to know each other as well as their brief association allowed.

Almost two years earlier during Bourke-White's extended absence, Caldwell had met and encouraged the Florida coed to follow him East. This time he again turned to a young woman for companionship. But there the comparison abruptly halted. In Tucson he was alone in a strange place; Margaret had abandoned him, her new house, and his needs.

Shortly Caldwell's "natural urges" toppled principles along with the love he repeatedly had professed to Margaret only days before. On October 27, 1942, three weeks after meeting June, he wooed the twenty-one-year-old through a mock memorandum—"Subject: Balance Sheet"—a statement that listed all his financial assets and liabilities. His net worth of $100,451.00—including good will arbitrarily estimated at $1.00—Caldwell offered to June Johnson upon whom he wished "all his love and worldly goods to bestowe (sic)."[5] He validated the document with the signature of a fictitious notary public whose commission expired on June 19, 1999.

That Caldwell and June so hastily had become smitten with each other seems predictable in retrospect. After his loneliness in Wilkes-Barre, Caldwell had met and shortly eloped with Helen so that he might "make an honest woman of her." Bourke-White and he had fallen into each other's arms only five days into their southern assignment. Only Bourke-White's professional commitments had prevented his marrying her. And when Caldwell had met June, he had been long separated from Bourke-White and those assurances her love provided. In retrospect, June believed that Caldwell "always felt he had to make an honest woman of whomever he slept with."[6]

To Helen, Caldwell had presented himself as a smolderingly intense writer. Bourke-White found his craftsmanlike skills, "closed-door" reserve, and openness to new experience intriguing. But to June, Caldwell offered himself not only as a well-known writer but also as one who loved her enough to bestow upon her all his worldly goods. What young woman of 1942 would not have been swayed by such fealty?

Born in Toledo, Ohio, as the only child of an electrical engineer and his wife, June had moved with them first to Memphis, then to New Mexico, and finally, when she was entering junior high school, to Phoenix. There her father held various professional positions and then operated small electronics-related businesses to provide his family with a modestly respectable position. After graduating from a Phoenix high school, June had attended the local community college before transferring to the University of Arizona to pursue her literary and writing interests.

Prior to meeting Caldwell, June's familiarity with his writing had been limited to reading *Tobacco Road* and seeing Henry Hull play Jeeter Lester in the Tucson road production. Beyond that, she knew him only by reputation. Initially, therefore, she saw Caldwell as a quietly modest and caring person who, for all his fame and experience, appeared hesitantly insecure and tentative. And so he was. A secure man would not have tried to impress a young woman with a carefully tallied balance sheet of assets—unless he had intuited that June expected signs of success in addition to love. That bending to meet the expectations of yet another woman, one more significant other, was to set Caldwell on still another tangential course.

Because Caldwell had come to Tucson to write, courting June notwithstanding, he worked to complete "a combination novel and book of short stories"—the adventures of a thirteen-year-old Georgia boy and a consistent cast of characters.[7] Long in the making, he first had introduced *Georgia Boy*'s people in 1937 through "The Night My Old Man Came Home."[8] Thereafter those characters must have festered within his writing canker until they began erupting in Moscow. During that time, or perhaps even earlier, he had fashioned five of his twenty published stories around the escapades of the three central characters. The plot essentially revolves about a boy's and his shiftless father's attempts to break from the restrictive confinements of a mother-wife's expectations. A black handyman helper only humorously complicates situations not unlike those of *Huckleberry Finn* and Faulkner's later work *The Reivers.*[9]

William Stroup of *Georgia Boy* devotedly cherishes a father dominated by the righteously good wife. So badgered, Morris Stroup offers lament: "The good Lord ought never put more than one woman in the world at a time."[10] Later Caldwell was to admit that *Georgia Boy* had been pretty close to him in its writing: "It was just one of those reminiscent kind of things," about a boy who lived as he once yearned to live, and sometimes had.[11] But even as he wrote his book about free-spirited men confounded by a woman's exacting expectations, he sought to free himself from one woman so he legally might be united with another.

Caldwell advised his agent and close friend Al Manuel in mid-December not to contact Bourke-White about signing some necessary contract waivers. Some changes were "in the process of taking place," and he wanted to avoid "any matters pertaining to the lady in question."[12] Those changes, however, had begun before the end of November.[13]

On the ninth of that month—almost two weeks after his proposal to June—Caldwell cabled Bourke-White. He had "REACHED THE MOST DIFFICULT DECISION OF LIFETIME." He had "DECIDED THAT PARTNERSHIP MUST DISSOLVE IMMEDIATELY. . . . EYE AM TRULY SORRY AND UNCONSOLABLE."[14] She was to contact Julius Weiss, their mutual attorney.

Margaret responded immediately by cable. She needed more reasons for the divorce and asked him to tell her "HONESTLY IF ANYONE ELSE INVOLVED." Caldwell's response on November 12 was evasive: "EYE HAVE WAITED FOUR YEARS FOR SOMETHING BETTER THAN THIS AND THE PRESENT AND FUTURE HAVE BECOME DISMAL APPARITIONS STOP SUCH IS LONELINESS." Her farewell sadly testified to how well she knew him, how clearly she could see his true motives: " 'SUCH IS LONELINESS AND SUCH IS POETRY BUT SUCH IS NOT THE ANSWER TO DIRECT QUESTION STOP THEREFORE CAN DRAW ONLY ONE CONCLUSION AND SORRY YOU COULD NOT TELL ME OPENLY."

Five days later Caldwell applied for a Mexican visa, after first seeking

more legal advice from Julius Weiss. By December 1, 1942, Caldwell
had registered at the Hotel Reforma in Mexico City to begin his twenty-
day waiting period. From there he immediately called Weiss again.
Since he had flown to Mexico to file for divorce, he wanted the attorney
to initiate the legal proceedings required for a division of property between him and Bourke-White. Margaret's cable to Weiss a few days earlier had contained essential information and the name of a counsel other
than Weiss for the proceedings. She would not oppose either Caldwell's
actions or his offer for property settlement.[15] She agreed to his making
the December payment on the Darien house and signing over to her his
half interest. For her part, Bourke-White immediately changed her will
and insurance policies, naming her brother and sister, rather than Caldwell, as beneficiaries. Beyond that, she later shipped Fluffy—the seven-
toed cat given by his children—to him. After a six-year relationship begun with cat fights and kisses, Caldwell's and Bourke-White's marriage
ended with a whimper.

How Bourke-White truly felt about the end of what had been both an
exciting, yet painfully taxing, relationship, no one really knew. Peggy
Smith-Sargent had heard that she "was ravaged by Erskine's abandonment."[16] It is difficult to know from whom she could have heard that. To
her casual associates Margaret did not even mention the breakup. In her
letter to Julius Weiss she was carefully reasoned:

> I suppose by all the rules governing what is considered proper for a lady in
> these circumstances I should have felt desperate and devastated. My one
> feeling was relief. I have felt for so long that such a disproportionate amount
> of my attention went into worrying about whether someone was in a good
> mood or not, whether he would be courteous or forbidding to others,
> whether day to day life would be liveable at all on normal terms, that I am
> delighted to drop all such problems for the more productive one of photo-
> graphy.[17]

She later confided to Caldwell's mother that she had not mourned the
break. For a long time their interests had been heading "in different directions," and she felt that Caldwell would be happier after the divorce
as she, "certainly—without any doubt," was.[18]

While Caldwell waited in Mexico City for the Cuernavaca divorce to become final, he did not waste his time "doing nothing." By December 16, he had "finished the book" as he had come there to do. The *Georgia Boy* manuscript, scheduled for spring 1943 publication, signaled that Caldwell had resumed his writing career. To do that, however, he had reached through space and time from Moscow to Tucson via Mexico City back to Georgia, telling through memory stories of people he once had known.

Judging from the reviews of Caldwell's just-published war novel, *All Night Long,* he had returned to the South as his writing territory none too soon. Most critics generally concurred with Margaret Marshall's estimation offered in *The Nation.* She regretted to say that *All Night Long* was one of the worst novels she had ever read. Though the Book League of America patriotically selected it for a member issue, not even Hollywood eventually capitalized upon its fifty-thousand-dollar investment.

While Caldwell wrote in Mexico City, June remained the lady-in-waiting in Tucson. On December 15, she purchased and sent a Christmas gift to Caldwell's nine-year-old daughter, Janet. But by the twentieth of that month the waiting was over. On that day, Caldwell checked out of the Hotel Reforma with the decree in hand.

For little more than twenty-four hours he remained an unwed man. On December 21, 1942, four days after his thirty-ninth birthday, Caldwell married June in a ceremony performed by a minister in Tucson's Central Methodist Church. Only June's parents and a few of June's friends attended. This sparse, traditional gathering, nonetheless, was the largest to witness any of Caldwell's legal bindings to the three women he had loved enough to marry.

This time, however, there were no burlesque shows in Baltimore or a long honeymoon in Hawaii. Instead June moved with Caldwell directly into the house he had purchased for Bourke-White. A two-day business trip took them to New York. Before their scheduled January 8 departure for Caldwell's proposed six-week lecture tour, Al Manuel called. Disregarding any breach-of-contract suits, they were to catch a train for Hollywood immediately. Al had negotiated a $1,500 per week script-writing contract for Caldwell with Twentieth Century Fox.

Less than three weeks after their marriage, the newlyweds had settled into the finest hotel Hollywood had to offer—the Beverly Wilshire. The impressive accommodations testified to the promise implied in that balance-sheet account Caldwell had offered as a courtship gesture. As an additional assurance to June, he had, since meeting her, finished a new book and snagged one of the largest writing contracts in Hollywood.

And Caldwell himself could feel securely pleased. This time his wife was neither in Mount Vernon with the children nor on the battlefields of Europe. Rather June was with him to provide the womanly assurance and comfort he required. Two days after arriving in Hollywood with his new wife, Caldwell confessed his satisfaction to Morang: "I'm mighty glad I did what I did on December 21st, because now I'm feeling right for the first time in my life. I'm sorry it didn't happen sooner."[19]

Although June perhaps initially felt like a princess in a Hollywood tower, she soon realized that such a position is not necessarily an envied one. While Caldwell hobnobbed with studio stars, attended parties, and shared his travel experiences with reporters, June stood either at his side, or aside, as an attractive appendage. Even the expensive Hollywood shops must have lost their appeal after a few weeks of browsing. Although Caldwell himself could get along in Hollywood "for two or three months at a time," he soon acknowledged that "June [didn't] like it there, and want[ed] to go back to Tucson."[20]

By March even Caldwell had tired of the Hollywood scene. Finagling a week's leave from the studio, he and June took a hasty trip to New York, stopping back en route to see Morang in Santa Fe. Although Morang still painted, wrote, and taught art in his studio, his and Dorothy's fortunes had not improved. Despite Caldwell's monthly subsidies, he often wrote to request an additional ten to twenty dollars for living essentials or art supplies. Most recently, one of Morang's Santa Fe friends had written confidentially to Caldwell. Morang had been sick, and unless the friend could forestall it, the Morangs would be evicted. Then, as always, Caldwell came to his friend's assistance. But in late March of 1943, he apparently wished not only to visit Morang but also to introduce him to June. Never one to lodge overnight with either friends or relatives, he, as usual, stayed at the La Fonda Hotel, but this time with June.

Upon their return to Hollywood, the Caldwells forsook their expensive suite at the Beverly Wilshire for more modest lodgings at 9118 Sunset Boulevard. With a concern become habit, Caldwell complained that the two of them were "practically living on bread and water" since he had to "scratch up $33,000 somewhere" for last year's taxes.[21] Although during the past eight years *Tobacco Road* royalties and other earnings brought Caldwell's yearly income to almost $100,000, he had saved little.

After the frugality of his years with Helen, he had learned to accommodate Bourke-White's lavish tastes. He had paid his share of their travel expenses while a *Life* expense account supported accommodations dictated by her expensive habits. And because she ordered tailor-made clothing in abundance, so had Caldwell. His careful lifetime habits had all but eroded as he had tried to keep in step with Bourke-White's splendid style. Yet even as he had accepted her "pound foolish" displays, he salved his conscience with "penny wise" practices. During the same week he purchased five dozen bottles of wine for a party, he rejected as too expensive a stonemason's bid of $260 for laying some two hundred feet of stone-fence. And even as he dreamed of saving $100,000 in 1939, he sought reimbursement for a one-dollar repair bill on a toaster.

Yet in other ways more crucial to his writing, Caldwell's associations with Bourke-White and comfortable affluence had changed his habits. The drinking of hard liquor, begun in her company, persisted through California parties and weekend Las Vegas trips with Al Manuel and friends. While married to Helen, Caldwell had lived frugally in Mount Vernon or in brown-front basement rooms with the impoverished as he wrote his stories about the poor. By the time he had married June, however, he had chosen to live at the Beverly Wilshire while he tinkered with other people's stories. Never after was Caldwell to live hungry and share poverty with the poor; he would only write about them from a comfortable distance.

After his New York–Santa Fe break, Caldwell returned to Hollywood to continue his $1,500-per-week chores for Fox. After finishing the script for *Grand Street Boys*, he worked on another for *The Russian People* and other miscellaneous war movies. But by the end of September,

Caldwell had had enough. He was "anxious to get away" to start a story of his own since he was "pretty sick of other guys' stories after nine months."[22]

The April publication of *Georgia Boy* met with the most universally positive fiction reviews Caldwell had earned since becoming involved with Bourke-White. Familiar though the book's landscape and characters were, its vision was not. Reviewers praised Caldwell's storytelling skills. According to one reviewer, not since reading *Huck Finn* had he met a more companionable storyteller than William in *Georgia Boy*.[23] Even the *Library Journal* recommended it. Others believed Caldwell to be back on track to fulfilling his early promise. And although his most recent offering paled in comparison to *Tobacco Road*, it was "the real thing."

Finally, before the end of October 1943, Caldwell broke free of Hollywood so that he and June could depart for Tucson. Having sold Bourke-White's house during their absence, they had purchased another located in the Catalina Foothills Estates. Her last two months in Hollywood June had spent working with Tucson decorators to furnish and appoint the house. Her reward came a few months later. A local paper featured the Caldwell residence as an example of good taste and gracious living. Apparently without complaint, Caldwell promptly paid the bills and adjusted to her orderliness, just as he had before to Bourke-White's domestic casualness.

After his extended hiatus working other people's words into script, Caldwell plunged into his writing with the energy of a destiny too long postponed. By the end of March 1944, therefore, the manuscript that was to be *Tragic Ground* was ready either "to be copied or tossed into the wastebasket." This time Caldwell told a story of red-clay rustics who are lured to a city with the promise of wartime jobs. Unskilled, uneducated, and unemployed, the Douthits are as victimized as the Lesters were by economic and social forces beyond their understanding. God-hungers no longer offer hope; they yearn but to return home to the land. Otherwise confused and lost, the Douthits are stranded victims ministered to only by unfeeling social workers.[24]

Speaking through *Tragic Ground*, Caldwell, who had lived in Maine and Connecticut before coming to Arizona, has a character say, "You just can't keep digging a man up by the roots and setting him down in different parts of the country and expect him to be satisfied for the rest of his life."[25] Yet before the end of that March 1945, Caldwell and June relocated yet again. Al Manuel had negotiated a year's script-writing contract with Twentieth Century Fox. For a figure of over a hundred thousand dollars, Caldwell once again agreed to return to Hollywood.

But the Caldwells had barely settled into their Los Angeles residence before the long-familiar Caldwell-versus-producer disagreements took an unfamiliar turn. After less than a month, a Fox executive decided the studio had had enough. "Caldwell was a complete loss to Fox," because everything he wrote was unusable and because none of the producers wanted to work with him.[26] Twentieth Century wanted to settle the contract. Caldwell inflexibly rejected their nominal offer. Six months later he finally accepted an amount that would provide for "a good year's living." In the interim he had turned down an offer from MGM, hoping to be "free of Movietown for all time."[27]

More than the completion of *Tragic Ground* and contract difficulties had consumed Caldwell's energies since the beginning of 1944. His father and a brother-in-law had wished to purchase an Allendale, South Carolina, weekly and two other allied weekly papers. They had asked Caldwell to provide the twenty thousand dollars and remain as the majority stockholder. Aware of his father's lifelong interest in newspapers, Caldwell did not refuse him. By mid-February he thus made Ira Sylvester's dream a reality. And before midsummer, another reality made itself known: he and June were to have a baby before year's end.

Before the Caldwells could anticipate an addition to the family, however, they had to mourn the demise of another family member. Although Ira's health had been failing since 1937, his death on August 18, 1944, nonetheless, shocked the family and the many others who loved and respected him. As they returned him to the earth in Prosperity, South Carolina, all were there—Helen, Pix, Dee, and Janet—except Caldwell. Although he had tried diligently to gain airline priority during a period of wartime travel restrictions, he had failed.[28]

Personally inexpressive as Caldwell was, none of his remaining letters ever mentioned any grief for his father. Only in later years did Caldwell translate—through *Call It Experience, Deep South,* and various other autobiographical works—the sense of loss he had felt with Ira Sylvester's death.

During that period also, Duell, Sloan and Pearce issued a short-story volume edited by Henry Seidel Canby. In his introduction to *Stories by Erskine Caldwell,* Canby argued convincingly that Caldwell's stories placed him within the ranks of Irving, Hawthorne, and Poe as one of the nation's most distinguished storytellers. Yet despite other similar recognition of his talents in that genre, Caldwell had, by then, all but abandoned that format. In the decade between 1942 and 1952, he published only one short story, "Sylvia," in 1944. Why he forsook the short story for so long is speculative at best. As he was to claim, perhaps he had tired of that particular challenge. But more pragmatically, he most likely realized that short stories published singly earned little and collections not much more. For whatever reasons, commencing with *Georgia Boy,* Caldwell published only novellas almost annually until 1953. The autobiographical *Call It Experience,* published in 1951, provided the lone exception.

The October 1944 publication of *Tragic Ground* gathered solidly favorable but muted reviews. *Tragic Ground* had the sort of theme in which Caldwell excelled; "His heart was still in the backlands," as one reviewer observed, and another commented, "For those who liked strong humor or raw sex," there could be no question of *Tragic Ground*'s merit.[29] But like the book's characters and theme, reviewers' comments appeared to have worn thin through repetition.

Possibly more telling than any reviewer's response to *Tragic Ground,* however, had been Caldwell's own concern about the worth of his most recent novel. Not since he had agonized over the merits of *Journeyman* had he written to Morang or anyone else with as much doubt regarding the quality of his writing. Once more his concerns spun around questions and convictions unexpressed for a decade. When the work first appeared, he admitted that it wasn't much, or at least it wasn't as much as he'd have liked for it to be. Someday, Caldwell allowed, he might write a book that would satisfy him, but the trouble was that if he did, no one else would be satisfied.[30]

A short time later, Caldwell continued his musings. He mulled the dilemmas of a conscientious writer. When a book was finished, he was "pretty well full of it," not able to read it with a critical eye. Six months later, he would reread it only to recognize that "the thing was all thumbs." The ideal would be to write a work, put it away for a year, and then reread it, but if that were practiced, the book might be thrown "in the waste basket," leaving the writer nothing to publish. Ultimately Caldwell accepted the reality that the best a writer could do was "to plug along, doing the best" he could to write "one book after another, and God willing, at the end of fifty years maybe one book of the lot would be worthwhile."[31] For the rest of his life he was to do just that.

Such private realizations not withstanding, Caldwell again leaped to reviewers' baits with all the vigor of an all-but-forgotten literary righteousness. Caldwell could admit to himself the shortcomings of his books, but other criticisms drew his ire as they had not since before his meeting Bourke-White. At those few who categorized *Tragic Ground* as a "dirty book," he privately leveled his wrath. Sure the book had been dirty, in the same sense that people are dirty, but to him there was no such thing as dirtiness. People are what they are, and making them appear different would label the writer a fraud. Real people did not enjoy only the good, highly polished things of life, and because they had to "grunt and . . . groan in an effort to win an existance [*sic*], it [was] not always pleasant to watch or to hear about."[32] But if making a story real made it dirty, then he stood guilty since he could not be a fraud. Caldwell did not pretend that *Tragic Ground* was a great book—"the greatest ever written—" because he knew it wasn't. Nonetheless, he knew that it was "not dirt for dirt's sake any more than it [was] art for art's sake." In this work, as in his others, he merely had tried "to reveal life."

Only E. B. Burgum, writing for the *New York Times* won Caldwell's approval.[33] Because he alone caught that moment of transcendent power that lighted each of Caldwell's better novels, his observation is worth summary and expansion. *Tragic Ground*, better than any of Caldwell's other works, directed attention "to those more serious emotions which are always to be found beneath the comic exterior." By way of example, Burgum used one of the novel's most sensitive scenes. Returning home from an evening's casual soliciting, thirteen-year-old Mavis is

tired. Her father, afraid that upbraiding her might cause her to leave
again, "talks to her, as though she were still an innocent child." Her
crust of hardness, her pretense of maturity, dissolved and she fell asleep
on the bed as she had in an earlier time.

Though Burgum did not acknowledge it, similar moments likewise
shimmered through those other novels wherein Caldwell's characters
grunted and groaned to win an existence. Jeeter Lester in *Tobacco Road*
had remained transfixed by the memory of Pearl's eyes, "early in the
morning before the sun . . . threw too much light in them." Ty Ty Walden mourned for his children like an Old Testament figure, gazing
across God's little acre, keening, "Blood on my land. Blood on my land."
In *Journeyman*, God's abandoned and ragged clowns stared through a
barn-wall crack to marvel about feeling "like heaven can't be so dog-
gone far away." That Burgum, therefore, saw through *Tragic Ground*'s
"dirty situations," to its essential dignity—in fact, declared it the best of
all Caldwell's novels—only could have boosted Caldwell's spirits.

But before Caldwell had a chance to pursue the writing ambitions
stirred by the success of *Tragic Ground*, a host of personal situations
fragmented almost a year's time. He taped Treasury Department an-
nouncements and traveled the Southwest signing Defense Stamps at
War Bond rallies. With a pained bemusement, he read of the Boston
judge who had dismissed the pornography complaints lodged against
Tragic Ground. In the magistrate's opinion, the book was dull, "one you
had to chain yourself to a chair to read."[34] But on a more positive note,
Jay Erskine Caldwell was born on December 28, 1944. Although a nurse
would help June care for the child until he entered school, no doubt his
birth called for some major household readjustments.

Mingling with such distractions were worries about Carrie. Because
her friends were in the area, she had decided to continue teaching in
Wrens. She would defer living with Caldwell and June until later. He
agitated additionally about some of the problems his uncle experienced
in trying to run the South Carolina newspapers. And the year had barely
begun before Alvin Manuel again dangled golden chains before him. A
fledgling company, Electra Picture Corporation, offered two thousand
dollars per week for Caldwell to adapt Thomas Wolfe's *Look Homeward,*

Angel. He agreed, if Arthur Ripley, a company co-owner, would come to Tucson since Caldwell refused to return to Hollywood. That settled, he scarcely had begun writing before the Caldwells hurried to Pensacola, Florida, where Pix was stationed.

Torpedoed and wounded off the coast of Casablanca two years earlier, Pix had been reassigned to the Florida base through Bourke-White's influence with the military.[35] There, already decorated but only eighteen and confused, he had sought his father's direction and aid as he coped with coming of age. This time Caldwell came, at considerable personal sacrifice, when Pix needed him.

When the Caldwells returned to Tucson, they found Ripley sitting "at the Santa Rita yelling for something to read."[36] Before a month had passed, business called Caldwell and June to New York. While he was gone, Ripley seethed. Caldwell was too often absent and what he did write proved unacceptable. In short, Thomas Wolfe, Erskine Caldwell, and Arthur Ripley just did "not make bed fellows."[37] Again, Caldwell refused the negotiated compensation. He simmered with resentment for six months before he won the settlement he demanded.

Unable to write among such confusion, Caldwell packed himself, the family, a nurse, and a domestic couple to a rented ranch in the lakes region some twenty miles from Tucson. There he settled down to a "six-hours a day, six days a week" regimen of writing another novel. That readjustment was not easy. It was at such times that he kicked himself "for not learning bricklaying at an early age."[38]

The uninterrupted writing time Caldwell had anticipated at the ranch became too often interrupted. For one thing, he continued stewing about the Electra situation. For another, in Tucson proper, June had kept busy with Women's Junior League activities and miscellaneous volunteer activities. Too distant for such involvements while in the country she then had turned to writing. In another time, Helen had acted as Caldwell's adviser-critic; he now accepted that role for June.[39] Before that autumn was over, June had published her first story, "Frances," in the winter issue of the *Arizona Quarterly*.

Summertime on an Arizona ranch also invited visits from Caldwell's other children, Dabney and Janet. Dee, by then a freshman English ma-

jor at Bowdoin, shortly was scheduled for induction into the marines' in-
telligence section. During his brief visit, nonetheless, he and his young
stepmother appreciated each other almost as peers. Twelve-year-old
Janet stayed longer. At one point, Caldwell objected to her riding horseback with a local rancher's daughter.[40] It was then that he discovered
that the little girl he never had a chance to know well had become a person with a strong will of her own.

Such distractions, combined with wartime shortages, kept them confined to the ranch and made Caldwell vow "never again" before summer's end. Not knowing whether the book that was to be *House in the
Uplands* was "good, bad, or indifferent," he nevertheless kept grinding
away through August. At times he felt as if he could quit and live off a
rich wife, if he had a rich wife.[41] But as he wrote, he promised himself
rewards that, along with almost everything else, had become wartime
scarcities.

Always addicted to travel by automobile, Caldwell found those war-
time restrictions especially trying. But with the Japanese surrender on
August 14, 1945, he looked forward to resuming his customary travels.
If the book were finished, he planned to attend a Dallas Book Fair in
November, fly to New York in December, and to go to Miami in January.
Before the year was done, Caldwell told Morang, he and June hoped to
resume their too-long-interrupted visits.

During the almost three years of their marriage, Caldwell and June
apparently had settled into a relationship of unspoken compromise and
mutual acceptance. He tried to hide his annoyance about her numerous
social activities and telephone calls; she attempted to cope with his
moody silences. Provided with a nurse for Jay's care and domestic help
for other chores, she could accompany Caldwell as he always wanted. In
other ways as well Caldwell silently spoke his love. Never before a gregarious sort who needed elite social-club camaraderie, he joined and
helped found such groups after marrying June. Enrolled in both the
Tucson Country Club and the Press Club, Caldwell went so far as to
write skits for the latter's amateur shows. He became a charter member
of the local Saddle and Sirloin Club.

Erskine and Jay Caldwell with Crackerjack, Tucson, Ariz., 1946. Printed by permission of June Caldwell Martin, Tucson.

Such associations naturally enough encouraged business ventures. Caldwell joined with his father-in-law to purchase an electrical contracting company in October of 1945. Shortly thereafter he selectively purchased undeveloped real estate properties, and over the next two years became a majority stockholder and functioning board chairman of the local KCNA radio station. Though Caldwell had previously purchased stock during his later years with Helen, never before had he become as directly involved in business situations so unrelated to his writing career.

His activities of the next few years also reflected departures from Caldwell's previous behavior. He encouraged, and seemed to enjoy, parties and social gatherings in the home. Consistently, according to June, he had acted the perfect host as he mingled from group to group, telling stories and generally appearing to enjoy the attentions his reputation

Alfred Morang, Santa Fe, N.M., ca. 1950. Printed by permission of Z. B. Con-
ley, Jr., the Jamison Galleries, Santa Fe.

Jay and June Caldwell, Tucson, Ariz., 1946. Printed by permission of June Caldwell Martin, Tucson.

brought.[42] That stiff and sometimes silent man that Bourke-White described had become a consciously different person during his early years of marriage to June.

In other more symbolic ways, Caldwell's patterns likewise apparently changed as he bent to the expectations of a young woman he had wooed with a statement of financial account. Always, like his father before him, he had purchased and driven Ford automobiles. Yet as soon as cars became available again after the war, he had bought a Lincoln Continental for June and a Ford for himself. Soon Caldwell was driving a Cadillac while June zipped around Tucson in her Corvette.

Chapter 16

The anticipated Dallas Book Fair trip and the later one to New York were more than pleasure excursions. They marked the beginnings of a literary-business venture that was to bring Caldwell more fame—and literary notoriety—than ever he had enjoyed before. Those two trips introduced him to the mass-marketing techniques and demands associated with his entry into the then-infant paperback-publishing industry.

A few years before, Kurt Enoch, a young Nazi-displaced German editor, and Victor Weybright, a wealthy Maryland native, had combined talents and resources to purchase the unprofitable Penguin line from the British firm Ballantine. They planned various tactics to stimulate their sales. They would offer titles with popular appeal under the Penguin insignia and more traditionally respectable books under the Mentor standard. Catering to Americans' fascination with pictures, Enoch wished to make a book's "sales-pitch" as accessible as the cover itself.[1] Glossy cover photos would do that.

Without any distribution system of their own, the partners contracted first with Curtiss Publishing, and later with Fawcett Books, to place the Penguin-Mentor editions. Accordingly, their attractively packaged and invitingly priced twenty-five-cent books would appear on the magazine racks and stands in popular locations such as drugstores, transportation depots, and newsstands. These innovations promised to appeal to an untapped market—people whose schedules, interests, and economic levels did not include bookstores among their essential stops.

Without writers of their own, Enoch and Weybright approached traditional publishers about purchasing reprint rights to books by established authors under their contracts. Negotiating through Max Lieber with Duell, Sloan and Pearce, they thus acquired paperback reprint rights to all of Caldwell's fiction. Mickey Spillane and Ian Fleming were also to be consistent winners in their stable of popular thoroughbreds. The authors themselves were to receive an initial fifty thousand dollars plus a small percentage—one to two cents on twenty-five cent editions—of the wholesale book sales. The arrangement proved to be financially profitable for all concerned.

There were dangers, however, for a writer of Caldwell's literary reputation. Name association with inexpensive reprints known for their arresting cover-pictures and unconventional merchandising and distribution methods were but some of the disadvantages. There were, nonetheless, compensations. Millions of readers would spend a quarter to read what they had not been able to afford in hardcover editions. Caldwell, Spillane, and Fleming would become pioneers in democratizing the modern novel in America.

Many literary elite never would forgive Caldwell for allowing his unwashed characters to mingle so cheaply and promiscuously with the undiscriminating masses. But Caldwell could not have known that at the time. Even if he had, he most likely would have scorned such considerations as unworthy of a person who wrote stories about common people for common people.

Caldwell's November 1945 trip to the Dallas Book Fair had been but the first of what were to be many such personal appearances to promote his books. Time consuming and demanding though such stints were, Caldwell perhaps accepted them as necessary evils. At the time, he was one of America's few serious authors who supported himself and others exclusively with direct and indirect earnings from his writings. Beyond the cost of those life-style comforts he and June had come to expect, others periodically depended upon him for support. As in Morang's instance, he always had offered his mother supplements, first, to her sparse salary and, later, her retirement benefits. He continued to provide support payments for his younger children. Beyond that, Caldwell generally responded favorably to Dabney's requests for college-expense money and to Pix's often-strained financial situations. At times it must have seemed to Caldwell that as his writing efforts became more strenuous, his financial obligations grew heavier.

Writing had come easily to Caldwell early in his career. *Tobacco Road* and *God's Little Acre* literally spilled pell-mell from a combination of experience and desire. Yet writing his most recent, *A House in the Uplands*, had consumed the last six months of 1945. Reviews in April of 1946 did little to support the religious dictum that "a man will be rewarded according to his labors." Only two among the host of critical responses could be construed as positive. One writer observed that the book was almost classic, with a compactness like that of a Shakespearean tragedy. The other felt that, like Caldwell's other books, the *Uplands* novel appeared well constructed and well paced, but tempered this faint praise with the warning that only "so many crops of cotton or harvests of fiction" could be gathered off "one of God's gullied little acres."

The even harsher reviews beat a yet more painfully strident tattoo. "Frivolous" and "unconvincing," the book seemed but "a calculated attempt to produce a sensation in sales." Caldwell had been "too good a writer to so indulge himself." The *New Yorker* critic judged *Uplands* to be the most disastrous piece of pretentiousness he ever had read by an author of presumably "serious intentions."[2] Caldwell might have gained some solace, however, from a fan letter. The woman claimed that her husband had seen himself in the villainous Grady Dunbar. Reading the book made him a reformed man, thanks to Erskine Caldwell.[3]

Those numerous and affirming fan letters that followed each paperback issue of his books may have offered some consolation for the Professor Perkins–type gnashings. Otherwise, he might have realized the truth of Ira's caution that Caldwell had been away from the South too long. During his absence the region had changed by more than the military airfield that had paved the Tobacco Road area. Other southern writers emphasized those transitions. Looking beneath the surfaces, they gazed more deeply to tell, with more-modulated voices, stories that explored the mysteries of human hearts in conflict with themselves. During the same month that *Uplands* appeared, Eudora Welty published *Delta Wedding*, and Carson McCullers, her *Member of the Wedding*. And before long, other southerners—Truman Capote, Flannery O'Connor, and Richard Wright—would be writing about Caldwell's South in a new manner, with a different emphasis. Increasingly his books would provoke charges of his literary plowing of the same eroded fields of memory.

Though the war's end emphasized those changes that had divorced Caldwell from his once-familiar South, people were now anxious to read about the countries that had been involved in their wartime victories and defeats. Publishers in Europe—France, Italy, England, the Eastern European countries large and small—and South America as well, printed translations of Caldwell, Steinbeck, Hemingway, Faulkner, and others. And perhaps because his writing style, with its directness and democratic concerns, translated so easily, Caldwell's writings were foremost among them all. But in 1946, he could not know of the international fame that would offset America's neglect.

Placing critical disdain behind, Caldwell hurried in that spring of 1946 to place other business in order so that by the end of May he and June would be ready for their first trip abroad together. He completed corporate arrangements to purchase the Catalina Broadcasting Company with its then-promising television possibilities. He cultivated his interests with local businessmen, whom June believed he "infinitely preferred" above the local literary people.[4] All interests attended, including Jay's care during their absence, the Caldwells departed for a two-month excursion to Latin America.

Throughout their journey, whether in Cuba, Peru, or Brazil, the patterns were to be the same. Pictures of Erskine Caldwell and the beautiful young Mrs. Caldwell departing their plane splashed across the front pages of newspapers. Interviews about his work, and reviews of his books appeared with predictable regularity. Then as ever later, meetings with the press, editors, and agents consumed the time that others might have used for relaxation. Instead each day became a regimented exercise in exhaustion: radio—and later, television—appearances, sessions with local writing groups, embassy parties, and whatever other functions Caldwell's editors and agents had arranged for their famous client. Breaks from his ordinary routine they were, but carefree they were not.

After returning to Tucson by the end of July, Caldwell plunged into his more-familiar work routine. During his absence, his partners in the Catalina Broadcasting venture had brought the project to the point of being operational.[5] Enoch and Weybright had also done their work. Their twenty-five-cent Penguin edition of *God's Little Acre* approached the million mark in sales. He learned with satisfaction that the *Caldwell Caravan* potpourri—*Tobacco Road* and *God's Little Acre*, plus twenty short stories with a brief introduction by the author—was headed toward its second printing in August of that year. Some of his introductory comments were aimed perhaps both at defusing the critics and explaining his writing intentions. He had no delusions about his artistry. Without any earthshaking importance, his writing was intended to do only one thing—to tell stories, or else something had gone "wrong somewhere." About one thing Caldwell assured the *Caravan* readers: the pieces were "readable, honest, and the result of hard work."[6] His criteria for evaluation and justification were telling. Readability and integrity—signed by hard work—marked good writing.

Caught up in the details surrounding the opening of KCNA–TV and other business transactions, Caldwell did not sit down to write another novel until the first day of 1947. Necessary distractions associated with the radio station and one or two other things "kept him in a stew" as he worked hard to write. After Pix's release from the service, he had gone to Mount Vernon to live with Helen and Norm Cushman. By 1947, however, he had come to live briefly with June and Caldwell while he worked as an instructor at a military school in Tucson. The responsibilities and confusions associated with Pix's readjustment to civilian life perhaps contributed to what Caldwell felt as he labored over his novel. After three and a half months, "working on it from 9 to 5 it had become all a big blur."[7] He planned, nonetheless, to complete it by June 1.

Probably allowing some leeway in his projections, Caldwell that past January had already scheduled an August 1 European departure as a reward for his hard work completed. Then he and June would enjoy a four-week trip to London and Paris. Once again he complained to Morang about his "begging and borrowing" the necessary travel money somewhere. Against that lament he offered consolations. Projected end-of-the-year estimates indicated that Penguin's sales for *God's Little Acre* would reach the three million mark. *Tobacco Road*, issued only in mid-March, promised to add another million to the grand total. Without a doubt, Enoch and Weybright had come up with a successful combination. Caldwell's reputation, the provocative four-color covers, and an aggressive distribution system had earned big money for their company. For Caldwell it meant a modest amount of wealth and an immodest degree of fame mixed with notoriety.

Not only his past work accounted for the flood of dollars that increasingly flowed from Caldwell's paperback sales. His personal and career costs just as surely directly contributed to their measure. As a portion of his agreement with Enoch and Weybright, he had agreed to help them promote his books. Accordingly, even as he struggled "in a big blur" to write his next novel, between April and September of that year he attended distributors' promotional meetings in Detroit, New York, and twice in Chicago. Beyond delivering brief talks, the workhorse author was expected to do little more than meet and shake the hands of those newsdealers who tended the racks for Curtiss Publishing Company. The books of a famous hail-fellow-well-met author certainly would merit first-rack display prominence rather than back-stack limbo.

Neither the aggressive publishers, their merchandisers, nor Caldwell himself had considered the long-range costs such tactics exacted. Each marketing meeting eroded the crucial time, energy, and creativity that Caldwell's present writing required. Like the sharecroppers of Caldwell's early works, no one recognized that creativity, like the land itself, feeds upon rest. Career-regeneration required more than merchandising-guano; it demanded fallow periods of unbroken creative time.

Increasingly those flurried activities of the past decade combined to shatter the uninterrupted writing growth Caldwell had once so jealously nurtured in Mount Vernon. Hollywood stints, travels with Bourke-White, Tucson business concerns, and finally those activities promoted by his paperback publishers all conspired against the solitude so essential to his best work. Caldwell recognized that those demands exhausted his creative genius. Occasionally he yearned for a quiet retreat such as it had been his "good fortune to enjoy in Mount Vernon for years."[8]

Lacking a comforting and productive retreat, Caldwell, nonetheless, drove himself to complete his annual novel, and mailed the manuscript for *The Sure Hand of God* to Duell, Sloan and Pearce before August 1, 1947. Then he and June departed as scheduled for London, Paris, and

other European cities. There, as in South America before, the public all
but lionized Erskine Caldwell. Daily papers printed pictures of the celebrity and his young wife; he appeared as a featured guest on radio interview shows, and was quoted and feted as a respected literary figure. In
addition to Caldwell's earlier releases on the Continent, his English
publisher issued *Georgia Boy*, and a French house, *Trouble in July*, to
coincide with his trips to those respective countries.

And in both nations, as in America more than a decade earlier, then-
current stage versions of *Tobacco Road* won him a recognition even
broader than his books might have claimed. Later in Czechoslovakia,
moreover, the people greeted Caldwell as a fondly remembered guest.
Since his earlier visit, recent translations of *Tobacco Road* and *Southways* had added to the fame—and nontransferrable royalties—that
God's Little Acre had brought him over the past decade. As tightly scheduled and exhausting as this and subsequent trips proved to be, he relished them. Appearing reticent and socially withdrawn, he yet savored
that expression of literary acclaim too often denied in his native land. As
Kurt Enoch was to observe, Caldwell "wanted to entertain you like a star
and be treated like a star."[9]

But while the Europeans orbited Erskine Caldwell like a literary star,
June hovered deferentially—attractive, gracious, smiling—at his side.
In traditional Europe even more than in the United States, she felt ignored as a person, perceived only as the companion-wife. An unusual
exception stands alone in her memories.[10] One evening a reporter at the
British House of Commons talked with her almost exclusively. The following day's paper featured what she, and not Erskine Caldwell, had
said the night before. Otherwise she remembered the European trips
only as scheduled rushes from country to country, city to city, and appointment to appointment. The Caldwells enjoyed few lazily intimate
continental sightseeing days, strolls, or browsing excursions. What
Caldwell seemed to anticipate as pleasurable reward for work completed
was merely business as usual set in a different scene.

When the Caldwells returned to Tucson in September of 1947, he still
basked in the afterglow of European admiration for his early writings.
Immediately after his return, he forwarded a copy of his just-issued *The*

Sure Hand of God to Morang. Alfred responded with all the enthusiasm that close friendship and financial dependence might have evoked. His interpretation, as usual, was as sympathetically revealing as the reviewers' were to be disappointedly damning:

> In this book you have accomplished what I have been waiting for, the thing I knew you could do, and the thing no writer can do when young. The woman [Molly Bowser] in this story is not a single character; rather she is a symbol of a stratum of society that is the pawn of other groups of society. Her vulgarity is a statement of the self-defense of a mass fighting to stay alive, and thus it ceases to be vulgarity. You have taken the smallest things and used them to build up a solid literary structure. The red wine is no longer wine, it becomes a dream in daylight, a dream that effaces the grim reality of the too tangible things of daily life. You will be accused of repeating yourself in subject matter. That you do use subject matter along the lines of previous subjects in your books is good. Picasso paints a subject until he has become part of that subject. It is only the writer who is weak who depends upon the always new. In this book you proved yourself able to come to grips with a whole social structure, and to present it in a small space of a town. After all, a small town contains all of life's reactions, and you have the common sense to realize that fact.[11]

But the thematic coherence and Picasso-like repetition that Morang cited escaped most reviewers.

A precious few critics pointed to the novel's strengths: a type of Rabelaisian humor lurked beneath those deeper feelings extended to characters lost in their existential gropings.[12] Another saw *The Sure Hand of God* as but a continuing example of Caldwell's "creative vitality." Other reviewers, however, countered those few tributes. He had created slapstick characters, touched his job lightly without devotion, and if he wasn't joking, he was slipping.[13]

One reviewer of note looked at Caldwell's latest book more reflectively. James Baldwin cited for comparison "profound" works such as *God's Little Acre* and "Kneel to the Rising Sun" as he offered lament. Caldwell's twenty-third volume argued that his storytelling had become mechanical, his former passion "almost a study in the slow conquest of immobility." Baldwin sadly feared that, unless Caldwell's future writings could resurrect his earlier force and passion, his career would die from a virus similar to the one that had claimed so many other American writers.[14]

Such requiems forwarded to Caldwell by his clipping service perhaps confounded as much as they pained him. He worked at his writing as hard as ever before but gathered mostly critical rejections as reward. He perhaps questioned what had changed. Had he been able emotionally to distance himself as he compared his early writings with his more recent, he might have perceived the changing patterns. Caldwell's comic-vision had refocused.

Bogus though Caldwell's early religious figures appeared, their lives quivered, nonetheless, with cosmic hope and trust. Despite preachers like Sister Bessie and Semon Dye, who used people's faith to gain selfish advantages, the victims yet believed in a personalized, beneficent deity. The Jeeter Lesters, Ty Ty Waldens, and Clay Horeys blundered faithfully past the preachers toward sustaining moments of transcendence. Theirs was a dignity rooted in things of the earth, in natural God-given urges that carried their generations beyond the present comic writhings. What Baldwin perhaps missed in Caldwell's post-forties fiction was an essential faith, a belief in human dignity that for its own heroic sake transcended existential struggle.

That saving spark of divine hope did not shine through Caldwell's later figures. Instead they grotesquely stumbled through lives gripped by existential confusion and meaninglessness. *Trouble in July, Tragic Ground, A House in the Uplands,* and *The Sure Hand of God*—a cynically ironic title?—all focused upon victims variously exploited beyond hope. The cosmically infused struggles of Caldwell's thirties creations became the hopeless squirmings of forlorn caricatures in his post-forties fiction. Caught in mechanistic webs of social and economic circumstances, they, like Caldwell's stories themselves, lost their redemptive cosmic vitality.

That loss perhaps was as elemental as Caldwell's reduction of his religious heritage to that of a more comfortable humanism. Early in his career he had wrestled with his religious confusion. Questioned about his faith much later, Caldwell admitted that his Presbyterian background encouraged a belief in "what is going to be is going to be."[15] But based upon what he had experienced in the past, he "couldn't believe in God"; he "had no evidence" there was such a person.[16] When that divine spark that once had fueled both Caldwell's life and fiction died only can be guessed.

Caldwell's experiences during that period perhaps smothered something else almost as vital to his writing as that divine spark. Early in his career, stories burst from his consciousness like flames from a haystack on fire. But by the mid-forties, he more frequently wished that he had learned bricklaying or observed that it was "a hell of a life to be a writer and be so dumb you can't do anything else."[17] On another occasion, he even set August 15, 1950, as the date "he was going to retire if he could hold out that long."[18]

Behind such miseries, however, stood other symptoms of his artistic malaise. In the thirties, Caldwell apologized to Max Perkins because when stories boiled up, he could do nothing else until he wrote them. By the early forties, he claimed to be working on a preplanned cyclorama, with each succeeding novel painting but a facet of the larger scene. Later in that decade he told reporters that he revised each page as many as fifteen times. And by 1950 at least, he sometimes typed preliminary character-identification charts, notes, and time sequences.[19] Therefore while reviewers shot their critical darts, Caldwell only could shake them off. With more and more wearied acceptance it seems, he increasingly sat down to write as if fate, duty, honor, and justification would always demand one more book as long as he lived.

After the 1947 European trip, Caldwell wasted little time beginning a new novel. Excusing himself from a November trip to Las Vegas with the Manuels, he offered hope that he "could take New Year's Day off" to attend the Rose Bowl game with them. Later that January he was "very tempted" to attend some European openings of *Tobacco Road* with Marcel Duhamel, a French writer and casual friend.[20] If it weren't for trying to finish a novel, which was more important to him right then, he probably would have gone. Caldwell again impressed upon Morang that his writing obligations came before pleasure.

By mid-April, Caldwell personally delivered the manuscript for *This*

Very Earth to Duell, Sloan and Pearce. Normally Caldwell did not hand-carry finished copy to his publishers, but in this instance a special occasion called him to New York. Because *God's Little Acre* had sold four million copies and five other Caldwell reprints another eight, Penguin–Mentor Books planned a five-day celebration spree. With thanks and pride, those responsible wished to mark that singular achievement with a merchandising extravaganza.

Organized by Victor Weybright in conjunction with Fawcett Publications—the by-then distributors—the fete was a boisterous departure from traditional publishing-company celebrations. This was no sedate gathering of those with honeyed voices speaking reverently of good writing that earned modest sales. Rather, it represented an exuberant celebration for all who had helped promote the paperback as that extraordinary, mass-marketing bonanza of the written word. And the honored guest, who had made the gala-event possible was Erskine Caldwell.

Newspapers and trade journals carried full-page accounts of the observance. They pictured Caldwell with Weybright and Enoch, with Roscoe Fawcett, regional distribution representatives, and with newsstand managers. Dominating the spreads was a photograph of Caldwell cutting a tiered cake so tall that it dwarfed even him—a sweet symbol of the wealth that *God's Little Acre* had divided among them all.[21] Pieces of the communal cake were forwarded to those distributors and newsdealers who had not been able to attend.

Never before, not even in Europe, had anyone so lavishly honored Caldwell's writing. But more satisfying than the money, the honor, and the back-slapping, good-ole-boy conviviality of the *God's Little Acre* tribute, lay a greater recognition. Millions of people finally were reading Erskine Caldwell's stories. Fielding a question about the possible causes for this general burst of popularity, Caldwell seemed almost awed: "I don't know. I don't know. It may be that the people I was writing about have begun to buy the books now that they cost only 25 cents a piece."[22]

Since one of the greatest rewards of writing was being read, Caldwell publicly expressed his appreciation for what the extravaganza represented. It was "probably the biggest lift of [his] writing career."[23] He never was to forget what Roscoe Fawcett, Weybright, and Enoch had done for him. Always afterwards, it appears, he slavishly accepted their overly inflated opinions and impressions and those of others like them, as more valid than those balanced ones offered by hardcover publishers, paid reviewers, or agents.

By the summer of 1948, as Caldwell's popular reputation continued to grow, June must have looked more critically at her own personal situation. By then twenty-seven years old, she perhaps questioned her accomplishments, her identity, and the satisfactions of her marriage. After its promising start, her writing career had faltered. Beyond that, she helped care for Jay, accompanied Caldwell's mother whenever she stayed in Tucson, and decorated the residential Tucson house the Caldwells recently had purchased. That location allowed more Junior League and Red Cross volunteer work, but was that all? she must have asked.

June was no Helen with three children and an eighteenth-century house to manage. Neither did she revise and edit Caldwell's writing. Unlike Margaret Bourke-White, whose career made her identity as Caldwell's wife a secondary consideration, June was only the wife of Erskine Caldwell, the mother of his child, and mistress of his household. The Signet-Fawcett affair only reconfirmed her role as appendage that she had felt so obviously in Europe. Like Ibsen's Nora in her dollhouse, June seemed increasingly to see herself as a gracious, smiling accessory to Caldwell's husbandly fact and career.

That role may have fed other domestic tensions. Since three years after their marriage, June had periodically consulted a local psychoanalyst. As one who fiercely had rejected such direction himself, Caldwell objected to that expression of dissatisfaction more than he did to the numerous phone calls that had followed from her other activities. He, conversely, had not abandoned his periods of punishing silences. These tensions may have encouraged June to decide against accompanying him on his next scheduled trip.

Caldwell had not traveled extensively by automobile since before the war. In June of 1948, therefore, he planned to revisit the South, stopping en route to do promotional stints for the Fawcett distributors. After spending a week in Georgia, he would drive to Baltimore for an examination of his bad eye at Johns Hopkins before departing for Lawrence,

Kansas, where he was to participate in the university's writer's conference. Since June refused to accompany Caldwell the full length of his
tour, they arranged for her to meet him at Lawrence. During that week-
long seminar, he at least would share her company.

The details of that trip are provocative for a number of reasons. They
not only reflect the dimensions of Fawcett's promotional tactics but also
offer insights into Caldwell's writing perceptions during his first extended return to the South in over a decade. Yet more compellingly, they
reveal how Caldwell, feeling rejected by June because she had refused to
travel with him, responded to her abandonment.[24]

After promotional stops in El Paso and Dallas, Caldwell arrived in
New Orleans, where Eddie Lewis, the Fawcett advance man, had arranged his grand reception. Mayor Chip Morrison welcomed him offi-
cially to the city, an event both pictured and reported in the local papers.
Asked about writing, Caldwell admitted to sitting daily at his typewriter
from nine to five, sometimes without a line to show for his work. More
generally, he perceived American writing in cyclical terms. The thirties
offered the apex, the forties, through loss of creativity, reflected a
"second-rate" downswing which would reverse itself in the fifties.
Whether personal experience and hope had anything to do with Caldwell's predictions is only speculative.

Leaving promotions, reporters, and predictions behind, Caldwell
turned to the past, as it were, driving to Natchitoches to meet with James
Aswell. A classmate from Hench's seminar, Aswell and Caldwell renewed a literary friendship all-but-neglected since their university days.
A bourbon-drinking, humorous type, the Louisianan wrote novels with
mixed success. Their conversations may have centered around an estimation Aswell later shared with Caldwell. A local reviewer felt that
James M. Cain's *The Moth*, Caldwell's next issue, *This Very Earth*, and
Aswell's *Midsummer Fires* virtually tied for the "most nauseating book"
of 1948. Aswell's won "by a matter of split infinitives."[25]

Stopping next in Georgia, Caldwell wandered around in old clothes,
talked a little, and listened a lot to old voices from a once-familiar South.
Nothing had changed, he thought[26] As a consequence of machine politics and benign neglect, the region was only more dilapidated, giving it

the honor of having the poorest roads and highest taxes. Otherwise, he believed that federal policies that tried "to stuff civil rights down the throats of Southerners" would prove counterproductive.

After a Johns Hopkins eye specialist confirmed that his eye condition remained inoperable, Caldwell had attended a party in his honor at Victor Weybright's Maryland estate. Then he had headed for Kansas City, en route to Lawrence and the University of Kansas. There he had discovered that the indefatigable Eddie Lewis once more had been at work.

As he entered the city limits, a patrolman pulled him over, directing that Caldwell follow him to the Kansas City municipal building. With photographers and reporters in attendance, the mayor presented Caldwell with a scroll designating him an honorary member of the City. That tactic, Lewis correctly assumed, would direct readers to an advertisement in the local papers: "Meet the author of *God's Little Acre* and have your copies autographed by Erskine Caldwell at the grand opening of Katz's twenty-fifth drug store." On June 26 the author faithfully sat for one-and-a-half hours by the book rack at Katz's new store. He signed some three hundred copies of his twenty-five-cent books.

From there, Caldwell drove immediately to Lawrence where writing method, not promotion, was to be the focus. June, who was to have helped him endure five days of academic palaver and literary jousting, did not arrive. Instead he registered alone at a downtown hotel. All the other authors assembled by Professor Ray B. West, Jr.—Katherine Anne Porter, Allen Tate, John Frederick Nims, Robert W. Stallman, Caroline Gordon, Walter Van Tilburg Clark, and *Mademoiselle* fiction editor George Davis—lodged as a group at a university fraternity house. The spatial distance Caldwell symbolically placed between himself and the others held until July 2 when the conference ended. What the others perhaps thought of him, he attempted to shrug off; what he thought of them he couched within the claim that he liked "to associate with people."[27] That Caldwell felt like a popular pariah consciously excluded by a different species of the fiction breed is understandable.

A scarcely unbiased account written by a young reporter for the *Beaumont Enterprise*, contained the seeds of her special sympathy and his polite discontent. Because Caldwell was not scheduled for lecture or panel participation until six days after the seminar formally began, his belated arrival fresh from the commercial hustings immediately set him apart from the established group. Art for art's sake seemed the established theme.[28]

Katherine Anne Porter boasted of her standards by admitting to two trunks of unpublished manuscripts. With reverent voices, other writers read from their own stories. The interested young reporter noted that Erskine Caldwell "fidgeted politely" when one of them read aloud the entirety of James Joyce's "The Dead." He appeared more interested in Caroline Gordon's pronouncement of Ernest Hemingway's literary demise and Katherine Porter's wonder about D. H. Lawrence's surrounding himself with corpses. Both as a panelist and as a figure apart during coffee breaks, Caldwell seemed "almost totally unaware of the sniping" that the others aimed at his commercialism. Obviously the young reporter empathized with the "freckled, genial Caldwell" who responded both to questions and covert jibes "with his tongue practically glued in his cheek."

When Caldwell lectured about his Russian experiences of almost a decade past, other writers were conspicuously absent; they were attending "a private dinner in the ivory tower." The young woman reporter was not. Obviously the literary "lone-wolf" intrigued her; feeling so recently rejected and unloved by June, Caldwell found her also openly appealing.

It was she who discovered that he was staying alone at a local hotel. There, in reporter fashion, she uncovered details about his education, interests, and family life. The ex-Georgian had a mongrel appropriately named Cracker, and was a big man, blonder than he had appeared in his photographs.

Two weeks after Caldwell returned to June and Tucson, and the reporter to her Beaumont job, her extended summary of the Kansas Writer's Conference appeared in nationally syndicated papers. Her biting criticism of the other writers, slanted to Caldwell's advantage, invited his appreciation in the form of a letter to the editor. As an innocent bystander, he wanted to let people know that he thought their reporter's piece about the Kansas Writer's Conference was a wonderful piece of journalism. "If there were more writing of this standard on book pages, there would be many more readers of books," he observed by way of conclusion.[29] Whether or not Caldwell also privately thanked the young woman personally is unclear.[30]

More than domestic tensions stirred Caldwell's ire upon his return to Tucson. Without any foundation in fact, it seems, Helen feared he would renege on paying the children's college expenses after they turned twenty-one. She, therefore, filed suit to have the original divorce agreement modified. Under the new terms, Caldwell would pay continued support—a portion to the children and the rest to Helen—for each of the three until Janet either turned either twenty-one or married. Although Caldwell and June forgot their differences long enough to seethe and rail mutually, the judge somehow ruled in Helen and the children's favor. Caldwell chafed under a legal decree dictating conditions that he felt he had fulfilled honorably without judicial sanctions.

Another source of distress was related to the signals that Duell, Sloan and Pearce began sending at about the same time. Pleading financial concerns, they objected to the cost associated with the Folkways Series. Though the seventeen volumes already in print did in fact earn profits and a contract obligated them to the remainder, they attempted to withhold $1,500 owed to Caldwell from reprint earnings. Such tactics understandably eroded some of the good will that had characterized Caldwell's eight-year history with the firm. Although hardcover sales of his recent books had earned them little if any profits, their portion of Caldwell's paperback sales made him too valuable a property to lose. That symbiotic situation allowed their relationship to settle into one of mutually wary watchfulness.

Amid such generalized festerings, the reviews that followed the August 1 publication of *This Very Earth*, reopened some painful wounds. Although one reviewer claimed that the novel read "startlingly like Sartre's play, *The Respectful Prostitute,*" and another thought it was valid because the world was "becoming increasingly artificial instead of deeply felt," others proved less kind. "Old Caldwellians" might be satisfied, but his latest read like "the worst kind of melodrama." Or, though Caldwell's work occasionally emanated a spirit akin to Twain's, he evidently had written himself out: "If not, he would hardly have made such a slip-shod job of *This Very Earth.*"[31]

Not even Morang's elaborate praise could balance the painful cruelty of another review Caldwell placed within his clipping files. Written in the form of a personal letter, it began:

> Dear Erskine Caldwell,
> It takes colossal nerve or immense stupidity to publish the childish novels you have been giving us of late. How long do you think readers of *Tobacco Road* and *God's Little Acre* will buy your books on a vanished reputation?[32]

If his name had not been assigned to *A House in the Uplands, The Sure Hand of God,* and *This Very Earth,* the disillusioned critic guessed, no one would have known that the old master himself had written these novels. He continued by offering some folksy advice. Caldwell first should go apologize to his editors, then find himself some spotted hounds, get himself a gun, and go tree possums instead of writing novels.

Such personally directed and devastating advice would have wounded any writer, even one more securely callused than Caldwell. How deeply such reviews cut him became evident only six days after that particular public letter appeared. Then Caldwell dutifully sat in California signing copies of his paperbound books, participating in a "San Francisco Caldwell Week" extravaganza promoted by his paperback cohorts. There he uncharacteristically and publicly retaliated with all the defenses he could muster.

During Caldwell's first few years as a writer, ninety-nine out of a hundred reviews had been favorable, but no one had bought his books. In the second decade, ninety-nine out of a hundred reviews were unfavorable but everybody read his books. As a portion of his defense, he then had cited evidence. His paperback reprints had sold over nine million copies, while the Russian State Publishing House alone had printed over a hundred thousand copies of his stories. Then turning at bay, Caldwell attacked those who hounded him. Critics took themselves too seriously, using an assumed literary sophistication and aestheticism that only exalted them even as their reviews exceeded their readers' understanding. Because their audiences consequently had lost faith in them, the critics had "outlived their usefulness."[33] As Caldwell had signed his reprints, what he had failed to acknowledge—possibly did not recognize—was that while *God's Little Acre, Tobacco Road,* and his early works had sold millions, reprints of his more recent books had sold only in the thousands.

Whatever Caldwell felt about the negative reviews evidently stirred even June's sympathy, because she leaped to his defense during that embattled time. To Harry Hansen, the long-friendly reviewer for the *World Telegram*—he who had compared Caldwell to Twain but judged *This Very Earth* as slipshod—she wrote:

> You seem to be unaware of the fact that Mr. Caldwell is writing a series of novels not of recurrent themes but against a unified background. Each novel portrays a phase of community life such as politics in *Trouble in July*, religion in *Journeyman*, and, of course, family disintegration in *This Very Earth*. No doubt you mistook for repetition Mr. Caldwell's consistent search for the true components of man's happiness and grief.
>
> I am sure that you will want to take back your statement that the key to Mr. Caldwell's secret of success is that he is primarily a most interesting storyteller, etc. There is, as you know much more than story telling ability involved.[34]

June's defense, that Caldwell was writing a series of novels, a southern cyclorama united by a common background, is interesting. First, her rhetoric seemed borrowed from Hollywood agents or paperback promoters. More basically, however, it implied that calculated reason and planning rather than stories boiling up to be told now determined his writing. And June lashed out at Harry Hansen as one among many because always before his reviews had been almost invariably positive.

During the midst of this critical assault, Caldwell received a satisfying letter of request from a William and Mary English professor. William W. Seward praised Caldwell's *This Very Earth* as a work, which, like his more recent ones, was on par with *Tobacco Road* and *God's Little Acre*. As a short-story writer, moreover, Caldwell ranked along with Hemingway as the twentieth century's best. He required his students to read selections from both. His request for an autographed copy of *This Very Earth* must have gratified Caldwell. Apologizing for having no hardbound copies of that issue on hand, he instead immediately forwarded an inscribed copy of *Tragic Ground*.

The more public responses to *This Very Earth* shook not only Caldwell and June but also his profit-minded publishers. Donald Demarest, an associate editor at New American Library, scurried about during the next four months trying to repair the damage.[35] Apparently he promoted a treatment of *This Very Earth* with *Time* magazine—an analysis that was to have placed Caldwell's latest issue into cycloramic context. He ruefully admitted that the story "sure panned out badly." *Time* featured Caldwell's picture in a review that judged his most recent novel to be "as scrawny a literary turkey as has been hatched in 1948." In that work, the reviewer remarked, Caldwell performed like a once-talented dancer who still remembered all the steps and postures but had forgotten how to dance. Demarest hoped that *Time* would print June's rebuttal. Weybright and Enoch likewise wrote to the *Saturday Review* protesting its review of *This Very Earth.*

Demarest tried other tactics to salvage Caldwell's sagging literary reputation. Seeking somebody of stature to reevaluate Caldwell's "tremendous mass appeal" within the context of his southern-panorama intentions, he approached both Maxwell Geismar and Henry Canby.[36] Each excused himself from the undertaking. Not so easily defeated, Demarest tried other ploys. Since Caldwell had been the first author to autograph twenty-five-cent books in drugstores, perhaps *Look* magazine could "hang their picture angle" on such a session. *Look* passed on that opportunity. Those to whom Demarest appealed perhaps saw through his scheming. New American Library was trying "to stir up a big controversy pro and con Caldwell to boil over" coincident with their reprint issue of *House in the Uplands.*[37]

Although he had not been approached, Irving Howe, a "critic of stature," did briefly evaluate Caldwell's career in an article for the *American Mercury.* His conclusion was scarcely what Demarest would have desired:

> How to explain this spectacular disintegration of Caldwell's talent? The influence of Stalinism with its totalitarian habits of mind? A desire to cash in quick while the cashing is good? Or some more subtle and treacherous internal collapse of his creative impulse, already observable in his recent book; some perilous self-dispersal of talent? Frankly, I cannot say, and at the mo-

ment it hardly matters, for the sheer fact of the collapse is itself so over-whelming. It is as if one could see nothing but an endlessly barren desert piled with bleached and ugly bones.[38]

Critics who carefully had been reading Caldwell's stories during the past decade might have questioned Howe's leading assumption. The "spectacular disintegration" had not been as precipitous as he implied. Knowledgeable intimates like Ira and Helen and astute readers and critics alike had been sounding the warnings ever since Caldwell's domestic traumas had begun. When Caldwell divorced Helen, he separated himself from that sure editorial eye of one who knew him and his once-familiar territory better than he knew himself.

Chapter 17

As reviewers, critics, and New American Library personnel stewed over Caldwell's literary fate, he dutifully continued to write. Forty-five years old, he worked on *A Place Called Estherville* from August of 1948 until he finished it early in February of 1949. Working as if his personal salvation, honor, and reputation depended upon it, he was "just about out" on his feet before the book was done. Though he liked it better than anything else he'd written in the last five years, he'd just have to wait and see how it was received.[1] Before the Caldwells could embark on that two-month European trip he had scheduled as reward, however, he had "to wrangle with Charlie Duell over a new contract."

Advising the Texas reporter that June would accompany him on this particular trip, the Caldwells departed for New York so that he could confirm what he suspected. Charlie Duell and Cap Pearce claimed misgivings about renewing his contract. The costs of the Folkways Series and his declining hardbound sales made renewal a marginal gamble. Caldwell countered their arguments with some of his own. His hardcover titles lagged in sales because the firm had failed to promote them enthusiastically. Questions about profits, furthermore, represented canards. Their share of reprint money more than compensated for any losses they might have incurred through association with him. Duell and Pearce could not refute Caldwell's claim about their share of the paperback earnings. When all the wrangling was done, they realized that a continuing five-year contract would benefit them all. Yet that agreement proved not to allay the respective suspicions all of them excused as cautions.

No matter the coolness with which Duell and Pearce had greeted Caldwell, Enoch and Weybright compensated for it. Weybright once more hosted a party for the Caldwells at his Maryland country place. The evening was remarkable only because Victor introduced Caldwell to a vivaciously warm and attractive young woman, Virginia Moffett

Fletcher. Separated from her husband and a neighbor to the Wey-brights, she had attended only at the urging of her wealthy Fletcher in-laws. As Virginia left the gathering that evening, Caldwell followed her outside; he wished to see her again in the future. Properly reluctant, she gracefully avoided his request, slipping away from his life for the next two years.

Shortly after their New York visit, the Caldwells departed for Europe, with extended stopovers in Poland, Switzerland, France, Belgium, England, and Sweden preceding their longer visit to Italy. Perhaps with some hyperbole, Caldwell charted their activities for his New American Library associates. During their travels they weekly averaged some "three radio programs, four dinners, five cocktail parties, fourteen interviews, and one motion picture script for good measure."[2] And he could not count the bookshops where he had autographed his translations in each country along the way. Yet beneath Caldwell's Olympian boast seemed to hide a quiet satisfaction with the international recognition his writing had earned.

In Europe Erskine Caldwell's reputation in Italy ranked second only to his fame in France. Valentino Bompiani, his Italian publisher, felt that the visit would be his country's important literary event of the year.[3] To assure that importance, Bompiani planned functions both to promote Caldwell's literary respectability and to generate publicity encouraging readers to buy his books.

Italian reporters puzzled about both the man and the behavior of that author who had created such haunting figures as the ragged Jeeter Lester and Ty Ty Walden. Impeccably dressed in a grey suit, he stood aloof like an urbane, martini-drinking diplomat who shook hands "with a smile that became cold every time." That in itself appeared remarkable since one reporter had not seen him smile for two days. Nonetheless, as June sipped orange juice by his side, Erskine Caldwell's "calm silence said something that intrigued everyone."

While his disquieting reserve proved embarrassing, what Caldwell said during interviews bemused them. Refusing to participate in small talk, he knew only three Italian authors by name, had never studied Italian literature, could not speak French, and ignored Italian. He never initiated a conversation and answered but briefly when questioned. Concluding a reply, his eyes cooled down, and he looked "to a point of the room as if attracted by an obsessive sight."[4] Close to him throughout, June "bowed her head with grace." Reporters did not realize how many times in so many countries Caldwell patiently had suffered the same questions. Neither could they know that calm silence and abstraction were the most natural expressions he could assume in the glare of that fame that was both so profitably satisfying and, at the same time, discomforting.

Only a few differences marked the Caldwells' return to Tucson. Caldwell's mother had gone back to Prosperity, and Pix had moved to Los Angeles to seek his fortune. He worked briefly at various jobs, trying all the time to find a satisfying one. In the meantime he had married, but the Caldwells continued to worry. Sometimes Pix seemed unsure of himself, as if overwhelmed by his father's large shadow. For a while he even attempted to write short stories of his own.[5] Keeping it secret from Pix, Caldwell asked Al Manuel to help the young man personally and financially whenever he seemed in need of it. Caldwell would repay his agent later.

In other respects Caldwell also resumed his habitual patterns, but this time with a difference. During a time when his own marriage was strained, when he had kept the young—now *Houston Post*—reporter advised of his comings and goings, when he recently had been attracted to a Virginia Fletcher, he planned carefully in July of 1949 for the novel that was to be *Episode in Palmetto*. About the work, critic Sylvia Cook would one day observe: "The novel is populated by single people trying desperately to marry and married people living bitterly and rebelliously in their joint estate."[6] More obviously Caldwell would plot around a young woman teacher who fell in love with a mature seventh-grade student. Her situation would be complicated by a local married man who argued that marrying him would free them both even as it helped his political career.

Caldwell charted the story's thirty-three characters.[7] Certain ones would repeat phrases keyed to their identities. "Mortifying my soul," "A half-assed canary," and "The whole all-over situation in general," signed just some of them. Names such as Reverend John Couchmanly, Jack Cash, Cato Pharr, and Dolly Kno suggest that Caldwell perhaps intended to tell his version of a modern southern morality tale about men and women caught between the demands of their public roles and private needs. But as he attempted to write what would prove to be his last novel for five years, he apparently struggled as never before. Indeed, as he regularly confessed to Morang, his writing no longer seemed to come with the ease of stories waiting to be told.

Through sheer perseverance, Caldwell finished the novel before the end of 1950. This time as reward for work completed, he wished to travel by car to places south. In what was a telling departure from the usual, he planned to visit with old acquaintances from his university days—first Jim Aswell and later Gordon Lewis with whom he had lost touch shortly after his and Helen's visit more than fifteen years earlier.

The Caldwells attended the Sugar Bowl game with the Aswells and then departed for a two-week stay in Sarasota and Key West. Disappointingly, Lewis had moved to Cuernavaca, something Caldwell did not discover until they had arrived in Florida. Tensions had flared between him and June during the New Orleans outing with the Aswells, but Caldwell persisted in trying to reach Gordon Lewis. A feeling of rejection might have made Caldwell seek his old acquaintance more persistently than he would have otherwise.

Once in correspondence with Lewis, Caldwell talked June and Jay into making the Cuernavaca trip. Lodged in private accommodations there, he visited much with Lewis and the John Steinbecks, who also were guests at the time. Although Lewis was but a dissolute writer at best—with only a Florida fishing guide to his published credit—he cultivated literary hopes. Perhaps those, as much as the three men's congeniality, made the five-day visit satisfying for Caldwell. After the Caldwells departed, the Lewises discussed both Caldwell's literary and personal career.

During his university days, Caldwell supposedly had vowed to Lewis: "I'm going to be the best known writer in this world."[8] Guessing about Caldwell's personal circumstances, Lewis surmised that "Helen finally gave Caldwell the divorce so he might marry [Margaret] and salve his

Presbyterian conscience." As for his current marriage, the Lewises felt that "June didn't seem to care" about her husband's writing. But then, they had not read any of her letters written in defense of Caldwell and *This Very Earth.* Nor did they know that June regularly checked bookstands for displays of Caldwell's reprints, afterwards directing any complaints to Roscoe Fawcett, a tactic the distributor failed to appreciate.

Back in Tucson in less than two weeks, the Caldwells took to the road again. What June could not have known was that their western trek—like the Mexico trip—represented a retracing of routes Caldwell and Bourke-White had once traveled together. After a three-day visit to Santa Fe with the Morangs, the Caldwells departed for the Broadmoor in Colorado Springs and other towns west. Always on the move, Caldwell would remain in each town, whether Rapid City, Kalispell, Elko, Reno, or Las Vegas, no more than two days before departing once again.

After three months of almost uninterrupted travel, the Caldwells returned to Tucson. Whether consciously or unconsciously, Caldwell revisited acquaintances and friends, regions and locations where he had gathered experiences during his adult past. With his long habit of justifying work as pleasure—or vice-versa—Caldwell was apparently preparing for his next book, a radical departure from anything he had written previously. Selectively autobiographical, *Call It Experience* was to become a carefully calculated attempt to construct an account of those experiences that he believed had contributed to his becoming and remaining a writer.

Sometime after Caldwell had selected the format for his new work but before its writing, the reviews for *Episode in Palmetto* began to appear. Generally they almost universally confirmed that his decision to abandon the novel for a while had been a sound one. The *Chicago Tribune*'s assessment carried within it a tone of regret. Although Caldwell's stories once deservedly had ranked him among the leading novelists of the country, currently one only could "speak of his achievement in the past tense."[9]

Caldwell's own perceptions and public admissions during that time gave credibility to such a judgment. In various ways he seemed to have conceded his fiction-writing demise. *Trouble in July*—written ten years earlier—most nearly had said what he had wanted. That "book wrapped a lot of things in a package. . . . I felt I put everything I wanted there."[10] Later that summer a note of weary resignation crept into another of Caldwell's observations. As he grew older, he used more and more typewriter ribbons and sometimes sat at the typewriter staring "at it for three days without writing a word."[11] He feared he might be in a rut. As if such admission were not gall bitter enough, a respected voice from the past seemed to confirm it.

Interviewed by the *Virginia Spectator,* a university alumni publication, Atcheson Hench responded to questions about his famous student. The flavor that gave vitality to Caldwell's early stories about the underprivileged recently had been missing. He felt that if Erskine Caldwell "would return to his native Georgia, and again capture the additive of his youth in the area in which he received his inspiration, then his present writing might be greatly improved."[12] With echoes of Ira's earlier cautions, Hench offered professorial and fatherly advice.

In August and September of 1950, before Caldwell could settle down to sort through and write about his past and literary experience, distractions intruded. An official from Peace College—a safely respectable Presbyterian women's institution that Caldwell's mother had favored—wrote to Caldwell. Janet had steadfastly refused to register for a required religion course. Mere, who had moved to Raleigh to act as Janet's guide and chaperon, offered her analysis of the situation. For all her good qualities, Helen had failed to provide Janet with either appropriate religious example or knowledge of her religious heritage. Dabney more realistically provided the explanation. Janet never had wanted to attend the Presbyterian junior college. She had enrolled only because Caldwell and Mere had insisted. By refusing to fulfill the religion requirements, she had hoped to be expelled so she could then go to the University of North Carolina.

Conveniently ignoring his own dissatisfactions at a Presbyterian college, Caldwell yielded to his mother rather than his own experience. He refused to pay Janet's expenses anywhere else. The next semester, with a single stroke, she successfully confounded the inflexibility of the college, her father, and her grandmother. In a ceremony Caldwell and June failed to attend, she married Guy Gooding, a rural North Carolinian attending the university. By freeing herself, however, she also freed Caldwell from the support payments that Helen had legally enforced only two years earlier.

Other people from Caldwell's past likewise began to resurface hauntingly at this time. Howard Fast, an acquaintance from his proletarian-leaning years, had been imprisoned as Martin Dies's House Un-American Activities Committee sniffed among American writers to ferret out suspected "Reds." Fast's wife sought Caldwell's intercession. Similarly Arthur Miller requested his participation in a radio program protesting the committee's intimidation and jailing of American writers. He either ignored or denied both requests. More than a decade separated Erskine Caldwell from the time when he would have come to the aid of such people and their causes.

One of Caldwell's own oblique requests concerning an entirely different matter likewise received polite deferral in September of that year. Some eight years earlier, he, with much relief, had left the Florida coed in Hollywood. This time Caldwell wrote from Tucson, hoping to meet her during one of his future California trips. Though genuinely pleased by his remembering her, she had recently married. She made clear, nonetheless, that she and her husband would welcome Caldwell to their home whenever he was in the vicinity.[13] There is no indication that he ever responded to that offer.

After completing a series of promotional stints in St. Louis, Chicago, and Cincinnati, Caldwell finally sat down in mid-October to work in earnest on his next book. Because most of his records and correspondence had remained either with Helen or Margaret, he relied almost wholly upon memory for all his pre-1942 reconstructions. Only a few confirmations of fact from Frank Daniel at the *Atlanta Journal* otherwise helped inform his work.

Throughout his career Caldwell had shared with reporters and publishers only enough biographical details to satisfy their needs, to create and reinforce myths about his experiences and literary beginnings. *Call It Experience* might have offered much more; as an autobiography it could have set his record straight, providing some insight into Caldwell's personal life. It consciously did none of that: "What is to be found here is less a personal history than it is an informal recollection of authorship. Some things have been left out unintentionally; other things have been omitted purposely."[14] Consequently, except for his parents and an almost casual mention of Margaret Bourke-White as his wife, Caldwell carefully hid all significant others—Helen, June, and his children—behind the veil of this public account. All else that likewise might have revealed him as a complex person with feelings and needs and weaknesses he also hid behind that same veil. His was to be the story of the writer as public figure, rather than private person.

When Caldwell had courted Helen, he had "constructed a writer's account" to justify his otherwise inexplicable experiences, to create for both her and himself a credible identity. Then he also had fabricated a vocabulary of motives to support that identity. In *Experience* Caldwell did not need to create an identity, but—as recent criticisms and his own admissions argued—he needed to reaffirm for himself and the public the "signs" of his calling as a writer of fiction.

What those first signs were, Caldwell could not recall. Perhaps something had happened when he was "fifteen or sixteen or seventeen." Without mentioning Helen as either catalyst, influence, or companion, he did acknowledge accurately that at age "twenty-one or twenty-two, [he] realized [he] wanted to write more than do anything else in the world."[15] Between that candid beginning and the book's telling epilogue, Caldwell selected and recreated experiences that he believed had marked him as a writer responding to the sacred demands of his calling. Like Benjamin Franklin's classic, Caldwell's autobiography most essentially celebrated work, frugality, and those other secularized puritan values that he believed had been central to his success.

After the stories came Caldwell's "Epilogue." It was more revealing than those stories, real and apocryphal, that constituted the body of the work. "Born with the gift," a writer sacrificed all for its sake: "This state of mind is an almost uncontrollable desire that seeks fulfillment at any cost."[16] For that born storyteller, the desire to create became as compelling as those needs for "love and companionship," or for food and drink. More crucial than a willingness "to endure hardships," moreover, were the other covert costs Caldwell considered as necessary conditions for writing success:

> The desire to be a writer is composed of, for one thing, a spirit of aggressive-
> ness that impels a man or woman to strive to overcome anything that stands
> in the way of success. More common than wealth and ease, poverty and hun-
> ger are both symbolic and real, and the would-be writer is encouraged to
> greater effort as he sees himself gradually overcoming them. . . . [Nonethe-
> less] the reward of accomplishment, in the mind of the majority of authors,
> rich and poor, is the primary motive for writing, and the making of money is
> a secondary one.[17]

Having left hunger and poverty behind, first in Georgia and then in Maine, Caldwell may have failed to realize the effects of their loss. Hollywood salaries, stage and film royalties, and finally earnings from suggestively packaged reprints had freed him from those deprivations. That loss of his writing edge, the emotional costs of his involvements with women, and the physical demands of promotional activities, had by that time all conspired to betray him. No matter his intentions, the other factors negated both "the gift" and the hard work he offered almost as sacrificial tribute.

Even as Caldwell then wrote, a national magazine advertisement symbolically measured the distance between where he was and where he had been during his most creative years. In that feature, Caldwell, attended by a faithful Dalmatian, sat in his writing study promoting the smooth satisfaction of Calvert whiskey. The Presbyterian Georgia boy of the twenties, the impoverished writer of the early thirties, by 1950 had become a public figure promoting sophisticated living.

How writing a book like *Call It Experience* affected Caldwell he only hinted to Morang; he had "been all tied up in knots" as he had worked to finish the book by his self-imposed January 1951, deadline.[18] Of course he met it.

Over the previous few years Caldwell's letters to Morang had become increasingly infrequent and abbreviated. Just as invariably Morang's long letters to Caldwell offered interminable litanies ending on the same refrain. Although he was writing-painting-teaching-giving-radio-talks with the same old effort, he badly needed money. Once again the rent was in arrears, and he and Dorothy, threatened with eviction. Two years later Caldwell laid that to rest by buying Morang's house. Meanwhile, nonetheless, he answered his friend's every request with a check. Morang's drinking had increased despite hospitalization and treatment sometime before, that too at Caldwell's expense.

Within the year Morang's personality distortions became so extreme that they forced an end to his and Dorothy's marriage. During his deranged states especially, he falsely accused her of infidelities even as he hid his involvement with one of his older women students. Finally she could do nothing to brake his wild careening toward the divorce he requested. Afterwards he vacillated between seeking Dorothy's return and proposing to various women who showed him the slightest degree of personal sympathy.

Despite his own record, Caldwell in principle staunchly opposed divorce. Yet in this instance, he forgave Morang with a patient latitude that seldom excused others—wives, children, and associates—from those strict standards his principles imposed upon others as well as himself. In fact, as Morang proposed to woman after woman, Caldwell offered him some either humorously ironic or ruefully retrospective advice: "Don't rush into getting married too soon—there are too many women in the world who have too little to offer. It's a lot better to wait it out until the right one comes along, and in the meantime you can be looking over the field and doing as you please. Once you get tied up, it's difficult to get rid of a woman."[19]

More than just Caldwell's tentative letter to the former Florida girl and his continuing correspondence with the young Houston reporter indicated that the scope of his and June's difficulties had grown. Although Caldwell objected, she sought a degree of independent direction first by taking psychology and, later, prelaw courses at the University of Arizona. More reprehensibly yet, she had increased her sessions with Dr. Sarlin, the Freudian psychoanalyst she had begun seeing only three years into their marriage. Impatient with people who could neither solve nor bear their own problems, Caldwell disdained those practitioners who charged large fees to probe into people's secret places. Such disturbances, no doubt, brewed within him as he had shared his sage wisdom with Morang.

As if such personal concerns were not strain enough, the tensions between Caldwell and his publishers intensified as each looked more suspiciously at the other. Duell, Sloan and Pearce continued to question the profitability of keeping Caldwell on their list; he, in turn, stewed over their share of the reprint monies. He additionally grumbled about what he perceived as their less-than-enthusiastic promotional efforts. Such were merely portents, like those in his marriage, that another longstanding relationship was faltering.

The Caldwells relocated to Santa Barbara for the summer of 1951, a move Caldwell apparently made from no motive other than to revitalize their marriage through a change of scenery and pattern. They entertained and were entertained more than usual. And while he still maintained his formal work schedule—though no new book compelled him to write—the domestic situation was more relaxed. As evidence June offered what she estimated to have been Caldwell's largest and most appreciated gift. Every Thursday, beginning at 9:30 A.M., he allowed her the day off, the first unconstrained time he had granted during their marriage. Without pressures, she went to the hairdresser's, visited art galleries, or merely browsed at will through shops and walks. Returning about 4:30, June would change so the two of them could go out for the evening while a sitter cared for Jay. June guessed, "If he had done this sort of thing more often, our marriage might have lasted, and perhaps the other ones as well."[20]

Dabney likewise remembered that summer of rare exceptions; it had been a carefree, relaxed time when the Caldwells all seemed to enjoy one another. The barriers between Dee and Skinny no longer seemed quite as insurmountable as they once were. Long before, he had recognized that Caldwell could not "stand warmth," could not "handle that," an awareness that made him call Skinny "Sir" whenever they were together. A similar reluctance precluded his discussing his father's stories with him. As an English major who had read them all, he wished to share his impressions and questions but did not. Skinny's attitude and short comments made clear how uncomfortable he was with that subject. Dabney, nonetheless, had already come to his own conclusions:

Helen had been his "best editor" because Skinny had done his "sharpest writing then," had been "hungry at that time as he [hadn't] been since."[21]

Released from the marines and in Malibu for summer-school courses, Dee gratefully enjoyed his father's unusual generosity. He gave his son the use of his car; sometimes June and Dee would go out together for the day, "to have the greatest time, laughing." He always had appreciated his thirty-year-old stepmother who "was so beautiful . . . , so vivacious . . . and one of the funniest warmest girls" he ever had met.[22]

That Santa Barbara summer then, became a gift Caldwell quietly shared with those he loved. Not since the other California summer of 1936 had he been so free from his writing chores, so carefully devoted to the pleasures of his family. Their respective warm memories of those special times stand as measures against other times lost, occasions when Caldwell's work and personal character denied them all such luxuries.

On the public level, however, Caldwell's involvements became more strained during that period. Maxim Lieber tried with single-minded determination to sell Victor Weybright the reprint rights to *All Night Long*. Weybright, usually so uncritically enthusiastic, waffled. Only recently Whittaker Chambers had testified before the Un-American Activities Committee to Lieber's earlier membership in the Communist Party. Lieber never had denied the charge. His "pushing *All Night Long* so ardently," therefore, seemed impolitic.[23] Reprinted, the book's sympathetic view of the Communist guerrillas might lead readers to paint Caldwell with the same red brush. New American Library decided that everyone's self-interest dictated against reissuing the work.

Apparently chagrined, unconvinced, or in dire need of money, Lieber covertly tried to peddle the reprint rights elsewhere. Almat Publishing Company proposed what over a ten-year period could have been a $660,000 contract.[24] They anticipated a digest-sized monthly called *Erskine Caldwell's Magazine*, which would serialize Caldwell's books and stories under his "pro-forma" editor's imprimatur. Hearing rumors of the deal, Weybright and Enoch became "much wrought up." They correctly perceived that the magazine idea was merely a camouflage-operation that would undermine their Caldwell reprint sales.

Even while Lieber stirred that opportunistic pot, he stoked the fires,

with encouragement from Duell, Sloan and Pearce, for another profitable coup. Little, Brown and Company would issue selected Caldwell titles under their imprint but give credit to Duell, Sloan and Pearce. Under that arrangement the financially troubled company would receive a
percentage from Little, Brown without assuming the full risks their own
imprint alone might represent. These complex negotiations must have
made Caldwell feel as much used as confused, but one fact seemed clear.
Through a more assiduous gleaning of his stories and popular reputation, everyone except he, who had sacrificed to write them, would profit.
Like heirs before a burial, his business-associate friends finagled and
connived to parcel out that which he believed was only his to bequeath.
Worse yet, in the midst of these complex emotional and legal entanglements, Caldwell's long trusted associate-friend selfishly betrayed him.

Without hint or warning Max Lieber fled the country. Possibly hoping
to continue his agent's duties safely from afar, he took with him to Mexico all those Caldwell files and contracts dating from 1933 to November
of 1951.[25] Had he planned his escape as a form of revenge, Lieber's de-
fection could not have been more damaging. Without those files, without their contractual conditions and verifications, Caldwell stood de-
fenseless in the midst of negotiations that, at best, threatened both his
former security and future publishing fortunes.

But perhaps more personally devastating for Caldwell was what appeared as a selfish denial of a client and friend. He had known and
trusted Max Lieber for eighteen years—longer than anyone else except
Morang. In the beginning Caldwell had shared Lieber's leftist sympathies, had attended a Foster-Ford rally with him, and with his encouragement had contributed freely to *New Masses*. From the beginning he
had trusted him so totally that he left first Scribner's and then Viking to
follow the agent's promises. When Lieber fled the United States, he took
with him much more than Caldwell's contracts and files.

Weybright proved more perceptive than Caldwell perhaps credited
him to be at the time. Lieber must have realized that he could not successfully have countered Chambers's accusations during those xenophobic times. But whether or not Lieber had anticipated his departure
prior to the forestalled Almat Publishing bonanza is speculative. The re-

ality was that legally and emotionally Lieber had left his client and friend in a most vulnerable position.

The reasoned approaches of Julius Weiss, lawyer and increasingly respected friend, resolved Caldwell's contractual and publishing dilemmas. Even prior to Lieber's departure, his counsel advised against Caldwell's accepting the Almat gambit. Perhaps as compensation, Weiss afterwards negotiated an even better contract with NAL.

For Lieber's replacement, Weiss recommended a lawyer by degree and editor by former experience. Somewhat younger than Caldwell, James Oliver Brown had left Little, Brown and Company a few years before to form his own literary agency. Before the end of 1952, therefore, Caldwell and Jim Brown entered into an association that would bind them more essentially than the legal contract they had signed.

Until Brown, however, could reconstruct Caldwell's publishing history and sort through the confusion that Lieber had left in his wake, Weiss offered another suggestion. Caldwell's relationship with DS&P had long been uneasy and financially insecure. Why not accept the DS&P–Little, Brown alliance? Yes, they would receive the 50 percent NAL reprint royalty fee even on *Tobacco Road* and *God's Little Acre*, books they had not published, but that was accepted and standard publishing procedure. When his present contract expired, he and Brown could sign with whomever he pleased. Recognizing the practicality of Weiss's suggestion, Caldwell glumly accepted what he always had perceived as an unjust practice.

The turmoil surrounding Caldwell's publishing situation made public reactions to *Call It Experience* pale by comparison. Most of its reviews must have seemed lukewarm to one who had been "tied up in knots" during its writing. It was "smoothly written, and smoothly readable," its story told "honestly, simply and in complete seriousness." What reviews did not catch, one querulous fan did. The family he only hinted at, and Caldwell's other "sins of omission" seriously had flawed the work. His "cool calculatedness issued throughout the book like carefully measured ice-cakes." Then she struck perceptively close to the heart: "You put the knife in deeply for all the sad ones you've seen, but you can't stand the pinprick in your own skin, can you?"[26]

The pain such barbs inflicted was perhaps minor compared to the other assaults Caldwell then felt he was enduring. In addition to the DS&P battles, he realized that during the Santa Barbara summer he had not accomplished all he might have hoped. June's numerous volunteer-related telephone calls continued to disturb him, and she persisted in regularly visiting the psychoanalyst. Caldwell justifiably questioned some of what June claimed were Dr. Sarlin's most recent therapeutic methods. She had abandoned the couple's usual sleeping arrangements for the independent privacy of her own room.

What June denied, other women would provide. Caldwell had continued corresponding with the young Houston reporter. And almost as if by fate, a woman he earlier had tried to locate reentered his life through a letter. It told of a painting done by her art instructor, Stanley Goddard. "Cracker-Porch" reminded her so much of Caldwell's earlier works, that she thought he might be interested if he were not "tired of that sort of thing."[27]

What intrigued Caldwell even more was the signature: "Ginny Fletcher." In case he wondered who might be writing, Ginny gave him the clue; they had met at Victor Weybright's in Baltimore ages ago. He responded immediately.[28] Ginny was never to think for a minute that he could ever forget her. He merely had lost her after that Maryland goodnight.

Caldwell was not to lose Ginny again. During the next three months, as the old year passed into the new, they corresponded more and more frequently. And Caldwell, then forty-eight years of age, entered a new cycle of life, but one still shadowed by the old.

Part 5

"Outcast among the Literary Guys"

Chapter 18

Early in January 1952 Caldwell attempted to satisfy a variety of past obligations. He established trusts for each of his children; he satisfied Pix's several requests for small loans urged by the birth of a child and other complications. Later that year he assumed the mortgage for his Aunt Sallie Bell's modest house in Prosperity. Though Caldwell continued sending money upon request to Morang, he resisted his new wife Lucynda's efforts to play upon his generosity. He countered her alcoholic pleas by suggesting that she go to work.

And finally, always so prompt in paying bills, Caldwell that year remitted only one-fourth of Dr. Sarlin's more than four-hundred-dollar monthly charges for June's counseling sessions. Minimally fulfilling the letter of the law, Caldwell certainly begrudged paying for what he considered questionable services. Additionally his "capacity for tolerance was not enhanced by the subtle and usually vulgar jokes about analysts and their adulterous female patients" he overheard among his club associates.[1]

And as Caldwell juggled responsibilities that his sense of duty imposed, he likewise sought to assure his other private needs. His letters to Ginny appealingly anticipated their early March meeting in Sarasota. Apparently hedging those hopes, he likewise broached a May meeting in Houston with the young reporter, then teaching and writing a regular column for the *Houston Post*. She welcomed his coming but cautioned that she was older and "tireder" than when she last had chased him around the pillars of his Kansas hotel.[2] Perhaps when Caldwell made his reservations at the exclusive Shamrock Hotel, he should request a room with two rocking chairs. And although a June date would be more convenient to her, she assured him she was never out of town.

Before those arrangements could be completed, however, Caldwell flew to see Ginny.[3] Talking far into their two nights at the Hotel Sarasota

Terrace, they discovered how much they shared in common. Conceived in Richmond, Virginia, she had that and her name to offer as her southern origins. Her father, furthermore, was also a minister, though of the Seventh-Day Adventist persuasion. Like Caldwell, she had moved frequently during her childhood and adolescence.

Born in New Jersey, Virginia Moffet had been packed from Maine to Massachusetts, from Canada to West Virginia, and finally to Baltimore by the time she was fourteen.[4] After attending first a Seventh-Day Adventist boarding school and then public institutions, she completed her secondary schooling at a Washington, D.C., high school. Advised by her mother to follow her interests in art, Virginia nonetheless entered a pre-med program at the University of Maryland. Remaining there until her junior year, she withdrew to enter the Maryland Institute Art School. Like Caldwell she had never earned her degree.

During those Sarasota spring evenings Virginia and Caldwell discovered other sympathies. Virginia's mother, like Caldwell's, had been one with "strong character and a lot of pride."[5] An English teacher also, Mrs. Moffet gave up her career to raise the two daughters. Otherwise like Carrie, she too liked "lovely, material things," but felt "guilty for her yearnings" because religious beliefs reinforced by ministerial poverty denied such luxuries. The fathers too shared similarities. Both were "totally dedicated to their work and helping others," a situation families and children were forced to accept no matter the emotional costs. With loving respect and understanding, Virginia nonetheless observed that in such instances "there *CAN* be a feeling of neglect, there can be an actual 'loving' neglect, all unintentional."[6]

But such psychological considerations did not occupy Caldwell and Virginia in Sarasota that March, and again a month and a half later in April. Instead they talked about their respective feelings—Virginia about her little boy Drew and her solitary walks along Sarasota's beaches as she explored her feelings about her separation from her husband. Caldwell mused about his situation with June, his feelings of rejection. "It was just like a well overflowing," she noted, as he compared himself with a turtle; he had been hurt so much and so often that he feared coming out of his shell. Virginia felt then as always that Caldwell once had been a lonely little child, in fact, had "been lonely his whole life."[7]

Virginia's sympathy and understanding must have made Caldwell yearn for what he felt he had been missing with June. Either that or again his honor perhaps compelled him "to make an honest woman" of his new love. For whatever reasons, before he departed Sarasota after his second visit, he had asked Virginia if she could consider one day becoming the fourth Mrs. Erskine Caldwell. Her own situation allowed her to defer such a decision. With honesty and sympathy she neither had accepted nor rejected that possibility.

Returned to Tucson after a four-day Las Vegas stint with Al Manuel, Caldwell admitted to Virginia that their past week represented his idea of something worthwhile. It had been "no fun going away" from her and even less fun later. From Tucson Caldwell confirmed that things with June were "pretty poor" and getting no better with time. "It's hell," he concluded.[8]

But Virginia was not one so easily swayed by complaints that, had she known, were similar to the refrains Caldwell had used twice before, first with Margaret and then with June. As much as he appealed to Ginny in so many ways, she first had to think of her own unresolved domestic situation. In fact she had fled Baltimore for Sarasota seeking distance to sort through her own emotions.

Shortly after she had enrolled in the Maryland art school, Virginia had met Drew Fletcher, Jr., a handsome and sophisticated son of the St. Joe Lead Company Fletchers. Twenty-two at the time and forced by a mild case of polio to forsake her medical studies, she then had felt "exactly like meeting someone on the rebound." As a young woman of her decade and background, Virginia must have seen him as Prince Charming come to seek Cinderella. On his part Fletcher no doubt recognized vivacious beauty and charm despite its scullery beginnings. And to their credit, the elder Fletchers had liked Virginia almost immediately. Thus during that emotional surge accompanying the country's immersion in another war, Virginia married Drew Fletcher on December 19, 1942.

Deferred from the draft by his work in a Maryland shipyard, Drew pulled Virginia into a social whirl spinning with rich dreams. As heady as the attractions proved, their fairy-tale glitter through time appeared more and more like dross. Her early values had made Virginia question not only such activities but also a marriage awash within them. Yet some year and a half after their marriage she and Drew had a child, Drew III.

Familiarity gradually made her recognize that her young husband could not comfortably wear the heavy mantle of Fletcher family expectations. His insecurity combined with Virginia's differing value system provoked serious marital problems by 1947. Their unofficial separation became legal and permanent two years later.

Victor Weybright's party where Virginia first had met Caldwell in April of 1949—"a week before the Maryland Hunt Cup"— represented her first tentative step back into the social world after her legal break from Drew. Always sympathetic and understanding, the elder Fletchers had encouraged her to attend the function. After that, she socialized and dated little. Trying to rediscover who she was, Virginia and little Drew had been in Sarasota less than two months when she wrote Caldwell with her "Cracker-Porch" invitation.

When Caldwell, therefore, had asked if she would consider becoming the fourth Mrs. Erskine Caldwell, Virginia waffled, because she needed more time on the "sands of Siesta Key" for self evaluation. Her seven-year-old son came first, and she wondered at that point if she ever would marry again. Beyond those considerations, moreover, was an equally large one. She recognized that Caldwell's needs would totally consume her life. Virginia, therefore, remained in Sarasota while Caldwell suffered his "hell" in Tucson.

Although Caldwell was having to deal with his own emotional upheaval, his new association with the Duell, Sloan and Pearce–Little, Brown combine almost certainly called for a new book. What was he to do? During his harrowing of the past for *Call It Experience*, he must have unearthed the oft-rejected *Autumn Hill* manuscript of some twenty years earlier. In those early months of 1952 Caldwell apparently had dusted, revised, and retitled the old work as *A Lamp for Nightfall*, because that is what he submitted to his old-new publishers that spring. Either he had considerably improved the story, or his new editor was more easily pleased than the redoubtable Max Perkins. Edwin Seavor, writing for Little, Brown, boosted it as "one of the finest books" Caldwell had written.[9] Only Morang concurred. None of the reviewers was to share that opinion once the book appeared later that year. Critics commonly reconfirmed Perkins's earlier judgment.

Less than a month after his return from Sarasota, Caldwell was off once more—definitely driving alone this time—on one of his multipurpose, city-hopping tours which he habitually used as excuses for pleasure. His stop in Santa Fe only reconfirmed that, despite his earlier advice, Morang's domestic situation had not improved. Following an itinerary mapped out by Fawcett, Caldwell afterwards made promotional stops in Amarillo and Oklahoma City. Then he swung down to Houston on May 28 and 29 to engage a room at the Shamrock Hotel—with or without rocking chairs is unknown. After meeting with the Houston reporter, Caldwell promotion-hopped through Kansas City and Des Moines on his way to the Mayo Clinic in Rochester, Minnesota. Persistent abdominal pains had been feeding cancer fears. His subsequent seventeen-day exam, however, confirmed only remediable colon difficulties and fungi problems.

Only a day into his trip, Caldwell had found three letters from Virginia awaiting him at his Santa Fe stop. Each assured him that she would meet him in Rochester as planned. His answering letter confessed Caldwell's usual tentativeness. He hoped that this time when they got together, there wouldn't be any holding back: "The whole trouble is that I've been put in my place so often, I've become afraid of anyone. I like you so much that I hope this will be different."[10] Wanting her and her love, Caldwell hoped they could get so close together that he wouldn't "be afraid any more." Virginia did not disappoint him. She came to Rochester when June had refused. There she helped ease both his immediate and more essential fears at a time when he obviously needed such comfort.

Before Ginny had arrived, however, Caldwell had reverted to a tactic only Helen would have recognized. That first Sunday in Rochester he had reached back to his lawful wife requesting her reassurance of love. In the process Caldwell unequivocally shared both his fears and feelings with June:

I want to write this note before I go to the hospital to tell you that I love you and want your love more than anything else in the world and to let you know that if I don't come out of this thing tomorrow or the next day or if something should go wrong that you will know I love you. I am lonely without you all the time and I don't understand why life has to be incomplete not to be one with you [*sic*]. You may have reasons why it has to be like this but I don't under-stand them and maybe I never shall. I will only know if you tell me and I wish you would tell me your reasons. It may be that you've grown to have dif-ferent feelings or something but I have the same feeling for you that I've had all the time since I first knew you. I wish you could return to that and let us be happy together because that is all I want in life.[11]

Whether or not June responded to Caldwell's appeals became imma-terial. Virginia shortly did.

Departing the clinic alone on June 17, Caldwell detoured on business via South Carolina before arriving some two weeks later in New York. There more urgent concerns demanded his attention. His annual earn-ings had been slipping. From their high of one hundred thousand dol-lars, they had decreased to fifty thousand dollars, a situation Caldwell no doubt wished to mull with his new agent, Jim Brown. They liked each other immediately, but more than Jim Brown's enthusiasm and good humor commended him to Caldwell.

For the past seven months Jim Brown had worked unremittingly—and written Caldwell almost daily—as he diplomatically had sought to untangle Caldwell's confused publishing situation. Without abandon-ing his other clients, but saved by personal circumstances from estima-ting the financial costs too closely, he labored slavishly to revitalize Cald-well's literary reputation and sense of personal security. Caldwell always had expected that type of allegiance from wives, editors, and writing as-sociates. In Jim Brown he apparently had found that happy combination of both a dedicated agent and personal friend.

More than enthusiasm for his work bound Brown so devotedly to his famous client. Though long familiar with Caldwell's writings, Brown had reacted to the man almost with awe: "Erskine Caldwell was a gi-ant."[12] True enough, he seemed an untalkative giant, but Brown was comfortable with that trait, and the example of his own Presbyterian grandfather had made him sympathetic to Caldwell's almost inflexible sense of justice. That he yet objected to DS&P's 50-percent share of reprint monies and blamed them for his declining book sales was not unusual. All the writers Brown had ever known had done the same.

Caldwell's aggravation, however, was more intense than most. Earlier he had vowed never again to issue another book under the DS&P imprint. Confronted by that resolution, Brown had negotiated a compromise. Little, Brown would become Caldwell's de facto publisher with their Stan Salmen as his editor. Although the Boston firm likewise would exact their 50 percent share of reprint income, they would direct 10 percent of that for promoting Caldwell's titles. All intricacies of the agreement except one satisfied Duell, Sloan and Pearce. Strangely enough, they refused to release Caldwell from his Folkways contract. That slender tie alone remained to bind him. Otherwise Brown had extricated Caldwell from the firm and the consequences of his vow.

Before Caldwell left New York, all matters seemed comfortably resolved. Arthur Thornhill, the paterfamilias of Little, Brown, genuinely liked Caldwell, and only Victor Weybright's usual geniality seemed reserved. Resisting all of Caldwell's pleas, he claimed no decision had been reached about issuing a Signet edition of *Call It Experience*. Somewhat puzzled, Caldwell nonetheless seemed more professionally secure as he departed New York on July 25. Jim Brown's watchful concern and Arthur Thornhill's integrity seemed to warrant that ease.

From New York Caldwell traveled to Colorado Springs and the Broadmoor Hotel, where June and Jay met him. As in Santa Barbara the year before, he apparently tried to mend frayed family ties. On one or two occasions Caldwell even took Jay trout fishing. But sadly enough, June and he could not resolve what recently had become a central issue between them.

For whatever reasons—perhaps to break what Caldwell considered June's unhealthy dependence upon Dr. Sarlin and her Tucson volunteer associations—he, for a year or so, had wanted to move the family to Phoenix. But June had not agreed to Caldwell's plans, no matter their motivations. First and foremost, she could not relocate to Phoenix because that city had no analyst. Countering Caldwell's complaints about his lack of privacy for writing, June suggested that they either build a small dwelling near the main house or rearrange the floor plan of their present home to meet his needs. If that were unacceptable, then Caldwell could rent a small house in Tucson where he could write undisturbed. In response to his argument that he psychologically required a change of scene, June had granted him almost carte blanche; as he desired, he could take frequent or infrequent trips "to relieve tension."[13]

June could not totally discount Caldwell's concerns about the analyst's fees. She nonetheless did offer some extenuating circumstances so that $3,550 of the annual $4,800 charges could be deducted from taxable income. Concluding her response to his litany of complaints, she appended some advice for both of them. Each should allow a suitable length of time to think over the proposals without accusing the other. She did not wish to thwart his intentions but offered points they could talk about completely and freely.

Whatever talks they might have had apparently accomplished little because after their return to Tucson on September 5, the Caldwells reverted to their prior living arrangements, activities, and patterns. A possible legal suit about reprint rights for *The Bastard* and *Poor Fool* became "just one more headache" to add to the others.[14] Unable to write while so burdened with personal and professional concerns, he was "pretty far behind," but gave himself a starting deadline of November 1. He wanted enough time on the next book he wrote. Not contractually bound to any rigid production schedule, Caldwell's estimation of being "pretty far behind" was strictly that of his own internalized and goading sense of duty. As Jim Brown later had observed, Skinny always had been a "compulsive writer" because "he [was] a Presbyterian, . . . driven to produce."[15] That Caldwell himself was aware of his compulsions became obvious from his next book—one like nothing else he had written before.

Although *The Sacrilege of Alan Kent* was a personal and poetic chronicle of sorts, it built upon memory, presenting Caldwell's retrospective interpretation of experience. The book that was to become *Love and Money*, however, he wrote during the midst of his personal confusions, perhaps as a form of cathartic exercise in the form of fiction. Although

Stan Salmen cautioned that readers might interpret it as autobiographical, Caldwell discounted that concern. All fiction grew from the seeds of experience.

Though firmly rooted in Caldwell's factual experience, *Love and Money*'s introspections crawled ivy-like into the recesses of his conscious self, wound through those secret places where he agonized about himself, his art, and those ideals that had always haunted his realities. The story's central character, a popular writer named Rick Sutter, finds himself "lonely and restless" in an "early April" period between books. "Fallen into a rut," he wishes "to write a different kind of novel" but has trouble starting it, is "already six months behind" schedule. To ease the pain of his writing frustration, the writer seeks a woman—"any woman who can qualify."

Sutter finds such a woman in Sarasota. His Tess, like Caldwell's Ginny, had "thick dark hair, cut somewhat short and framing her face."[16] After he spends an innocent night nestled in her arms "on the sands of Siesta Key," Sutter is obsessed. Offering reluctance and excuses, she becomes a quest figure whose promise lures him to follow wherever she flees. That odyssey becomes a listing of those place names where Caldwell himself had had varying encounters with women: Sarasota and New Orleans, Houston and Colorado Springs, and finally Santa Barbara. And of course, Sutter cannot write because he is caught between "Duty and desire, desire and duty. . . . A man—the masculine—has to argue with himself in order to shirk duty and indulge desire."[17]

In essence, duty and desire rather than love and money seemed a more appropriate title for Caldwell's novel. At one extreme Sutter has "a driving urge to be a story-teller in the written word," working on novel after novel whether or not they are worth writing. On the other, he seeks woman because there are times that man wants her with an appetite like that for salt or music. "I crave her mentally, morally, spiritually and physically. She fills a need—and a void," Caldwell has Sutter confess.[18] That mixing of artistic and psychological desires forces Sutter to an examination of both since each consumes different aspects of his life.

Employing a professor friend as a type of alter ego, Caldwell confronts the weaknesses and strengths of his character's writing. "Is it better to write a poor novel than not write a novel at all?" And what if the millions who buy and read Sutter's books are only "in search of a thrill"? Just because he has published some "shoddy books," should he have special consideration and attention? In fact, the friend steams, Sutter is conceited and loathsome, "an inferior being . . . taking up space on God's green earth."[19] If he could not write better novels in the future than he had in the past, he argues, Sutter should close up shop then and there.

During the course of their exchanges Caldwell has the protagonists agree on at least the issue of woman. The professor celebrates her "mothering instinct," her "ability and capacity and imagination to be fulfilling of any demands [men] make of her." He ultimately enshrines woman: "There should be a worshipful statue of her at every crossroad, every hamlet, in every public park. In all human existence there is nothing to take her place . . . in the life of a normal man."[20] And thus Caldwell, during the period of his own struggle between duty and desire, fused experience and imagination to create fiction. The emerging figure was a woman-mother on a pedestal.

In other ways also *Love and Money* reflects those attitudes, experiences, and confusions that variously confounded Caldwell then as they had before. Seeking the fleeing Tess, Caldwell's character rejects those women who too casually grant him sexual convenience; they fail to satisfy more essential yearnings. One he discounts because she had "wanted to be independent or some fool thing like that."

Eventually finding Tess, Sutter is forced into self-examination by her careful rejection. Writers, he admits, cannot help being "selfish, cruel and scoundrelly" because their calling becomes a consuming priority. Perhaps they "ought to be kept in cages so they can't mingle with decent human beings." Ultimately Caldwell forces his protagonist to confront the truth of a painful analysis offered by an understanding woman friend:

> There's no future in your frantic attempts, when you're between books, to
> find the ideal woman. There's no such creature, Rick. Believe me, there
> isn't. There'll always be the same futile ending—you'll never be able to find
> her because she doesn't exist outside your imagination. Most writers have

the same telltale occupational malady—you too. You get in the habit of making fictional women so attractive and desirable—when you're not making
them despicable and crude—that you'll always be disappointed with every
one of them in real life.[21]

Immersed in his writing, a storyteller plunges into an abstract world so
consuming that people and events from the real world become distracting intrusions. When the work is completed, however, and he attempts
to resume normal living, he finds himself out of practice and lost.

Platonic ideals cast shadows more appealing than any reality, or so
Caldwell wrote while he hid himself behind *Love and Money*'s gossamer
veil.

Between books, not yet bound by his November deadline for beginning *Love and Money*, Caldwell used June's offer of freedom of movement to schedule a late October meeting in Tampa with Ginny. As in
Rochester before, he had argued that while she remained too unsettled
to marry him, she nonetheless should move to Phoenix to work as his
writing assistant and secretary. As before, Virginia deferred even that
degree of commitment. She needed more time to sort through her feelings. So stymied, feeling rejected again, Caldwell abandoned desire for
the demands of duty.

Faithful to his schedule, Caldwell entered that world of focused con-
centration where outside people and events represented intrusions. He
did not write to Ginny until some two months later when he briefly acknowledged her Christmas gift as a "fine example of bookbinding."
Then he lapsed once more into a three-month silence. This time Caldwell used it not only to hide and cause pain but also to struggle through
the book that so nakedly told his painful story.

Even before he had completed the work, Caldwell anticipated the
1953 trip to Europe he had promised himself as reward. June would not
interrupt her appointments with Dr. Sarlin for that month, and Virginia
scarcely could have accompanied him even if he had dared ask her. Not
wishing to travel alone, Caldwell then sought male companions to keep
him company. Jim Aswell, his old college acquaintance, passed up his

invitation, characteristically bantering regrets that he couldn't go along to act as alcoholic and sexual chaperon.[22] Jim Brown, however, could not argue with Caldwell's assertion that an American agent should meet those European publishers whose interests he represented. More persuasively, he perhaps recognized that the man who claimed never to have been lonely did not want to travel alone.

Before Caldwell could either finish the book or leave, however, two other distractions must have brought him a degree of satisfaction. His home state inducted him, along with other Georgia luminaries such as Bernard Baruch, John Nance Garner, Helen Keller, and golfing great Bobby Jones, into the South's Hall of Fame for the Living. Caldwell did not attend the ceremony because he had to go to Ottawa to defend the dramatization of *Tobacco Road* against obscenity charges. Perhaps more than annoyed, he was both bemused and gratified that the play still provoked indignant public reactions.

During this lonely period of his life, Caldwell was probably no less gratified by the infatuated attentions of the twenty-five-year-old actress who played *Tobacco Road*'s Ellie May. This Canadian woman, like Sutter's Colorado Springs love-surrogate about whom he then was writing, offered him her version of reality, but as in Sutter's instance, that was not enough. She thereafter wrote him unaffected letters, signed "love, deep love."[23] Yet he was taken aback when, some three months later, she arrived baggage-in-hand upon his Phoenix doorstep. Caldwell embarrassedly shoved some money at his secretary, instructing her to take the young actress back to the Greyhound bus station.[24] She later sadly admitted that staying away from Phoenix was probably best for her acting career.

Despite Caldwell's fame, the reception Caldwell enjoyed in Europe upon their February 1953 arrival caught Jim Brown by surprise. London, the capital of sophisticated decorum, particularly provided a spectacle that amazed him. Unlike Americans, English newspaper and television reporters waited as Caldwell stepped off the plane. Almost besieged, he and Brown hurried through customs to be "rushed off in a taxi to Claridges." That sedate establishment seemed a trifle shocked by Caldwell's reception, but "Skinny, of course, loved it."[25] Throughout

England, France, Italy, and the other countries where they traveled, the greetings were similar and the pace increasingly hectic.

More than Caldwell's stamina and relish amazed Brown. One night at the Saudeen Bar in Paris he marveled at the number of beautiful hookers who "were all going for Skinny." Leaving for a few minutes, he returned to find Caldwell gone and the girls scattered. Assuming what he considered the obvious, Brown retired alone to his own room. Not until the next morning did he discover that Caldwell also had used that opportunity to escape and sleep alone. That incident confirmed Brown's beliefs about Caldwell's essentially puritan background. He then only half-correctly assumed that if Caldwell "were going to sleep with a woman, he had to be married to her." In this instance Caldwell had remained faithful to June. He moreover sent her almost daily postcards stressing how much he missed and loved her: "Sure wish you were here because I guess I love you."[26] Despite such reassurances, the relationship between Caldwell and June did not improve subsequent to his return from Europe. Yet neither did he have occasion to dwell upon his unresolved situation with Virginia.

Before Little, Brown issued *Love and Money,* they had hoped to present a respectable, complete collection of Caldwell's short stories. Toward that end, Stan Salmen requested some recent contributions that would help reestablish Caldwell's importance "in the critical mind." Caldwell responded in those early months of 1953 with five stories—his first since nine years earlier.[27] After considering them, however, Salmen decided against their inclusion.[28] Reviewers would inevitably compare the later stories with the earlier ones and question what had happened to Caldwell during the interim. Better that Caldwell's contributions to American literature rest upon his previous work than to provoke unnecessary speculation, Salmen argued.

Other publishing matters likewise awaited Caldwell's consideration early that year. Weybright and Enoch, apparently with Arthur Thornhill's encouragement, had made an offer Caldwell found difficult to refuse. They would give him a cash advance of $100,800—to be paid in monthly installments of $5,600—for all the Caldwell reprints NAL would reissue subsequent to January 1, 1953. Jim Brown tried gently to dis-

suade him from accepting the offer; so large an advance would leave Caldwell helplessly in the publisher's debt. For years to come, moreover—
until sales canceled the advance—he would have little influence over
their selection of titles, covers, or promotional efforts. Caldwell countered such reservations with the belief that NAL's investment would
stimulate that firm's, and indirectly Little, Brown's, promotion of his
forthcoming titles. In times to come Jim Brown would not allow Caldwell to forget his prophetic warnings.

On the personal level, Carrie must have guessed that something was
amiss in Caldwell and June's marriage. As her solution to their problems, she reminded him of his forefathers' legacy. They had exiled
themselves for the privilege of worshipping according to their beliefs.[29]
If at least he and June would participate actively in the church of which
they were members—. Apparently both June and Caldwell, however,
had felt that their marriage was beyond either human or divine repair.
By the end of that March, Caldwell moved to a Phoenix house he had
purchased. Publicly, husband and wife cooperated to justify his relocation; he went there to gain quiet for his writing since "eight year old boys
get lively after school."

Alone, apparently feeling rejected and forlorn, Caldwell reached out
once again, not to the willing Houston reporter or the Canadian actress,
but to Virginia, who had kept her distance during the previous three
months. He wrote that since he had moved to Phoenix he had been
wishing for a letter from her.[30] Her warm replies provoked his immediate pressures, first for Virginia to visit, then to relocate in Phoenix. He
remembered vividly the pleasures they had shared in Sarasota; his secretary was resigning; he needed "a house-cleaner" and "a lot of other
things too."[31] Finally Caldwell's pleas gained the advantage. Virginia
and young Drew planned to arrive for a week's visit on July 11. Caldwell
accordingly made reservations for them at the Arizona Manor Motel.

After Caldwell's previous trip to Houston, he and the young *Post* reporter had exchanged letters more regularly.[32] But by June—as he anticipated Ginny's visit—the young woman began writing more invitingly
and candidly. When a letter complaining about her suffering sex-life
went unanswered, she followed six days later with one of mild lament.[33]

She was glad to hear that he was working on the new novel, but was lonely not hearing from him. No doubt distracted by Virginia's visit, he did not respond until late September, when he proposed a mid-October meeting. That was "agreeable and desireable" with her; he was to call when he arrived and got settled in Houston.[34]

But Caldwell's concerns were not only the basic ones relating to his writing and financial security. Family, business, and fame concomitantly exacted their dues. Between March of 1952 and December of 1954, Caldwell commuted often between Phoenix and Tucson as he and June initially continued to maintain the facade of a stable marriage. He hesitated to sue for divorce because he feared losing Jay, whom he loved deeply.[35] She possibly postponed action because marriage provided at least some emotional and financial security. For whatever reasons, both persisted in a misalliance that overtly provoked more antagonism than satisfaction.

Among his other family, Dabney had married almost three years earlier. Although Caldwell and June had not attended the wedding, Norm Cushman stood in Caldwell's place. Caldwell, nonetheless, continued sending monthly payments of two hundred dollars to supplement the stipend Dee earned as a graduate assistant in hydrogeology at Brown University. Seeking to preserve some equity among the children, he likewise somewhat grudgingly lent financial assistance upon request to Pix and his growing family. Only Janet and her young husband preserved their independence by never asking for help. With a second child they nonetheless scrimped along on whatever Guy earned as a teaching assistant in plant pathology at the University of North Carolina. Otherwise Caldwell sometimes augmented his mother's meager retirement income, and of course, sent checks upon request also to Morang. He additionally overlooked those rental payments that should have been his due as then-owner of Morang's house. All such responsibilities must have weighed upon his honor because his then-secretary recalled that "everywhere Caldwell looked, . . . he saw a hole in his ship of funds and everything was going out."[36]

Such financial drains, perhaps, help explain the income-producing activities Caldwell pursued so actively during that period. They balanced against Brown's reservations about the NAL advance; they urged increasing his stock and active participation in the operations of the Catalina Broadcasting Company. Though Caldwell earned only $450 per month as president of the board, the capital growth potential promised to compensate for the additional demands. Pyramiding as it were, he likewise had expanded his real estate holdings during the past few years.

Such commercially related ventures encouraged Caldwell's membership in the Phoenix Press Club, whose members were not primarily writers—as he later claimed in *With All My Might*—but Phoenix's entrepreneurial elites. Their knowledge and associations supported his financial interests far more than his literary interests. If these activities were aimed at securing his financial gains as well as honoring his initial commitment to June, they succeeded on both counts. She was convinced then and thereafter that he was a most astute businessman. But such activities, added to Caldwell's promotional business trips to Rapid City, New York, Houston, and finally, Beverly Hills, necessarily took away from his creative time and energies.

By December of 1953 Caldwell had finally completed *Love and Money*, a book which, much interrupted by personal and professional obligations, had been more than a year in the writing. Stan Salmen found it interesting but "not the book we had hoped for." Jim Brown, nonetheless, enthusiastically praised the first book Caldwell had written during their association. He only cautioned him about staying away from women like its Tess and Charlotte.

Obviously Brown's warning arrived belatedly, because after Virginia's Phoenix summer visit, she returned to Sarasota and initiated divorce proceedings. With the elder Fletchers' approval, she planned to relocate to Phoenix. Once there and resettled into a rented house of her own, Virginia had told herself, she could supplement her small monthly divorce settlement by finding work of some sort. She did not yet wish to work for Caldwell. He might mistake that association as her first cautious step toward marriage, a commitment she was not ready to make. She and young Drew, therefore, moved to Phoenix before September so she could ready him for his entry into Tucson's exclusive Judson School, where Virginia had registered him.

Thus as 1953 drew to a close, Caldwell's woman-ideal had moved closer to him. But because she then had refused marriage, that rejection had goaded Caldwell to follow some advice he once had offered to Morang. He "looked over the field" by dating other women in Phoenix and elsewhere, even as he continued seeing Ginny during the following year.

Chapter 19

The years between January 1, 1954, and the first minute of 1957 appear to have been the most embattled of Caldwell's life and career. During that nadir period, nonetheless, he dutifully wrote—with a difference—and continued to function with a persistence strengthened by lifetime habit. Throughout that time—a span when Caldwell functioned without being legally bound to a woman he loved but beset by women offering their love—he wrote stories almost exclusively about women.

Certainly women had always been central to Caldwell's fiction. In his foreword to *God's Little Acre* he pithily revealed his underlying attitude: "No man as yet has reached the depths to which a woman can sink."[1] Without women, many of his best stories and all of his novels would have lacked essential motive force. Whether acting as sexual catalysts stimulating men's natural instincts or as mother figures restricting their freedom, women shaped his fiction. James Devlin, relying almost exclusively upon evidence gleaned from Caldwell's pre-fifties fiction, identifies some provocative patterns. They argue that Caldwell's experience with women infused all of his fiction more than he or anyone else had previously realized.

Accurately noting Caldwell's "lifelong concern with the role of women," Devlin estimates his "barely repressed fear of their domination."[2] This he perceives most obviously in both *The Bastard* and *Poor Fool*. The latter work "terrifyingly objectified his concept of smothering womanhood in a menacing female figure tagged blatantly as Mrs. Boxx," she who literally castrates her husband and prepares to do the same to the novel's young protagonist.[3] Working also only from literary evidence, Sylvia Cook found that "certainly the only good mothers in Caldwell are the dead ones."[4] Devlin acknowledges more benign variations of that figure even in the deceptively slight *Georgia Boy*. There Mrs. Stroup—justified as she is—always keeps "careful watch" over both William and his rambunctiously inclined father. The message for the boy seems to be "that the company of men is more edifying and cleaner than that of women, that women corrupt and destroy the candid interaction of males."[5] Devlin's reading echoes those resonances that would hum through Caldwell's reminiscences in *Summertime Island* and *Afternoons in Mid-America;* there also a boy and his father could be comfortably companionable "away from home." When Caldwell scholar Edwin Arnold questioned him only months before his death specifically about Devlin's impressions of *The Bastard* and *Poor Fool,* Caldwell justified the works as experimental creations. About the characters, however, he concluded: "I'm sure psychologists could explain why I gravitated toward certain characters, for example the 'big woman.' You know, that it says something about my views towards the matrix, the mother in life. The bigger the woman, the stronger her influence, I suppose, for the good or the bad. But I can't explain where these characters come from, and I don't want to."[6]

Neither might Caldwell have "wanted to" try to defend some of the other characterizations Devlin had intuited. In none of Caldwell's fiction does he perceive any bonds of love or sympathy between women and men. Though partners may mutually exploit one another, "A woman is fickle . . . until she has been mastered," and is "by nature [a] slight creature . . . drawn to the powerful male."[7] Because men are physically attracted toward only beautiful women, Devlin claims that Caldwell derided "Ellie May's sex drive" in *Tobacco Road* and snickered at Sister Bessie's. That attitude, he felt, displayed Caldwell's "personal prejudice" that "sex may not ennoble a man, but it always degrades a woman."[8] And those men in Caldwell's fictional universe? Devlin implies that most are insensitive creatures uncontrollably drawn toward women who, like Ellie May or *God's Little Acre*'s Darling Jill, horse around until they attract a male. But even Caldwell's portrayal of Will Thompson, his most powerful male, leaves Devlin uncomfortable and questioning: "And there is undoubtedly something immature in a world view that demands woman be a submissive animal permanently cowed by a potent lover."[9] But is the lover faultlessly potent or maternally flawed? Devlin uses persuasive evidence to conclude that Will "is an irresponsible little boy who stirs maternal solicitude in [women] and who needs them even more than they need him."[10] Even after Will has overwhelmed Griselda with his dynamolike sexual force, Devlin claims that "she wants to serve him and mother him because 'there was a painful plea in his eyes, a look that she had seen wounded animals have.'"[11]

It is clear that during the period when Caldwell found himself separated from one woman and not yet married to another, his writing about women was more obsessive than ever before. Most likely his earlier renditions of women had been unconscious. During this period, however, his writings reflected a conscious attempt to write with greater understanding as he tried to define women.

The first, *Gretta*, apparently played sympathetically upon the theme that woman is more debased than man. And almost without exception, his selections in the 1956 *Gulf Coast Stories* present women protagonists. His next year's book, entitled *Certain Women*, contained a collection of seven stories, all of which he titled with women's names—Anneve, Clementine, Hilda, and others. Stories published separately from books during those years appeared exclusively in men's magazines—four in *Manhunt*, one each in *Dude, Swank, Cavalier, Gent, Magasinet* (Denmark), and *Playboy*. The latter also printed a Caldwell selection called "Advice about Women" in its January 1956 issue. Not until 1962 would Caldwell write a book whose central character was a man.

As Caldwell began work on *Gretta* in the early months of 1954, real women directly and indirectly distracted him from his writing. To Morang's relief, Lucynda divorced him in February, sparing Caldwell any more rounds of mutual accusations. But by early March he began receiving other complaints, this time from June, who demanded a prompt resolution to a problem. Caldwell's minimal payments on Dr. Sarlin's bills had placed him so far in arrears that the psychoanalyst threatened to discontinue her treatments. He rejected both Caldwell's claim of financial exigency and his request for a discounted adjustment. June, furthermore, was "tired of having to ask for money like a child." If Caldwell truly did not have the money, he could use their various properties, bonds, or stocks as collateral for a loan. Otherwise she had already placed a call to their realtor. Unless Caldwell offered other solutions, she would advise the agent to sell either the thirty-acre Foothills property or the Tanque Verde parcel. And because her two-hundred-dollar monthly allotment failed to meet household and personal expenses, June requested a reasonable increase.[12]

How either of June's requests was resolved is unclear, but local opinion in conservative Tucson only supported Caldwell's reservations about paying Sarlin for what he perceived as questionable services. It seems likely, moreover, that he in fact was experiencing some justifiable cashflow fears. Always before, reprint monies had compensated for income lost through declining hardcover sales and decreasing royalties from *Tobacco Road*. But by mid-March of 1954, Jim Brown reported that the paperback business was "not good," and that meant a loss of earnings for all concerned. An even more ominous warning shortly followed. Whatever Caldwell's financial difficulties, NAL would "not be able to bail him out. His reading audience was not expanding."[13]

How Caldwell responded privately to what could have seemed a breach of both friendship and faith in his future can be gathered only from his public actions. First, and perhaps most painfully, he advised Julius Weiss to begin legal procedures preliminary to selling Morang's house, a foreclosure he justified as necessary to help secure some of their debts.[14] Julius approved that move since both Morang and the house had been deteriorating rapidly. Whether he or Caldwell consulted with Morang about that decision remains unclear, but Morang appealed immediately to Caldwell for delay.

Morang claimed to have understood Caldwell's necessity but could the sale be deferred until he could reopen his school? He had been in an auto accident and only help from friends had allowed his water and lights to be turned back on. Seeking income on his own, he was selling postcards of his paintings, but he earned so little that he suffered from lack of money and food. His mental anguish was in fact so severe that he was ready to take pills and end it all.[15]

That Caldwell proceeded with the sale despite his oldest friend's pleas is perhaps a measure of the mental anguish he himself suffered at the time. Or perhaps he pursued that tactic to convince June, and himself, that her demands forced his abandoning Morang to satisfy her petulant interests.

Beleaguered by financial and emotional concerns though he was, that

summer Caldwell took to the road again. Before completing the manuscript for *Gretta*, he and eight-year-old Jay took a six-week automobile
trip that was to carry them through the Dakotas, to New York, and then to
Maine before their return to Arizona. Jay had come to accept his father's
laconic manner. During their travels he listened to "the Lone Ranger
and read the maps."[16] In New York he spent time with Virginia and
Drew, who had flown east to visit relatives and friends. Otherwise when
Virginia and Caldwell went out together or when Caldwell fulfilled his
numerous professional and social obligations, the boy remained at the
hotel with a hired companion.

Subsequent to their New York visit, Caldwell and Jay spent two days
with Dabney at his geological survey site in Maine.[17] Following promotional appearances in Washington and Kansas City, they headed west to
the South Platte River, where Caldwell and the boy fished. After that
excursion—which as an adult Jay only vaguely recalled—they returned
to Arizona in mid-August. Dropping the boy off in Tucson, Caldwell returned to Phoenix alone—to finish writing *Gretta* and confront other
problems.

Almost daily, letters from Jim Brown heaped professional worry upon
worry. *Love and Money* sales seriously lagged. Always sensitive to Caldwell's feelings, Brown offered the excuse that perhaps the book's provocative dust jacket had betrayed it, but little could be done about such selection policies. The contract Lieber had signed with Duell, Sloan and
Pearce transferred its conditions to the Little, Brown arrangement.[18]
Caldwell seethed. As much as the Folkways Series meant to him, he resigned as editor. Neither he nor Charlie Duell could tolerate each other
any longer. He threatened, furthermore, that if he could not be freed
from Lieber's old restrictive covenant, he had no alternative but to quit
writing.

Because Weybright refused to reprint *Call It Experience* unless in tan-
dem with *Love and Money*, Caldwell contacted Julius Weiss about the
possibility of breaking the NAL contract.[19] Under the standing arrangements the earnings from both books would come under the terms of the
pre-1953 agreement, a condition subtracting their future earnings from
the hundred-thousand-dollar advance. At that rate, Caldwell moaned,

he would be "indentured for perpetuity." Seeking the causes for Weybright's unusual truculence, Brown discovered that Caldwell's emphasis in *Experience* had hurt Victor's feelings. There he unjustly had given Roscoe Fawcett rather than Victor the credit for his paperback success. That, compounded with Caldwell's catering to every Fawcett-contrived promotional whim, made Weybright feel unappreciated.

Through patient negotiations Brown eventually healed both the Caldwell-NAL rift and the confusion between Little, Brown and DS&P.[20] But the reprint firm as well as the hardcover one would have to abandon book-cover appeals like those of "the NAL trash." Money-making though they were, they cheapened Caldwell's reputation. If Caldwell were to be brought back "where he belong[ed] in the field of American literature," then his future works would have to be packaged "in a more dignified way, more in keeping with the quality of his writing."[21]

In other more personal ways Brown lent Caldwell that support that not only saved him from himself but also filled those empty spaces left by the withdrawal of others. June's increasingly critical distance and Morang's now-only-occasional letters deprived him of those companions his silent nature required. Although financial and domestic concerns would not allow Brown to accompany Caldwell on another European whirlwind tour, he otherwise offered assurances of his faithful allegiance. The heavy demands of Caldwell's projects were not too burdensome; Brown appreciated working with him more than anyone else. After reading the *Gretta* manuscript, which in book form critics universally would pan, Brown proclaimed, "[It] is a fine book. You have another ready to go."[22] Stan Salmen likewise offered praise rather than reservations. There could be no improvement over *Gretta* in craftsmanship, but he hoped Caldwell's next work would be three times as large.[23]

Later questioned about why neither he nor the editors ever challenged the quality of *Gretta* and Caldwell's subsequent books, Jim Brown mused: "I suppose we were being two-faced, but we loved Skinny. He was a great writer." Because Erskine Caldwell had not enjoyed the recognition that his earlier writings warranted, those who admired him as a person and writer perhaps overcompensated with undiluted praise. But at that time it was obvious that "Skinny would not accept editorial advice," so Brown and the others accepted this reality, went along with him, and hoped.[24]

What neither Brown nor anyone else recognized—except possibly Caldwell and his first wife, Helen, in another time—was that during that other time Caldwell had indeed accepted and valued editorial advice. Then Helen, with her directing assurances, and Max Perkins, with his sensitive firmness, had nudged Caldwell's writing to quality. But soon Lieber came along to convince a hungry and naive Georgia boy that monied contracts were more valuable than editorial supervision. With similar promises, Lieber perhaps had led the trusting Caldwell down the path toward future difficulties.

Almost from his literary beginnings, Caldwell's writings had been widely read and acclaimed in Russia. When the Union of Soviet Writers, therefore, offered him an expenses-paid invitation to the Moscow All-Union Congress of Soviet Writers, Caldwell enthusiastically wired his tentative acceptance. In that otherwise bleak November of 1954, that honor seemed especially appealing. As Brown, Thornhill, and Weybright all warned, however, the situation and times were scarcely auspicious for such a trip. Alone among all American writers, the Russians had invited Caldwell. And with memories of the McCarthy hearings still fresh, with labels like the "Russian menace" and "Red Scare" yet current, his visa request would raise questions about his associations with Lieber. In fact, Brown only recently had muted some covert inquiries. But Caldwell could not be dissuaded; he applied for his passport.

The Department of State's prompt response argues that they only had to open already assembled files for Caldwell's associations with Lieber to haunt him. His name was signed to a pamphlet entitled "Culture and Crisis," which supported the Communist candidates Foster and Ford in 1932.[25] Other accounts identified Caldwell's "connection with several front organizations during the late 30's and 40's."[26] The Passport Office would await his response before acting upon his visa request.

Incensed and shaken, Caldwell outlined a cogently reasoned and candidly honest defense. Perhaps his name was on the Foster-Ford literature, but he remembered signing no such pamphlet. As for the "front organizations," he then had been a "joiner" of almost anything in order to advance his literary career. As evidence of his conversion from previous leanings, Caldwell cited his recent resignations from the leftist-leaning League of American Writers and the Nation Associates. More positively he reminded the Department of his wartime correspondence work and the two U.S. Treasury citations given him for promoting War Bonds and stamps. He had "no interest whatsoever in the Communist cause," would do, in fact, all he could to hinder it.[27]

But reasonable evidence seldom counters xenophobic paranoia. The Passport Office rejected Caldwell's request.[28] The presence of an American writer of his reputation at such a meeting would be used for Communist propaganda purposes. Whatever disappointment Caldwell felt, he swallowed, answering the rejection with respectful obedience.

If Caldwell did not already feel like an embattled Job by mid-November of 1954, that was merely because the trying year had not ended. On the twenty-fourth of that month—during her thirty-third year and his fiftieth—June filed suit to dissolve their twelve-year marriage. She requested custody of Jay, one-half of their community property and assets, and monthly child-support payments. What Caldwell felt about this situation, with the threatened loss of both Jay and half his assets, he shared only with Virginia. That evening he had plucked a red garden rose for her before taking her to dinner at their favorite restaurant.

Although Caldwell immediately turned to Ginny after receiving the divorce papers, he almost as hastily wrote to advise his mother of the recent developments. As before, she responded not only with sympathy but also with suggestions for salvaging the marriage. That was beyond hope, he answered, since he had already exhausted all possibilities:

> June is set and determined. I have tried to persuade her to reconsider for many reasons, among them being the fact that it will hurt me a great deal not to be able to grow up with Jay during the next few years. Aside from my own feelings, it will be harmful to Jay in many ways, and that is more important than anything that happens to me. For his sake, I wish it were possible for her to take another look at what she's wanting to do. I think her parents feel the same way you do.[29]

After that there was nothing he could do except to wait for the legal process and further developments to unfold.

Both public rumors of the divorce and the beginning of the 1955 New

Year prompted various people to offer Caldwell their sympathies. A few
Tucson locals claimed that June's seeking the divorce was not "fair at
all." Otherwise Caldwell turned almost immediately to still one more
woman for understanding and sympathy. Six days after the decree's issue, Ruth Carnall responded to Caldwell's recent letter. She was sorry
for his loss but hurt that during his many California visits he had never
contacted her. Why? she wanted to know. Nine months later, Ruth must
have come to her own conclusions. She admitted to being "mature
enough (at last) to recognize," as he apparently did, that which was
"dead and gone." Just in case, nonetheless, she sent her own phone
number "for old time's sake."[30]

Two years earlier Caldwell had told Brown that he would write no
more short stories, yet beginning in 1955 and for the year thereafter, that
is all he wrote or was to write. Despite Salmen's broad hints, he worked
on no "big novel." Instead he apparently tried to forget through motion
what disturbed him in place.

Increasingly Caldwell traveled to Beverly Hills, where he and Al Manuel laid plans for a production company to film a movie version of *God's
Little Acre.* He dated Anne St. John, a newspaper writer for Hollywood's
lighter scene. For the next four months they wrote casually and met occasionally in either Beverly Hills or Las Vegas, where Caldwell enjoyed
people watching. She could not make it for a March 1 trip to New York,
but would he settle for a weekend in Beverly Hills instead? At Phoenix's
Concho Room he met a Vivianne, who wrote to thank him for showing
her around the town one night.

While divorce proceedings were in their initial stages, Caldwell sent
June two-hundred-dollar monthly payments to support her and Jay. He
also paid most of their household and medical bills. Although Caldwell
did not visit Jay in Tucson, the boy came to Phoenix in mid-March to see
"Papa" and to spend some time with Virginia and Drew.

Mid-February marked the beginning of a series of disassociations
which further wrenched Caldwell's sense of professional and personal
security. Stan Salmen unexpectedly resigned from his Little, Brown editing position. Caldwell barely had a chance to become comfortable with
Nick Wreden, his replacement editor, before that young man died of

pneumonia. Then followed the more permanent Ned Bradford. Within the space of those few months, Caldwell had to confront yet more harrowing losses. A February 23 telegram informed him that his old University of Virginia friend James Aswell had died of a cerebral hemorrhage. A few months later Caldwell's recent romantic companion Anne St. John, perhaps depressed by loneliness and distance from her native England, committed suicide. Those endings, in conjunction with June's divorce action, served as painful reminders of the sadly closing circle of his narrowing friendships, associations, and mortality.

In the meantime, nonetheless, the living continued to exact their due. Morang's occasional letters expressed his loneliness and unabated financial strains. Through their Little, Brown connection, Caldwell and Charlie Duell still exchanged dissatisfactions without resolution. But looming yet more prominently in his life were Caldwell's frustrated attempts to balance what he perceived as justice against what he saw as June's sometimes irresponsible extravagance. Knowing each other too well, the two of them pricked with pikes to avoid swords, both jousting to draw bloodied advantage from the other's secret vulnerabilities.

During Jay's 1955 summer's residence with Caldwell, June planned to take classes in Mexico. He cautioned that Jay's absence would reduce her allowance proportionately, a reality she should consider. She said that she would. Beyond that, moreover, Caldwell issued other warnings. Her last month's Pueblo Club bill had been sixty-five dollars. Unless she pared that unseemly amount in the future, he would cancel their membership.[31] There seemed little doubt that he would follow through on his threat. Earlier, when she had flaunted his instructions about buying supermarket eggs that were fifteen to twenty cents per dozen cheaper than those delivered by the dairy, he had closed the account. In retaliation, she had demanded a twelve-dollar monthly payment increase to compensate for the cost of Jay's milk, which she consequently also had to buy at the supermarket.

And so it went throughout most of the year. Caldwell charged against June a list of unnecessary and calculating grievances. She, in turn, accused him of using pathetically humorous tactics. Yet she could not budget as independently as she had anticipated. Three times during that summer she had written from Mexico to request additional money. Each time Caldwell forwarded it.

More than June's financial wants consumed Caldwell's attention that summer. He also bent to the more essential needs of some of his children. After Jay had completed his stint at a boy's camp, he and his Papa took another cross-country automobile tour. That unspoken traveling companionship Caldwell always expected from wives fell comfortably to the son. In Chicago Caldwell noted that the two of them had explored all the tunnels and visited all the zoos en route. They had visited the Newton Crumleys at their Elko, Nevada, dude ranch, and since Jay was a railroad enthusiast, he treated the boy to an all-day freight-train trip from Ogden, Utah, to Park City. While Jay divided his journey between the caboose and engine, Caldwell spent his hours gazing out the caboose window. Possibly he remembered an earlier time when he had ridden freights with an equally elusive companion.

But the youngest son did not receive all of Caldwell's fatherly concern that summer. Occasionally he placed concerned calls to Dabney. By then twenty-eight, married five years with two young children, Dabney was experiencing serious marital difficulties. Circumstances prevented his working on his dissertation and worries about the larger losses of divorce consumed him. All of this Caldwell knew, and so he called.

Always before, Caldwell had filled Dabney's carefully estimated and written requests for necessary money. Yet during this period of his son's crisis, he could not bring himself to offer personal comfort and advice. During Pix's earlier confusions, he had asked Al Manuel to stand in his behalf on the West Coast. This time Caldwell asked an East Coast agent-friend to meet in his place with another troubled son. Accordingly Jim Brown flew up to Boston in early November for a four-hour meeting with Dabney. His report spoke highly of Dee but promised little hope for the marriage. Once more confronted by the pain of those he loved, Caldwell had stood helplessly mute, unable to offer consolation. Instead he had stoically suffered, victim of a nature shaped by solitary experience and the conditions of his calling.

Prior to that summer's discontents, however, one of Caldwell's most persistent hopes had been satisfied. Because his long-time secretary was leaving, Virginia finally had agreed to accept that position. Seeking advice from the departing Betty Pustarfi, Virginia was only reconfirmed in what she had already suspected. Betty generally cautioned, "He'll drive you buggy at first. Until he's convinced you're 'sincere'! Keep your sense of humor. Whatever else, Caldwell does have that priceless quality—he can laugh at himself."[32]

An undergraduate student in English, Betty Pustarfi was not only romantically uninterested in Caldwell but had also been an astute observer of his behavior during that difficult period of his life. Some of her observations and stories, therefore, are worth sharing. But first a bare rendering of her impressions: "A very oblique man" captures their essence. He exuded an aura of sadness and disappointment, one that seemed to expect others to let him down. A southern gentleman, Caldwell never swore or exhibited anger before ladies, and though a gentle man, his relentless teasing sometimes seemed almost cruel. His only unqualified dislikes were aimed toward lawyers, taxes, and literary agents, and he hated to have anyone around him when he was working.

Pustarfi's stories, both in summary and detail, reveal further dimensions of his character. So financially close that he carefully tallied each expensive restaurant's tab, Caldwell, nevertheless, left his liquor cabinet unlocked and signed blank checks for Pustarfi's secretarial use during his frequent absences. During those times everyone—secretary, housekeeper, gardener, pool-skimmer—all worked like beavers not to disappoint him upon his return. And though never romantically interested in her, he occasionally felt compelled to take Pustarfi to all the "smart dinner houses in Phoenix." They then swilled martinis and exchanged long silences: "A filet mignon will never taste the same as it did when it fed not only me but also the conversation."

Incident after incident, situation upon situation, multiplied to confirm Pustarfi's reading of Caldwell's character and habits. Acquiring a kitten, he had named it "Mister." Afterwards he had asked Betty, with a sly grin, if he had chosen the proper generic name: "With delight he watched both the feline and me squirm as we examined the cat's nether parts." Further parrying about the cat: since Caldwell's frequent trips required that he take it to a boarding kennel, he had asked Betty to buy a cat carrier. After she had purchased one at a pet shop, they had spent that afternoon discussing whether or not the box had enough air holes in it. Was she *"really* convinced" that Mister would get enough air? Betty answered the question with a "silent expletive." Yet when she arrived the next afternoon, there was Caldwell, sitting on the floor of her work area—not in the privacy of his office—hacking slits in the box with a kitchen knife. His sheepish grin and the timeliness of his chore convinced Betty that he had been "disappointed in the purchase."

"Caldwell is a very STUBBORN man." For a year Betty typed with a portable machine, one that she liked. But Caldwell wanted to provide her with a heavier one. Attempting to sway her, he had brought literature about standard machines. She had read it but insisted that she liked and wanted to keep the familiar one. One day a new standard model stood in the place of the old. Though Caldwell was in the next room, he had left a note in the carriage; why didn't she try the new heavy platen? She used it; that evening she left her own cryptic note. She had not noticed any difference between the two machines except that she typed faster on the old one. The next day the new typewriter was once more back where the old had been, another note in its carriage: "Don't you *really* think the type is darker using the standard?" Her noted response: "No."

Although Caldwell and Pustarfi talked daily during midafternoon work breaks, their written dialogue about the typewriter went on for days. Finally Caldwell won. Her conclusions about Caldwell's will-toward-submission are both forgiving and illuminating:

> After awhile, Caldwell doesn't drive you buggy. Perhaps because of the mischievous grin and sparkling eye. He seems to communicate obliquely, and all is well as long as he eventually gets his own way. The little games added some zest and humanity to the job, and I'm sure he got just as much fun out of the resistance as the victory. All of Caldwell's employees apparently were subjected to the same treatment. He practiced a type of "isometric karate": just gently lean on someone's arm long enough, and sooner or later it will break! But we couldn't do enough for him.

Yet Caldwell recognized his practices for what they were. Having been accused of being "hardheaded, perverse, single-minded, stubborn, and [taking] delight in inflicting mental cruelty on other persons by insisting on having [his] own way without compromise," he did not deny such charges. He only justified them: "I considered my job more important than anything else."[33]

In every other respect also, Pustarfi perceived Caldwell as a regimented person and writer. He cherished the mechanical tools of his trade, appeared preoccupied equally with typewriters and erasers, sharpened editorial pencils and proper paper. Not incidentally, that regard extended also to royalty ledgers and financial forms. Speaking through her summary of Caldwell's writing routine, Pustarfi was convincing:

> I do not know about the *big* incidents in E.C.'s life. Except perhaps that the
> biggest of all incidents in his life is his writing—and his care in arranging his
> life so he *can* write. I lived with that daily for two years, have periodically wit-
> nessed it for [the twenty-eight years since]. He is a professional writer who
> does not wait for the muse, but arranges his life so he can use, or perhaps
> drain, the hell out of whatever it is that people call the muse. Daily, with the
> exception of travel and cat and typewriter incidents, for two years I would en-
> ter the studio to find him at the typewriter, the air reeking of his lunch of
> cheese and bermuda onion sandwiches, and lots of canary paper piled high
> in the waste basket. And when he finished his writing for the day, he would
> take the same intense care arranging the rest of his life so he could go on
> writing [the] next day and the next and the next.

Betty Pustarfi's memories of her two years as secretary to Caldwell are especially revealing by reason of time and circumstance. They embraced that period of his separation from June and Jay, his alienation from significant women, and his turbulent confrontations with publishers and negative reviews. In the midst of all such personal turmoil he, nonetheless, always presented an unvarying public face to his young secretary. Obviously anything less would have represented a serious breach of his southern manners as well as a violation of both his rigid values and private habits.

In the meantime the legal process of the divorce dragged along with each spouse blaming the other for the delays. June's Mexican absence and a mid-proceedings switch of lawyers contributed to the lag. She further balked about Caldwell's proposed alimony payments. If he died, she would receive nothing under his terms. He, in turn, claimed not to understand the problem. Would an insurance policy naming her as beneficiary resolve some of her delaying tactics? The tardiness, she shot back, was not her fault. His correspondence was so laggard that she could assume only either or both of two deliberate measures: he was unhurriedly transcribing it from Sanskrit or else sending his counterproposals via Pony Express. Such countering slings only reinforced the mutual distrust that was to hound their relationship for years after the legal decree declared them unbound.

Before Caldwell and Jay departed for their 1955 ritualistic summer trip, June's lawyer had submitted a proposal that, with some modifications, was to formalize their postmarital relationship.[34] Its conditions perhaps caused Caldwell to think almost nostalgically of those earlier and less costly agreements that Helen and Margaret had signed. Their household furnishings were to be equally divided. Because most of the other real estate already had been sold, she would accept either the Tanque Verde acreage plus five thousand dollars, or a twenty-five-thousand-dollar lump sum to be paid by Caldwell over a period of three years. Her five-thousand-dollar attorney's fees he likewise was to satisfy. Such assignments seemed agreeable to both.

The last three settlement stipulations, however, would fuel most future conflicts between Caldwell and June. As a "rock bottom" alimony proposal, she would accept "until either her remarriage or death" $450 per month annually or 20 percent of Caldwell's adjusted gross income before deduction of personal expenses, "whichever be greater," with these funds to be secured by a trust account. Jay's support payments were to be two hundred dollars monthly up to age twenty-one. That obligation would be halved during his sojourns with Caldwell or periods of military obligation. And finally Caldwell would assume payments for June's $15,000 endowment policy that would be transferred to Jay's name to secure his future education. During the next five months of negotiated bickering, Caldwell succeeded only in reducing the alimony payment to $425 per month.

Caldwell's then-declining annual income perhaps emphasized the specterlike conditions that would stalk him for a lifetime. Even were June to remarry, he would be obligated to half that amount for the rest of his days. If June happened not to remarry, he would be obligated to her until death did them part. He, nevertheless, had few alternatives when confronted by laws more inexorable than his own will. His imprudently signed fealty account might have exempted him from division of at least $100,800 in assets, but he could not locate it. Eventually he capitulated, because psychologically he never could endure extended conflicts. If Caldwell wished freedom from turmoil, if someday Virginia agreed to marry him, and if he wanted a measure of tranquility for his writing, he had no choice. He had to agree to those conditions listed by June's lawyer. With reservations he accepted the November 25, 1955, decree as final. The year's hassle left him fifty-one years old and tired.

Throughout that roiled year Caldwell somehow persisted in writing his *Gulf Coast* story collection. Unhappy with what the Little, Brown–DS&P combination had done for *Love and Money,* he wished to switch publishers. Brown advised against it.[35] First, no other firm likely would do any better, and second, Arthur Thornhill so liked Caldwell that Brown "had got nowhere" with the proposal. What he failed to mention was that a collection of stories all about women, written by a man during the midst of his own difficulties with women defied all but the the most generic promotional efforts.

With one past association dissolved, but another break denied, Caldwell nonetheless wished to sever one more tie with his past. Only two oblique hints help explain a decision he made without any apparent forewarning almost immediately after the divorce.

The day before Thanksgiving he listed his Phoenix house with a realtor, rented another at 29 St. Germain in San Francisco, and shortly thereafter moved to that city. The clues to his behavior are tantalizing. Two days before Caldwell listed the property, he had received a letter from June.[36] She mentioned almost too casually that both Jay and Carrie, then visiting in Arizona, would be spending Thanksgiving Day with her. Jay could come see Caldwell later that week. The cumulative and exasperating affront of ostensibly co-opting his own mother was too much. Caldwell apparently decided there and then to place as much psychological and spatial distance as possible between him and what he felt was June's deliberate cruelty. But one more nagging question remains. Why did he choose so unfamiliar a city as San Francisco?

Abandoned and perhaps feeling rejected by those who should have cared the most, Caldwell spent Thanksgiving Day with Virginia and Drew. As they discussed arrangements for his move, Virginia, almost casually, had expressed a wish to live someday in San Francisco. Except for his unspoken desire to please her, she knew of no other reason why he might have selected that place.

If that were Caldwell's motive, it would have fit a consistent pattern. Presenting himself to Helen as a writer, he had become one. Since Margaret Bourke-White had desired a roving journalist, he had written commentary for her photos. Then he had multiplied more than twofold the balance statement with which he had pledged troth to June. Surely therefore, a relocation to the city of Ginny's dreams might have seemed slight by comparison.

With the change of scene Caldwell assumed, by either design or circumstances, a different life-style. Although Ginny had placed her house for sale when Caldwell did his, she remained in Phoenix to care for his remaining concerns. Except when she flew up for a weekend or long holiday, he was—perhaps for the first time in his life or at least for the last twenty-four years—woman-free. True enough, Carrie shortly moved to a nearby apartment, but except for her, he was alone. Apparently Caldwell's dalmatian Belinda and cat Mister gave him as much uncritical daily companionship as he needed.

Occasionally people from his past reminded him that they had not forgotten. Having read of his divorce, the *Houston Post* reporter wrote, telling of her marriage to a wealthy bachelor somewhat older than Caldwell; nonetheless, should he ever pass through Houston, she would like to see him once more.[37] Teasing, June informed him that she was having a cocktail party on February 29. Would he like to come? Caldwell responded by asking what time the party would begin. Another time on a more serious note, she suggested the convenience of her keeping Caldwell's American Airlines credit card to facilitate Jay's traveling back and forth. The following day he requested that American Airlines cancel the card. And once again, the Soviet Writers Union invited Caldwell to an all-expenses-paid Moscow conference, this time honoring Dostoyevsky. Caldwell did not even bother the State Department, even though the USIA had requested permission to use his materials for their purposes the previous year.

Caldwell gradually became a recognized solitary figure at San Francisco's Trader Henry's and other fashionable—and some more risqué—"watering holes." His evening activities became the stuff of Herb Caen's popular *San Francisco Chronicle* columns. Obviously, the two enjoyed a friendly mutual banter.

And swinging more richly into the California scene, Caldwell with increasing regularity had begun hobnobbing with the Al Manuels. In fact, that early spring Manuel had negotiated two of Caldwell's works into lucrative deals. As part of one, Caldwell joined the company of Anthony Mann, Phil Yordan, and Sid Harmon to produce a filmed version of *God's Little Acre*. Yordan immediately began writing the script. And despite *Gretta*'s bad reviews, Manuel used his persuasive magic to peddle those film rights for $22,500. Possibly as assurance that he had not forgotten respectable eastern friends and associations, Caldwell forwarded 5 percent of that amount to Jim Brown.

As Caldwell's literary agent, Brown was not entitled to any of the money; the film commission belonged by contract only to Manuel, a right Caldwell did not deny him. Rather the money he forwarded to Brown was subtracted from his own earnings, payments that in the past Brown had refused to accept. This time, however, Caldwell—he who always checked his restaurant bills and quibbled about dairy egg prices—insisted that Brown keep the $1,125. Since Brown had helped promote *Gretta*, Caldwell felt he was entitled to the money and wanted "to hear no more about it."

Placed in that delicate situation, Brown diplomatically advised that he would use the amount to purchase a portrait of Caldwell painted by an Arizona artist. Virginia, however, frustrated that plan; she purchased it for herself. Caldwell's generosity and Brown's and Virginia's mutual appreciation confirmed a common bond; words could not have stated more clearly what each of them felt for one another.

Chapter 20

Virginia's sensitivity to Caldwell's numerous needs seemed then, and thereafter, to be always present. Gently, with gestures and symbols more than words, she had settled ever more comfortably into his life. During her annual trip east with Drew, she had written warmly to Jay, a little boy she saw as confused by his mother's too many words and his father's too few: "How are your father and Belinda and Mister? Is your father resting every afternoon as he promised? If he does, I will give him gold stars for every time he's good."[1]

Whether guided by Virginia's example or urged by his own feelings, Caldwell tentatively reached out to Jay during the boy's 1956 summer-camp experience: "I wish I was hardboiled because then I wouldn't miss you so." Such a naked admission he could never have offered to his older children, but during that earlier time he had not known himself, the children, or Virginia so maturely.

Perceiving himself as one born with the gift, Caldwell did not leave it behind; he wrote in San Francisco as doggedly he had before. With the *Gulf Coast* collection completed but not yet issued, he began working, despite continuously intruding publishing difficulties, on those seven vignettes that would be published as *Certain Women*. Brown only hinted at the scope of those hassles relating to Caldwell's situation. Recognizing that details of the DS&P–Little, Brown difficulties reduced Caldwell to the level of impotent frustration, he maintained a prudent silence about that unrelenting skirmish. The financially tottering firm had valued its NAL reprint royalties more and more, but Cap Pearce finally had said it all with his "to hell with Erskine Caldwell and Little Brown."[2] That had been enough for Arthur Thornhill. Before midyear he had paid Duell, Sloan and Pearce for the satisfaction of alone representing and publishing future Caldwell titles.

Flying in the face of Brown's once-pessimistic predictions, NAL reprint sales promised to erase the hundred-thousand-dollar advance before year's end. Because Thornhill liked Caldwell enough to have purchased his contract and since he did not weigh everything by profits, Brown urged that Caldwell boost the firm's forty-sixty reprint royalty share to the usual fifty-fifty division. Although Caldwell grumbled his reluctance through many letters, Brown finally persuaded him that no one would promote his books any better than the respected Boston firm. Beyond that assurance, moreover, the manuscript for *Certain Women* was so much better than either *Gretta* or his *Gulf Coast* stories that it surely would generate larger sales. Caldwell gratuitously had accepted that estimation.

Brown's politic praise hid what careful readers and later critics would wonder about those three works, as well as the others so pointedly written about women. Sylvia Cook identified some of those gender-defined themes characterizing Caldwell's later works. His male characters were "often childish, exploitative and selfish" but maintained "economic and physical power over women." His women, conversely, countered only with "their sexual wiles" and through ingenious manipulations of "scheming and bargaining."[3] Ultimately Cook cited the recognitions offered by *Annette*'s central character as evidence of the limited options Caldwell granted his fictional women: "We need a man. And that's why there are two kinds of us—loving wives . . . and wide-legged prostitutes."[4]

But by Christmas of 1956 Caldwell had a more personal and singular concern about women. Arranging for Jay's holiday visit, he advised June that the boy could remain with him only until December 30, because after that he himself would be traveling. What he had told no one except Al Manuel was that he and Virginia had planned to begin the new year of 1957 by being married in Reno. Although marriage had been an unspoken agreement between them for over a year, they had not set the actual date until late summer of 1956. He, at last, must have learned his lesson about hasty marriages.

Or perhaps Caldwell actually believed what later he lightly offered through a newspaper article as advice for avoiding "marital pitfalls." The lamentable plight of contemporary American women, he believed, "had to be blamed on women themselves." Ever since gaining voting and community-property rights through some hocus-pocus, they believed they were qualified for choosing a man; instead they picked "the wrong one for marriage each and every time." After summarizing the signs and consequences of such wrong-headed actions, Caldwell offered his own solution:

> As everybody knows by now, a man has the instinctive ability to seek and select the right woman for a wife; and if he could have his way, a man would never make the mistake of marrying the wrong one. The trouble is, of course, that he is never given the opportunity to make this choice. Stalked, waylaid, and compromised, a man is then in the position to be easily persuaded that the noble thing to do is go ahead and marry the girl. After that, it is only a matter of time until he realizes that, instead of marrying her, she married him.[5]

Implicit in such mock-serious estimates are those attitudes that Cook also had perceptively inferred from the canon of Caldwell's fiction. What he had implied covertly, she had deduced: "All his men and women exist in a relationship of sexual barter to each other, most often with women's beauty and nurturing offered in variable proportions for men's equally variable economic support and comfort."[6] And finally, speaking about *Annette*, the work that one day would be his last acknowledged piece of fiction, she summarized: "He also takes up again that more interesting and murky area of men's and women's lives in which women's innate tendencies to lure and depend upon men contend with men's responsibility for both abusing and protecting women, so that his women seem both seductresses and victims, while his men both idealize and mistreat them."[7]

At the time of Caldwell's more public admission, however, only a person with an understanding of his past marital experiences would have recognized the private seriousness that lurked beneath the public smile. But from whatever motives, Caldwell uncharacteristically did not rush pell-mell into marriage with Virginia. This time he acted with deliberative caution, assuring that he, rather than she, had selected the right marriage partner. This time also Caldwell had not had either to create or recreate an identity to meet the needs and earn the love, of his significant other. Virginia's artistic interests, unlike Margaret Bourke-White's, had not demanded his accommodation, a redirection of interests and habits. Because he had not proposed with a statement of worth, he had not felt driven to prove himself an able businessman, to invest in real estate and communication ventures or to join socially elite clubs. Instead he could be himself, the dedicated writer whom he had vowed to become when he had met Helen. Only in oblique, nonessential ways would Caldwell feel urged to meet Virginia's needs, and those, not so much to earn her love as to reaffirm his.

Up to the time of the marriage itself, however, Virginia had not been totally without qualms. Against her awareness of the many women in Caldwell's past, she had balanced her feelings for a sensitive man so many times hurt that, turtlelike, he feared emerging from his shell. Unlike the other wives, Virginia had understood that being married to Erskine Caldwell would be "a full time occupation."[8] Caldwell's priorities, those allied with writing and traveling, his habits and whims, his various human and domestic needs, all would thereafter take priority over whatever her own personal needs and preferences might be. On the other hand, she knew that he truly loved her, and like none of his other wives, she felt that she had the maturity to "fine tune and pick up" his subtleties.[9]

Perhaps just as persuasively, Virginia had accepted a "revisionist's" interpretation of Caldwell's marital history. About Helen she had known only as much as she could gather from him and the children. But she truly had believed that Erskine did not want "to get married a second time," that he had leaped "from the frying pan to the fire because Margaret was interested in HERSELF." But his worst mistake of all, she was convinced, had been his "rushing to Mexico to get a quick divorce to marry June, and here again he wanted even LESS to get married." Rather, she concluded, Erskine had been manipulated by a woman "who knew a good thing when she saw it."[10] But Virginia, of course, had not known what Caldwell had repressed and forgotten: that years before he had been mighty glad he had married June, feeling right for the first time in his life and sorry it hadn't happened sooner. Yet Virginia did know herself and him well enough to be sure that she could make him happy, if any wife ever could.

Married at the Park Wedding Chapel at 12:01 on January 1, 1957, the Caldwells almost immediately began one of those trips that afterward would pattern their lives. Ostensibly embarking upon a honeymoon, they boarded the *S.S. Queen Mary* in New York on January 4 for a voyage to London, Milan, and Paris.

Never again during the Caldwells' life together would he, then fifty-three, ever have to travel alone for so much as a day. Neither would Virginia, then thirty-seven-years-old, ever again be free of what it meant to be Mrs. Erskine Caldwell at home and abroad. That involved being besieged by correspondents and photographers wherever the Caldwells went in Europe; publishers and agents provided that assurance. In London Caldwell observed that there was "too much easy money" in America, a situation "bad for the human spirit." In Paris he and Virginia attended Marcel Duhamel's stage adaptation of *God's Little Acre.* If she had not recognized it before, that honeymoon period must have shown Virginia that for Caldwell pleasure and business were one and the same. Therefore, for Virginia as well, they would have to masquerade as luxury and fame.

The Caldwells were home in San Francisco for less than a month before Caldwell had bought a new Chevrolet—no Cadillac this time—in preparation for their departure on a ten-thousand-mile tour across America. Possibly he had justified the trip as merely another experience-gathering venture, but it also had allowed him to introduce Ginny to his worlds past and present. Each stop along the way confirmed that present: Salt Lake City, Denver, and Houston, where he did not visit the *Houston Post* reporter; then on to New Orleans, Miami, and Augusta, Georgia, where they toured Tobacco Road country; other stops included New York City, St. Louis, Kansas City as part of a carefully orchestrated, promotional effort. Agents for Security Pictures worked with NAL representatives to prepare newspaper people and book distributors for the signal event in each scheduled city and town along the route. The Caldwells were coming—to generate publicity for the forthcoming *God's Little Acre* and to help sell books. Caldwell and Virginia left in their wake front-page pictures accompanied by interview accounts. Appropriately enough, he was quoted on this "typical vacation": "Never spend more than a day or two anywhere. Keep moving."

New American Library, through Fawcett publications, had insured that newsstands and paperback racks in those along-the-way places prominently displayed Caldwell titles. Observing carefully those tactics used to ballyhoo a "hot property," Caldwell later advanced them as evidence against publishers whose promotional methods had been less flamboyant. His increasing associations with large-spending, hard-selling publicity types had made him scorn the less profitable but more genteel realities of the hardcover publishing world.

Parables about the multiplication of talents, memories of his poverty years, and Caldwell's then-declining income perhaps increased his vulnerability to those who offered advice with monied voices. Their marketplace practices overwhelmed consideration of any other critical values. Al Manuel, Victor Weybright, Roscoe Fawcett, and his sales representative Eddie Lewis, had known all the techniques for making Erskine Caldwell a household name, for peddling his works with seductive promises. Without literary friends or trusted advisers, Caldwell had been easily gulled; he had accepted their indiscriminate praise offered for the sake of profitable fellowship. Who could argue their success? Their merchandising methods had made them all wealthy. Their magic had transformed his hardcover "sow's ears" into gaudy paperback purses dispensing riches for them all.

Flattered by their backslapping conviviality and camaraderie, Caldwell possibly failed to realize that for reprint publishers, distributors, and promoters alike he was a "hot property," that his name was a valuable commodity. Thus early in 1957 he accepted seven thousand dollars from Fawcett's *Cavalier* magazine for serial rights to his *Certain Women*. Beginning in July of that year, each successive month's issue of that "action and adventure" magazine for men had bannered Caldwell cover stories: "Selma: Her Hunger for a Man Made Her Bold,"[11] or "Hilda: Every Man's Dream of Sex"[12] by Erskine Caldwell, "the man who knows more about women than Kinsey."[13]

Eyeing the slant of Caldwell's inclinations, Jim Brown had hoisted his warnings.[14] Why should Caldwell damage his reputation by placing his stories in "girlie" magazines? Although Brown was too discreet to say so directly, such cheap exposure made Little, Brown's efforts to dignify his books for the hardcover market almost impossible. Publishers and readers would not take seriously a writer who allowed his stories to be flaunted so promiscuously. Moreover, Brown earlier had passed along to Arthur Thornhill some of Virginia's broad hints: justice seemed to demand that Caldwell be promoted for membership in the prestigious American Academy of Arts and Letters.[15] Thornhill agreed, yet both he and Brown realized that each lurid association detracted from Erskine Caldwell's literary credibility.

In a variety of ways the "quantity means quality" formula had helped sabotage whatever hopes for literary recognition Virginia and Caldwell might have held. Victor Weybright had thought that Caldwell should appear with the paperback wholesalers' wives at their May convention in San Francisco. Such publicity would help generate interest in the forthcoming film version of *God's Little Acre* and the thousands of paperback copies with which NAL planned to inundate the cities where the film played. Similarly he had touted the advantages of Caldwell's addressing the three-day Pacific Coast Independent Magazine Wholesaler's Association meeting that October in Seattle. Citing the same golden muse, Roscoe Fawcett had wanted him to endorse certain Gold Medal books with large-type "Erskine Caldwell Selects" on paperbacks written by other authors. Fawcett promised him one to two hundred dollars weekly for these services. Jim Brown, Arthur Thornhill and, this time, even Victor Weybright—who in this instance had something to lose— successfully argued against this ploy to trade upon Caldwell's name.

And by July of 1957 Caldwell had found himself caught within a vortex sucking him to the level of promoting the screen version of *God's Little Acre*. A bevy of leggy southern belles had met him, Virginia, and Anthony Mann in Augusta, Georgia, where they had flown to negotiate an authentic location for filming. Caldwell and Virginia were pictured admiring pigs in Wrens; Caldwell alone had appeared in photos with local dignitaries. Eventually, however, the local power structure had refused location rights. They had feared the film would promote an even more odious picture of the region than the novel had inspired a quarter-century earlier.

Shooting the film in Stockton, California, had demanded additional promotional dues from Caldwell. The Ted Loeff agency had displayed him with a scantily clad Tina Louise playing the part of Griselda, with Robert Ryan as Ty Ty, and Aldo Ray portraying Will. Erskine Caldwell appeared in shots standing between Buddy Hackett as Pluto Swint and Faye Spain as Darling Jill. He had looked on as a young Michael Landon, playing the albino, had wrestled suggestively in his nocturnal encounter with Darling Jill. Later spreads in *Playboy, Life,* and a host of lesser magazines and Sunday supplements featured the actresses in provocative disarray. Sultry smiles and heaving bosoms invited audiences to see Erskine Caldwell's soon-to-be-released *God's Little Acre.* No doubt such features publicized his movie and helped sell his paperbacks, but they had not enhanced his reputation as a serious storyteller and writer. Such panderings only fixed Caldwell's reputation more securely within the amber of a public's imagination.

Promotional demands and public displays certainly had taxed that time and privacy so essential to Caldwell's writing. But as if those were not distractions enough, he had become increasingly embroiled in a legal harangue that was to strain him emotionally for almost a decade to come. Consequent to Caldwell's and June's divorce, two forces still bound them. One revolved around their common love for Jay; the other evolved from their respectively rigid interpretations of justice as outlined by the terms of the decree. For each, the letter of the law—prosecuted by a healthy measure of ordinary self-interest—became the mote in the other's eye.

Jay's visit each summer and holiday had provided an additional occasion for battles to be fought upon the grounds of justice. Caldwell's monthly support payments of two hundred dollars were to have provided for all the boy's essential needs. When Jay, therefore, had come to San Francisco, Caldwell had deducted each jot and tittle—purchases of heavier clothing and shoes, bills for medical shots and wart removal—from June's next child-support allotment. She, in turn, had seethed at what she believed to be but other instances of Caldwell's pettiness. If he had lived at the North Pole, should she be responsible also for paying the cost of suitable clothing? Caldwell had retaliated. The following month he additionally had subtracted the expense of Jay's weekly dollar allowance. These, and other legalistic thrusts too numerous to recount, Caldwell and June had parried against each other during the years of their discontent.

Such picayunish, recriminatory tactics perhaps were only diversionary skirmishes each waged respectively around the perimeters of righteously disputed ground. The divorce decree had assured June of monthly payments of $425 for a yearly minimum of $5,100 *or* 20 percent of Caldwell's annual income *before deductions for personal exemptions* and charitable purposes—depending upon whichever amount was greater. Knowing that Erskine never had earned less than $50,000 annually during the years of their marriage, she anticipated considerably more than her guaranteed minimum. When 1956, then brought her only the minimal $5,100, June sought the causes of that disappointment. There she was confounded first by Caldwell's sense of justice and then by a rigid interpretation of the divorce legalities themselves.

When Caldwell's lifetime accountant, Owen Golden, had forwarded the required statement of his client's adjusted earnings to June, she must have studied the figures with disbelief. How had he managed to avoid paying the extra alimony? She requested a copy of his income tax return. Golden had refused to release it. June's lawyer had appealed to Caldwell's Tucson attorney who had suggested that he comply with her request. Rejecting that advice, Caldwell had turned, as usual, to Julius Weiss, his trusted final arbiter. He had confirmed that the Certified Public Accountant's statement was legally sufficient.

June's frustrations wedged in that legal crevice between what the document actually stated and what she and her lawyer carelessly assumed it provided. They had expected 20 percent of Caldwell's income *before* deduction of business-related expenses. Instead a closer reading of the document granted that allowance only before *"personal exemptions* and charitable deductions," but *after* business-related subtractions. That meant that almost all expenses—Caldwell's travels, dinners with Herb Caen, and Las Vegas trips with Al Manuel, gratuitous payments to agents and even June's alimony charges—had been subtracted as business-related expenses from his yearly gross to arrive at the adjusted figure of June's entitlement. Only Caldwell's $600 personal income tax exemption and his charitable deductions were not subtracted from his earnings before June gained her percentage. And in future years, when his income so had escalated that June then might yet have received more than her minimum, California's community-property laws entitled Virginia to half his earnings. And so Caldwell had sliced legally through June's Gordian knot.

Although Caldwell had solved that conundrum to his advantage, he was not to enjoy the spoils of victory. Within a few months June had filed suit through Arizona courts asking that he show cause why he should not provide a copy of his yearly income tax return. Julius correctly advised that she had no chance of winning such a judgment, but cautioned, nonetheless, that Caldwell should avoid trips to Arizona lest he be subpoenaed to offer testimony. Immediately he had canceled a speaking engagement in the state. He moreover used that caution as his justification for never returning, even to see Jay win dual recognitions as an all-state football performer and scholar. For those deprivations he also had blamed June. He and Virginia further believed that her written complaints instigated two tax audits during the years of their feud. Though June had lost her legal battles with Caldwell, her emotional sniping eventually declared her winner in their war of wills and nerves.

The unquestioning support that Virginia had offered Caldwell during these stressful periods became a constant within their marriage. When he told interviewers that he had sat at his "typewriter every single day from 9 a.m. to 5 p.m.,"[16] for the ten months to a year he spent grinding out a novel, she had never challenged his claims. Truthfully Caldwell did exactly that when he was home. The discrepancy was that in almost any given year promotional obligations and various other trips generally consumed more than half his writing time.[17]

With care and sensitivity Virginia had stressed Caldwell's positive qualities even as she minimized the negative ones. That he avoided "any discussion of his inner feelings" became an accepted given. Caldwell's silences she had learned to weather. She had balanced such idiosyncrasies against "his devotion to his mother, children, and wife, his care of his dogs and cats, his pleasure in his home and home-life, his delight in a simple dinner of black-eyed peas and cornbread."[18] She moreover had marveled at Caldwell's ability to empathize with worried family members, at his always trying to extend sympathy. Finally Virginia concluded those praises she shared with his mother: more than anything else she appreciated his being "so good, so kind, this son of yours," and she hated "to add anything to his own problems."[19] Actually she need not have worried because increasingly Ginny and his mother became the only people Caldwell could depend upon for the uncritical support he would require in the years to come.

When *Certain Women* finally appeared under the Little, Brown imprint in September of 1957, many of the traditionally respectable papers failed to review it. Those that did offered lukewarm comments at best. Even Luther Nichols, one of Caldwell's "watering hole" buddies, had expressed reservations. Although the stories were not top-grade Caldwell, he had needed only "to restoke those old fires and write with more burning passion and less tidy and consciously dramatic plotting."[20] That advice apparently had come too late, because Caldwell was already writing *Claudelle Inglish*, whose reception the following April would be just as cool.

Against the chilliness of that public world, Virginia had offered the warm haven of a secure home. Although he disliked the formal trappings and gift giving of Christmas, there was a small potted tree in the Twin Peaks house during that 1957 holiday season. Under the tree were modest gifts for Jay and Drew and a few also for Virginia and Caldwell. The family had capped the season by staying up until midnight, donning paper hats and shaking noisemakers to celebrate both the New Year and the Caldwells' first anniversary.[21]

In one saddening respect at least, the beginning of 1958 marked another transition in Caldwell's life. A January 28 telegram from June had informed him that Alfred Morang had died. Not until some days later, however, could he have read it. When the death notice arrived, the Caldwells had been in Arizona meeting secretly with their lawyer. Even had Caldwell known earlier, whether or not he would have attended Morang's funeral is debatable.

The friendship between the two had cooled perceptibly after Caldwell's sale of the Santa Fe house. Morang's long letters and his glowing estimates of Caldwell's books had become things from the past as they had exchanged only occasional brief notes. In fact, by the time of Morang's death Caldwell had forwarded his last loan-on-account two years before, and they had not visited for five years or more. Almost as telling perhaps, Caldwell had neglected to introduce Virginia to him, although their previous year's tour had taken them near Santa Fe. Always in the past he had taken new wives to meet Morang as soon as conveniently possible.

Perhaps the clue to what Caldwell felt even six months before his old friend's death hid beneath some of his public denials. His friendships, he explained, were very limited because he was "the type who join[ed] a crowd to be alone," who preferred mingling with people as a group rather than individually. He furthermore avoided literary people, since their endless talking only violated that rigid writing schedule he kept.[22] But once, ages ago and afterwards, Caldwell and Morang had shared long conversations and letters. They had exchanged dreams as well as troubles, and to Morang alone Caldwell had tried to explain the depths of his feelings about his writing and career. That and much more had died with Morang, but even had it been within Caldwell's desire or nature, he had not been there publicly to mourn.

But in 1958 Caldwell hardly had had time or opportunity to consider Morang's death. Compensating for that immeasurable loss had been measurable gains. That very month, in fact, Al Manuel had sold the film rights for *Gulf Coast Stories* to Twentieth Century Fox. Estimates, moreover, indicated that by the end of September *God's Little Acre* would have paid for itself after only a six-month run. Manuel accordingly had thought that Caldwell probably would realize between three and four hundred thousand dollars—paid in annual installments of fifty-two thousand dollars—from the royalties on *God's Little Acre* alone.

Beyond that, however, *God's Little Acre* was being touted as an Academy Award nominee and had already been selected as an American offering at the 1958 Venice Film Festival. "Large money" and much effort had gone into promoting both the movie and NAL's reissue of the book. Manuel had boasted to Weybright the degree of their workhorse's involvement; in the space of three days Skinny had made at least ten appearances. Weybright and Enoch should have seen the performances so they might learn how "merchandising" was done on the West Coast.[23] The Ted Loeff agency certainly had left nothing to chance in the merchandising of *God's Little Acre.*

In addition to the *Playboy* and *Life* features, *Sports Illustrated* had resurrected Caldwell's Platte River fishing adventure with Jay, purchased four years earlier but then judged unworthy to issue. This time, however, they printed it to coincide with the showing of *God's Little Acre.* The Loeff agency also had "firm plants" in *Argosy, Cavalier, Pageant,* and *Tempo,* and in unlikely publications such as *Popular Photography, Photoplay, Weekend,* and *Atlantic Monthly.*

On the East Coast, Weybright likewise had done everything NAL could to advance the movie—and thereby the book. He and his young public relations person, Jay Tower, had approached the *Atlantic Monthly* about running a feature on Erskine Caldwell. After being refused, they had enlisted Arthur Thornhill's more prestigious help; his "pressure" had worked.[24] *The Atlantic* put Caldwell on the cover as well as inside that venerable old Boston periodical, "the inside, a Carvel Collins interview with the author of *God's Little Acre.*" Caldwell apparently had shared little but the usual. Collins summarized: "He's not a great mind, he's not a great thinker, he's not a great philosopher, he's a storyteller."[25]

The publicity attending the movie and NAL reissue apparently had moved even Caldwell's mother to reread the book. Her interpretation certainly embroidered upon Caldwell's simple storyteller's identity. *God's Little Acre,* she read as

> an allegory, not just a parable. Man, made of the particles of earth, in the image of God. . . . Ty Ty exemplified the Beatitudes. He was merciful to others, . . . he was a peace-maker among the members of his family, . . . he was pure in heart, so he was spiritually able to see God . . . . I like Ty Ty as I like Jeeter Lester. They both encourage me to cherish the divine spark in myself, and to search for it in my neighbors.[26]

Those who read the paperback and saw the movie, without doubt, likewise placed their own constructions upon Caldwell's timeless story written a quarter-century before. That fact, with its possible consequences, he had recognized and accepted. Thanking Phil Yordan for a screenplay that could not have been "excelled by anyone else," Caldwell guessed: "It may make me an outcast among the literary guys, but I'll always maintain that I'm very pleased with the picture made of my novel."[27]

To imply that others alone had contrived *God's Little Acre*'s financial success would slight Caldwell's own efforts. He and Virginia—later joined by Carrie, perhaps so she might experience firsthand her son's celebrity status—had spent ten days in New York in late-February, early-March. Guided by the Meyer P. Beck public relations agency, Caldwell had appeared on the Tex and Jinx, Dave Garroway, and Ed Sullivan television shows, and had been interviewed by Monitor radio and numerous publications. At Eddie Lewis's request, he had even appeared at the American Legion Infantry Post #307, a group commanded by Lewis and a part of that larger organization which had cast communistic stones at Caldwell. In the evenings he and Virginia had attended Broadway productions of *Auntie Mame, West Side Story,* and *Two for the Seesaw.*

Less than two months later the Caldwells were off again, this time on tour to cities as diverse as Boston, New York, Chicago, Dallas, New Orleans, and Memphis. During that three-week period in May the promoters had scheduled Erskine Caldwell wherever *God's Little Acre* opened, shunting him to a daily average of ten promotional meetings, luncheons, or interviews. But he had not complained. In fact, he had written Phil Yordan his letter of appreciation immediately after that taxing stint.

Then for almost two uninterrupted months—save for annoying letters from June and her lawyer—Caldwell might have found time to write. After that he had departed for a two-week auto trip to the West with Virginia and the boys. Two weeks later the family had flown to Atlanta for speeches and honors, and then to the University of Georgia for more of the same.

Ten days later yet the merchandisers had moved the Caldwells and their *God's Little Acre* extravaganza to the Continent. All were there—the Erskine Caldwells and Tina Louise, Tony Mann, Sid Harmon and Phil Yordan—as the Venice Film Festival judges had sat unimpressed through Hollywood's version of a quality production. From Venice the

Caldwells followed the film to its London premiere before they traveled to France for meetings with publishers and agents and then back to London to pursue similar business. During those frenzied times, Virginia had marked one notable and one memorable exception. One evening they had enjoyed a dinner with Art Buchwald, Caldwell's acquaintance from earlier days. On another day the Caldwells had rented a car to drive as a family through England's peaceful and cow-specked countryside.

Back in the States by mid-September, Caldwell and Virginia had devoted three days to mending literary fences. Much of that time he had spent with Jim Brown as his agent summarized the details of Caldwell's writing affairs. During his promotional absences Virginia and Drew's favorite Caldwell story, *Molly Cottontail*, appeared as a children's work. Otherwise Brown had resisted Caldwell's intention that his next book directly bypass hardcover publication for first issue in the more profitable paperback market. His literary reputation was too great to demean it through paper publication alone, Brown had argued. But still exhilarated by the impressive results of marketplace book promotions, Caldwell had been more than a little impatient with the traditional approaches he expected Little, Brown to use in promoting his next book.

His six-year association with Brown had sensitized Caldwell to his agent's disdain for the type of promoting Al Manuel and his Hollywood cohorts thumped. Yet more than concerns about hucksterlike methods had ruffled Brown's sensibilities. Almost from their beginnings Brown had thought of Caldwell as more than an ordinary client. He had admired and respected him as a loyal friend. After the *Cavalier* serializations, however, their association had become strained. More and more Caldwell had challenged Brown with suggestions advanced by Manuel and others. He had resisted them, but after Caldwell's merchandising conversion, Brown's earlier almost-daily correspondence dwindled to once-or-twice-a-week notes. During his New York promotion visits, moreover, Caldwell had spent most of his time at the call of Meyer Beck and Jay Tower. For Brown and his literary concerns, he only had had time for hurried meetings. Possibly, therefore, Brown had smarted from more than Caldwell's seduction by commercialism. He likewise feared the loss of his friend's regard and allegiance.

If indeed Brown harbored such suspicions, Caldwell sought to allay them. Since he was dissatisfied with some of his European agents and publishers, would Brown accompany him and Virginia on their March 1959 trip? Brown waffled. His business could not stand his absence, and he could not afford the expense. Perhaps compensating for the friendship lost through Morang's death, Caldwell had nudged and cajoled Brown. He had offered to pay his expenses if necessary, but he also had reminded him of a verifiable fact. Brown received a generous 5-percent royalty from the film version of *God's Little Acre*, in addition to his normal 10 percent from reprint earnings. He was implying that if one eats bacon, he should not turn his nose away from barnyard smells. Whatever the reasons, Brown reluctantly agreed to meet the Caldwells in Europe.

A variety of concerns occupied the Caldwells upon their return to San Francisco. They attempted to discount June's continuing aggravations, this time revolving about her attempts to gain control of Jay's fifteen-thousand-dollar educational trust. Following the Manuels' urgings, they accompanied them on another "people watching" Las Vegas trip, where Caldwell could be alone in the crowd. Within a few weeks Virginia and Caldwell took a train to Rochester, Minnesota, for his physical exam before continuing to New York for meetings with assorted publishing-related people, Brown among them. By the end of December the Caldwells had moved from the Nob Hill house with its twenty-four-hour view of the Pacific Ocean, the Golden Gate Bridge, and what appeared "to be a child's town of a city." The house had been too small and the boys' noises carried up three floors through the elevator shaft, they had felt. Their next Nob Hill place Herb Caen described as one "complete with iron gate and haughty exterior."[28]

And so the pace of the old year had taken them into 1959 and the new. Caldwell and Virginia had spent their second anniversary attending the Rose Bowl game with the Manuels, a visit that extended for the next two weeks as Manuel and Caldwell pursued film and reprint interests. Despite Brown's impatience with the ideas Manuel had planted in his client's imagination, Caldwell seemed mesmerized by the agent whose schemes always reaped financial bonanzas. Yet neither did he want Brown to feel excluded from both his friendship and what tricks the east-

Virginia and Drew Fletcher, *rear*, with Erskine and Jay Caldwell, *front*, San
Francisco, ca. 1958. Printed by permission of the Estate of Erskine Caldwell.

erner might learn from Manuel. He asked Brown to join them in their
Los Angeles visit. Whatever Brown's deep-seated reasons, he claimed
he could spare neither the time nor the money for such a trip. Conceiva-
bly, Caldwell had felt hurt and puzzled by such a rejection. Regardless of
Brown's qualms about Hollywood publicity methods, his principles did
not prevent his accepting royalties equal to those that Manuel himself
earned.[29]

The beginnings of the dispute between Brown and Caldwell had taken
shape even before their trip to Europe in March. Within days after Caldwell's visit with Manuel, he had advanced another ploy. Because his

Erskine and Virginia Caldwell at the Lido in Paris, 1958. Printed by permission of the Estate of Erskine Caldwell.

hardbound issues sold so poorly, Caldwell offered to use his own funds for hiring a New York public-relations agency to promote the forthcoming novel. Bristling, Brown had defended Little, Brown's projected methods. He lashed Manuel and the West Coast people for planting seeds of suspicion about established and respectable publishing practices.[30]

But Caldwell had not allowed the issue to lie. The matter of promotion-merchandising had become one of those situations in which he was determined to have his own way. Once again he spoke at the Northern California Booksellers Convention. Through his topic, "This Business of Books," he had leveled a critical charge at publishers in general:

> As much as we might like to protest against the country-cousin treatment we receive from publishers, we must remember that they live by a strict code of business ethics every bit as practical and honorable as any to be found among the cannibal tribes of the African jungle.[31]

The bitterness of what he had perceived as a personalized form of inequity rolled forth with his evidence:

> We see proof of this every day. For example, a publisher will ship $5 books to booksellers at 40 per cent discount with one hand, and at the same time sell the same books to book clubs for a dollar a copy with his other hand. But that is not all. With the third or really astute hand, he is selling the reprint rights to the same book to a 25 cent paper back publisher.

Persuaded by myopic business-friends—as by Max Lieber before—Caldwell had discounted Brown's often-repeated arguments. Hardcover publishers seldom recouped their expenses from the hundreds of titles they published yearly. Only occasional book-club sales and reprint incomes allowed them to survive another day to give their writers hardcover credibility. But Caldwell had rejected that reasoned propriety with as much obstinacy as he had proposed the legitimacy of using public-relations firms to sell books. Brown must have been increasingly disheartened by a letter whose oblique criticism of Little, Brown, and by implication him, once more had signified Caldwell's dissatisfactions.

As the time approached for Little, Brown's release of *Claudelle Inglish,* Caldwell had lodged an observing complaint. He had seen no full-fledged campaign to benefit from his name. Had Brown thought his idea of employing the Ted Loeff agency, so successful in promoting the movie, a good one?[32] Brown had hedged. Past practices indicated that such strategies satisfied "the egos of authors" but accomplished little else. Finally Brown's will had broken under pressure from Caldwell's form of "isometric karate." He allowed that using the Ted Loeff agency might help and that he would cooperate in any way he could.

Caldwell's persistence in flouting Brown's judgment in the promotional matter may have had many origins. Undoubtedly Manuel's experience and arguments had been convincing. He, moreover, had sold film rights for *Claudelle Inglish* even prior to publication; energetic promotion of the book would enhance the movie's chances for earning big dollars. Pragmatic estimations alone then might have caused Caldwell to have cast his lot with Manuel.

But deeper, more psychological forces perhaps led him to value Manuel's advice more than Brown's. Manuel, from North Carolina, was also a southern country boy at heart. Innate ambition, shrewdness, and persistence had enabled him to squeeze wealth from Hollywood moguls and indirectly from the public. Brown, on the other hand, embodied all those characteristics that rural southerners were suspicious of. He was a well-educated easterner, a lawyer by degree, and allied with a publishing establishment that had built its fortunes upon work performed by others. Caldwell's expectation, moreover, of "having others let him down," had found a stereotypically perfect subject in Brown. As lawyer and literary agent, he represented two categories of those Caldwell most disliked. Such preconceived expectations and reservations might have strained any friendship, even one less tainted by money and more subtle complexities.

Thus the die of conflict between Caldwell and Brown had been cast long before the Caldwells' departure for Europe on March 5, 1959 and their later Paris meeting with Brown. Once at sea, they had made an enjoyable discovery; John and Elaine Steinbeck were also aboard the *Liberté*. Remembering each other, the men shortly had renewed an acquaintance whose "equality of position," in the literary field encouraged them to talk, and later write, with a familiar commonality, or so Virginia had believed. And the wives soon had recognized their common bond. They shared a sympathy for "what being married to famous, demanding personalities involved."[33] Later Virginia and Elaine discovered that both their husbands, even as children, had been accustomed to being "waited on . . . hand and foot." But from Le Havre, the Steinbecks had departed for their rented cottage in Wales while Caldwell and Virginia left to spend their holiday attending to business as usual.

At Claridge's, Virginia, rather than Brown this time, had marveled at the considerations granted to Caldwell. Their lavish accommodations included a maid, valet, and waiter, all perhaps contributing to her estimation that "EC is without a doubt the favorite American author in England." Public behavior had boosted that opinion. Newspaper reporters sandwiched themselves into the Caldwell's otherwise busy schedule to record their impressions of the famous American writer and his wife. One correspondent observed that "Mr. Caldwell sits quietly with his thoughts, letting his trim, charming, tiny wife answer the door, answer the phone, answer the questions. It is a harmonious, dutifully maintained arrangement."[34] Another London reporter more generally summarized Virginia's role: "She keeps the accounts. She turns away visitors during writing hours. She does not ask what her husband is writing for he won't tell her. She says bravely that Caldwell is never difficult when he is creating. . . . Mrs. Caldwell is obviously the perfect writer's wife."[35]

On yet a more personal level Virginia had tried to shield Caldwell from those situations that he found both tiring and emotionally taxing. During "the luncheons, dinners, and long drives between places," she allowed him to sit back while she carried the conversation.[36] Yet ironically, this type of vigilant protection and care only confirmed Caldwell's lifelong habit of solitary isolation, deprived him of a writer's necessary experience and social interaction. Much later he pithily acknowledged the degree of his dependence: "Friends? Why would I need them? I have Virginia. She talks and I listen."[37]

From London the Caldwells had traveled to Paris, where they met Brown, who later accompanied them to Rome, Zurich, and the Scandinavian countries. There Caldwell had checked his publishing affairs. Uncharacteristically he had "changed two publishers and a French agent as well."[38] Possibly he merely had acted upon Manuel's advice, or perhaps Caldwell had wished to show Brown through example how either a writer or agent should expedite matters to his advantage. Brown, however, had been unimpressed by his methods and offended by his manner. Because Caldwell had tried to tell him what to do in the "Paris mess," he as the agent had been placed in an "embarrassing position" and Caldwell, "in an unhappy light." Feeling that he worked more effectively alone, Brown thought that in the future everyone might be happier if Caldwell "were not to be on the scene."[39]

Within that same memo of his discontent, Brown had touched upon a more sensitive complication: "As to our personal relationship, that can't be as close as it was in the sense of seeing each other as much. It is not as easy for me to work with you and Virginia as it was with you alone." Brown's honest statement of his feelings laid bare the psychological intricacies of a relationship more binding than that merely between agent and client. For three more years the two friends stepped awkwardly to a refrain of allegiance marked by the relentless beat of money and the dissonance of merchandising.

Perhaps only coincidentally, both Caldwell and Brown had experienced debilitating ailments almost immediately after their European return. By mid-April Caldwell had to undergo surgery for an excruciatingly painful thumb malady. About the same time doctors had diagnosed Brown's more generally bilious complaints as the result of hepatitis. Caldwell remained in the hospital for four days. Brown only tried to get more rest, to put his office and finances in repair, and complained about how the trip had irreparably damaged his health and business.

Shortly after his hospitalization, Caldwell had returned to his writing. With the injured hand tied to a hoist in the ceiling, he had typed with the unaffected one. Brown, meanwhile, had strained Caldwell's patience with a variety of complaints. His health was poor. His financial accounts were strained because he had to devote so much time to sorting out Caldwell's foreign royalties. To make matters worse, his marriage was headed toward divorce. Such oblique criticisms caused Caldwell to question whether or not Brown wished to continue representing him.

Immediately Brown responded with a long, emotionally charged and handwritten letter of contrition: "What I'm trying to say—and badly—is that I want to do everything you want me to do. Above all else is a friendship I value as one of the very few of the great relationships any human can have. Maybe the only one. And it hurts not to be able to do everything for you—but to be limited by money and lack of energy."[40] Caldwell's stoic reserve had appeared confounded. He had little tolerance either for sentiment or for what he interpreted as weak-willed excuses in situations demanding strong-willed fortitude. He accordingly had responded with a cool rationality: "It could be put this way: I write, you sell, and we maintain friendship at all times."[41] As if to reinforce his prescriptive remedy, he had reminded Brown that he had two new Caldwell titles to "spread around the world."

Though Caldwell perhaps had wished to stress that he worked instead of complaining, he had written precious little during the past year of combined activity and emotional struggle. Only three new stories had complemented *Claudelle Inglish* as the sum of that period's writing.[42] Although a fan thought the novella excellent—"like a Greek tragedy"— almost all reviewers lined up with one, who began with classical smirking: " 'Tis a pity she's a bore.' " Another from Herb Caen's *San Francisco Chronicle* aptly noted that "it [had] a later-day sheen . . . as commercial as the marquee on a down town movie house."[43]

Warner Brothers rather than Caldwell finally had pumped $25,000 into Meyer Beck's campaign to help Little, Brown promote Caldwell's latest. That boost logged measurable results. Although the firm's earlier Caldwell hardbound issues averaged sales of a bare 5,500 copies, *Claudelle Inglish* after three months had sold 12,581—at a per-volume increased cost of some three-and-a-half dollars, one might figure. With such visible assurance as evidence, Caldwell had wanted to pour some of his own money into increased advertising. Brown's response was accusingly blunt: "Don't cheapen yourself in New York."[44] But not even the film royalties generated by the hastily produced *Claudelle Inglish* satisfied Caldwell and Al Manuel. Manuel questioned accounting personnel about why Caldwell's 25 percent of a $3.5 million gross amounted only to $158,000.

Chapter 21

Poor reviews, Caldwell's continuing struggles with June, and his puzzled confusion about Brown muted his spirits in 1959. That summer he had spent some time attending baseball and football games with Jay and Drew and generated ideas for travel and home activities. Beyond that he and Virginia had attended the Indianapolis Speedway Memorial Day Races with Carvel Collins and his wife. During Khrushchev's West Coast visit, Caldwell had met with the writer Sholokhov, an acquaintance from pre–World War II days.

That visit apparently confirmed for Caldwell how much royalty money awaited him in various Communist-restricted countries. Perhaps to circumvent Immigration Department suspicions, he approached the U.S. Information Service (USIS) in the autumn of 1959 with a proposal. Could he ever be of use to them during his European travels? Indeed Erskine Caldwell could. They would provide a per diem stipend if he would meet with groups convened by the various foreign embassies.

During their travels abroad that autumn, the Caldwells had certainly wasted no time. In addition to their usual continental visits, they had journeyed to Prague, Istanbul, and Russia. They discovered that in Turkey twenty-eight Caldwell titles had been published clandestinely and without royalty. Caldwell charged Brown with the task of that attempted recovery. Caldwell and Virginia had found Moscow terribly depressing because while his young audiences wanted to learn about America, they remained obvious victims of Communist ideology. While there the Caldwells had lodged that early November in the same hotel where he and Bourke-White had headquartered in 1941. And although they also had dined lavishly with caviar and wines, their four-day expenses barely tapped his growing ruble accounts.

Back in New York, Caldwell met with his usual people, including Jim Brown, and the Caldwells spent an evening over dinner with the Steinbecks. But with increasing frequency the name of Jay Tower, NAL's promotional agent, appeared in their meeting schedule. Before Caldwell's movie involvement in 1957, he and Virginia had presented Jim with a captain's chair as a gesture of their gratitude. In 1959 they gave Ms. Tower a gold watch for her loyal work.

Subsequent to the Caldwells' New York departure they traveled to Washington for a USIS debriefing and afterwards had spent five days in South Carolina with Mere, staying with relatives and friends. They were home for two weeks before departing for Erskine College and Caldwell's induction into its prestigious Euphemian Society. Robert E. Lee had once excused himself from that honor by pleading sickness, but Erskine Caldwell did not. Shortly they departed for Atlanta, where Virginia had marked his fifty-sixth birthday in a special way. She had served him breakfast in bed and later surprised him with an arranged visit from Frank Daniel, his old associate from the *Atlanta Journal.* Then they had awaited the arrival of Jay and Drew for Christmas vacation.

The Caldwells spent Christmas Day—without a tree—in Sarasota. As a treat Caldwell had scheduled the family for a deep-sea fishing trip out of Key West. At the last minute, however, he had decided that he did not want to go along. Since the rest refused to go without him, he finally and reluctantly went but was "miserable the whole trip." That experience taught Virginia a lesson: never again would she "even *let* Erskine do anything he didn't whole heartedly want to do."[1]

How he displayed his misery she did not say, yet in the past she had confessed that he wasn't exactly "an 'easy' person to live with." Those " 'freeze ups' as MBW called them" remained as patterns within Caldwell's behavior. But Virginia had continued to believe that if a wife were "willing to take the time and effort to understand them," she might find the key to their cause. Yet beyond that she had remained puzzled because, as Bourke-White had pointed out in *Portrait of Myself,* he was "TERRIBLY possessive," and Virginia still didn't "know WHY exactly."[2] Her painful confusion about Caldwell's possessiveness and mysterious silences would remain a constant in their relationship. Virginia could neither trace them to their childhood sources nor discern their present causes.

With the beginning of a new decade, the Caldwells had been married for three years, time enough to have settled into predictable patterns. Circumstances changed but the two of them essentially did not. They merely became more confirmed in those obligations and habits revolving around Caldwell's career and his personal propensities.

As Jay and Drew grew through adolescence into adulthood, family concerns—evolving both from Caldwell's first family and his and Virginia's common one—caused some necessary and temporary adjustments. But beyond that, only that which proved remarkable punctuated what had become ordinary. This is not to imply that Caldwell's life—and accordingly, Virginia's—was without conflict. Rather it presumes that his rigorous conscience and principled righteousness assured varying levels of conflict and tension as constants in his life. Yet Virginia's gifts of devotion and security, accommodation and protection, had granted Caldwell a greater measure of peace than he perhaps had ever before experienced.

But those puritanlike exactions imposed upon a person "born with the gift" had denied Caldwell a truly comfortable sense of serenity. Early in the sixties Virginia mused:

> Erskine appears to be so calm that only those . . . who know him well . . . realize the level of his tension. Ernest Hemingway is here [at the Mayo Clinic] now with hypertension. Elaine Steinbeck lives with the same concern over John. He worries constantly. . . . In many fields it [tension] is outgoing whereas Erskine and John are burning themselves up inside. Instead of becoming less [troubled] with the achievement of success, it [anxiety] becomes more intense because time seems shorter.[3]

Virginia had understood, but there had been little that she, or Caldwell himself for that matter, could have done. He could no more have rejected his history with its exacting values than he could have denied his ancestral blood.

Beginning with New Year's Day of 1960, Caldwell had tried unsuccessfully to relax by giving more attention to his family. Again the Caldwells had attended a football game on their anniversary, but this time it was the Orange Bowl with Jay and Drew. Later that winter they had

given Dabney—then divorced and disconsolate without his children—
the gift of transportation, and more exceptionally yet, lodging in their
home so he could attend the Squaw Valley Olympics. But in the midst
of a Tokyo literary visit, Caldwell's schedule and tension had combined
to grip him. Doctors had guessed either exhaustion or a slight heart at-
tack. He would have to slow down, relax, and exercise, they had cautioned.

All of those things would have been difficult, but for Caldwell relaxation had remained all but impossible. Throughout, he and June had
continued their exchange of mutually accusing letters. He and Brown
only delicately had balanced their tenuous relationship. His first income
tax audit had uncovered only a $155 error, and that not in June's favor.
Another accounting by Little, Brown, however, had not proven so satisfying.

When they had received Caldwell's October manuscript for *Jenny by
Nature*, Arthur Thornhill perhaps had used that as an occasion to examine Caldwell's literary account. His hardcover sales had been so slight
that without the firm's share of reprint earnings, it would have lost almost $20,000. Even so, their three-year profits from his ledger had come
to a measly $3,500. Not willing to bind Erskine Caldwell to the com-
pany's imprint for so marginal an amount, Thornhill had encouraged
him to find someone who might do better for his titles. Long convinced
that Little, Brown's lackadaisical promotion policies had been responsible for his dismal earnings, Caldwell gladly accepted the offer.[4]

Shortly afterwards, Erskine Caldwell signed a contract with Farrar,
Straus and Cudahy, his fifth publisher in his thirty-year career. Naturally enough Roger Straus knew much about Caldwell's writing history.
He was old enough to remember the quality of Caldwell's earlier works
and young enough to believe that with direction, his firm could build
upon the promise that still lurked beneath the surface of Caldwell's
more recent writings. He, furthermore, knew and liked Ginny through
associations they had shared while she was still a Fletcher. Although
Straus would not offend Caldwell by assigning him to a junior editor—
that duty he took to himself—he would rely heavily upon Robert
Giroux's astute criticism. As the next five years revealed, not since Max

Perkins had editors as sensitively and honestly attempted to redirect Caldwell's work.

Relieved of some uncertainties and without either of the boys scheduled for Christmas vacations, the Caldwells took the Canadian Pacific Railroad cross-country from Vancouver to Quebec and Ontario. Caldwell had wanted to stay in the Hotel Frontenac—where he and Helen spent an autumn in 1936—"in the winter for years." There he and Virginia drank champagne on Christmas Day before leaving for Augusta, Georgia, where they quietly celebrated their fourth anniversary alone.

Two weeks later, and prior to the couple's departure for a six-week European jaunt, Caldwell talked publicly about *Jenny by Nature*, miscegenation, and himself. Through his book, he did not propagandize for interracial marriages; through time nature itself would take care of that. Instead its message was that a true democracy cannot allow selected individuals to exist as "second-class citizens." Then on a more personal note, Caldwell had sketched the scope and measure of his interests. Annually he had devoted nine months to writing and "as a basis for comparison," three months to traveling: "Otherwise I am isolated. I'd like to write books twelve months of the year because that's all I like to do, nothing else."[5]

Pausing in New York after their European trip, the Caldwells hosted a cocktail party in their Statler Hotel suite. In addition to his publishing associates, some different types of people had attended. Like Tina Louise and the John Steinbecks, the Harry Behns from Caldwell's Hollywood-Tucson days were there. More remarkably yet, Mr. and Mrs. Shelley Berman likewise came.

The inclusion of the then popular comic hinted at a tendency which later became more obvious in Caldwell's choice of associates. Like some celebrated tragic figures of old, more and more he seemed to have valued the distractions offered by professional and private jesters. The list was to be selectively impressive. Among the professionals, in addition to Berman, were Dan Rowan, Art Buchwald, and Herb Caen. Among the lesser-known but consciously striving comedian-types were Marvin Belli, Roscoe Fawcett, Eddie Lewis, and the Minneapolis people's pundit, Eddie Schwartz. For a man who seemed dour to many and whose own humor was quietly sardonic, Caldwell's choice of jokester companions seems to have been almost contradictory. Yet he always had looked at life as a mixture of the comic and tragic.

During this period those who truly respected Caldwell apparently sought to burnish his literary reputation. Roger Straus touted his credentials to the University of Missouri School of Journalism. They should invite Caldwell to lecture because he was a damn good speaker who took "his writing extremely seriously—as well he should." Following that endorsement, Caldwell delivered his "Wordsmanship" talk on April 30, 1961, which the University's Crippled Turtle Press later printed in pamphlet form.

Hearing from Elaine Steinbeck that someone was doing John's biography, Virginia tried to promote a similar recognition for Caldwell. Like his mother who always tilted towards things English, Caldwell first had approached Britisher David Lewin to write the work. He genteelly had excused himself since his time was too limited for such a consuming and important endeavor. Finally Carvel Collins tentatively agreed to pursue the project, only to beg off after he received a grant to support a Faulkner life-study. Once again Erskine Caldwell found himself outside that pale of luminaries whose reputations cast his efforts in their shadows.

Such covert disappointments perhaps only intensified that sense of aggrievement that June's legal hagglings and Brown's complaints continually stirred. Retaliating against June, Caldwell drew "the line on paying for the boy's [summer] haircuts."[6] To Brown he offered an increased percentage of foreign royalties in addition to a weary request: "Tell me anything you have in mind."[7]

Apparently only Virginia recognized the painful toll the dual aggravations had exacted from Caldwell. Denying June any gloating satisfaction, she instead defended him by attacking Brown with abandon:

> EC is trying to write a book from early in the morning until very late at night almost everyday of the week. This is something he does because he is a creative writer who WANTS to write and because he is making a living for a great number of people and contributing to the living of many others. During the past years he has done this in the face of many obstacles. . . .

You are *fully* aware of Erskine's sensitivity. You have often expressed to me your anger over the humiliating treatment he received from June. And yet you turn around and use the same technique you deplored in her. Perhaps you don't realize it, but for the past four years you have berated Erskine for first one thing and then another and there has been constant upheaval and disention [*sic*] in your attitude toward him. You must realize the effect constant criticism has upon him.[8]

Why hadn't Brown ended the prolonged confusion by quietly telling Caldwell what the problems were? As a friend, his motives for helping Caldwell should have been no less complicated than her own:

It is something far greater than the money. . . . It is my desire to contribute my efforts to help give a great author an opportunity to write something that will even surpass the previous best and let him win the so-called competition with himself.

By this time, however, Brown was consumed by his own pain. Throughout the period of conflict Caldwell likewise had obliquely criticized him. Brown had not been aggressive enough; he had been too disorganized to transact Caldwell's business properly. Emotionally strained by his divorce and anxious about realigning his agency and accounts, Brown had blown hot and cold in the face of Caldwell's expectations. He had valued Caldwell's friendship too much to give up the account, but on the other hand he had neither the emotional energy nor the necessary time to conduct Caldwell's business as he seemed to expect. And so the mutual accusations, accommodations, and agonies continued long past mercy. Finally in May of 1962, Caldwell released Brown from his duties.

After Caldwell took "the final step," Virginia probably expressed his attitudes to Victor Weybright, who, along with Al Manuel, had urged Brown's dismissal: "Erskine felt he could no longer afford a literary dilettante who lacked the aggressive personality so necessary to a good agent, for . . . an agent needs to be a salesman as well as a keeper of records."[9] The line of argument as well as its rhetoric seemed borrowed from the Hollywood types who profitably boosted a product no matter its quality. But whatever his motives, Caldwell's dismissal of Brown did not end their association. Its after-effects would confound them mutually for another three years.

But throughout the emotional melées of 1961, further complicated by his other usual interruptions, Caldwell had continued to write his next novel. When he remitted the finished manuscript to Farrar, Straus and Cudahy in February of 1962, John Farrar fell into that familiar pattern of his earlier publishers.[10] *Close to Home* represented one of Caldwell's very best. During its reading he had been "moved, gripped, horrified," an estimate that Straus and Giroux apparently could not second.

Immediately after forwarding the manuscript, the Caldwells took another extended automobile tour, one that took Erskine close to home. Uninterrupted this time by promotional sorties, Caldwell apparently wished to reacquaint himself with the South. Perhaps that distance and period of reflection allowed him to recognize that the San Francisco scene merely multiplied those intrusions which had subtracted from the privacy his best writing demanded. Not only "watering hole" types such as Herb Caen and Luther Nichols, but also Marvin Belli, counted among those who expected Caldwell to go along for the sake of fellowship. Belli, in fact, urged that Caldwell write his biography, a different type of project that kindled Caldwell's enthusiasm. Even the usually reckless Weybright, however, advised against it. Roger Straus finally dashed the scheme.[11] He liked the idea of Caldwell's doing a nonfiction book but not about a character as controversial as Belli.

Effectively forced once again to belabor the familiar, Caldwell sought escape from his doldrums through a change of scene. He wanted to get away from San Francisco and its "rich people kind of houses."[12] Some fifty miles east of the city, in the Rheem Valley near Orinda, Caldwell and Virginia found a house that made "him all excited." Situated on a one and one-half acre hill site, dotted with shrubs and trees, the place invited the deer that would be central to his children's book *The Deer at Our House*. The day of its purchase Caldwell had awakened at 4:30, anxious about whether or not his offer would be accepted. It was. Even before he had completed his novel, the Caldwells moved.

In their new home the Caldwells cultivated a privacy so essential that they used a post office box mailing address and gave their unlisted telephone number only to relatives and a few select friends. Caldwell left no doubt about his feelings: "I don't have any friends. I don't like the individual person, but I like the person in abstract. Friends try to influence you and you have no independence."[13]

That relocation, moreover, encouraged more than Caldwell's isolation; it also redirected his writing interests. Although he completed the novel begun in San Francisco there in Orinda, for the next four years he would write no more fiction. Instead he turned to nonfiction accounts— some analytical, others almost meditative, and two works unusually nostalgic in their focus.

Virginia tried in every way to reinforce that sense of uninterrupted serenity that the Rheem location invited. She forced herself "to creep around like a shadow," agonized over those noises—the phone's ringing, furnace's running, the sounds of water coursing through the pipes— which all disturbed Caldwell.[14] Because "the cost of his emotional upset [had been] incalculable" she had to make his life peaceful enough to "restore his self-confidence and trust in people."[15] And finally, Virginia had foreseen that she had to help heal the ruptures that had separated him from his children, especially the older ones.

Caldwell always assumed a public diffidence about kin: "I move away from relatives as far as I can go . . . . [Like friends, they] take advantage of you, not consciously, but they have the wrong impression of writers. They think you don't have a job, so they just come around and sit."[16] Despite Caldwell's abrupt dismissals, Virginia had known that his true feelings were more sentimental, that his children meant more to him than he could openly admit. As evidence she offered a saying he often repeated as his ideal: "Your first responsibility is your children, who will supplant and survive you. Give them love, care, and discipline when they are young . . . prepare them for their independence, and 'wean' them when they are ready."[17]

Throughout the years Caldwell had given freely, although sometimes hesitantly and grudgingly, whenever the children had requested money. And all, except the fiercely independent Janet and Guy, had. There remained, nonetheless, a barrier between him and those first children.

They perhaps could not bridge the gap that Caldwell's reserve, physical distance, and fame had created throughout their lifetimes. And apparently forgetting his and Helen's long dependence on relatives, Caldwell on his part failed to empathize with the financial strains that growing families placed upon his children.

Admittedly with some compelling evidence, Caldwell believed that Pix and Dee had tried to live beyond their incomes. But as much as that he suspected that "their mother had brought them up with the idea they should get all they could out of their father." He, therefore, eventually responded to his sons' requests for help with suggestions instead of checks. He offered to lend Pix and his wife budget counsel in lieu of money. He told Dee much the same but, apparently blind to irony, offered him a little more. If Dabney needed advice about "bringing up children," he should let him know since through experience he "might be able to help."[18]

Through time Caldwell perhaps had forgotten his occasionally trying experiences with the young Pix and Dee. Some of those scars had healed, because Virginia noted that Caldwell had good "rapport with Dabney, and would with Janet and Guy if they would just get to know him better."[19] But the situation with Pix, she had felt, was different: "It has seemed to me . . . that what Pix needed most of all was love and reassurance, and he needed it most from Erskine, his father, and the one who meant the most to him."[20] What immaturity, impatience, and the will to succeed had not allowed Caldwell to offer his older children, he silently had cultivated with Jay.

But Caldwell apparently feared that even that might not be enough. He wished for the boy to spend as much time as possible with Mere "so that Jay would learn some of the precepts [she] had embedded in Erskine's mind, and which he appreciate[d] *very* much."[21] Naturally enough, there had been the usual conflicts between father and son. Disdaining any show of elitism, Jay had rebelled against joining a post-high-school European tour and attending Harvard. In both instances, nonetheless, "as usual Erskine's tenacity paid off."

Always family-oriented and sensitive, Virginia recognized so many of Caldwell's unspoken needs that in 1963 she proposed a common Caldwell-Moffett Christmas gathering. Caldwell had been "talked into it" after she volunteered to pay the various expenses from her personal funds. Accordingly, before their autumn trip to Europe, the Balkans, and Russia, Virginia hurried to complete arrangements for the Sarasota reunion. Withdrawing the necessary three thousand dollars from her private account, she paid for the lodging and forwarded transportation expenses to all the members of both clans. She wanted Caldwell to, for the first time, experience the gathering of all of his children, grandchildren, and their paternal grandmother. Eventually all were gathered for the four-day holiday. The Caldwells gave small presents to the little grandchildren, but Virginia felt that Caldwell, more than anyone else, had "enjoyed the Christmas reunion." As evidence she cited one incident. All of Caldwell's children had come to the Caldwells' room for a cocktail when suddenly he said, " 'Janet, come over here and sit in my lap. I haven't held you since you were a little girl.' So Janet [had], and it was very touching."[22]

Working from that tenuous foundation of tradition, Virginia arranged another Christmas reunion at Lake Tahoe for the following year. This time even Caldwell seemed "excited about the Christmas plans."[23] Again, they had a "wonderful" time, but Virginia and Caldwell came away feeling used. Dabney had failed to send so much as a thank-you note; instead he, and later Pix, had requested another loan. Upon that occasion Virginia also must have felt as Caldwell had earlier, "that relatives take advantage of you."

That lack of appreciation, followed so soon by more requests for money, made Caldwell realize it was time to wean all his children. Carefully tallying all records, he discovered that his gifts to Janet had fallen far behind. The Caldwells, therefore, combined theirs and the Goodings' old cars for trade, paid the difference, and purchased a new one for Janet and her family of by-then five children. Not to feel compromised, Guy had pulled Caldwell aside to confirm that "the car was for Janet and not him." Once all the accounts had been balanced, Caldwell had sent a letter to each of them. Because he, as were they all, was growing older, he had to set money aside for his and Virginia's future security. Hereafter, each of the children equally could expect a check for a hundred dollars per year, other requests notwithstanding.

Other financial specters haunted Caldwell throughout the early sixties. He agonized over June's extended legal wrangling and Brown's fresh complaints following Caldwell's most recent tactics. By late December of 1963, therefore, Caldwell appeared "just totally morose." Despite the personal turmoil, not until some two years later did he wearily surrender to June's persistence. In exchange for abandoning her intentions of taking her claims to the Arizona Supreme Court, Caldwell agreed to an arbitrated settlement. In lieu of her monthly payments, he established a $125,000 trust; interest accruing from the principal would provide her yearly income. With her remarriage or Caldwell's death, whichever came first, half the principle amount would revert either to him or his estate. As Virginia was to fume: "Quite a request from a woman who refused to travel, move, or live with her husband and divorced him."[24]

Almost a decade of struggle between will and principle had passed before that spring of 1965 when the issue finally came to rest. Within a month June remarried, forfeiting $62,500, but certainly registering a victorious gain. Under her earlier agreement she would have received nothing after marriage. And thus Caldwell painfully had borrowed from his annuities to satisfy this obligation.

Caldwell had been so stung by this defeat that afterwards he regularly exaggerated: "I've been married four times and the Caldwell estate has been split down the middle three times. Uncle Sam has taken care of the rest."[25] As a matter of record, Helen had received only $12,000, and Margaret had asked for, and received, nothing. June's settlement, therefore, apparently symbolized a financial scourge that, in Caldwell's vision, had devastated his financial situation and future security.

Just as Caldwell's righteous frugality had drawn out his struggles with June, so it troubled that peace that should have settled over his terminated association with Brown. But as he successfully had with the exiled Lieber before, Caldwell tried to place a three-year limitation on the royalties Brown could earn from the contracts he had negotiated. That provoked a contest that would embattle both for three years to come.

Brown rightfully argued accepted practice; agents retained royalty rights from such works ad infinitum. Caldwell had refused to budge. Brown appealed.[26] He hoped Caldwell hadn't forgotten their good years together, the most important of his own life. Discounting that consideration, Caldwell wrote all his domestic and foreign publishers and agents, instructing that they should send all royalties directly to him. When Eric Linder, his long-time London agent, refused, Caldwell released him. Firms like NAL, which followed his orders, Brown threatened with suit. Farrar, Straus subtracted the agent's royalties from their own earnings, through that generous ploy satisfying both Caldwell and Brown. Little, Brown placed all royalties in escrow.

Not even Julius Weiss's circumspect mediation helped span the breach. Caldwell refused his opinion that Brown's arguments seemed legally founded. For his part, Brown refused to meet with Weiss even to discuss the issue. He, in fact, requested the return of all his archival files from Caldwell's Dartmouth collection and threatened to go through the courts to secure his rights. Although he did not, such sound and fury intermittently ragged the two adversary-friends until both eventually accepted a guarded truce. Brown received the commissions he had been entitled to and Caldwell wearily said no more.

Possibly Caldwell finally realized that neither staunch principle nor money was worth the personal turmoil and larger career costs his bouts with June and Brown had exacted. After those defeats and truces, he pulled back into his shell, jealously guarded his isolated retreat. Thereafter Caldwell allowed no one—friends or business associates—close enough that they might hurt him.

During those years two of Caldwell's more profit-motivated friends drifted away to pursue their own interests. Al Manuel abandoned his agent's role early in 1963 to become a Paramount Pictures executive. Victor Weybright and Kurt Enoch sold their interest in NAL shortly thereafter to the Times Mirror Syndicate for a rumored $8.5 million. Victor remained as an executive with the firm but had lost much of his power even before his 1965 release. Casting about for new agents to represent him, Caldwell followed Steinbeck's suggestion of Elizabeth Otis of McIntosh and Otis. On the West Coast he chose Annie Laurie Williams as his movie agent, and to oversee his foreign rights, Lawrence Pollinger. Their professional briskness combined with Caldwell's reserve assured that none would ever be more than a literary-business associate. And as for the trusted people from Caldwell's past, only the loyal Julius Weiss and Owen Golden remained.

Before the move to San Francisco and after settling in Orinda, throughout family adjustments and financial tensions, Caldwell, of course, religiously continued to write. *Close to Home*, which John Farrar had accepted with praise, the reviewers almost universally rejected. *The Last Night of Summer*, completed after the retreat to Orinda, this time provoked strained silence from Farrar and a call for revision from Robert Giroux. Anticipating Caldwell's reaction, Roger Straus offered an alternative through Elizabeth Otis.[27] If she wished to try placing the book elsewhere, they would offer single release on the condition that it did not jeopardize their future association with Caldwell. Caldwell's response to both suggestions must be guessed from the telegram Straus hastily sent to his prickly writer: "Delighted we will be doing *The Last Night.* "[28]

Anticipating what most reviewers would say about the Caldwell novel, Straus and Giroux offered a different direction for Caldwell's next three books. Without citing the successful example of Steinbeck's *Travels With Charley*, they wanted the first to present a travel summary of American life, the next to explore blacks and society in the South, and finally WASPs in America as focus of the third. Ripe for the change symbolized by the relocation to Orinda, Caldwell accepted the contract and the challenges. But before beginning, he had hedged his future somewhat. The Newsday organization had agreed to syndicate the chapters from the first work, his and Virginia's *Around-About America*.

After twenty-five years a return to the type of assignment Caldwell had once shared with Margaret Bourke-White might have appealed as a form of ritual and renewal. The woman sharing his work this time, however, would not be snapping pictures and observing, but sketching pictures and noting:

> He can hardly wait to get started in the morning and sets the alarm for six. I hop out of bed and make each of us a cup of hot instant coffee. We . . . carry our own cups, spoons, coffee and powdered "Pream." We are usually packed and in the car in half an hour and then stop for breakfast at the first "open" sign we see, which is usually what we call a "Greasy Diner." All day we wan-

der and I make occasional sketches and Erskine talks to various "Natives."
At about four P.M. we find a motel, then both go to work—E. with the portable typewriter and me with India ink and the drawing pad. At six we have a
cocktail but keep on "at the job" until E. reaches a stopping point, then have
dinner, wash our drip-dry shirts and read for awhile.[29]

That was the daily record of what was to be Caldwell's method for most
of his following nonfiction books. His "idea" folders had not bulged.
Cryptic notes—"The Old South will live again."—and place names,
Chamber of Commerce brochures and atlas figures gave him the facts.
Such bits and pieces interwoven with those "reconstituted essences" he
had gleaned from the "Natives," Caldwell presented, without any eye-
twinkling denials, as factual chronicle. Virginia could not help being
amused:

> I wonder how many readers will separate the fact from the fiction in *AAA*.
> For instance, there was no "Aunt Martha" on Long Island, no "Betty of
> Huron" *etc, etc, etc.* I have explained to my parents that we really don't spend
> most of our time in bars and poolrooms—that this is "creative license"!
> Erskine merely used these props (and I was one of them) for an interesting
> "vehicle" in making his point, using his imagination to create the scenes and
> "put words in people's mouths," (Mine included).[30]

"Because he wrote [*Around-About America*] for newspaper syndication,
not for the book," Caldwell was saved from more frustrations with
critics.[31] Few of them praised it. More painful was the inevitable question: "Did you write this because Steinbeck's *Travels* did so well?"[32]
Though Caldwell seldom responded, Virginia did. He and Margaret
Bourke-White had written travel books decades before Steinbeck had
issued his. Caldwell merely had brought his earlier observations up-to-
date.

The Steinbeck comparison, nonetheless, may have touched some
sensitive spots. True enough, Elaine and John were close friends, and
Steinbeck had signed Caldwell's copy of *Travels* "with respect and affection." Yet that Steinbeck's "dog book"—as he humorously called it—
had stimulated the recognition that ultimately had earned him the 1962

Nobel Prize for Literature must have seemed cruelly misdirected. The citation for "realistic and imaginative writings, distinguished as they are by a sympathetic humor and a social perception," just as accurately described Caldwell's contributions to literature.

Except for Fortune's turn, Caldwell's name might have appeared in place of Steinbeck's, and few would have recognized the difference. In fact, so credible a critic as Malcolm Cowley had judged Caldwell's work as seminal and Steinbeck's but an elaboration on the same theme. And then there was the matter of work itself meriting reward. While Steinbeck had sailed his boat through long afternoons, Caldwell had hunched over a typewriter, pecking with one hand, the other hoisted to the ceiling to diminish pain. As the Steinbecks, furthermore, had vacationed during the summer in Wales entertaining Adlai Stevenson, the Caldwells had tended to European business and performed chores for the USIS.

And at least Virginia had made other provoking comparisons. At that time Caldwell had led all authors in worldwide sales. Against Steinbeck's relatively few publications, she weighed Caldwell's dozens and his 150 short stories to boot. While no one had written biographies of Erskine Caldwell, she knew from Elaine that John Steinbeck would shortly have two. She may have questioned the fundamental puritan doctrine of reward following from work, but Caldwell gave his own accommodating explanation. The Nobel Prize was "never given for the first two or three books a person writes but to his subsequent work as a whole." He further concluded that a writer had "to be over 60 to get it."[33] Since he had turned sixty just recently, Virginia possibly had hoped for the future.

Even before the reviews for *Around-About America* appeared, Caldwell had plunged into his next work. The book, eventually called *In Search of Bisco*, engaged him more essentially than any other since *Georgia Boy*. Additionally Orinda's peaceful setting provided the isolation that Caldwell required to write at his best.

Hardly anyone disturbed the Caldwells, and 1964 became the exceptional year when they did not travel extensively. Only in that March did they make a brief tour through the South as a refreshing prelude to the writing.[34] It could not have been intensive, for as Caldwell had begun *Bisco,* Virginia had observed: "I know how Erskine feels. Life is too short to do all he wants with his work. To him every minute counts towards that end, and he doesn't want to deviate for *a second.* "[35]

By May 1 Caldwell had announced that his "work was right on schedule," and on May 19 he had told Virginia to be ready to leave for a two-day trip to Lake Tahoe. Then, Caldwell had packed his typewriter and materials so that he could write in a different environment.[36] Back home again Virginia had guessed the book's general topic pretty much from his somber attitude: "He apparently got a lot of his feeling about the subject out of his system in his early stories . . . 'Candy-Man Beechum,' 'The People vs. Abe Latham,' etc. But present day events seem to bring it all home to him. There is a lot of tension in him about it now."[37] Caldwell's manuscript about "a treatment of blacks and society in the South" was ready for first editing by June 14.

Uninterrupted by promotion obligations and other travels, Caldwell had regained the momentum of his early career. He had finished *Bisco*'s rough draft in little more than three months of concentrated writing effort. Before mid-September and after three months of revision, he had declared himself ready for a real, four-day vacation at the Tropicana in Las Vegas: "It is an atmosphere that relaxes Erskine. [He] enjoys watching people 'in the abstract,' so he'll be vacationing."[38] But this time no Al Manuels or Roscoe Fawcetts had met them there. They vacationed alone as they would almost exclusively in future years. As long as Caldwell had Virginia, he did not need either friends or other companions.

America's black/white dilemma was much in Caldwell's consciousness as he probed the experience through his own writing. During that period he complimented Shirley Ann Grau after reading her sensitive analysis "The Southern Mind, Black/White" in the August issue of *Cosmopolitan* magazine.[39] After Martin Luther King, Jr., had won the 1964 Nobel Peace Prize, Caldwell had written also to him: "Of all contemporary Americans, you are the most deserving of such an award. I am proud to be one of your fellow citizens."[40] Caldwell's interests were not those of a voguish parvenu. Rather, other white Americans had only belatedly recognized concerns that had been his since childhood.

As in so many of his other best stories, Caldwell had dredged the most evocative situation in *Bisco* from his childhood reservoir of memory. As a lonely child he sadly had left Bisco's home because his mother would neither allow him to spend the night nor play with him in the future. In most other matters perhaps, Carrie might have been more liberal, but she could not escape the values of her culture in this instance. Even in the sixties, she had rejected the goals and tactics of Martin Luther King and his sit-in disciples. People who "push against the tide" or engage in "lie-down, head-beating tactics" are whipped. Carrie drew upon example to make her point. As a child, Caldwell had beaten his head on the floor to get his way. Picking him up she had "paddled [his] other end."[41] But his letter to King as well as his strong-willed persistence indicate that Caldwell had not learned all of her lessons well.

Caldwell's initial manuscript submitted to Farrar, Straus and Company was not accepted without conditions. Robert Giroux did more than suggest a title change from *Southside USA* to *In Search of Bisco*. He had felt that Caldwell's *Southside* lacked coherence because it had mixed stories strained from memory with those gathered from contemporary black experience. His "reporting stance" had neglected so many obvious facts that readers would recognize it as a superficial facade covering impressions stitched together in California. As remedy, Giroux had directed that Caldwell "take the best thing in the book, [his] personal reminiscences, and capitalize on them."[42] That refocusing, plus the more personalized title, would strengthen the work considerably, he thought.

Within little more than a month had Caldwell reworked the *Bisco* manuscript to incorporate some of Giroux's suggestions. Subsequent reviews offered strong evidence of a lamentable fact: if editors other than Perkins and Giroux had dared confront Caldwell's displeasure, they might have saved him from himself, prevented him from uncritically publishing everything he wrote. If others had cared more for quality than profit, he perhaps would have followed their lead to the fulfillment of his early literary promise. But thirty years of stubbornly profitable habit had separated that reputation from the possibilities that lay ahead in Caldwell's future.

Although a few nagging critics had hoped for more from Caldwell's

Bisco, almost all other judgments rang with praise similar to that offered by the *Saturday Review:*

> Through some weird literary alchemy, Erskine Caldwell has been typed with the colors of backwoods racism and unholy miscegenation. This is unfortunate, for his are the most photographically accurate and lyrically incisive narratives ever done about the grotesque "American Problem." In this latest most powerful book by him, the voices of the Deep South cry forth in one collective lament from the obscene corpse of an antebellum "tradition."[43]

Such accolades confirmed that Giroux's instincts had been sound.

Americans in the agonized mid-sixties perhaps were ripe for a book that went beyond the scenes flashed across screens with the evening news. More important for Caldwell, however, Giroux had directed him to a more "personal kind" of book, one that had forced him to abandon the formulaic method that had characterized his fiction since the early forties. For too many years his "message" had told the story. But *Bisco*, like Caldwell's earlier works, was different because its story was the message. Its mythic search for a once-forbidden friend, for innocence lost somewhere among the labyrinthine horrors of a southern childhood, touched chords too long ignored—both within Caldwell himself and among his readers.

Everyone connected with *Bisco* had basked in the satisfaction of work well done. As evidence, Bob Giroux had pointed to the long *New Yorker* review, which perceptively noted, "Quite properly, Caldwell never finds Bisco."[44] Virginia had bubbled with a type of battle-won elation: "Everyone is saying that this book puts him back on top as a writer."[45] But more essentially she had rejoiced because Caldwell finally had seemed relieved from the pressure of "winning that competition with himself."

The secrets of *Bisco*'s success are tantalizing. For the first time since leaving Maine, Caldwell had written with unqualified emotional support from the significant woman in his life. No trips broke the isolation of his Orinda retreat. Neither San Francisco friends, Hollywood merchandisers, nor paperback distributors had interrupted his flow of creativity. With an undaunted editor's help, the result had promised to put him back on top as a writer.

Yet even as critics proclaimed what seemed to promise Caldwell's literary rebirth, his well-meaning friend, Arthur Thornhill, perhaps
tarnished that hope.[46] He had "pulled off the sale" of eighteen reprint titles—a negotiated deal that would bring money upon both their
houses. Royalties from the MacFadden-Bartell issues—with covers as
cheaply suggestive as the ones Signet still used—would carry a $90,000
guarantee for Caldwell alone. At a time when he had worried about
money enough to establish June's trust, that temptation had been too
attractive to resist.

Balanced against such massive trading upon Erskine Caldwell's
name, came a more respectable but exhausting offer, which he accepted.
Beginning in 1965 and extending for the next two years, he signed a contract with the Colson Leigh Lecture Agency.[47] For stipends ranging
from $250 to $500 per talk, Caldwell would travel the country annually
delivering sixteen to twenty lectures within each month's contract period. The speech would be the same. Only the city and audience would
be different. Although the pace had been consuming, Virginia boasted
that Caldwell had spoken to standing-room-only audiences and had
been "gratified by the response from his young readers."[48] Understandably he had come to dread the formalities, the luncheons, and long, talk-
filled rides to and from airports.

With *Bisco*'s success still sweet, the Caldwells had left their Rheem
Valley hideaway for almost six months of scarcely interrupted travel. After the February Colson tour, they departed almost immediately for
Florida, where Jay had joined them in watching spring-training baseball. Visiting briefly in South Carolina with Mere, the Caldwells then
had turned to the University of Virginia, where a wealthy University
alumnus, C. Waller Barrett had arranged a special celebration in Caldwell's honor.

That recognition, like a later one staged by the University of Georgia's
Rick Harwell, had come somewhat belatedly. Caldwell's two "home"
universities welcomed the prodigal with fatted calves, but decades before, Caldwell had followed Charlie Duell's suggestion and directed
most of his collection to Dartmouth.

After swinging through Washington and Baltimore for mid-April visits, the Caldwells returned home so Caldwell could resume writing his third contract work for Farrar, Straus—and now—Giroux. Needing more regional reacquaintance for the WASP book, they shortly caught a plane for Knoxville, where they rented a car whose in-state license plates would not attract attention during those difficult times in the South. Caldwell stopped occasionally to talk with locals as they drove through various countryside places. In McComb, Mississippi, he and Virginia attended the same Assembly of God church he and Bourke-White had recorded three decades before. A new experience for Virginia, she exulted: "We've been going to church!! Baptist, Full Gospel—you name it, we've been there and I've had a fine time shouting the old hymns."[49]

Back home again by July 22 Caldwell wrote until mid-October, when he mailed the manuscript to his publishers. The following day he enjoyed his reward for work completed. He and Virginia caught a plane to Las Vegas, where they slept very late the next morning. Then they walked some, and "spent most of the next two days catching up on sleep."[50]

Roger Straus's response to *In the Shadow of the Steeple* almost beat them home.[51] Caldwell's treatment had not been what they had hoped. Instead of the expected in-depth analysis of southern establishment WASPs, Caldwell had interwoven too much memory with his observations. True enough, his father had stood strong against the railings of "the fire-and-brimstone types," but he, nonetheless, had seemed "thin and unreal," the "vehicle" which carried the book's interspersed sections. In short, Caldwell's manuscript was really two books requiring separate development. This time neither Giroux nor Straus had offered any suggestions for revisions.

Straus's reaction caught Caldwell "with his hands behind his back."[52] Disappointed in not meeting the firm's expectations, he nonetheless remained satisfied with what he had done—namely "contrasting WASP religious practices of the Sixties with those of the Twenties." Caldwell issued a challenge; the book would have to be accepted or rejected as it was. He had "no ambition" either to abandon his original idea or to dilute it by making "two-out-of-one." As "publisher and friend," Straus argued just as strongly that unrevised publication of the work "would be a mistake for *both*" of them. "With sorrow but with understanding," therefore, the hardcover firm would not object if he wished "to show *In the Shadow of the Steeple* to the NAL crowd."[53]

Caldwell promptly returned the $2,500 royalty advance, but Elizabeth Otis, echoing Straus's impressions of the manuscript, advised prudence. She believed he might want "to put it aside for the time being and either do the real WASP book, or something else."[54] Neither Straus nor Otis knew the measure of Caldwell's persistence. After more than two decades he earlier somehow had pumped the often-rejected *Autumn Hill* to publication as *A Lamp for Nightfall.* Caldwell was not one to allow even his sparse literary crops to go unharvested.

Hampered somewhat because by this time he and Virginia already were traveling in Europe, Caldwell nonetheless submitted *Steeple* to Weybright, then still at NAL. Receiving Weybright's guarded but negative reaction, he urged a second reading. Weybright's reexamination produced almost a duplication of Straus's criticisms. Further, Tarrie— Mama—who Weybright knew was very real, had remained "only a shadow character in the saga."[55] Something else he did not mention was that of the some fifteen Caldwell titles then in print, their total 1965 royalties came to less than forty dollars.

Financial considerations were not Caldwell's primary motives for his urging publication of the book. *God's Little Acre* then still played around the world—in a total of forty-four foreign countries—eventually earning for Caldwell almost five hundred thousand dollars from those royalties alone. Television rights had added another forty-five thousand dollars. More than actual dollar increments demanded placing the writing. His usual persistence combined with a belief that no work should go unrewarded made Caldwell push it beyond others' advice. In fact, while yet in Europe he placed *Steeple* with London's Heinneman Press. That, however, had not satisfied him totally. When Elizabeth Otis had finally exhausted all her possibilities on the book's behalf, he had approached old acquaintances and editors such as Luther Nichols and Ned Bradford, who also rejected it with by-then familiar reasons.

Released from his publisher and unattached to another, Caldwell had apparently cast about without much sense of direction during most of

1966. Following Ginny's encouragement, he wrote *The Deer at Our House*, a work he had dismissed with self-effacing humor as "a reader for pre-school brats."[56] By September, however, Virginia recognized "all the familiar signs" of another book a-brewing. They traveled again, he tried "to pick arguments" with her, and seemed to enjoy literally pulling the cat's tail.[57]

Chapter 22

Caldwell began toiling on the book that was to become *Miss Mamma Aimee* almost immediately after his and Virginia's mid-October return to Orinda. In the midst of that work, one which signaled a return to his old fictional patterns, he answered a fan letter with a degree of defensiveness. He purposely did not read books by others because he wanted "to have [his] own way of writing."[1]

That independence was confirmed in one sense at least. Victor Weybright and Truman Talley, finally separated from NAL, had established their own press. They would publish *In the Shadow of the Steeple* if Caldwell would add a southern black religion section and retitle the work. He accepted that since nothing else interested him as much "as the rock-bottom religions of the South." The avowed agnostic remained curiously attracted to the human "shake-down experience at a church of Eternal Ecstasy."

Although Weybright and Talley were to publish the retitled *Shadow of the Steeple* as *Deep South*, Caldwell contracted with New American Library for issue of *Miss Mamma Aimee* and his subsequent fiction. Since that firm had recently added a hardcover division, his works would have hardcover respectability as well as paperbound profitability. *Miss Mamma* contributed only a little to the first and not much to the second.

Incorporating an earlier Caldwell theme of aristocracy in decline, Mamma Aimee, like Jeeter Lester before, futilely attempts to keep both her family and its mansion from internal disintegration. Erosion devastated *Tobacco Road*'s earth, but in the updated version, earth-moving machines ravage the land for shopping centers. And as Jeeter fell tragic victim to forces in which he had placed his future salvation, so does Aimee. A demented son in whom she blindly had placed her hopes shoots her to death at the novel's conclusion. Through this work as in his early most successful novels, Caldwell attempted again to blend the tragic and the comic.

Reviewers generally remained critically unsympathetic, failing either to recognize the novel's tragic dimensions or to appreciate its broad comic humor. A few acknowledged it as Caldwell's strongest in the recent past, but references to Martin Luther King, the civil rights movement, and folksingers were not enough. Another felt it was flawed because Caldwell had been unable to make up his mind whether he was writing low comedy or high tragedy, and in the absence of either, settled for easy ribaldry. Disappointingly, *Miss Mamma Aimee* failed in that delicate balance of the tragic and comic which had characterized some of Caldwell's early writings.

Caldwell's subsequent, almost annual, novellas gathered mixed reviews, but his *Summertime Island,* published in 1968, evoked especially mellow responses. Reviewers cast it as "a morality play in primitive colors," or as a skimpy version of a modern-day *Huckleberry Finn,* also set on the Mississippi. One saw thematic resemblances between Caldwell's story and both Faulkner's "The Bear" and *The Reivers,* but thought that Caldwell's "preaching" had marred the book. Almost all readers, nonetheless, felt the difference of mood that permeated the work.

Possibly the thematic longing that had tied *Mamma Aimee* to *Tobacco Road* had likewise translated Caldwell's sense of reverie into his most recent reworking of past experiences. Strains of his early 1930s story "Maude Island" played through this version of modified nostalgia. More than that, its fantasy situations appeared like those a son might have imagined during fishing trips with his father as they had shared time away from a respectively demanding mother and wife. After reading the book Virginia, in fact, had felt a sense of déjà vu as the Caldwells later drove around Atoka, Tennessee. There she saw the country store with cheese signs displayed just as they were in *Summertime Island.* Only then did she realize that many of the book's details and its "landscape were right out of his memory."[2]

Summertime's recasting of memory perhaps urged Caldwell to a more direct harrowing of his past. During that summer's "in-between-books restlessness," he and Ginny sorted through his twenty-year accumulation of correspondence and materials. Some they kept, some they boxed for shipment to Dartmouth, and the largest portion they burned. Caldwell "really enjoyed the burning part" as they prepared for a move Virginia had been promoting with oblique but dogged persistence.

Some months before, Caldwell's doctors in Phoenix had discovered some lung congestion that they had diagnosed as the beginning of emphysema. He had been "scared into" unsuccessfully trying to break his "two-three pack per day" smoking habit, but his condition also demanded more exercise. Caldwell just did not "want to take the time to take care of himself properly," but Virginia believed that if they moved to a warmer climate and if they purchased a house with a pool, her company would encourage him to swim daily. She accordingly had played upon Caldwell's restlessness to urge their relocation to a healthier environment.

Before those arrangements could be concluded, however, and shortly after the beginning of 1968, Caldwell, then aged sixty-four, had to lay to rest an even more essential part of his past. Three days into the new year his Allendale cousin Mary Maner called to advise that Mere was sinking fast. Despite his mother's ninety-five years, Caldwell seemed startled by the message: "Are you telling me that my mother's not going to get well?"[3] Since he and Virginia had visited her only two weeks earlier, had, in fact, taken her to dinner and for a ride, her imminent death perhaps seemed even more unbelievable.[4] But by January 4, Caldwell's Tarrie—Mere—had slipped away in her sleep to confront him with a new experience.

Upon his deathbed Ira had whispered, "Erskine will take care of you," before he had "sighed with relief" and died.[5] More than that assurance had guaranteed that Caldwell would be faithful to the charge. Over the years Virginia's letters had confirmed that filial respect which Caldwell always had felt—but could not express—for the first woman who so essentially had shaped his life. Her confirming values and presence had contributed to his own sense of determination and strength: "I'm sure the knowledge that *you* were always standing behind him has helped a lot in keeping up his courage, in fact I would say that your moral support has been the great sustaining factor in his ability to surmount prob-lems."[6] Or if Ginny had praised Caldwell in some way, he discounted it: "It is all thanks to my mother if you think I'm any good."[7] On another occasion he had called upon experience to advise his stepson: "Drew, your mother is the best friend you ever have. I know because that's the way it is with my mother."[8] Most tellingly, moreover, the man who was never lonely, the writer who suggested placing a worshipful statue of the woman-mother at every crossroads, only three years before his mother's death had confessed to Ginny, "My mother and you are all I've got."[9]

Janet and some of her family attended Mere's funeral. And although Caldwell had not accompanied Virginia to her own mother's recent burial, she stood beside him as they lowered his mother next to the father in a Prosperity cemetery. Both finally came to rest in that regional vine-yard where they had labored so strenuously and faithfully in fields white for harvest.

If his mother and Ginny were all that Caldwell felt he had had, he per-haps returned to California feeling more bereft than ever before. Except for Ginny and the children, his other significant people all had gone away. His parents, Alfred Morang, and Jim Aswell were dead; before year's end Steinbeck joined them. Caldwell's eventual reconciliation with Jim Brown was still in the future, and though Al Manuel and Victor Weybright yet remained, their associations had always been reckoned more accurately in dollars and sales than in essential friendship. The others—Roscoe Fawcett and Eddie Lewis, Herb Caen and Eddie Schwartz—he knew were in their respective worlds because he received their casual and gag-filled letters, saw them on special occasions or whenever passing through. His mother's death left Caldwell only with Ginny and his writing, but in his solitarily constricted universe, he ap-parently believed that was enough.

Following his mother's funeral, the Caldwells returned to a rented place in San Francisco, where they awaited completion of the house they had purchased in Dunedin, Florida. Its location met those "health po-tential" requirements Virginia had listed as essentials. Its low elevation would benefit Caldwell's suspected emphysema, the moist climate would be better for his tender "Scotch skin." With a pool, and proximity to good transportation, bars, and restaurants, it was large enough to ensure writing privacy for Caldwell and located in an area of "lowest living costs." Early in 1968, therefore, he returned to live in the region he, at least physically, had left some forty-two years before.

For the first time since Erskine Caldwell had begun *Tobacco Road* thirty-six years earlier, he lived in the South, as he wrote yet another story set in that region. Throughout the latter part of 1968 and into 1969 he tried to give life to that abstraction called miscegenation.

A weather shelter, normally used for storing hay, gave the novel its name. There, in a few scenes almost as darkly haunting as Thomas Hardy's or Poe's, the three principal characters, black and white, escape community censure to share a common loneliness, to gratify their otherwise unmet needs. From these matings, Caldwell implied, a different generation would come forth. A *Choice* critic was later to be so impressed that he said, "The symbols of the Shetland pony ranch and the weather shelter make this novel [Caldwell's] most effective indictment of Southern life since *God's Little Acre*.[10] Other reviewers were to bemoan the characters' one-dimensional simplicity and the book's regional stereotypes. They, nonetheless, seemed fascinated by the netherland confusion of the book's miscegenous character Jeff. Caldwell, the storyteller, yet managed to catch even sophisticated readers in his web.

The promise of *Weather Shelter* was dashed by *The Earnshaw Neighborhood*, his next regional novel. In 1933, he had used a jackass's braying in "Meddlesome Jack" as the clarion for the townswomen's sexual frenzy. Caldwell tried the same tactic in his 1970 novel. This time, however, readers were expected to believe that a bit of "pitty-pat, pitty-pat" doggerel made everyone and everything plunge and snort to happy conclusion in *The Earnshaw Neighborhood*.

Caldwell's long-standing popular reputation had encouraged publication of the work, but mercifully, most critics avoided reviewing it. Consequently for the first and only time since *Tobacco Road*, one of Caldwell's books did not gather enough reviews among the bellwether periodicals to earn inclusion in the annual *Book Review Digest*. Possibly most reviewers judged that after so many years he deserved a courtesy.

Before Caldwell was to write his next, and last, novel, Virginia urged him to submit to a complete physical examination at the Mayo Clinic. Increasingly she had worried about his health, taking as bad signs his unusual moodiness and irritability. The physicians there discovered some worrisome and potentially dangerous clues. Because an artery in one leg appeared seriously clogged, he would have to quit smoking, something he did immediately upon leaving the clinic. For his increasing lung congestion and shortness of breath, they prescribed medication and more exercise. The doctors otherwise generally recommended a regimen of relaxation, exercise, and medication.

Retirement might have seemed timely, because Caldwell once had told Virginia that he would quit writing when he reached age sixty-five. Yet before turning sixty, and some two weeks after the sailing Steinbeck had won the Nobel Prize, he more publicly had stated the fact: "I can't retire. I don't know anything else to do. I don't play golf or sail boats. How would I spend my time?"[11] Within Caldwell's system of self-justification he could spend time and life only through work.

Before the end of 1972, therefore, Caldwell once more sat before his typewriter pecking his "two-fingered" way through another novel. *Annette,* again a woman-centered work, explored the confused life of an attractive young woman whom men selfishly exploited. Caldwell's practice in this genre made her story come easily. Virginia worried. Instead of the usual staccato typing sounds, she some days heard nothing at all from his study. One late afternoon he emerged as if in a daze. Apparently he had sat before the typewriter for hours, had written nothing, and remembered little more. Virginia called the Mayo doctors. They hypothesized that the Caldwells' ritual evening cocktail or two might be causing an adverse reaction with his medications.

Ever since his Margaret Bourke-White days, Caldwell had enjoyed an after-luncheon or dinner cocktail as an excuse to relax. But if he wished to remain alert enough to continue writing, the doctors cautioned, that practice would have to stop. Like the smoking before, he quit hard liquor immediately and altogether. Only occasionally would he sip a glass of wine with a meal or guests. The occasional Caldwell visitors always could select from a full range of choices, but for himself, Caldwell's habits had come full circle. Religious convictions made his ancestors re-

ject alcohol. A concern for his writing and health exacted a similar accounting within Caldwell's adapted theology.

As always, critics and readers could not know the degree of self-willed
determination and struggle that had forced each of Caldwell's previous
works to completion. *Annette* demanded yet more, but its reception in
1973 earned little sympathy. With each passing Caldwell novel, the reviews in widely circulated newspapers and magazines had become more
sparse and delayed. In this instance those few that acknowledged *Annette* fell between two extremes. A reviewer for the usually lax *Best Sellers*
publication felt the book was not bad, but he never would "have paid a
dime for it let alone $6.95."[12] On the other hand, the more respectable
Choice magazine presented a subdued positive judgment. Caldwell retained his ability to shape a character even like the woman-child Annette, she who depended upon dreams for fulfillment and teddy bears
for friendship. More headily yet, "the expression of such talent as this
has made Caldwell one of America's most effective and successful novelists."[13]

Even before having written his last two novels, Caldwell had sounded
a note of change, if not one of almost tired resignation: "The feeling here
in this house" was that he should wait at least six months before beginning anything new. Despite Virginia's injunction, he immediately began
anticipating his next work: "I'm inclined toward the personal and sub-
jective, regional American life, visitation and revisitation, etc."[14] For-
saking novels permanently, Caldwell followed that inclination in all of
his subsequently published works.

The Caldwells had carried with them to Dunedin that jealously
guarded privacy of their Orinda days. As gentle reminder, a smiling
pumpkin-face at the front door cautioned, "The Occupant is occupied."
Daily, Caldwell drove the mile or so to the post office, but again only select relatives and associates who respected his antipathy to telephones
were given their unlisted number. In fact, during their two months in
San Francisco they had gone to a couple of Herb Caen's parties, saw all
the people they had avoided for the six-year "Orinda hibernation" period but had said good-bye to no one. Neither had they told anyone they

were leaving the Bay area. Their isolation had been a cautiously deliberate one willed by Caldwell and accepted by Virginia.

Occasionally the Caldwells rode their bikes around the peaceful
streets of Dunedin and otherwise preserved "a quiet, well balanced routine" with a weekly dinner out and a once-a-week maid coming in. Virginia cared for Caldwell, cooked the dishes he enjoyed, and helped him
as she had before; she kept accounts, answered all except the strictly literary correspondence, and maintained the files. As she had suspected,
being married to Caldwell was a full-time job.

During the Caldwells' "period of noncommunication with others"—
one that would become the rule rather than the exception—neither
lacked for work. Although fewer and fewer of Caldwell's works remained
in print, Virginia religiously charted the published copies that annually
added to Caldwell's worldwide total. By the mid-seventies, her count
had pushed beyond 75 million and gradually inched beyond.[15] Evidence of such international stature must have provided him some satisfaction.

Withdrawn from the world, Caldwell kept in touch with it through
reading as many newspapers and journals as he could, and answering
fan mail directed to his writings or philosophy. One Georgia man requested permission to use the "God's Little 'A' " logo for his "Model A"
restoration business. Caldwell agreed in exchange for two free-ride chits
in one of the cars. Upon request, he gave unpaid talks to the inmates of
Florida's Raiford State Prison, a maximum-security unit in Gainesville.

A college professor from a little-known midwestern college wished to
bring a group of college students to meet Caldwell in Dunedin. He deferred because Dunedin would force them too afar afield. Instead, would
they meet him in Augusta for an all-day tour of Tobacco Road country?[16]
And so Erskine Caldwell generously offered those measures of time otherwise devotedly saved for writing.

Without publishers and promoters hawking Erskine Caldwell's
name, his Dunedin retreat might have relegated him to oblivion, all-
but-forgotten and ignored by the nation, its readers, and its historians.
Yet the late sixties and early seventies offered some hope that he would

not forever be slighted especially in his native land. He was one of two Americans chosen among eight judges for the 1972 Cannes Film Festival. Without Caldwell's full-fledged cooperation two biographers raced against each other to complete his unofficial biography. Without his knowledge, other young academics otherwise explored his writings.

Many times previously the subject for scholarly study in Europe, Erskine Caldwell and his selected works had been the focus of two completed American Ph.D. dissertations near the turn of the decade. More valuable had been James Korges's *Erskine Caldwell*, a forty-eight-page contribution to the University of Minnesota Pamphlets of American Writers. Korges's acute revisionary assessment of Caldwell's works argued justice for the man and his writings and issued a warning. Unless American scholars awoke to the importance of Caldwell's work, their disgrace would be as well deserved as that which followed from their long neglect of Herman Melville's literary achievements.[17]

In other ways also Caldwell experienced the satisfaction of some belated recognitions. Edward Connery Lathem, the director of Baker Library at Dartmouth College, attempted to express that institution's appreciation for Caldwell's large gifts. He commissioned London's John Gilroy to paint Caldwell's portrait when he traveled to that city in the fall of 1971.[18] Upon its completion Dartmouth invited the Caldwells to the campus for its unveiling and continued display in the south entryway to the venerable library. Almost yearly thereafter Caldwell acted as writer-in-residence or joined others like Bernard Malamud and Wallace Stegner as campus Montgomery Fellows. No doubt he squirmed but also glowed beneath such respectable mantles.

Not to be outshown, the Universities of Georgia and Virginia otherwise paid tribute to Erskine Caldwell. The Georgia institution asked him to deliver the Phiney lectures, which he did. Later Caldwell sold to them—with a twinkle in his eye, "for a good price"—his entire 973-volume private library collection of domestic and foreign Caldwell first editions. At Virginia, C. Waller Barrett not only remained an avid collector of Caldwell's materials and writings but also came to appreciate Caldwell and Ginny as individuals. At one of the Barretts' social functions, a Virginia lady asked Caldwell for his dormitory residence number from his university days. She and a group of alumni wished to designate it appropriately with a plaque. Caldwell's honesty deflated such propriety: "I didn't live on the lawn but had a room at Miss Yeager's rooming house."[19]

After Caldwell had completed *Annette* early in 1973, Ed Lathem, by this time acting as his unofficial editor, suggested a different type of project. As an editor for a Dodd Mead series, Lathem thought Caldwell should write a personalized, visitation-revisitation account of regional American life for issue during the bicentennial year. In fact, Caldwell and the French writer Marcel Duhamel—with Alec Waugh, one of his two regular European correspondents—previously and seriously had considered such a collaborative work. Duhamel would travel with the Caldwells through what formerly had been France's territory in mid-America. Responding individually to their common observations, they would then collate and publish their balanced impressions as one book. Caldwell responded enthusiastically to Lathem's proposal.

Anxious to begin the trip in the summer of 1974, Caldwell confronted an obstacle. Duhamel was in the process of writing his autobiography and did not wish to interrupt that project; he urged Caldwell to proceed alone. If Caldwell wished to meet his bicentennial deadline, he had no alternative. And though Ginny's sketches rather than the Frenchman's impressions eventually complemented the work, Duhamel's presence nonetheless helped shape it. Caldwell interspersed the work with personal letters to his associate, a type of sharing that lent a somewhat unique perspective to *Afternoons in Mid-America*. In another way also his odyssey log was different from anything he previously had written.

Caldwell's foreword to a literary work that interwove memories, impressions, and associated experiences was fetchingly appropriate. At least by innuendo, he suggested that his father's dream had inspired it. When he and Ira last had camped on an eastside landing of the Mississippi, Ira had repeated a story he often told. An Arkansas traveler allegedly claimed that objects cast longer shadows on the afternoon side of the Mississippi than did identical objects on the morning side. Ira had dreamed of someday personally testing the accuracy of the man's tale, but death had not allowed him to satisfy that curiosity.

Caldwell implied, therefore, that his own meanderings west and north of the Great river were but part of a twofold obligatory quest. On one hand, he pursued his father's time-deferred dream; on the other, Caldwell vicariously experienced for Duhamel—who himself shortly died— that exploration of once-French territory he was denied. Imposing such mortality-laden associations upon *Afternoons* might seem exaggerated. Yet what Caldwell and Virginia confronted during their mid-America trip perhaps lends it psychological credibility.

Through that late spring and early summer of 1974 the Caldwells ambled and sketched their way through places as peaceful-sounding as Evening Shade, Arkansas; Lebanon, Missouri; and Shenandoah, Iowa. By late June they reached Rochester, where Caldwell was scheduled for his annual Mayo Clinic examination. The concluding Friday's medical conference struck fear into one even as stoic as Caldwell. Tests and X-rays revealed a growth in the bottom third of his left lung. The physicians scheduled surgery for the succeeding Monday.

Rather than remain in Rochester during an agonized weekend, Caldwell and Virginia drove the 250 miles to Brainerd, Minnesota, the next stop on their itinerary. Although they visited the Roscoe Fawcetts at their summer home, Caldwell also continued his work over the weekend. Driving about the area, he noted that at least twelve local establishments— from the Bunyan Burger to Paul Bunyan State Park—all celebrated the town's legendary Giant and Babe, his blue ox. Not the total stoic, he also was "glum and apprehensive about life thereafter . . . about what momentous events might take place in the world after [his] life had ended."[20] On Monday, August 20, the Caldwells were back at the clinic for Caldwell's surgery.

The long operation confirmed everybody's fears; because the growth was malignant, the doctors removed the lower third of Caldwell's lung. After a twelve-day convalescence in Rochester, Virginia slowly drove them home to Dunedin. Finally there, she made sure that he slavishly followed the postoperative directions for medication, rest, and gradually increasing schedule of exercises.

Because the mid-America project remained unfinished, Caldwell became restless by mid-October. Accordingly, they resumed the interrupted trip, but before they could reach their earlier Brainerd stopping place, midwestern weather conditions forced a return. Both Caldwell's susceptibility to pneumonia and winter driving hazards posed dangers not even he could ignore. Back in Dunedin once again he could only await the next spring-summer season, which would allow completion of their travels.

Every three months following surgery, Caldwell forwarded a sputum sample and current X-rays for Mayo analysis. All checks proved encouragingly clear until the one two weeks before the Caldwells were to resume their tour of the Midwest. Caldwell and Virginia flew to Rochester, where examination revealed a growth, identical to the first, in Caldwell's other lung.

Once more the physicians urged immediate surgery, but this time Caldwell refused. The operation would have to be postponed. If he did not finish the trip that summer as planned, he argued, the book would be delayed at least one more year. The doctors warned that if the surgery were not performed then and there, the work might never be completed at all. Caldwell rejected all their arguments. The Mayo surgeons would have to wait. His work always had come before all other considerations—except, of course, during those times he slavishly had followed Bourke-White and his later promotional obligations.

The Caldwells thereafter returned to Dunedin to pick up their car so he could continue with his travel plans and resume their interrupted gathering of impressions. He therefore reconstituted conversations, facts, and impressions while Virginia sketched in North and South Dakota, Nebraska, and Kansas, and finally Oklahoma. Only after completing that work did Caldwell return to the Mayo Clinic. On July 22 surgeons removed the cancerous bottom third of his other lung.

After a recuperative period in Rochester, the Caldwells flew back to Dunedin for Caldwell's convalescence. How long he endured that necessary luxury only can be guessed, but by spring he forwarded the completed manuscript for *Afternoons in Mid-America* to Ed Lathem for editing. Dodd, Mead and Company published the book, as scheduled, in 1976. Caldwell had met the deadline. Through rigorous observance of those American values the bicentennial celebrated, he had given the nation his book of remembrance.

For Caldwell those values strained from his own particular history perhaps provided saving grace. Work had not allowed him "to stop for death"; its charge had propelled him past the immediate moment. Not until some five years later did he realize how dangerously close he had come. Then the doctors expressed their amazement. Caldwell's survival beyond "the danger zone of post-op cancer surgery" and its lasting threats testified to his stubborn persistence reinforced by good health practices.

The *Afternoons* book, through which Caldwell had tried to capture "the emotional response to life," to sketch a "delineation of the human spirit,"[21] caught readers within its web. Within less than six months, *Afternoons'* sales reached into a third printing. No Caldwell hardbound issue had accomplished that in recent decades. One reviewer even allowed that it might represent Caldwell's best work of all. Other critics were not so totally enthusiastic, but most read it at least as "a nostalgic and variegated piece of Americana." Only the *New York Times* critic, unaware of the conditions involved in the book's writing, flailed away with the same reckless abandon the paper seemed to have reserved for most of Caldwell's more recent books.

Against the few nagging receptions, Caldwell and Virginia could balance a different type of publishing honor. Before Marcel Duhamel had died, he had negotiated for an illustrated folio edition of *The Sacrilege of Alan Kent*. Although Pablo Picasso's previous commitments would not allow the time, Alexander Calder, who personally liked Caldwell and appreciated his writings, accepted the assignment. Within a short time he produced some twenty-five plates to accompany Maeght Publishing Company's limited edition of the Caldwell-Calder work. Issued at fifteen hundred dollars each, the folios appeared as more than a world and fortune away from those gaudy twenty-five-cent drugstore copies of *God's Little Acre* Caldwell had once also inscribed.

Although Erskine Caldwell had earned international critical recognition in various forms by 1976, his literary credibility still lagged in his home country. The reevaluations that two unofficial but scholarly biographies—one by Dale Speer and the other by William Sutton— might have encouraged came to naught since neither of those works ever reached print. Otherwise both Caldwell's career and his literary reputation remained in limbo.

Despite the serenity that Caldwell's latest book and continuing good health reports encouraged, Virginia began making excuses for their moving from Dunedin. Visits from children and friends intruded upon Caldwell's necessary privacy. Familiarity with area people invited neighborly visits. Florida's humidity so inflamed her arthritis that she could not type. Her reasons urging their relocation to a different area and drier climate became legion.

Such complaints were absent from Virginia's seven-year Florida correspondence before Caldwell's 1976 surgery. Afterwards they became constants. She realized that the damp climate represented pneumonia-related threats to his weakened lungs. Yet she also acknowledged that her concerns about Caldwell's health would not persuade him to move. As she had before in Orinda, Virginia therefore carefully built upon those dual motives that would encourage him to relocate—his concerns for his writing and for her.

Among the options Caldwell would consider only Colorado Springs, Santa Fe, and Phoenix. As much as both tried to avoid "returns," Arizona's hot, dry climate convinced Ginny that Phoenix would be most congenial to his health. Their 1977 return to search for a house with the necessary space, privacy, and pool, however, ironically confounded her best intentions. One evening Caldwell mentioned that he did not feel well. His temperature already hovered above 103 degrees. By the time Virginia located a doctor and rushed him to a local hospital's emergency ward, his fever had climbed above 104 degrees. The doctor prescribed immediate alcohol and ice-water sponging, yet even as the nurses worked Caldwell shook so violently that the bed vibrated with his chills. Antibiotics and rest provided the rest of the cure. The pneumonia Virginia had feared in Florida gripped Caldwell in Arizona, a place she had hoped finally would be more kind.

Eventually the Caldwells found a comfortable, Spanish-style house with all the necessities in Scottsdale. Its pool would encourage Caldwell to exercise, but its automated sprinkler system, which individually watered each tree and shrub, would free him from that chore. And otherwise, as he was to say, "A good yardman, a pool serviceman, tax accountant, lawyer, and Ginny. What more would I need?"[22] The home's large wrought-iron vestibule-gate perhaps served more as a symbol than it accomplished in fact.

After their relocation to Scottsdale in late April of 1977, Ginny and Caldwell spent most of the summer settling in. They were happy with the location and had "total privacy." Virginia informed one of her former Phoenix friends that she was back, but otherwise told no one, not even "Caldwell's old Phoenix Press Club friends." But she hurried gracious explanation: "It sounds so MEAN, but we do have to hold to it until we have a stretch of peace and quiet to catch up on so many things that fell behind. We even needed more time for communication and that is working out perfectly."[23]

The Caldwells' return to Arizona came some two decades after their last Phoenix residence and their twenty years of marriage. Throughout that time those relatives and acquaintances who knew them well remarked that Virginia had been—as she had molded herself to be—the perfect wife for Caldwell. Although married to him through work as well as love and care, her appeals seldom penetrated his reserve. When she asked, "Do you love me?" he would reply, "I'm here, aren't I?" Her own expressions were more sentimental. No occasion was too small to provide an excuse for one of Virginia's personally crafted cards through which she expressed her love. She knew how essential such reassurances were for Caldwell.

Despite such efforts Caldwell's silences periodically still left blanks in the couple's emotional harmony. Guessing that the withdrawals masked his feelings of pained rejection, Virginia could not reconstruct their deep-seated origins. Finally she merely accepted and worked around them less painfully. Ira had threatened to leave Carrie if she did not abandon her own pouting silences. Yet Ginny's nature would not allow that tactic. Moreover, by the time she—or any of Caldwell's former wives—had entered his life, the problem was too emotionally complex for so simple a solution.

Chapter 23

A western ridge shielded the Caldwells' Scottsdale house from the setting sun's direct rays. Twilight's patterned regularity was little more predictable than the routine that marked their daily lives in Arizona. Virginia always prepared them a nutritious breakfast. By nine A.M. Caldwell was in his office, attending to correspondence and writing introductions for Bentley or Beehive Press reissues of *Tobacco Road* and other earlier books. Without any apparent signs of feeling, he wrote the introduction for a new edition of *Grapes of Wrath* illustrated by Dorothea Lange's photographs, scenes also from that other time. During one spell Virginia opened each of 27,500 copies of *God's Little Acre* and *Jackpot* for Caldwell so that he might sign each book. The Franklin Mint Library sold 12,500 copies of the first and 15,000 of the other to subscribers on their list. For his chore Caldwell received two dollars per signature; for hers, Virginia was paid four dollars per hour.

Daily before lunch, Caldwell left his office and drove to a postal branch to collect the day's mail. After eating Ginny's carefully balanced diet meal, they shared the mail before he retreated to his bedroom for a two-hour nap. If Virginia wished to shop or meet with one of her few friends, she did so during this time, but only after having switched off his bedroom phone so a possible call would not disturb him. Otherwise Caldwell became anxious if she were gone from home longer than an hour or two.

After arising from his nap, Caldwell returned to his office, perhaps speaking casually to Virginia as he passed by. At five-thirty he emerged to retire to a room where he kept his exercise bike and a television set. There he pedaled the bike as he watched local and national news. Afterwards he moved into the central great room where he read, but again, only newspapers and magazines. That habit made Virginia marvel at the type of reading he and Helen once had shared. During their own life

Erskine and Virginia Caldwell, 1963. Printed by permission of the Estate of
Erskine Caldwell and Dartmouth College Library.

Erskine and Virginia Caldwell in their Scottsdale, Ariz., home, 1982. Printed by permission of the Estate of Erskine Caldwell.

together Caldwell didn't "WANT to read other people's writing, see their films, or know their ideas;" he just wasn't "interested in them."[1]

So Caldwell would read as he wished until Ginny announced supper. Then they talked until he returned to office work or else puttered about. They no longer took evening walks or bike rides since the threat of violence had extended even into Scottsdale. Once a week they disrupted their routine to dine out, alone together, at a local restaurant. Sometimes on Sundays they took a drive or otherwise diverted themselves if Caldwell were not immersed in writing a book. They had been in Arizona for two years before Caldwell began another lengthy manuscript.

During that period, various trips—to Europe, to New York, California, and eventually Oregon—had taken the Caldwells away from home. He accepted government-sponsored seminar engagements first in Santo

Erskine Caldwell in his Scottsdale study, 1982. Printed by permission of the
Estate of Erskine Caldwell.

Domingo and, in 1978, in Guatemala. They also flew almost annually to
Dartmouth, where Ed Lathem arranged scholarly assignments and formal dinners to honor Caldwell.

And thus the Caldwells marked their Arizona years. Except for special
events and trips and yet one more book to be written, each day, each year
became but a repetition of the last. Increasingly Caldwell's lifetime
habits became more confirmed during his declining years.

One of the special events which was to lure Caldwell from the comforts of his solitude was the 1978 celebration of his birthday. December
17 marked his seventy-five years of living and fifty years of writing. To
honor that occasion, C. Waller Barrett arranged an elaborate recognition dinner at the University of Virginia. About sixty-five people attended the meal and ceremony in the prestigious Barrett Library of
American Literature. Barrett himself delivered the address, which em-

Erskine Caldwell in his Scottsdale home, 1983. Printed by permission of the Estate of Erskine Caldwell.

phasized Erskine Caldwell's generous contributions to the body of American literature. Except for numerous letters and telegrams—one from President Carter among them—America and her literary establishment otherwise generally ignored both his birthday and his contributions to the nation's literary heritage. The exception was a brief squib in *The New York Times*. With superficial disdain rather than tribute, it reported the occasion with a "Caldwell 'Rehabilitated'" head-note.

But a people's memories are short. Whatever the quality of Erskine Caldwell's post-forties fiction, his earlier novels and stories alone should have merited a measure of recognition. Earlier that year Caldwell humbly had admitted the impossibility of reaching the level of literary excellence that his conscience, more strenuously than literary critics, demanded: "When you're young, it's easy. Very easy. Maybe too easy. . . . As time goes on, you realize how difficult your profession is and how you're failing at it. You begin finding flaws in your work, and realizing it's not perfect. So you rewrite in order to achieve some semblance of perfection. And finally, you discover—there is no perfection."[2] His advancing years forced from Caldwell not only a large human truth but also what must have become a haunting admission: "Age tells on you. You feel you should achieve greater ability as a writer as you grow older, but you discover there is no greater ability."[3]

Discounting Caldwell's longevity, but conceding the suspect quality of some of his later works, the occasion of his seventy-fifth birthday should have provoked questioning rather than veiled disdain. Why had Caldwell and his writings been so critically rejected? True, he had won no literary prizes or awards, yet some eighty million readers had spent money to read his stories.

Possibly the reason for the scant attention given to Caldwell's writings is as simple as the stories themselves. Critics, like *Jackpot*'s straw-man Professor Perkins, usually wrote volumes about books explaining how feeling might follow from obscured meaning. Caldwell's writings did not lend themselves to such literary dissection in either written or classroom explication. In his sparse, simple stories meaning flowed from the reader's feelings. As Caldwell had approached his seventy-fifth year, he elaborated upon that quality: "Fiction should be poetry in prose. It should have the same quality and feeling. . . . For the reader as well as the writer, it must go through the whole range of emotions."[4]

Yet if the literary establishment had ignored Caldwell's three-quarters of a century of life and achievement, those who respected and loved him did not. "The biggest . . . birthday surprise was from Jay and his wife Diana. They sent E. two round trip tickets to Anchorage where Jay and his family had relocated and he practiced medicine. Erskine was absolutely overcome by the magnitude of their thoughtfulness," Virginia observed.[5] After opening the gift card, he held the tickets, walking around the room with a sense of almost amazed disbelief. They perhaps made him realize that others beside Ginny were willing to spend money so they might enjoy his company.

But before departing for Anchorage, the Caldwells enjoyed Virginia's gift to Caldwell. From among her list of many options he could have selected, he had decided upon a San Francisco dinner with Herb Caen. She had rejoiced at his choice since he generally refused to see almost all of his friends and acquaintances. The dinner with the Caens proved to be not only enjoyable but also a subject for one of his daily columns in the *San Francisco Chronicle.* As usual, Caen granted Caldwell his hyperbole. " 'At Mayo . . . they took off half of each lung. . . . They took me off the hard stuff too. I was drinking a fifth of bourbon per day.' And, "How many books?" 'Oh, 50, 55.' Reprinted in how many languages? 'Oh, 50, 55.' "[6] After those allowances Herb Caen offered his pithy impressions:

> Dinner over, Caldwell puts on his long overcoat, his 20-year-old hat that he wears with the brim turned down all around, like Dashiell Hammett. "Have to go back to Mayo soon," he confides. "My left eye is getting weak. Old age, y'know. Haven't had any sight in my right eye since I was a little kid, about five. Well, be seein' you—I hope!"
>
> He and Virginia walk off into the rainy night, he looking like somebody from another age. Which he is. An age of people slightly larger than life.[7]

By the time the small recognitions for the large man were over, another year had well begun. Only a slight exception altered its predictability.

For the first time since Morang's death, the Caldwells began taking annual vacations to Santa Fe. Meanwhile signs had begun to appear as literary wonders.

Caldwell read Malcolm Cowley's *And I Worked At the Writer's Trade*
"cover-to-cover, nonstop." The aging critic's observation that Caldwell's
"contribution to American Letters," to the body of American folklore,
merited reevaluation met with Caldwell's appreciation. He bristled,
however, because Cowley had accepted as fact an unpublished biographer's estimation that Caldwell habitually lied for his own advantage.
Somewhat later he enjoyed the two hundred pages that *Pembroke Magazine* devoted to his life and writing in its annual 1979 issue. More satisfyingly yet, Scott MacDonald published a 1981 collection of Caldwell
criticism and commentary, which included convincing arguments for
the excellence of his short stories as well as some of his longer works.
And by 1984 the Twayne Series editors admitted him to the respectability of their canon of significant writers. *Erskine Caldwell*, James Devlin's
perceptive study, did not tout Caldwell's greatness, but it coherently argued both the strengths and weaknesses of at least his earlier writings.

Yet eventually that praise for past achievements was not to be enough
for Caldwell. The present demanded its own productive accounting.
Subsequent to Ed Lathem's 1979 Scottsdale visit, Caldwell started
showing the telltale restlessness that indicated a book idea was ger-
minating. Shortly he, Virginia, and his typewriter made trips to Santa Fe
as first stops of two extended tours of states and places west. As usual he
said very little to Virginia about the subject of his latest effort.

Perhaps the nature of the subject, or aging itself, made the writing of
Caldwell's last long work more exacting than usual. After almost a year
he sent the manuscript for *With All My Might*, his final autobiographical
accounting, to Ed Lathem for editing. He and Virginia, meanwhile departed for "a recycled honeymoon" to Lake Louise, the same place he
and Helen had first vacationed almost a half-century earlier. Who
knows what associations the second visit stirred? But back in Scottsdale
Caldwell asked Lathem to return the text for some added work. What he
wanted to add or revise, he did not say. A few months later he again forwarded the amended copy for Lathem's suggestions.

But after that what was Caldwell to do? He attended to day-to-day details. The Caldwells visited Disneyland with Drew's children. But for Caldwell to whom "anything else [but writing] would be unnatural," such activities became thin. Virginia noted that "the between books syndrome is not the best time for him, and even through he is quite pleased with life in general, he is happier when there is action. And at the moment there is none."[8] Writing and action—through such activities, he could, as he shortly before had admitted, stay "too busy to reflect upon the past."[9]

That autumn the Solidarity movement in Poland caught Caldwell's interest. He and Virginia accordingly spent ten days in that beleaguered nation. There the Polish Ministry of Culture conferred upon him its Order of Cultural Merit. Subsequently he and Virginia observed the people in action and used his blocked royalties to purchase some folk art. After their return to Scottsdale, Caldwell's restlessness took them to New York to see about business affairs. The Caldwells dined again with Jim Brown and visited with Julius Weiss. Home once more, they anticipated another trip that would carry them from one year into the next.

In Honolulu at 12:01 A.M., January 1, 1982, the Caldwells celebrated their twenty-fifth wedding anniversary. As evidence of the reality, they sent friends and associates a colored commemorative picture that showed a smiling, unusually relaxed Caldwell holding Virginia, attractive and exuberant, upon his knee. Its message, "We Wish You Years of Happiness, Too" might have said it all, except one photo at least also carried the postscript, "We made it!" Indeed the Caldwells had, both to Honolulu and through twenty-five years of life together.

That recognition behind them, the Caldwells returned home to await the unfolding of yet another year. The following spring they flew to Japan. Caldwell scholars there hosted a number of activities, calling attention to the man whose Georgia stories still fascinated people in different parts of the world. In America, meanwhile, the Friends of the Library at the University of Minnesota and the Caldwell Literary Society in Phoenix both had planned summer events recognizing his accomplishments. The Caldwells attended the Minneapolis opening of a three-month display of his first editions, now considered rare books. A Phoenix telecast of *Tobacco Road* and the Arizona governor's declaration of November as Erskine Caldwell Month called attention to his accomplishments even as it forced him uncomfortably out of seclusion.

Caldwell became increasingly restless. He wanted to move again, this time to a smaller house without landscaping concerns and expenses. Virginia touted the advantages of locating in Ashland, Oregon, where both the environment and her grandchildren attracted her. Still wary of being so distractingly close to relatives, Caldwell resisted. He wished to remain in the Phoenix area, but until their house could be sold, they would wait and see.

Caldwell also awaited word of the disposition of his autobiography, *With All My Might.* Written with such dutiful effort, the book that was to be his last extended work, failed to excite those publishers who considered it. Like most of his later fiction, this final personal accounting was both repetitious and lacking in vitality. Many of its events and details he already had shared in his 1951 autobiographical effort, *Call It Experience.*

Unlike that carefully censored memoir, however, Caldwell's last attempt to step from behind the veil did lend some insight into his personal life. He acknowledged that he and Helen had been sleeping together before their elopement. Correcting the false impressions projected through *Experience,* he this time accurately assigned ownership of the Maine home to Helen's parents. His and Helen's children belatedly became a part of this life story. Caldwell also included Alfred and Dorothy Morang but omitted mention of the lasting depths and bonds of their friendship. He hinted the sexual beginnings of those involvements with, first, Margaret, and later, June, but so reinterpreted the events from each occasion that he appeared to be blameless in the subsequent divorces. Caldwell otherwise also used his "creative license" to rearrange facts and reinterpret situations to his advantage. Sequencing of events, associations with former publishers and agents, and motives for behavior all were creatively embroidered with a dual design: to reaffirm his writer's constancy and to justify himself in almost every instance as a righteous victim.

One other essence, and that not as patently self-serving, haunted

Caldwell's past accountings. In at least three instances he confessed to a longing for life as he once had enjoyed it in Mount Vernon. The contexts of those admissions were provocative. Reflecting upon that time when he had been married to June and immersed in Al Manuel's efforts to squeeze ever more Hollywood money from his writings, he had counted the costs: "Even though I knew I would continue living the life I had made for myself, often there were yearnings for a quiet retreat as comforting and productive as it had been my good fortune to enjoy in Mount Vernon for many years."[10] On another occasion when he had gained a span of uninterrupted time for writing, he had felt "as if [he] had been granted a continuation of the early days of tranquil living in Mount Vernon."[11] Such musings reckoned two sad truths; there, in another time, he had enjoyed a comfortable world; there too he had written most productively.

Despite such oblique admissions and revisionary inclusions, *With All My Might* otherwise seemed almost clinical in its rendering of Caldwell's life and career. Not his relationships with people but rather his participation in life events structured the work. Figures and occasions, professional associations, trips and changes of home locations dictated the final one-third portion of his account. Just as Caldwell's fiction and writings had progressively marked a disengagement with life subsequent to his marriages to Margaret and June, so his life's story seemed to trace a similar pattern. A couplet from one of Robert Frost's poems perhaps best describes *With All My Might:* "It couldn't be called ungentle. But how thoroughly departmental."

Not until four years after its completion was *With All My Might* to be issued in America. How much the work's dispassionate quality, Caldwell's failing reputation and diminished readership, and an economic decline in publishing each contributed to the delay cannot be determined. Whatever the cause, the sad fact remains that during the last few years of his life Caldwell had to be satisfied with those recognitions accumulated from his body of writings rather than from his most recent autobiographical work.

In October 1983 the Caldwells departed for Nice, France, where Caldwell had been invited to attend a gathering of French writers. Unbeknown to him, the invitation to participate had been a partial ruse. Invited to center stage at the gathering, Caldwell belatedly realized that he was the guest of honor; he received France's highest literary honor: Commander of the Order of Arts and Letters. After the banquet that evening, the lights dimmed and a band played "Happy Birthday" music. On signal each of the five hundred participants was given a lighted candle and sang birthday greetings as Caldwell cut a huge cake. The tribute was so "unexpected and unbelievable" that he was moved to tears.[12] The actual celebration of Caldwell's eightieth birthday, he and Virginia noted alone with a short trip to Little America in Flagstaff, Arizona.

Travels, both in America and abroad, punctuated the Caldwells' lives during the next year. That spring he was participant in a Writer's Conference at Birmingham Southern College in Alabama. In April they journeyed to Milan, Zurich, and Lucerne to meet Caldwell's agent and representatives. By mid-May they were in Augusta, Georgia. That summer they drove to Santa Fe, to Utah's Monument Valley, and to Ashland, Oregon. In early October, they attended a New Haven opening of *Tobacco Road*, but by October 21 the Caldwells were in Sofia, Bulgaria, for an international writers meeting. There he received the Ministry of Culture's Medal of Merit and was the guest of honor at a reception given by the Bulgarian president. At the conference's close he gave a speech that earned a standing ovation.

Though such international honors were signal events in Caldwell's life, more meaningful yet were recognitions granted him during the following year, 1985. They affirmed that at long last his home country was willing to give him some of his dues. The most satisfyingly honorific was Caldwell's May 15 induction into the prestigious American Academy and Institute of Arts and Letters. Finally "the literary guys" had formally accepted him into their ranks.

Shortly thereafter even Caldwell's home state acknowledged its native son. Georgia's first lady, Mrs. Joe Frank Harris, invited him to the governor's mansion to sign her collection of Caldwell first editions. That following autumn Caldwell traveled to several state locations. A consortium of public libraries had received a grant from the Georgia Endowment for the Humanities to bring him back home to small-town

Georgia communities. During two separate two-week stints he was the honored speaker and designated resource person for programs recalling readers to his works. Places as diverse as Atlanta, Fitzgerald, and Burrus, Decatur, Stone Mountain, and Covington celebrated and feted the author who, a half century before, had been all-but-anathema almost everywhere in the state.

Such international, national, and regional academic plaudits provided quiet satisfactions for Caldwell. Though he had "never been totally at peace," Virginia estimated that he was more at ease with himself during those last few years than he had ever before been.[13] For one such as Caldwell who had placed his writing duties before almost all else, recognitions of that sort offered at least a small measure of solace and reward.

Between the trips, when at home, Caldwell became increasingly reclusive. He wanted only peace and quiet, to read the newspapers, answer the mail, watch the news or football games and just to be with Virginia. He did not want to see people or even to go out and eat. Though he readily granted almost all interviews, he allowed such intrusions because they were a part of "his work, his duty."[14]

Those who came seeking more information, more insights into Caldwell's writings, into the details of either his life or the lives of those once a part of his experience, confronted a now aging titan who had always resisted such prying. If a query provoked a story or snippet of reminiscence, he was congenial and talkative. But in private matters he still hid behind a more creviced version of his self-same mask. Goldberg's impressions subsequent to her 1984 interview about Margaret Bourke-White capture the spirit of what most interviewers confronted: "Did I tell you the great man himself finally granted me a brief interview? It was timed as if with a stop watch, but he was surprisingly loquacious. I'm still in correspondence with him, chiefly through Virginia. The correspondence is amusing. If he can find a monosyllabic answer to a question, he does; if not, he'll go a syllable to two farther."[15]

In other more generalized interview sessions, Caldwell usually repeated only what he had said so many times before to so many interviewers through so many years. Yet occasionally either old truths or fresh insights crept in. In 1982 he allowed that his mother's influence, her emphasis upon education, had led him to write.[16] But just as obliquely that influence and heritage did not always sing true. He perceived nothing divine about human beings; life is a chance.[17]

Those interviews Caldwell granted after he knew that death was impending offered some more reflective conclusions. About his writings: why, beginning in 1946, did women start becoming the main characters in his novels? Edwin Arnold asked forty years later. Well, maybe because he had begun "to have a lot of personal experiences with women. . . . You become disillusioned as time goes on, so you start reflecting about it, and maybe that leads to creation of female characters. . . . Women are, to a great extent, victims in a male dominated society."[18] And more about his life: "I didn't expect to have anything except the pain of living. I did expect that. Not the ecstasy but the pain of living."[19] When questioned not directly about the pain but about his self-admitted single-mindedness, Caldwell "shifted uncomfortably in his armchair and said, 'When I was having domestic trouble, I did not hesitate to get out of it. I was not a nice guy. I considered my job more important than anything else. But I had to take a stand selfishly, not thinking of anybody, just myself.' "[20] All things considered, all personal and career matters weighed, Caldwell implied that he would stand firm until death itself forced the measure.

As the years passed, moreover, there were fewer and fewer nonprofessionals who might have imposed upon Caldwell's privacy. His children from his first marriage, Pix, Dabney, and Janet, sometimes still uneasily balanced what they remembered against what he perhaps had forgotten. All involved in careers and families of their own, they, through the passing years, had visited and stayed in touch. More than any other of Caldwell's children, Janet, and later her daughter Becky, made special efforts to visit the Caldwells at least every few years. Caldwell, on the other hand, did not visit any of his older children during the last decade of his life.

Because Jay and his family had remained in Alaska, he was separated by distance from his father and visited him but rarely. Virginia's son Drew and his family had moved to Ashland, Oregon, where the Caldwells traveled often for visits and anticipated eventually moving. Though they still had not sold the Scottsdale home, they actively sought a place to buy in Ashland.

Otherwise all of those people who once had been so intimately a part of Caldwell's life had drifted away or died. Widowed, Helen had lived out her summer days in the Mount Vernon home, and spent the winters traveling among Pix's, Dee's, and Janet's families. She occupied herself by writing newspaper columns, generously assisting Caldwell scholars, and each Halloween by playing the part of "a green witch" for neighboring children. Vivacious and vital, she had laid the past to rest through her exuberance for the present. Finally in the fall of 1986 she died, a victim of cancer. Learning of her death, Caldwell made no comment whatsoever.[21]

Margaret Bourke-White's career had been severely arrested by Parkinson's disease in the mid-fifties. On a couple of occasions thereafter she had written Caldwell before passing through Phoenix. Might he want to meet over lunch? He always had excused himself. After almost two decades of crippling pain, Bourke-White had died in 1971.

June, Margaret's successor in Caldwell's life, achieved a secure independence from any identity her second marriage may have offered. Beginning in the late sixties she earned local renown through columns written for Tucson's *Arizona Daily Star* under the byline of June Caldwell Martin. Though the tensions between the Caldwells and her did not ease, Virginia became a warm friend of June's mother and visited the elderly woman often in her Scottsdale home.

And the other Caldwell associates? Most had gone away year by passing year. First, of course, Alfred Morang and then Al Manuel and Duhamel, Calder and John Steinbeck and Victor Weybright. By the mid-eighties Julius Weiss, Caldwell's first and only lawyer-adviser, also had died. Maxim Lieber, his first agent, had returned from his exile in Mexico and unsuccessfully tried to argue for past commissions he felt had been his due. That tension between them, the two did not meet again. The fracture between Caldwell and Jim Brown, Lieber's successor, had eventually been healed. Beyond a few shared dinners, however, that association failed to renew itself before Brown finally retired in the mid-eighties. Owen Golden, Caldwell's long-time accountant continued to function in that capacity, but who else remained? Roscoe and Elizabeth Fawcett alone maintained that friendship that had its beginnings when Caldwell had autographed paperbacks among drugstore racks across the nation. Otherwise only Virginia remained as Caldwell's wife, confidant, and friend. He who always had been so woman-centered and dependent remained so until the end of his days.

How frightfully few those would prove to be was first impressed upon the Caldwells in late August of 1986. Caldwell had experienced pneumonia symptoms in July. Tests associated with that illness eventually revealed that he had lung cancer once again. This was no recurrence of the old cancers which had been removed. Rather it was a new and virulent form.

Caldwell's response to the diagnosis was stoical. Dr. Bradley Gordon, his physician specialist, felt Caldwell was almost "presidential or regal" as he intellectualized about the diagnosis and treatment process.[22] Because his oxygen levels were so low, he was placed on oxygen almost immediately. Thereafter until his death some seven months later, Caldwell remained attached to his fifty-foot respiratory lifeline.

Virginia's reaction was to intensify those efforts that always had flowed from her love and concern for his well-being. She cared for his every need and stuffed him with those nutritious foods she and the doctors determined would be most beneficial. Otherwise she accompanied him for his twice-weekly chemotherapy treatments and allowed him the freedom to function as he always had. He gave up riding his exercise bike but otherwise continued to go to his office where he sometimes "wrote into the night." What he was writing remains unclear but he "was obsessed with working. Either driven or obsessed or both."[23] In fact, three days before his death, Caldwell insisted on being dressed so he could be wheeled into his office ready for work. As always in times of crisis, Caldwell worked as if his life and salvation depended upon that grace. How consciously this religious legacy variously motivated him became evident in a statement made to Doctor Gordon; "He said he was a Presbyterian and therefore not to be shaken by cancer."[24]

And work would merit reward, as Caldwell again had reconfirmed. A

French publishing house finally accepted *With All My Might* for publication in that country—and shortly thereafter, Peachtree Publishers, here—and invited the Caldwells there for its release. Caldwell wanted to go "come hell or high water." After all arrangements for oxygen use in air facilities had been made, however, he eventually canceled his plans and hopes. An interruption of the chemotherapy treatments would allow the cancer rampant growth.

Caldwell's last birthday celebration was subdued, but the Christmas season brought a visit from Jay and his family. Fears of infection from outside sources limited the family's interaction. Caldwell's granddaughters merely hugged him and then returned to the car. Janet likewise came to say her last good-bye after Caldwell was wheelchair-bound in late January. His grown grandchildren, Pix's son, Hayden, and Janet's daughter Becky, also visited during his final months. And Pix himself, who hadn't seen his father for three years, pleaded to come. Caldwell agreed but only to a "twenty minute" period.[25] Dabney alone maintained his distance during the term of his father's illness.

The chemotherapy treatments only controlled the cancer's virulence. When those were concluded, Doctor Gordon made weekly house calls primarily to offer whatever comfort he could. Explaining this to Caldwell, he concluded by asking, "What else can I do for you?" "I want a miracle," Caldwell replied.[26] But he, like everyone else, recognized that there would be no miracles in this instance.

As Caldwell's condition worsened, it seemed that he was observing—as had been his wont—observing and wishing to write about his experience.[27] Yet the details of his parting also became a matter for resolution. During the final week of his illness, Drew Fletcher, Virginia's son, came to Scottsdale to help Virginia care for, and make final arrangements for, her husband. Always before Caldwell casually had noted that he wished to be cremated and to have his ashes scattered over water. As the end approached, however, he asked Drew to call the mortuary and make the arrangements. Scattering the ashes had been "a silly idea." "The thing to do," he directed, "is to get a shovel, go find a dead-end street and dig a big hole." "A dead end street?" Drew queried; "Isn't that appropriate?" Caldwell replied.[28]

Beyond such darkly humorous directions, he offered little else. He did not care to have his ashes buried either in Georgia or near his parents in Prosperity, South Carolina. Neither did he wish to have his remains interred because he did not wish to be "shut in." On one issue Caldwell was insistent: he did not want a memorial service of any sort. Characteristically, he apparently wished that all who knew him well accept his ending as stoically as he himself had endured life and its conclusions. The scope of those conclusions he had charted for all a few years earlier: "I would not willingly consent to relive my life for the purpose of rectifying the mistakes I have made and attempt to correct the errors I have committed along the way. I accept my own failings together with the knowledge that my writings and I must exist with all our imperfections to the end of time."[29]

The scope of Caldwell's mortal time painfully narrowed. By Saturday, April 11, 1987, Virginia sadly realized that his hold on life was weakening. That evening, not knowing what else to do, she asked a psychiatrist neighbor whom Caldwell liked to come offer his opinion about whether or not he thought Caldwell should be moved to a hospital. When the psychiatrist entered, Caldwell roused himself enough to ask, "What are you charging for house calls?"[30] Shortly thereafter, at 7:30 that evening, the eighty-three-year-old Caldwell, attended by Virginia and Drew, drifted away into his last solitary sleep.

On an Ashland, Oregon, hillside surrounded by pastures and looking out on mountains, Caldwell's ashes are kept in a glass-doored crypt within a windowed mausoleum. He is not shut in. The Georgia boy grown mortally old rests a continent away from his White Oak beginnings, from Tobacco Road country. Virginia hovers near. Having sold the Scottsdale home, she purchased a condominium cottage in Medford, Oregon, near Ashland, family, and new friends. In December of 1991 she married Ralph Hibbs, a medical doctor and a friend from that new place and new life.

Erskine Caldwell wanted it all that way.

Notes

Introduction

1. Joseph Warren Beach, "American Fiction: 1920–1940," in *Critical Essays on Erskine Caldwell*, ed. Scott MacDonald (Boston: G. K. Hall & Co., 1981), 186, 188, 195.
2. W. M. Frohock, "Erskine Caldwell: Sentimental Gentleman from Georgia," in MacDonald, ed., *Critical Essays*, 211.
3. James Korges, *Erskine Caldwell*. Univ. of Minnesota Pamphlet Series. (Minneapolis: Univ. of Minnesota Press, 1969).
4. Scott MacDonald, "Repetition as Technique in the Short Stories of Erskine Caldwell," in MacDonald, ed., *Critical Essays*, 330–41.
5. Scott MacDonald, Introduction to *Critical Essays*, xxviii.
6. James E. Devlin, *Erskine Caldwell* (Boston: Twayne Publishers, 1984), passim.
7. Sylvia Cook, *Erskine Caldwell and the Fiction of Poverty* (Baton Rouge: Louisana State Univ. Press, 1991), 266.
8. Ibid., 280.
9. Virginia Caldwell in conversation with author, May 23, 1992, Waterloo, Iowa.
10. Erskine Caldwell, letter to author, Jan. 17, 1978.
11. Cook, *Erskine Caldwell*, 103.

Part 1. The Web the Story Spins

Chapter 1

1. This house was moved from White Oak to the Moreland community in 1989, largely through the efforts of Winston Skinner of the *Newnan Times Herald* and Sara Haynes, the mayor of Moreland. There it has been restored and is to be used as a Caldwell museum.
2. This incident is one June Caldwell Martin remembers Carrie Caldwell's reciting often. Telephone interview with author, Sept. 21, 1980.
3. Marilyn D. Staats, "Erskine Caldwell at Eighty-One: An Interview," in *Conversations with Erskine Caldwell*, ed. Edwin T. Arnold (Jackson: Univ. Press of Mississippi, 1988), 259.

4. Caroline Preston Caldwell to Erskine Caldwell, July 1952, otherwise undated, Erskine Caldwell Collection, Baker Library, Dartmouth College
   (hereafter cited as Caldwell Collection).
5. Details of this story came from various sources, most important among
   them Mary Maner, Caldwell's maternal cousin. Mary Maner, interview
   with author, January 21, 1979, Louisville, Ga., and telephone interview,
   Oct. 30, 1980.
6. Erskine Caldwell, *Deep South: Memory and Observation* (New York:
   Weybright and Talley, 1968), 180–82.
7. Blanche Bowers Hemphill to Erskine Caldwell, Oct. 10, 1958, Caldwell
   Collection.
8. Undated marginal notes made by Caroline Caldwell on letter received from
   Robert Cantwell, August 23, 1950, Caldwell Collection. Mrs. I. S. Caldwell
   contributed often to the *Monthly Bulletin*, a publication of the Woman's
   Presbyterian Missionary Union. Often her essays or poems stressed the
   value of duty: "Each one must bear his own burden of individual work"
   (*Monthly Bulletin* 6 [Apr. 1913]), or more obviously:

   > "Home Missions"
   > The day had been long and trying,
   > I was worn with work and care,
   > My lips were too weary for song—
   > My heart too heavy for prayer.

   The poem continues through ten eight-line stanzas with the concluding one
   indicating that the person flew back to her task to make a fabric "fit for the
   Master's use" (*Monthly Bulletin* 3 [Apr. 1916]). For sending me copies of
   Mrs. I. S. Caldwell's various contributions to the *Monthly Bulletin*, I am
   deeply indebted to Professor Benjamin Farley of Erskine College. Without
   his kindness I would have remained unaware of their existence.
9. Because Caldwell had been born at the end of one year and before the beginning of the other, the family believed that Ira, when making the entry,
   erroneously had subtracted by one year. In the late forties, the elder Caldwells sent a notarized affidavit to Erskine for passport purposes. It attested
   that he had been born in 1903. On the other hand, one Joe Leigh Camp
   wrote Caldwell in 1965 stating that he and Amy Walton had been the first
   couple Ira had ever married—on December 17, 1902, supposedly the day of
   Caldwell's birth. Informed of this, Carrie countered with the explanation for
   the confusion. As further evidence, she concluded, "[Aunt Edna] wrote me

you were born the year she married (1903)." Another person, Mrs. L. B. Walthall of Newnan, writing to Caldwell in his later years, offered confirming evidence: "You were born the same year I was married, 1903" (Mrs. L. B. Walthall to Erskine Caldwell, Jan. 21, 1965, Caldwell Collection).

An earlier unpublished Caldwell biographer, relied wholly upon the misdated biblical entry to conclude that Caldwell regularly dissembled to his own advantage. Working from that biographer's interpretation, Malcolm Cowley unfortunately presented that assumption as fact in his book *And I Worked at the Writer's Trade*. Among Georgia folk, communal memory and story are more trustworthy than written figures. I, therefore, accept the correct date as December 17, 1903. Appropriately, even the date of the storyteller's birth must be reconstructed through story.

10. *Newnan Times Herald*, July 6, 1978.
11. Undated notes Carrie made in response to Virginia Caldwell's request that she record some of Erskine's childhood anecdotes. Special Collections, Univ. of Georgia Library (hereafter cited as Georgia Collection).
12. Virginia Caldwell to Harvey Klevar, Nov. 28, 1978; telephone interview, June 21, 1981.
13. Erskine Caldwell, *The Sacrilege of Alan Kent* (Portland, Maine: Falmouth Book House, 1936), 8.
14. Mary Maner, interview with author, Louisville, Ga., Jan. 21, 1979.
15. Ibid.
16. Ibid.
17. Undated, handwritten memorandum, Georgia Collection.
18. Richard B. Sale, "An Interview in Florida with Erskine Caldwell," in Arnold, *Conversations*, 132.
19. Mary Maner, interview with author, Louisville, Ga., Jan. 21, 1979.
20. Erskine Caldwell, interview with author, Scottsdale, Ariz., May 30, 1978.
21. The summary of the Bisco story follows that told by Caldwell in his *In Search of Bisco* (New York: Farrar, Straus and Giroux, 1965), 1–7.
22. Excerpted and quoted from an unpublished submission by June Caldwell (Martin) to the Department of Amplification, *The New Yorker*, Nov. 8, 1951, Caldwell Collection.
23. Erskine Caldwell, *With All My Might* (Atlanta: Peachtree Publishers, Ltd., 1987), 13.
24. Ibid.
25. Ibid., 14.
26. Ibid., 20.

27. Ibid., 21.

28. *Afternoons in Mid-America* (New York: Dodd, Mead, and Co., 1976), 1–11.

29. Helen Caldwell Cushman, interview with author, Mount Vernon, Maine, July 19, 1977.

30. Virginia Caldwell, telephone interview with author, June 20, 1991.

Chapter 2

1. Erskine Caldwell, interview with author, Scottsdale, Ariz., May 30, 1978.

2. *Sacrilege*, 13–14.

3. Ibid., 14.

4. Quoted in an unspecified Shelby, N.C., newspaper article, June 23, 1953, 1952–53 correspondence files, Caldwell Collection.

5. Mary Maner, interview with author, Louisville, Ga., Jan. 21, 1979.

6. *Sacrilege*, 12–13.

7. Caldwell recalls having occasionally attended school in Staunton. Since the family never properly lived there, Carrie must have enrolled him during their visits. If she did, her actions lend credence to the supposition that she did not object to formal education for her son. She merely mistrusted what he might or might not have learned in schools less sophisticated than her background would merit.

8. Mary Maner, interview with author, Louisville, Ga., Jan. 21, 1979.

9. Erskine Caldwell, interview with author, Scottsdale, Ariz., May 30, 1978.

10. *With All My Might*, 40.

11. *Deep South*, 115.

12. The Sesquicentennial Issue of Erskine College's alumni magazine assigns Ira Caldwell to Timber Ridge, Virginia, between the years of 1911 and 1915. However, Caldwell recalled that the family moved from Prosperity to Charlotte, North Carolina, in 1910. Trusting implicitly his memory for places but respectfully assuming his chronology might be misplaced by a year, I adopt 1911 as the year the Caldwells moved, not to Timber Ridge, but to Charlotte. I am assuming that since Ira Sylvester's assignments during the next ten years were so various and brief in time and place, the editors of the Erskine College record probably for the sake of convenience assigned him to Timber Ridge and subsequently to Atoka, Tennessee. Hereafter I will follow the more specific charting provided by Caldwell's memory of places.

13. Mrs. I. S. Caldwell, *Women's Presbyterian Missionary Union Monthly Bulletin* 4 (June 1910), 6.

14. *Monthly Bulletin* 5 (Feb. 1912), 6; and *Monthly Bulletin* 5 (Dec. 1911), unpaginated.

15. *Deep South*, 1.

16. Quoted from the Rochester (Minn.) *Post Bulletin*, Oct. 17, 1958, Erskine Caldwell Scrapbook #5.

17. Edwin T. Arnold, "Interview with Erskine Caldwell," in Arnold, *Conversations*, 265.

18. Erskine Caldwell, interview with author, May 30, 1978; and *Sacrilege*, 34.

19. *With All My Might*, 20.

20. *Sacrilege*, 12.

21. *With All My Might*, 25.

22. Ibid., 34.

23. Carvel Collins in *Conversations*, 46.

24. "The Trouble with Knickerbockers," *San Francisco Chronicle*, undated clipping, Erskine Caldwell Scrapbook #5, Caldwell Collection.

25. M. G. Boyce to William A. Sutton, Oct. 15, 1970, Caldwell Collection.

26. *With All My Might*, 16–17.

27. Ibid., 24–25.

28. Ibid., 21–22.

29. *Sacrilege*, 15.

30. A work first published in *Story* 1 (Jan-Feb. 1932), 3–15. First issued in the short-story collection *We Are the Living* (New York: Viking, 1933).

31. Erskine Caldwell, *In Search of Bisco* (New York: Farrar, Straus and Giroux, 1965), 8–11.

32. M. G. Boyce to W. A. Sutton, Oct. 15, 1970, Caldwell Collection.

33. Ibid.

34. *With All My Might* places this experience in time prior to Caldwell's entering school. The earlier sequencing from *In Search of Bisco* is the correct one. What happened sexually to Caldwell during this sojourn is not clear. In the *Bisco* work he boasts that he was seduced by the YMCA secretary's wife. In the later work he claims that the secretary's prostitute-date for the night left his bed to come sleep innocently with Caldwell. Since both accounts include variations upon the sexual theme, it seems likely that—either in fantasy or reality—Caldwell had some sort of memorable sexual encounter during this time away from home.

Chapter 3

1. Erskine Caldwell, interview with author, Scottsdale, Ariz., May 30, 1978.

2. Elizabeth Pell Broadwell and Ronald Wesley Hoag, "'A Writer First': An Interview with Erskine Caldwell," in Arnold, *Conversations*, 179.

3. Edwin T. Arnold, "Interview with Erskine Caldwell," in Arnold, *Conversations*, 266.

4. Rev. Amplus Howard, letter to author, Jan. 20, 1979.

5. Erskine Caldwell, interview with author, Scottsdale, Ariz., May 29, 1978.

6. *Deep South*, 118.

7. Rev. Amplus Howard, letter to author, Jan. 20, 1979.

8. *Call It Experience*, 25.

9. Ibid., 23–24.

10. Erskine Caldwell, interview with author, Scottsdale, Ariz., May 30, 1978.

11. *Call It Experience*, 14. Beyond such claims, Caldwell's earliest novel, *The Bastard*, presumes some knowledge of a mill and its people, at least enough to confirm what might have been gained through some adolescent or later working experience.

12. Erskine Caldwell, interview with author, Scottsdale, Ariz., May 30, 1978.

13. Caldwell's full account of this experience is found in *Call It Experience*, 16–18.

14. Very likely the scope of Caldwell's duties at the paper were much exaggerated and almost certainly from another time. Based on the evidence of spelling, grammatical, and structural errors in later letters to his parents, any unedited newspaper articles he then might have written would have been laughably rustic at best. In fact, except for Caldwell's claims, there is no evidence that he owned a typewriter until much later.

15. *Call It Experience*, 20.

16. Ibid., 22–23.

17. *With All My Might*, 44–45.

18. First published in *Pagany* 1 (Winter 1930), 34–36; first reprinted in the short-story collection *American Earth* (New York: Scribner's, 1931).

19. First published in *Contempo* 2 (May 25, 1932), 1–8; first reprinted in *We Are the Living*.

20. Numerous older Wrens residents told essentially the same story. The woman whose relationship apparently sparked the story refused to be interviewed and thereby confirm or deny either local rumors or the details of Caldwell's published story. First issued in *Lion and Crown* 1, no. 2, 1933, 1–6.

21. *With All My Might*, 47.

22. Erskine Caldwell, interview with author, Scottsdale, Ariz., May 30, 1978.

Chapter 4

1. Jac Lyndon Tharpe, *Interview with Mr. Erskine Caldwell*, Mississippi Oral History Program of the Univ. of Southern Mississippi, vol. 13 (Hattiesburg, 1973), 69.

2. *Eighty-Third Annual Catalogue of Erskine College*, Collegiate Year, 1920–21, Rules and Regulations, 18.

3. Tharpe, *Interview with Caldwell*, 69.

4. *Call It Experience*, 27–28.

5. Cy Hood to W. A. Sutton, Dec. 6, 1976, Caldwell Collection. Although the teammate allegedly remembers every detail so accurately that he cites November 18, 1921, as the date for the Clemson game, there are some discrepancies. Caldwell was a freshman in November of 1920, not 1921, and if the game had been played on the cited day, it would have fallen on a Friday, an unusual time for a football game. Nonetheless, the "regular" seems to have been accurate in remembering the young Caldwell as a "long-legged, shut-mouth."

6. Erskine Caldwell, interview with author, Scottsdale, Ariz., May 30, 1978.

7. Jesse S. Agnew to William A. Sutton, Sept. 25, 1970, Caldwell Collection.

8. Tharpe, *Interview with Caldwell*, 60.

9. Ibid.

10. Erskine Caldwell, interview with author, Scottsdale, Ariz., May 30, 1978.

11. Erskine Caldwell to Caroline Preston Caldwell, July 30, 1920, Georgia Collection.

12. Erskine Caldwell to Caroline Preston Caldwell, July 2, 1920, Georgia Collection.

13. *With All My Might*, 54–55. Typically, Caldwell spins an elaborately contrived conceit to chart the details of his sexual initiation.

14. Erskine Caldwell, interview with author, Scottsdale, Ariz., May 30, 1978.

15. In Caldwell's account in *With All My Might* (56), he mistakenly cites an "April or May" departure.

16. An earlier, unpublished biographer apparently believed that Caldwell shared his New Orleans odyssey with a college companion. That assumption may or may not be correct, but its validity seems immaterial. Caldwell's reconstructions of that experience, through both his telling and his writing, always present him as the solitary figure, alone and experiencing.

17. Erskine Caldwell, interview with author, Scottsdale, Ariz., May 30, 1978.

18. *Sacrilege*, 20–21.

19. Al Hansen to William A. Sutton, Feb. 11, 1972, Caldwell Collection.

20. Affidavit of Arrest, Bogalusa City Court, Feb. 2, 1922, J. E. Branch, Presiding Magistrate, Caldwell Collection.
21. *Call It Experience*, 32.

Part 2. "That's Why God Made Words"

Chapter 5

1. Erskine Caldwell, interview with author, Scottsdale, Ariz., Nov. 30, 1978.
2. *With All My Might*, 65.
3. Ibid., 66
4. Ibid., 70.
5. Erskine Caldwell to Rev. and Mrs. I. S. Caldwell, Sept. 5, 1924, Georgia Collection.
6. Erskine Caldwell, interview with author, Scottsdale, Ariz., Nov. 30, 1978.
7. Erskine Caldwell to I. S. Caldwells, Sept. 5, 1924.
8. Ibid.
9. Kresge records from that period indicate that Caldwell worked at the Wilkes-Barre store only two weeks. However, his letters to his parents, dated during that autumn of 1924, reveal that he worked at the store for about four months—as he had correctly recalled, without the assistance of that misplaced correspondence, in his 1951 work *Call It Experience*. These detailed letters, as much as other documents, compellingly attest to Caldwell's accurate recall of most public facts about his life—save those touching upon his writings and personal relationships.
10. Erskine Caldwell to I. S. Caldwells, Sept. 24, 1924, Georgia Collection.
11. Ibid.
12. *Sacrilege*, 22.
13. Ibid., 50.
14. Ibid., 22.
15. Ibid., 54.
16. Ibid., 31, 39, 49.
17. Ibid., 54.
18. Erskine Caldwell to I. S. Caldwells, Nov. 6, 1924, Georgia Collection.
19. Ibid.
20. *With All My Might*, 75, 77.
21. Erskine Caldwell to I. S. Caldwells, Nov. 6, 1924, Georgia Collection.
22. Helen Caldwell Cushman, interview with author, July 19, 1977, Mount Vernon, Maine.
23. *With All My Might*, 77.

24. Hans Gerth, *Character and Social Structure* (New York: Harcourt, Brace and World, 1953), 114–15.

25. *With All My Might*, 77.

26. Edwin T. Arnold in Arnold, *Conversations*, 295.

27. Louis Ballou, interview with author, Richmond, Va., Jan. 29, 1978.

28. Helen Caldwell Cushman, interview with author, Mount Vernon, Maine, July 19, 1977.

29. Helen Caldwell Cushman, telephone interview with author, Nov. 12, 1980.

30. *With All My Might*, 77.

Chapter 6

 1. *With All My Might*, 78–81.

 2. Helen Caldwell Cushman, interview with author, Mount Vernon, Maine, July 20, 1977.

 3. Erskine Caldwell, interview by Michael Bandry, Univ. of Nice, Aug. 20, 1975, Dunedin, Fla., transcribed copy, Caldwell Collection.

 4. Helen Caldwell Cushman, interview with author, Mount Vernon, Maine, July 20, 1977.

 5. *With All My Might*, 81.

 6. Again, Caldwell's autobiographical sequencing of events is skewed. He does not mention this initial summer's sojourn in Maine.

 7. *With All My Might*, 82.

 8. Frank Daniel, interview with author, Atlanta, June 7, 1977.

 9. *Call It Experience*, 41.

10. Helen Caldwell Cushman, interview with author, Mount Vernon, Maine, July 20, 1977.

11. *Call It Experience*, 51.

12. Helen Caldwell Cushman, interview with author, Mount Vernon, Maine, July 20, 1977.

13. Helen Caldwell Cushman, interview with author, Mount Vernon, Maine, July 19, 1977.

14. Ibid.

15. Helen Caldwell Cushman, interview with author, Jan. 23, 1979, Beaufort, N.C.

16. Helen Caldwell Cushman, interview with author, July 19, 1977, Mount Vernon, Maine.

17. Erskine Caldwell to Atcheson Hench, Apr. 26, 1939, Caldwell Files, Barrett Collection, Alderman Library, Univ. of Virginia (hereafter cited as Barrett Collection).

18. Journal entry responding to D. H. Lawrence's "Glad Ghosts," Mar. 15, 1927, Box 9150, Barrett Collection.

19. Barrett Collection. A comparison of the essay's class-submission and publication dates hints that Caldwell slyly may have been testing Hench's grading. He submitted it to Hench on October 28, 1926. Although the same work was printed in volume 4 of the November 1926 *Monthly*, the time differential is suspicious. A month would hardly have allowed sufficient time for the process of submission, acceptance, and printing of an article. Rather, Caldwell most likely had written the essay earlier in the year, submitted it, and then, after having received notice of its acceptance, handed it in as an assignment to Hench. Lending credence to such speculation is the biographic squib that accompanied the work. Caldwell was identified as a "student of literature at Columbia University." One can imagine a discouraged young man adopting this pose to enhance his credibility as a writer.

20. "The Georgia Cracker," *Haldeman-Julius Monthly* 4 , no. 6 (Nov. 1926): 39–42.

21. Inscription to Atcheson Hench found in *In Search of Bisco*, Caldwell Files, Barrett Collection, Aldeman Library, Univ. of Virginia.

22. Erskine Caldwell to Mr. Gilliam, Nov. 24, 1949, Barrett Collection.

23. Erskine Caldwell, untitled, undated manuscript for a speech, Caldwell Collection.

24. *Call It Experience*, 51.

25. Helen Caldwell Cushman, interview with author, Mount Vernon, Maine, July 19, 1977.

26. Ibid.

27. Helen Caldwell to Caroline Preston Caldwell, Aug. 5, 1927, Georgia Collection.

28. Caldwell had purchased the used car during his Atlanta reporting days. His memories of it were to be less than fond: "And a broken-down wreck of a car it came to be. HCS stood for Harry C. Stutz, who made his fame with the Stutz Bearcat. His failure in life was the HCS." Erskine Caldwell, letter to author, Feb. 19, 1981.

29. Mrs. Corrie Wren, interview with author, Wrens, Ga., June 26, 1977.

30. Helen Caldwell Cushman, interview with author, Mount Vernon, Maine, July 19, 1977.

31. Ibid.

32. Ibid.

33. Caroline Caldwell to Erskine Caldwell, July 27, 1937, Margaret Bourke-White Collection, George Arendts Research Library, Syracuse Univ. (hereafter cited as Bourke-White Collection).

34. Caroline Caldwell to Erskine Caldwell, July 1953, Caldwell Collection.

35. *With All My Might*, 96.

36. Helen Caldwell Cushman, interview with author, Mount Vernon, Maine, July 19, 1977.

37. *With All My Might*, 96.

38. *Call It Experience*, 57–59.

39. Erskine Caldwell, interview with author, Scottsdale, Ariz., Nov. 30, 1978.

40. Allegedly Caldwell burned most of his poetry after receiving discouraging comments about the few poems he had forwarded for criticism. Nonetheless, Helen gave what remained to North Carolina State University in Durham. Guy Owen's subsequent article "Erskine Caldwell's Unpublished Poems" (*South Atlantic Bulletin* 43 [May 1978], 55) uses some of these works to build an interesting argument for Caldwell's struggle between "church and [his] more personal relationship with God."

Chapter 7

1. Erskine Caldwell to I. S. Caldwells, Mar. 19, 1929, Georgia Collection.

2. Some four years later, Sherwood Anderson's "Death in the Woods" was to appear. Its similarity to Caldwell's story is a suspicious irony since Caldwell always admitted to having read Anderson with admiration and respect. Yet in this instance, a comparison and dating of the two stories indicates that the master may have looked to the apprentice's work for his own inspiration and edification.

3. Cook, *Fiction of Poverty*, 35.

4. Erskine Caldwell to Richard Johns, Oct. 4, 1929, Portland, Maine, Caldwell Collection.

5. Tharpe, *Interview with Caldwell*, 98.

6. Erskine Caldwell, *Jackpot* (New York: Duell, Sloan and Pearce, 1940), 526.

7. Erskine Caldwell to Richard Johns, Jan. 7, 1930, Caldwell Collection.

8. Maxwell Perkins to Erskine Caldwell, Feb. 13, 1930, Scribner's Archives.

9. Fritz (Alfred) Dashiell to Erskine Caldwell, June 12, 1929, Scribner's Archives; Erskine Caldwell to Maxwell Perkins, Mar. (no date but before Mar. 6), 1930, Scribner's Archives; Maxwell Perkins to Erskine Caldwell, Mar. 6, 1930, Scribner's Archives.

10. *Call It Experience*, 75–86.

11. Erskine Caldwell to Maxwell Perkins, June 12, 1929, Scribner's Archives.

12. This indiscretion would have shortly preceded Caldwell's writing of "A Very Late Spring," wherein a wife also forgives the husband's infidelity with a schoolteacher.

13. Helen Caldwell Cushman, interview with author, Mount Vernon, Maine, July 19, 1977.

14. Erskine Caldwell to I. S. Caldwells, Mar. 24, 1930.

15. Erskine Caldwell to Maxwell Perkins, Apr. 18, 1930, Mount Vernon, Maine, Scribner's Archives.

16. Maxwell Perkins to Erskine Caldwell, May 20, 1930, Scribner's Archives.

17. Erskine Caldwell to Maxwell Perkins, May 23, 1930, Scribner's Archives.

18. Erskine Caldwell to Maxwell Perkins, July 20, 1930, Scribner's Archives.

19. Maxwell Perkins to Erskine Caldwell, July 26, 1930, Scribner's Archives.

20. Maxwell Perkins to Erskine Caldwell, Aug. 5, 1930, Scribner's Archives.

21. Guy Owen, " 'The Bogus Ones': A Lost Erskine Caldwell Novel," *Southern Literary Journal* 11 (Fall 1978), 32–39.

22. In *Call It Experience* (86) Caldwell claimed that none was accepted. Although Scribner's rejected many stories, they had—as stated earlier—by summer's end, and within a period of about six months after first approaching Caldwell, accepted a total of four stories for the *Monthly*. Additionally, they had contracted for the twelve unpublished ones that were to be included in the collection. Since that agreement had been struck in May, some of the stories he wrote that summer must have been aimed at honoring the thirty thousand additional words the editors had suggested to round out the book.

23. Erskine Caldwell to Maxwell Perkins, Aug. 22, 1930, Scribner's Archives.

24. Ibid.

25. J. H. Wheelock to Erskine Caldwell, Nov. 12, 1930, Scribner's Archives.

26. Actually, he boarded shortly before mid-November. Otherwise Caldwell's self-description is carefully posed. Throughout his life, he was always to present himself as struggling and poor. His account in *Call It Experience* tallies as conscientiously as a Ben Franklin the general costs of his living. He details his bare menus and charts the daily expenses of food, lodging, and incidentals. Letters to Helen were always to reflect miserly worries and fears. Possibly a combination of Caldwell's childhood perceptions, his early, meager life-style, and the Depression all conspired to make him stress poverty as one of the conditions for his entitlement to reward. Whatever its ori-

gins, Caldwell's abiding concerns about poverty were to inform his fiction, shape his career, and threaten future business and personal relationships.

27. *Call It Experience*, 92–95.

28. Ibid., 102.

29. Under contract to Scribner's, he allowed another publisher to issue this work. When Heron Press accepted *The Bastard*, it signed Caldwell to a contract for his next two novels. Whether or not it had rejected *The Bogus Ones* before he had submitted it to Scribner's remains unknown. If it had, the firm would have been forced to give up its claim to the next work. Thus why Caldwell gave the third novel to Heron Press, even while he argued to Scribner's that he had nothing except *The Bogus Ones* to offer them, is puzzling. That situation was to lead him into a confusion of later difficulties—too convoluted to retrace in this work—with Harcourt Brace & World which had bought Caldwell's remaining one-book contract from Heron Press.

30. Devlin, *Erskine Caldwell*, 8.

31. Cook, *Fiction of Poverty*, 18–25.

Chapter 8

1. Edwin T. Arnold, in Arnold, *Conversations*, 274.

2. Erskine Caldwell, Introd. to *Tobacco Road*, Modern Library edition (New York: Random House, 1940).

3. "The Bunglers," *Eugenics* 3 (June 30, 1930), 207.

4. Ibid., 334.

5. Arnold, *Conversations*, 245.

6. Erskine Caldwell to Maxwell Perkins, Jan. 14, 1931, Scribner's Archives.

7. Erskine Caldwell to Maxwell Perkins, Jan. 27, 1931, Scribner's Archives.

8. Erskine Caldwell to Richard Johns, Apr. 12, 1931, Caldwell Collection.

9. Erskine Caldwell to Dick Johns, Apr. 12, 1931, Caldwell Collection.

10. Erskine Caldwell, *Tobacco Road*, (New York: Charles Scribner's Sons, 1932), 1.

11. Sale, "An Interview in Florida with Erskine Caldwell," 136.

12. Kay Bonetti, "A Good Listener Speaks," in Arnold, *Conversations*, 245.

13. Cook, *Fiction of Poverty*, 108.

14. Devlin, *Erskine Caldwell*, 25.

15. Erskine Caldwell to Richard Johns, Apr. 12, 1931, Caldwell Collection.

16. Erskine Caldwell to Alfred Morang, June 3, 1931, Alfred Morang Collection, Harry Elkins Widener Memorial Library, Harvard Univ. (hereafter cited as Morang Collection).

17. Malcolm Cowley, *The Dream of the Golden Mountains* (New York: Viking Press, 1980), 112, 271, 274.

18. Maxwell Perkins to Erskine Caldwell, June 9, 1931, Scribner's Archives.

19. Erskine Caldwell to Maxwell Perkins, June 11, 1931, Scribner's Archives.

20. Maxwell Perkins to Erskine Caldwell, June 12, 1931, Scribner's Archives.

21. Erskine Caldwell, 1931 Guggenheim Fellowship application statement, File Box 9150, Barrett Collection.

22. Atcheson Hench, Guggenheim recommendation letter, Barrett Collection, File Box 9150.

23. Undated, received by Guggenheim Foundation, Nov. 2, 1931, Scribner's Archives.

24. Erskine Caldwell to Alfred Morang, Morang Collection.

25. Erskine Caldwell to Maxwell Perkins, Mar. 1, 1932, Scribner's Archives.

26. Maxwell Perkins to Erskine Caldwell, Mar. 4, 1932, Scribner's Archives.

27. Erskine Caldwell to Helen Caldwell, Apr. 1, 1932 (internally dated), Caldwell Collection.

28. Ibid.

29. Ibid.

30. Erskine Caldwell to Maxwell Perkins, Apr. 21, 1932, Scribner's Archives.

31. Erskine Caldwell to Stan Salomon, May 2, 1932, Caldwell Collection.

32. Erskine Caldwell to Alfred Morang, Mar. 1, 1932, Morang Collection.

33. Maxwell Perkins to Erskine Caldwell, June 18, 1932, Scribner's Archives.

34. Erskine Caldwell to Maxwell Perkins, June 20, 1932, Scribner's Archives.

35. *Call It Experience*, 120. Caldwell's variations upon the theme of rejection were inconsistent. His reactions to the Scribner's decision as recalled in 1951 in *Call It Experience* were honest ones. More puzzling are others implicitly responding to the same event. In a 1958 interview he claimed never to have had any editor make suggestions about any of his writings except about typographical mistakes (*Conversations*, 42). And in 1970 he further claimed never to have experienced any conflicts about revisons with publishers: "I've been with half a dozen publishers in my life, but not because of any editorial difficulties" (*Conversations*, 125). Or more directly, Caldwell claimed in 1986 that to his knowledge *Autumn Hill*, later retitled as *A Lamp for Nightfall*, had never been resubmitted anywhere else after Scribner's rejection (*Conversations*).

36. *Call It Experience*, 122.

37. Erskine Caldwell to Alfred Morang, Aug. 3, 1932, Morang Collection.

38. Helen Caldwell Cushman, interview with author, Mount Vernon, Maine, July 20, 1977.
39. Ibid.
40. Dabney Caldwell, interview with author, Boston, Jan. 18, 1978.
41. Erskine Caldwell to Stan Salomon, Mar. 26, 1933, Caldwell Collection.
42. Helen Caldwell Cushman, letter to author, Feb. 3, 1981; interview with author, Mount Vernon, Maine, July 20, 1977.
43. Erskine Caldwell to Helen Caldwell, Apr. 17, 1932, Caldwell Collection.
44. Helen Caldwell Cushman, interview with author, Mount Vernon, Maine, July 20, 1977.
45. Ibid.
46. Letter to Helen Caldwell, dated only "Tuesday, the 26th, Brookline, [Mass.]." Judging from internal evidence, it seems to have been written on December 26, 1933.
47. Erskine Caldwell to Alfred Morang, Sept. 22, 1932, Morang Collection.
48. Erskine Caldwell to Gordon Lewis, Sept. 23, 1932, Barrett Collection.
49. Sylvia Cook, in her "Erskine Caldwell and the Literary Left Wing," reprinted in *Critical Essays on Caldwell Caldwell*, ed. Scott MacDonald (Boston: G. K. Hall, 1980), 361–69, implies that Caldwell wrote some of his best stories and novels while stirred by radical sympathies. That hypothesis might be partially acceptable. But more than Caldwell's brief romance with radical sympathies contributed to that quality of his early writings. His later actions and values indicate that Caldwell's ideological persuasions were not essential beliefs. Rather, they seem to have been but naive gestures aimed at gaining approval from Max Lieber and *New Masses* editor Mike Gold. Nonetheless, William Foster's strike-breaking example and Lieber's approving nods may have influenced the resolution of *God's Little Acre*. Caldwell was completing that book even as he attended the Foster-Ford rally with Lieber.
50. Erskine Caldwell to Alfred Morang, Sept. 15, 1932, Morang Collection.
51. Erskine Caldwell to Alfred Morang, Nov. 1, 1932, Morang Collection.
52. Ibid.
53. *Call It Experience*, 125.
54. Caldwell's *Call It Experience* story includes also a lissome young Scandinavian woman among the visitors. Since she was the same with whom Helen had found Caldwell sexually engaged on their dock a few years earlier, his inclusion of her in association with *God's Little Acre* is provocative. Might

visions of "Signe-past" have shaped Griselda, she who also had blue-eyes and creamy skin, golden hair and "rising beauties"?

55. *Call It Experience*, 130.
56. Erskine Caldwell to Alfred Morang, Nov. 26, 1932, Morang Collection.
57. Erskine Caldwell to Alfred Morang, Dec. 1, 1932, Morang Collection.
58. Erskine Caldwell to Alfred Morang, Dec. 15, 1932, Morang Collection.
59. Erskine Caldwell to Gordon Lewis, Feb. 6, 1933, Barrett Collection.
60. Louis Kronenberger, *New York Times*, Feb. 5, 1933, 6.
61. Horace Gregory, *Books*, Feb. 5, 1933, 8.
62. Erskine Caldwell to Gordon Lewis, Feb. 6, 1933, Barrett Collection.
63. Robert Cantwell, *New Republic* 73: 356, Feb. 8, 1933.
64. Edward Dahlberg, "Erskine Caldwell and Other 'Proletarian' Novelists," *The Nation* 136 (Mar. 8, 1933), 265.
65. Erskine Caldwell to Stan Salomon, Dec. 16, 1933, Caldwell Collection.
66. Carvel Collins, "Erskine Caldwell at Work," in Arnold, *Conversations*, 39.
67. Devlin, *Erskine Caldwell*, 49–75; and Cook, *Fiction of Poverty*, 121–31.
68. Erskine Caldwell to Helen Caldwell, July 21, 1933, Caldwell Collection.

Chapter 9

1. Erskine Caldwell to Alfred Morang, June 26, 1933, Morang Collection.
2. Erskine Caldwell to Stan Salomon, Mar. 26, 1933, Caldwell Collection.
3. *Call It Experience*, 132.
4. For biographical purposes the 1978 resurrection of these many letters was fortuitously exciting. Becky Gooding, Erskine and Helen's granddaughter—Janet's daughter—was rummaging in the cavernous attic of the house where her mother had been born. There in a dusty box she found the letters from Caldwell to Helen—letters Helen had forgotten she had preserved. A young person's curiosity has thus enriched her grandparents' story. This correspondence is now a portion of the Caldwell Collection at Dartmouth College.
5. Erskine Caldwell to Alfred Morang, May 7, 1933, Morang Collection.
6. Erskine Caldwell to Helen Caldwell, May 6, 1933, Caldwell Collection.
7. Erskine Caldwell to Helen Caldwell, May 8, 1933, Caldwell Collection.
8. Erskine Caldwell to Helen Caldwell, May 13, 1933, Caldwell Collection.
9. Ibid.
10. Erskine Caldwell to Alfred Morang, May 26, 1933, Morang Collection.
11. Erskine Caldwell to Helen Caldwell, June 13, 1933, Caldwell Collection.
12. Sale, "An Interview in Florida with Erskine Caldwell," 132.

13. Erskine Caldwell to Helen Caldwell, May 28, 1933, Caldwell Collection.

14. Erskine Caldwell to Alfred Morang, July 11, 1933, Morang Collection.

15. Erskine Caldwell to Helen Caldwell, June 11, 1933, Caldwell Collection.

16. Erskine Caldwell to Helen Caldwell, June 1, 1933, Caldwell Collection; and Erskine Caldwell to Alfred Morang, May 29, 1933, Morang Collection.

17. Erskine Caldwell to Helen Caldwell, June 11, 1933, Caldwell Collection.

18. Ibid.

19. Erskine Caldwell to Helen Caldwell June 14, 1933, Caldwell Collection.

20. Erskine Caldwell to Helen Caldwell, July 24, 1933, Caldwell Collection.

21. Erskine Caldwell to Helen Caldwell, June 11, 1933, Caldwell Collection.

22. Erskine Caldwell, quoted in an interview published in the *Honolulu Star Bulletin*, Mar. 29, 1941.

23. Magistrate's Court, City of New York, Fourth District, Borough of Manhattan, Trial beginning May 2, 1922, cited from *God's Little Acre*, Modern Library edition, Fifth Printing, Appendix.

24. Erskine Caldwell to Helen Caldwell, May 7, 1933, Caldwell Collection.

25. Erskine Caldwell to Helen Caldwell, July 12, 1933, Caldwell Collection

26. Erskine Caldwell to Helen Caldwell, July 1, 1933, Caldwell Collection.

27. Erskine Caldwell to Helen Caldwell, internally dated, June 10, 1933, Caldwell Collection.

28. Erskine Caldwell to Helen Caldwell, undated but subsequent to one written on June 23, 1933, Caldwell Collection.

29. Erskine Caldwell to Helen Caldwell, July 22, 1933, Caldwell Collection.

30. Erskine Caldwell to Helen Caldwell, July 9, 1933, Caldwell Collection.

31. Erskine Caldwell to Helen Caldwell, July 20, 1933, Caldwell Collection.

32. Erskine Caldwell to Helen Caldwell, July 12, 1933, Caldwell Collection.

33. Erskine Caldwell to Helen Caldwell, July 22, 1933, Caldwell Collection.

34. Erskine Caldwell to Alfred Morang, July 17, 1933, Morang Collection.

35. Erskine Caldwell to Helen Caldwell, June 3, 1933, Caldwell Collection.

Chapter 10

1. Erskine Caldwell to Alfred Morang, Aug. 29, 1933, Morang Collection.

2. Erskine Caldwell to Stan Salomon, Aug. 29, 1933, Caldwell Collection.

3. Ibid.

4. In Caldwell's *Call It Experience*, his reconstruction of his writing of *Journeyman* (153–56) is misplaced in time. There he recalls its beginnings in February 1934, before his second trip to Hollywood. Actually he had begun it the previous February, before his first trip.

5. Erskine Caldwell to Alfred Morang, Sept. 17, 1933, Morang Collection.

6. Erskine Caldwell to Alfred Morang, Oct. 5, 1933, Morang Collection.

7. Ibid.

8. Erskine Caldwell to Alfred Morang, Oct. 29, 1933, Morang Collection.

9. Marshall Best to Erskine Caldwell, Nov. 10, 1933, Caldwell Collection.

10. Caldwell's *Call It Experience* story about this period is interesting in several respects. First, he honestly acknowledges the temperamental effects of his personality: "And as usual in recent years, I left home to write. I became disagreeable, morose, short-tempered, and unreasonably moody at such times, and it was asking too much for my family to endure me through such spells" (*Call It Experience*, 153). Secondly he claims that he took various bus trips—to Philadelphia, Baltimore, Washington, Scranton, Pittsburgh, Cleveland, Chicago, and Buffalo—to escape the cold of his basement room (154). These trips must have been confused with those of past experiences. This particular New York sojourn lasted little more than a week, and all of his letters to Helen stress his almost uninterrupted isolation during this writing stint.

11. Erskine Caldwell to Helen Caldwell, Nov. 15, 1933, and Nov. 17, 1933, Caldwell Collection.

12. Erskine Caldwell to Helen Caldwell, Nov. 15, 1933, and Nov. 18, 1933, Caldwell Collection.

13. Helen Caldwell to Stan Salomon, Feb. 26, 1934, Caldwell Collection.

14. Max Lieber to Erskine Caldwell, December 11, 1933, Bourke-White Collection.

15. Tharpe, *Interview with Caldwell*, 75.

16. Dec. 5, 1933, 31.

17. Stark Young, "Roads," *New Republic*, Dec. 20, 1933, 168–69.

18. Erskine Caldwell to Alfred Morang, Feb. 5, 1934, Morang Collection.

19. Ibid.

20. Erskine Caldwell to Alfred Morang, Feb. 15, 1934, Morang Collection.

21. Ibid.

22. ISC to Helen Caldwell, May 6, 1934, Bourke-White Collection.

23. 1934–37 Memoranda notebook, unpaginated, Caldwell Collection.

24. Caldwell mistakenly cited Al Manuel, a Hollywood agent, as negotiator in this process (*With All My Might*, 142). Because Manuel did not represent him in Hollywood until much later, Lieber acted as the film intermediary at this time. Considering how Lieber later treated Caldwell, he perhaps consciously refused to give Lieber his due in this instance.

25. Erskine Caldwell to Alfred Morang, June 10, 1934, Morang Collection.
26. Erskine Caldwell to Alfred Morang, June 23, 1934, Morang Collection.
27. Erskine Caldwell to Helen Caldwell, June 27, 1934, Caldwell Collection.
28. Erskine Caldwell to Alfred Morang, July 5, 1934, Morang Collection.
29. Erskine Caldwell to Alfred Morang, July 16, 1934, Morang Collection.
30. Erskine Caldwell to Alfred Morang, June 28, 1934, July 5, 1934, Morang Collection.
31. Erskine Caldwell to Alfred Morang, July 16, 1934, Morang Collection.
32. Erskine Caldwell, interview with author, Scottsdale, Ariz., Nov. 30, 1978.
33. Ibid.
34. Erskine Caldwell to Alfred Morang, dated "Thursday two days after return to Mount Vernon, Maine," Morang Collection.
35. Erskine Caldwell to Alfred Morang, Sept. 25, 1934, Morang Collection.
36. In a sense, Caldwell may have won a Pyrrhic victory in rejecting Viking's estimation of *Some American People.* For the second time in his publishing career, he had refused to bend to editorial advice. The first time Lieber had appealed to his client's pride to seduce him away from Scribner's and Max Perkins. This time Caldwell won his point without losing a publisher. But that same habit of self-resolve was eventually, work by work, to erode that enviable literary reputation Caldwell had achieved up to this point in his career. Against all advice and direction, he always was to insist that whatever he wrote be published. As various editors came to recognize this fact about Caldwell, they ceased either advising him or restricting what they published in his name. Because his name upon a book almost guaranteed profits, their reservations had to be compromised. But inevitably an editor would finally declare enough, thereby assuring himself that he had stood upon principle while losing a profitable author for his house.
37. Erskine Caldwell to Alfred Morang, Oct. 24, 1934 , Morang Collection.
38. *New York Post* series beginning Feb. 18, 1935.
39. Reckoning from Caldwell's memorandum log, the Caldwells had saved over $4,000 from *Tobacco Road* earnings alone. Added to this amount was whatever sum remained from the $4,800 Caldwell had earned during his eight weeks in Hollywood. In Depression-dollar terms, they were far from poor. Yet Caldwell retained the practices of their earlier married years. Often in his letters to Helen he mentioned the ten or twenty dollars forwarded specifically for train tickets and household or miscellaneous expenses: "I am sending a check for ten dollars, made out to you. It is to pay Oscar for cutting

wood. If he cuts less than five cords, you are to keep the rest." (Erskine Caldwell to Helen Caldwell, Jan. 19, 1935, Caldwell Collection, Dartmouth College).

40. Erskine Caldwell to Alfred Morang, Feb. 26, 1935, Morang Collection.
41. Erskine Caldwell to Helen Caldwell, Mar. 29, 1935, Caldwell Collection.
42. Erskine Caldwell to Alfred Morang, June 13, 1935, Morang Collection.
43. Erskine Caldwell to Alfred Morang, Feb. 6, 1935, Morang Collection.
44. Erskine Caldwell, "Violence in the Deep South," undated ms. for an address, Caldwell Collection.
45. *With All My Might*, 145.
46. Helen Caldwell Cushman, interview with author, July 20, 1977, Mount Vernon, Maine.
47. Erskine Caldwell to Alfred Morang, Aug. 11, 1935, Morang Collection.
48. Erskine Caldwell to Helen Caldwell, Sept. 11, 1935, Effingham, Ill., Caldwell Collection.
49. Ibid.
50. Erskine Caldwell to Alfred Morang, Nov. 13, 1935, Morang Collection.
51. Erskine Caldwell to Alfred Morang, Dec. 21, 1935, Burbank, Morang Collection.
52. Such as "Jesus Lopez" for *The Nation*, Apr. 29, 1936, 545–46-a casual piece on the conditions of Mexican-American produce workers in the San Fernando Valley.
53. Dabney Caldwell, interview with author, Boston, Jan. 18, 1978.

Part 3. "Trapped and Double-Crossed"

Chapter 11

1. Margaret Bourke-White, *Portrait of Myself* (New York: Simon and Schuster, 1963), 158.
2. Vol. 10, No. 4, Oct., 1934.
3. Bourke-White, *Portrait*, 170.
4. Margaret Bourke-White to Erskine Caldwell, Mar. 9, 1936, Bourke-White Collection.
5. Erskine Caldwell to Helen Caldwell, July 13, 1936, New York, Caldwell Collection.
6. Bourke-White, *Portrait*, 121.
7. Erskine Caldwell to Helen Caldwell, July 21, 1936, Caldwell Collection.
8. Bourke-White, *Portrait*, 124.
9. Erskine Caldwell to Helen Caldwell, July 26, 1936, Caldwell Collection.

10. Bourke-White, *Portrait*, 125.

11. During a July 19, 1977, interview, Helen recalled that Ruth had sent her a letter outlining her version of the events leading to her abandonment of the project. Questioned about this letter in a January 23, 1979 interview, however, Helen could not recall how she had learned the details of Bourke-White and Caldwell's romantic beginning.

12. Max Lieber, quoted by Vicki Goldberg in *Margaret Bourke-White: A Biography* (New York: Harper and Row, 1986), 167.

13. Bourke-White, *Portrait*, 125.

14. Ibid.

15. These materials are among the Erskine Caldwell materials filed in the Margaret Bourke-White Collection at Syracuse University.

16. Caldwell's dating of Carnall's departure in *With All My Might* (148) is miscalculated by three weeks.

17. To protect the privacy of these much-used people, Caldwell and Bourke-White departed from their working notes to place these relatives as unrelated, unidentified subjects in a fictional Locket, Georgia. Possibly Caldwell earlier had combined the first name Dude, and the surname Lester—a name borrowed from one of the employees of the Wrens cottonseed mill—to create a name for Dude Lester, the youngest son of the Jeeter Lester clan of Tobacco Road.

18. Erskine Caldwell to Helen Caldwell, Aug. 6, 1936, Caldwell Collection.

19. Erskine Caldwell to Helen Caldwell, Aug. 6, 1936, Caldwell Collection.

20. Before her death in 1971, Bourke-White must have destroyed most of that correspondence—except for three overlooked letters—whose sexual detail would have proved embarrassing. Those that remain are—with true lover's caution—designated only by day, not date. Thus their exact chronology cannot be determined. They reveal, nonetheless, that throughout that year, and even during their married absences, the two experienced an almost adolescent-like romantic ecstasy and frustrated desire shared via the U.S. mail and Western Union.

21. Erskine Caldwell to Margaret Bourke-White, internally dated, 1936, but before that autumn's Quebec trip, Bourke-White Collection.

22. Malcolm Cowley, *And I Worked at the Writer's Trade*, (New York: Viking Press, 1978), 116.

23. Bourke-White, *Portrait*, 159-60.

24. Erskine Caldwell to Helen Caldwell, Oct. 20, 1936, Caldwell Collection.

25. Such impressions are those condensed from her account in *Portrait*, further

reinforced from details within her letters, and finally argued most convincingly in Goldberg's brilliant study.

26. Elizabeth Ann Crotty, *Margaret Bourke-White as Seen from the Perspective of Selected Photographs, Writings and Associates* (Master of Science Dissertation), Syracuse Univ., 1978, 81.

27. Crotty, *Margaret Bourke-White*, 78.

28. Bourke-White, *Portrait*, 130.

29. Ibid., 114.

30. Crotty, *Margaret Bourke-White*, 53.

31. Margaret Bourke-White to Roger White, Aug. 26, 1936, Bourke-White Collection.

32. Crotty, *Margaret Bourke-White*, 53.

33. Goldberg, *Margaret Bourke-White*, 202.

34. Ibid.

35. Crotty, *Margaret Bourke-White*, 49.

36. Helen Caldwell Cushman, interview with author, Mount Vernon, Maine, July 20, 1977.

37. Erskine Caldwell to Helen Caldwell, Feb. 3, 1937, and Apr. 28, 1937, Caldwell Collection.

38. Bourke-White, *Portrait*, 196.

39. Goldberg, *Margaret Bourke-White*, 251.

40. These trips are charted by month, but not day, in Caldwell's claims for 1937 income tax exemptions (Bourke-White Collection). Apparently without qualms Caldwell included the costs of love among those expenses associated legitimately with his writing career.

Chapter 12

1. Erskine Caldwell to Helen Caldwell, Mar. 1, 1937, Caldwell Collection.

2. Erskine Caldwell to Margaret Bourke-White, 1937 (internally dated), Bourke-White Collection.

3. Erskine Caldwell to Margaret Bourke-White, Feb. 1937 (internally dated), Bourke-White Collection.

4. Erskine Caldwell, interview with author, Scottsdale, Ariz., Nov. 30, 1978.

5. Little more than a year later Caldwell would attempt unsuccessfully to subtract costs associated with his family's southern trip from the court-approved divorce settlement.

6. Erskine Caldwell to Helen Caldwell, telegram, Mar. 31, 1937, Bourke-White Collection.

7. Erskine Caldwell to Margaret Bourke-White, Mar. 31, 1937 (internally dated), Bourke-White Collection.

8. Erskine Caldwell to Helen Caldwell, Apr. 22, 1937 and Apr. 28, 1937, Caldwell Collection.

9. *Time*, Sept. 30, 1957, 102.

10. Caroline Preston Caldwell to Helen Caldwell, Sept. 3, 1937, Caldwell Collection.

11. Erskine Caldwell to Helen Caldwell, May 10, 1937, New York, Caldwell Collection.

12. Dabney Caldwell to Erskine Caldwell, Jan. 6, 1946, Caldwell Collection.

13. Erskine Preston Caldwell, Jr., interview with author, Nov. 30, 1978, Santa Monica, Calif.

14. Margaret Bourke-White to Erskine Caldwell, 1937 (internally dated), U.S.S. Distributor, Bourke-White Collection.

15. Erskine Caldwell to Margaret Bourke-White, 1937 (internally dated), Bourke-White Collection.

16. Ibid.

17. Caroline Preston Caldwell to Erskine Caldwell, July 27, 1937, Caldwell Collection.

18. Helen Caldwell Cushman, interview with author, Mount Vernon, Maine, July 20, 1977.

19. Caroline Preston Caldwell to Helen Caldwell, Sept. 3, 1937, Caldwell Collection.

20. Caroline Preston Caldwell to Erskine Caldwell, Aug. 9, 1937, Bourke-White Collection.

21. During the period from 1937 to 1942, Carrie was to earn only eighty dollars per month under the terms of a nine-month contract. Curiously, the Jefferson County Board of Education files contain no records of I. S. Caldwell's ever having taught in the system (Letter from O. W. Carter, superintendent, to author, Apr. 24, 1981). Yet community memories, school pictures, and family correspondence all verify that he did hold a position in that school until the fall of 1937.

22. Goldberg, *Margaret Bourke-White*, 203.

23. Erskine Caldwell to Helen Caldwell, Sept. 19, 1937, Santa Monica, Calif., Caldwell Collection.

24. S. A. Levine, *Books*, Nov. 21, 1937, 5.

25. *New Republic*, Nov. 24, 1937, 78.

26. Nov. 28, 1937, 11.

27. Bourke-White, *Portrait*, 170.

28. *With All My Might*, 196–97.

29. Helen Caldwell Cushman, interview with author, Mount Vernon, Maine, July 19, 1977.

30. Ibid.

31. Erskine Caldwell to Alfred Morang, undated, New York, Morang Collection.

32. Helen Caldwell to Erskine Caldwell, Jan. 23, 1938, Bourke-White Collection.

33. Ibid.

34. Helen Caldwell to Erskine Caldwell, summer 1938 (internally dated), Bourke-White Collection.

35. Helen Caldwell to Erskine Caldwell, Jan. 23, 1938, Bourke-White Collection.

36. Brooks Atkinson, *New York Times*, Jan. 31, 1938.

37. Joseph Wood Krutch, *The Nation*, Feb. 12, 1938, 190.

38. Erskine Caldwell, *New York World Telegram*, Feb. 12, 1938, Erskine Caldwell Scrapbook, #2, Caldwell Collection.

39. Ira Caldwell, *New York Post*, Feb. 12, 1938, Erskine Caldwell Scrapbook #2, Caldwell Collection.

Chapter 13

1. In both *Call It Experience* (176) and his *Might* record (160) Caldwell misdated the day of departure into late May.

2. *The Georgian*, Atlanta, Apr. 3, 1938, Erskine Caldwell Scrapbook #2, Caldwell Collection.

3. *New York Herald Tribune*, Apr. 10, 1938, Paris byline, Erskine Caldwell Scrapbook, Caldwell Collection.

4. Caldwell misdated the divorce date and to his advantage misrepresented the situation and terms of settlement in *With All My Might* (163).

5. 1938 Divorce Decree, Kennebec County, State of Maine, Apr. Term, Bourke-White Collection.

6. Bourke-White, *Portrait*, 170.

7. Helen Caldwell Cushman, interview with author, Beaufort, N.C., Jan. 23, 1979.

8. Erskine Caldwell to Alfred Morang, letters, May 11, 1938; May 30, 1938; June 16, 1938; and two undated but subsequent letters from Paris, Morang Collection.

9. Harold Strauss, *New York Times*, June 19, 1938, 7.

10. *Saturday Review of Literature*, 18:7, June 19, 1938.

11. *Books*, June 19, 1938, 5.

12. Erskine Caldwell to Alfred Morang, June 16, 1938, Paris, Morang Collection.

13. Goldberg, *Margaret Bourke-White*, 215.

14. Ira Caldwell to Erskine Caldwell and Margaret Bourke-White, undated Saturday letter, Bourke-White Collection.

15. Helen Caldwell Cushman to Erskine Caldwell, Dec. 2, 1938, Bourke-White Collection.

16. Through her marriage Helen thereby had reduced Caldwell's family support obligations from $2,600 to $1,950 annually. Her alimony payments, however, were to be paid annually until the $12,000 total had been gained. Helen perhaps rightly insisted that this amount was repayment for the house which her parents had previously sold to the Caldwells for a nominal figure.

17. Helen Caldwell Cushman to Erskine Caldwell, Dec. 6, 1938, internally dated, Bourke-White Collection.

18. *Booklist*, May 1, 1939, 288.

19. Crotty, *Margaret Bourke-White*, 49–50.

20. Erskine Caldwell to Margaret Bourke-White, telegram, Feb. 8, 1939, Bourke-White Collection.

21. Erskine Caldwell to Margaret Bourke-White, Feb. 9, 1939, Bourke-White Collection.

22. Goldberg, *Margaret Bourke-White*, 216.

23. Bourke-White, *Portrait*, 171.

24. Ibid., 72.

25. Erskine Caldwell to Alfred Morang, Apr. 25, 1939, Morang Collection.

26. Ibid.

27. Erskine Caldwell to Atcheson Hench, Apr. 26, 1939, Barrett Collection.

28. Marshall Best to Erskine Caldwell, May 26, 1939, Bourke-White Collection.

29. The details of Caldwell's association with Duell, Sloan and Pearce are all deduced from various sources and clues. They are, therefore, necessarily tentative and open to reinterpretation. When Caldwell finally departed from the firm in 1952, the editors imposed legal sanctions forbidding outside access to all correspondence and files relating to their association. Caldwell honorably abided by the terms of that stipulation. Efforts to locate

a representative of the now-defunct company who might have granted exception proved futile.

30. *Call It Experience*, 184.

31. Helen Caldwell Cushman to Erskine Caldwell, Friday, 1939, internally dated, Bourke-White Collection.

32. Helen Caldwell Cushman to Erskine Caldwell, Oct. 23, 1939, Bourke-White Collection.

33. Erskine Preston Caldwell, Jr., to Erskine Caldwell, Feb. 26, 1939, Bourke-White Collection.

34. Helen Caldwell Cushman to Erskine Caldwell, dated Sunday 1939, Bourke-White Collection.

35. Margaret Bourke-White to Erskine Caldwell, July 27, 1939, Bourke-White Collection.

36. Helen Caldwell Cushman to Erskine Caldwell, June 23, 1939, Bourke-White Collection.

37. Ira Caldwell to Erskine Caldwell, dated only Tuesday, Oct. 1939, Bourke-White Collection.

38. Possibly because of Ira Sylvester's continuing decline, the elder Caldwells never moved into the Augusta home Caldwell had purchased for them.

39. Margaret Bourke-White to Erskine Caldwell, Nov. 5, 1939, Bourke-White Collection.

40. Margaret Bourke-White to Erskine Caldwell, Dec. 12, 1939, Bourke-White Collection.

41. Margaret Bourke-White to Erskine Caldwell, Jan. 15, 1940, Bourke-White Collection.

42. Margaret Bourke-White to Erskine Caldwell, telegram, Nov. 24, 1939, Bourke-White Collection.

43. Margaret Bourke-White to Erskine Caldwell, Nov. 6, 1939, Bourke-White Collection. On two issues central to this letter Vicki Goldberg and I come to differing conclusions. Goldberg discounts a possible pregnancy for two reasons: neither Margaret nor Caldwell mentioned any physical discomforts, and Margaret allegedly purchased some "Kotex" that November. That is not evidence convincing enough to sway my readings of the possible pregnancy.

Goldberg also claims that Caldwell actually had seen Dr. Clara Thompson earlier that fall. Because I possibly could have missed evidence Goldberg apparently used to support her statment, I do not challenge her.

On the other hand nothing in the correspondence I read indicated any more association with Dr. Thompson than the appointment Caldwell failed to keep.

44. Clara Thompson to Erskine Caldwell, Nov. 25, 1939 and Dec. 14, 1939, Bourke-White Collection.
45. Erskine Caldwell to Margaret Bourke-White, letters, Jan. 10, 1939 and Jan. 16, 1939, Bourke-White Collection.
46. Margaret Smith to Erskine Caldwell, Jan. 25, 1940, Bourke-White Collection.
47. Erskine Caldwell to Margaret Salter, Nov. 22, 1939, Bourke-White Collection.
48. Erskine Caldwell to Margaret Bourke-White, Dec. 2, 1939, Bourke-White Collection.
49. Erskine Caldwell to Margaret Bourke-White, Dec. 4, 1939, Bourke-White Collection.
50. Erskine Caldwell to Margaret Bourke-White, Dec. 15, 1939, Bourke-White Collection.
51. Erskine Caldwell to Margaret Salter, Dec. 16, 1939, Bourke-White Collection.
52. ———— to Erskine Caldwell, Jan. 8, 1940, Bourke-White Collection.
53. Mrs. ————, Friday, (Aug.?) 25, 1939, and ca. Feb. 5, 1940, Bourke-White Collection.
54. *With All My Might,* 173.
55. If Kit had in fact carried Caldwell's child rather than a satisfying fantasy, she must have miscarried it shortly after January 31, 1940, probably in Romania. Caldwell seemed genuinely taken aback and somewhat incensed when asked, in May of 1978, whether or not he thought Margaret might have willfully aborted "Patricia." He did not wish further to discuss that "private matter."

If Margaret neither naturally had miscarried a pregnancy nor aborted it, the only far-fetched speculation is that "Patricia"—to whom *Faces* had been inscribed—had been a fantasy child, a projected troth of Skinny and Kit's love-union. (Margaret's letters written and addressed to Suzy and Fluffy hint that she might have been susceptible to such a fascination.) But *if* the actual conception of that child had been contingent upon Caldwell's accepting counseling from Dr. Thompson, and *if* he had failed, in spite of Margaret's demands, to meet with the psychiatrist on February 1, then that refusal might have forced Margaret sadly to abandon at the same time what had been only a mutually accepted delusion. But whatever the reality, after that date "Patricia" was no more.

Interestingly and somewhat fictitiously, Caldwell claimed in *With All My Might* (196) that Bourke-White's pleadings about his seeking psychiatric help to relieve his hostilities and loneliness had not been in vain. He identifies Harry Stack Sullivan as the analyst and places the event—one that occurred early in his relationship with Margaret—as a preface to her departure and his subsequent divorce from her. As usual, Caldwell carefully reconstructed a scenario wherein he emerged as almost blameless; he claimed to have done as Bourke-White, the woman, had requested, but she, unappreciatively, had abandoned him anyway.

Chapter 14

1. Feb. 13, 1940, Bourke-White Collection.
2. Richard Wright, *New Republic*, Feb. 25, 1940, 2.
3. Clifton Fadiman, *New Yorker*, Feb. 24, 1940, 74.
4. John Mair, *New Statesman and Nation*, Aug. 17, 1940.
5. Cook, *Fiction of Poverty*, 145.
6. Caldwell, "The Automobile That Wouldn't Run," in *Jackpot*, 323.
7. Caldwell claims September for the beginning of the venture (*Call It Experience*, 192), although photos in *U.S.A.* imply, as Margaret stated in the book's afterword, that the project had its beginning with their June trip to Monterey, San Diego, and other southern California points. Letters and records do not reveal that they traveled there subsequent to the summer of 1940. Further, Caldwell claims to have been in Mexico alone—writing. He was writing, as he claims, but letters from that period indicate that Margaret was with him at least part, if not all, of the time.
8. *Margaret Bourke-White*, 234.
9. Harry Stack Sullivan's appointment secretary to Erskine Caldwell, Sept. 5, 1940, Bourke-White Collection.
10. Goldberg, *Margaret Bourke-White*, 235.
11. Ibid., 235.
12. Ibid., 248.
13. During that year Caldwell published also "A Mexican Candidate Comes to Cuidad Tamaulipas," "An Evening in Nuevo Leon," and "The Thunderstorm"—none of them of the same quality as the other stories.

14. Theodore Dreiser to Erskine Caldwell, Oct. 15, 1940, Hollywood, Bourke-White Collection.
15. *Call It Experience*, 192.
16. Marion Manuel, interview with author, Beverly Hills, Calif., Dec. 1, 1978.
17. *Call It Experience*, 194; and Erskine Caldwell, interview with author, Scottsdale, Ariz. Nov. 29, 1978.
18. *American Earth*, 1936; *Tobacco Road*, 1938; *Trouble in July*, 1940; various selections from *The Rising Sun* and *We Are the Living* also had been issued.
19. Goldberg, *Margaret Bourke-White*, 239.
20. Bourke-White, *Portrait*, 178.
21. Anonymous review, *New Republic*, Mar. 23, 1942, 406.
22. Erskine Caldwell to Alfred Morang, Mar. 5, 1942, Morang Collection.
23. Bourke-White, *Portrait*, 197.
24. Ibid., 196.
25. Erskine Caldwell to Alfred Morang, June 11, 1942, Morang Collection.
26. On December 20, 1951, exactly ten years after the fact, Ms. Lynn wrote Caldwell a long apologetic and explanatory letter. Margaret had been "too much" for her, and feeling that she could bear no more of Bourke-White's "dynamic-ness," the young Oregon native had fled to Florida without notice to "save her reason." She wrote the letter belatedly to tell Caldwell that she had "always been proud and humble" to have worked as his secretary.
27. Erskine Caldwell to Alfred Morang, June 11, 1942, Morang Collection.

Part 4. "Grunting and Groaning—to Win an Existence"

Chapter 15

1. Goldberg, *Margaret Bourke-White*, 235.
2. Erskine Caldwell to Ira and Caroline Caldwell, Oct. 2, 1942, Georgia Collection.
3. Harry Behn, interview with author, Tucson, Ariz., Oct. 28, 1978.
4. June Caldwell Martin, interview with author, Tucson, Ariz., Oct. 28, 1978.
5. Undated memorandum, Caldwell Collection.
6. June Caldwell Martin, interview with author, Tucson, Ariz., Oct. 28, 1978.
7. Erskine Caldwell to Al Manuel, Dec. 16, 1942, Caldwell Collection.
8. Caldwell had published previously "Handsome Brown and the Aggravating Goats" (*New Republic*, Aug. 19, 1940); "My Old Man Hasn't Been the Same Since," (*Friday*, 1940); "My Old Man and the Grass Widow" (*Coronet*, Feb. 1941), "Handsome Brown and the Shirt-Tail Woodpeckers" (*Stag*, Feb.

1942), and "Handsome Brown's Day Off" (originally published as "Day Off," *Collier's*, May 30, 1942).

9. William Sutton in his *Black Like It Is/Was* argues that Caldwell sympathetically presents Handsome Brown as but another black man victimized by the insensitivity of a culture which had traditionally used his people as dupes. Such might have been Caldwell's intention but in this instance, as in his earlier works, he so inextricably blended the comic with the tragic that they became uncomfortably one.

10. *Georgia Boy* (New York: Duell, Sloan and Pearce, 1943), 9.

11. Undated, unidentified newspaper clipping, Erskine Caldwell Scrapbook #3, 1943, Caldwell Collection.

12. Erskine Caldwell to Al Manuel, Dec. 16, 1942, Caldwell Collection.

13. Within a span of a few days Caldwell had talked with Weiss at least twice according to his November 1942 telephone billings. (Correspondence and Expense Files, 1940–1950, Caldwell Collection.

14. Goldberg, *Margaret Bourke-White*, 254.

15. Caldwell's claims in *With All My Might* concerning his divorce from Bourke-White were presented to his advantage in various ways. He did not file for divorce before meeting June. He did not fly back and forth three times between Tucson and the state of Morelos to meet Mexican divorce requirements. But most tellingly, Bourke-White was not at all firm and unyielding about the divison of property. Rather she was graciously cooperative in every way. The accurate aspects of Caldwell's story were gleaned from Vicki Goldberg's account in conjunction with documents and his correspondence from that time.

16. *Margaret Bourke-White*, 254.

17. Ibid.

18. Margaret Bourke-White to Caroline Preston Caldwell, Mar. 6, 1943, Georgia Collection.

19. Erskine Caldwell to Alfred Morang, Jan. 8, 1943, Morang Collection.

20. Erskine Caldwell to Alfred Morang, Feb. 4, 1943, Morang Collection.

21. Erskine Caldwell to Alfred Morang, Mar. 9, 1943, Morang Collection.

22. Erskine Caldwell to Alfred Morang, Sept. 24, 1943, Morang Collection.

23. William DuBois, *New York Times*, Apr. 25, 1943, 6.

24. Caldwell's choice of a subject for *Tragic Ground* might have been as simply dictated as adapting the Lester Douthit types he remembered from past experiences to a more contemporary situation. Yet in 1940 he had received a fan letter that could have inspired his story. One Paul Gillis had written that

Caldwell should consider writing a novel about "the trials and tribulations [of] a family on relief"—a modern family which had lost its employment and been forced into a public relief situation (Mar. 4, 1940, Latrobe, Pa., Caldwell Collection). True, Caldwell had received the suggestion four years before writing *Tragic Ground*, but that fan letter was one of very few not left at Darien with the other correspondence from that earlier period. Since it is included among Caldwell's materials lodged at Dartmouth, he must have taken it West with him—possibly as the basis for a novel he would write after he had completed *Georgia Boy*.

25. *Tragic Ground* (New York: Duell, Sloan and Pearce, 1944), 237.
26. Jules C. Goldstone to Al Manuel, notes, June 21, 1944, Caldwell Collection.
27. Erskine Caldwell to Alfred Morang, Oct. 5, 1944, Morang Collection.
28. In Los Angeles at the time, Caldwell was deeply grieved by the news of Ira's death. Within a period of two hours on that same day, he sent three telegrams to Carrie advising her of his futile attempts to secure a flight for the funeral trip. His last carried with it a note of resigned acceptance: "Please attend to all details for me." Caldwell would, nonetheless, continue trying to book a flight for the next day, an effort that also failed (Erskine Caldwell to Mrs. I. S. Caldwell, Aug. 18, 1944, Caldwell Collection).
29. Jonathan Daniels, *Saturday Review of Literature*, Oct. 14, 1944, 27: 46.
30. Erskine Caldwell to Alfred Morang, Oct. 5, 1944, Morang Collection.
31. Erskine Caldwell to Alfred Morang, Oct. 16, 1944, Morang Collection.
32. Erskine Caldwell to Alfred Morang, Oct. 23, 1944, Morang Collection.
33. E. B. Burgum, *New York Times*, Oct. 15, 1944, 6.
34. Anonymous news story, *Boston Post*, Dec. 29, 1944, Erskine Caldwell Scrapbook #3, Caldwell Collection.
35. Margaret's ship too had been torpedoed during passage between Italy and North Africa late in 1942. She was consequently to remark on the coincidence that placed her and Pix in similar misfortunes at about the same time and place. (Margaret Bourke-White to Mrs. I.S. Caldwell, Mar. 6, 1943, Georgia Collection).
36. Erskine Caldwell to Al Manuel, Jan. 21, 1945, Caldwell Collection.
37. Al Manuel to Erskine Caldwell, Apr. 13, 1945, Caldwell Collection.
38. Erskine Caldwell to Alfred Morang, June 11, 1945, Morang Collection.
39. Within the Caldwell Collection at Dartmouth are a few of June's manuscripts for stories and Arizona articles that reveal the scope of Caldwell's editing. Although he marked no major revisions, he suggested numerous

word and sentence substitutions in the script. June's first piece of published fiction was good enough to attract the attention of Houghton-Mifflin editors. Having come across her story, they wrote in February 1946, inviting her to submit to them anything else she had written or was then writing, or the outline of a longer work she might be planning to write (letter to June Caldwell, Feb. 26, 1946, Caldwell Collection).

40. Helen Caldwell Cushman, interview with author, July 19, 1977, Mount Vernon, Maine.
41. Erskine Caldwell to Alfred Morang, Aug. 26, 1945, Route 2, Morang Collection.
42. June Caldwell Martin, interview with author, Tuscon, Ariz., Nov. 28, 1978.

Chapter 16
  1. Kurt Enoch, interview with author, Jan. 16, 1979, New York.
  2. Hamilton Basso, *New Yorker*, May 11, 1946, 89.
  3. Fan letter folder, 1940–50, Caldwell Collection.
  4. June Caldwell Martin, telephone interview with author, May 5, 1981.
  5. The station did not formally open until the first week of April 1947.
  6. Introd. to *Caldwell Cavaran* (Cleveland: New World Publishing Co., 1946).
  7. Erskine Caldwell to Alfred Morang, Apr. 13, 1947, Morang Collection.
  8. *With All My Might*, 205.
  9. Kurt Enoch, interview with author, New York, Jan. 16, 1979.
 10. June Caldwell Martin, interview with author, Tucson, Ariz., Nov. 28, 1978.
 11. Alfred Morang to Erskine Caldwell, Oct. 12, 1947, Morang Collection.
 12. Undated, *Washington Star*, Erskine Caldwell Scrapbook #4, Caldwell Collection.
 13. *New York Times*, Oct. 12, 1947, 4.
 14. James Baldwin, *New Leader*, Dec. 6, 1947.
 15. Tharpe, *Interview with Caldwell*, 80.
 16. Erskine Caldwell to F. Aydelott and Christopher Brewster, transcribed interview, Hanover, N.H., Oct. 25, 1973, Caldwell Collection.
 17. Erskine Caldwell to Alfred Morang, June 11, 1945, and Apr. 13, 1947, Morang Collection.
 18. Erskine Caldwell to Alfred Morang, Aug. 26, 1945, Morang Collection.
 19. Notes for *Episode in Palmetto*, Barrett Collection.
 20. Erskine Caldwell to Alfred Morang, Jan. 24, 1948, Morang Collection.
 21. The accompanying news stories reported that Caldwell's share of reprint royalties to that date was almost $150,000, an average of over $50,000 per year.

22. Erskine Caldwell, *Item*, New Orleans, La., June 10, 1948.

23. *Tucson Magazine*, July 1948, Erskine Caldwell Scrapbook #3, Caldwell Collection.

24. *With All My Might*, 221.

25. James Aswell to Erskine Caldwell, Jan. 21, 1949 (misdated, 1948), quoting from an undated review by Elsie Beauchamp in the New Orleans *Times Picayune*, Caldwell Collection.

26. *Baltimore Evening Sun*, June 21, 1948, Erskine Caldwell Scrapbook #4, Caldwell Collection.

27. *Beaumont Enterprise*, July 4, 1948, 6.

28. *Dallas Morning News*, Sunday, July 18, 1948, Sec. 4, p. 1.

29. Undated, undesignated clipping, Erskine Caldwell Scrapbook #4, Caldwell Collection.

30. Some of the young reporter's subsequent letters to Caldwell remain in his files. Internal evidence, combined with Virginia Caldwell's memory of the event, suggests that others were destroyed when Caldwell selectively burned a mass of his personal correspondence in 1967 before depositing the remainder in the Dartmouth Collection.

31. Harry Hansen, interview in (New York) *World Telegram*, Aug. 20, 1948.

32. Wilbur Needham, unidentified publication, Aug. 21, 1948, Erskine Caldwell Scrapbook #4, Caldwell Collection.

33. *San Francisco Chronicle*, Aug. 27, 1948, Erskine Caldwell Scrapbook #4, Caldwell Collection.

34. Letter reprinted in Harry Hansen's column, *World Telegram*, Sept. 3, 1948, Erskine Caldwell Scrapbook, Caldwell Collection.

35. Penguin-Mentor Books had incorporated on January 31, 1948, under the new logo of New American Library of World Literature. In the process, the Penguin insignia became the Signet line.

36. Donald Demarest to Erskine Caldwell, Sept. 8, 1948, and Sept. 16, 1948, Caldwell Collection.

37. Donald Demarest to Erskine Caldwell, Sept. 16, 1948, Caldwell Collection.

38. Irving Howe, *American Mercury*, Oct. 1948, 494–503.

Chapter 17

1. Erskine Caldwell to Alfred Morang, Jan. 5, 1949, Morang Collection.

2. *Charlotte* (N.C.) *Observer*, July 19, 1949, quoting a letter received at New American Library and most likely copied and forwarded to newspapers for publicity purposes.

3. Valentino Bompiani to Erskine Caldwell, July 4, 1979, Caldwell Collection.

4. Undated, undesignated newspaper clippings, Erskine Caldwell Scrapbook #2, Caldwell Collection.

5. Erskine Preston Caldwell, Jr., interview with author, Santa Monica, Calif., Nov. 30, 1978.

6. Cook, *Fiction of Poverty*, 180.

7. Undated notes, Box 4976K, Barrett Collection.

8. Mrs. Ann (Gordon) Lewis, interview with author, Lake Worth, Fla., Jan. 18, 1979.

9. Kelsey Guilfoil, *Chicago Tribune*, Oct. 1, 1950, 4, Erskine Caldwell Scrapbook #4, Caldwell Collection.

10. *Colorado Springs Evening Free Press*, June 2, 1950, Erskine Caldwell Scrapbook #4, Caldwell Collection.

11. *Time*, undated, 1950, Erskine Caldwell Scrapbook #4, Caldwell Collection.

12. *Virginia Spectator* 111 (Feb. 1950), 10, Barrett Collection.

13. ——— to Erskine Caldwell, Sept. 6, 1950, Caldwell Collection.

14. *Call It Experience*, 5.

15. Ibid., 12

16. Ibid., 230.

17. Ibid., 231.

18. Erskine Caldwell to Alfred Morang, Jan. 27, 1951, Morang Collection.

19. Erskine Caldwell to Alfred Morang, May 28, 1951, Morang Collection.

20. June Caldwell Martin, interview with author, Tucson, Ariz., Nov. 28, 1978.

21. Dabney Caldwell, interview with author, Jan. 12, 1979, Boston.

22. Ibid.

23. Victor Weybright to Erskine Caldwell, July 25, 1951, Caldwell Collection.

24. Matthew Treasurer, Almat Publishing, to Julius Weiss, Aug. 25, 1951, Caldwell Collection.

25. In *With All My Might* (220) Caldwell mistakenly cited 1949 as Lieber's departure year.

26. Alice McGown, Apr. 1952, Calif., fan-letter correspondence file, Caldwell Collection.

27. Virginia Moffett Fletcher to Erskine Caldwell, internally dated, Nov. 6, 1951, privately held in the Caldwell correspondence files (hereafter identified as privately held).

28. Erskine Caldwell to Virginia Moffett Fletcher, Nov. 9, 1951, privately held.

Part 5. "Outcast among the Literary Guys"

Chapter 18

1. *With All My Might*, 228.
2. ——— to Erskine Caldwell, Feb. 24, 1952, Houston, Caldwell Collection.
3. In Caldwell's *With All My Might* (44) he makes their initial Sarasota meetings and Virginia's eventual move to Phoenix seem purely circumstantial. Actually other internal evidence confirms that all were carefully arranged through the various letters and conversations the two of them shared during that period.
4. Virginia Caldwell, telephone interview with author, June 5, 1981.
5. Ibid.
6. Ibid.
7. Interview, Nov. 30, 1978, Scottsdale, Ariz.
8. Erskine Caldwell to Virginia Moffett Fletcher, Apr. 1952, privately held.
9. Edwin Seavor to Erskine Caldwell, Mar. 26, 1952, Caldwell Collection.
10. Erskine Caldwell to Virginia Moffett Fletcher, May 25, 1952, privately held.
11. Erskine Caldwell to June Caldwell, June 1, 1952, Caldwell Collection.
12. Jim Brown, interview with author, New York, Jan. 10, 1978.
13. Internally dated, 1952 memo, June Caldwell to herself and Erskine: Topics for discussion, 1952 correspondence files, Caldwell Collection.
14. Erskine Caldwell to Alfred Morang, Oct. 3, 1952, Morang Collection.
15. Jim Brown, interview with author, New York, Jan. 10, 1978.
16. Erskine Caldwell, *Love and Money* (Boston: Little, Brown and Co., 1954), 31.
17. Caldwell, *Love and Money*, 61.
18. Ibid., 62.
19. Ibid., 67.
20. Ibid., 62.
21. Ibid., 237.
22. Jim Aswell to Erskine Caldwell, Jan. 27, 1953, Caldwell Collection.
23. ——— to Erskine Caldwell, Caldwell Collection.
24. Betty Pustarfi, interview with author, Nov. 30, 1978, Thousand Oaks, Calif.
25. Jim Brown, interview with author, New York, Jan. 10, 1978.
26. Erskine Caldwell to June Caldwell, postcard, Feb. 20, 1953, Milano, Caldwell Collection.

27. These works later were to be published and titled "A Gift for Sue," "Girl with Figurines," "Kathy," "To the Chaparral," and "Soquots." The first three were retitled without Caldwell's permission and published respectively as "Just a Quick One" in *Cavalier*, "Figurines of Love" in *Esquire*, and "The Motive" in *Manhunt*. Subsequent to Caldwell's May issue, *Esquire* published the fourth story with its original title in its December issue. "Soquots" was not to be published until October of 1954. *Manhunt* (Oct.) again retitled, this time choosing "Second Cousin" as more appealing than the original "Soquots." These magazines variously paid Caldwell from $500 to $750 for each selection. *The Complete Short Stories* was to be a misleading title. At least twenty stories, excluding those so classified but excerpted from other, longer writings, were not to be included in the "complete" edition.

28. Stan Salmen to James Brown, enclosed with a June 22, 1953, letter from James Brown to Erskine Caldwell, Caldwell Collection. Always sensitive, Brown defended Caldwell against Salmen's oblique judgment with the excuse that Caldwell's reputation had lapsed through mismanagement, no fault of Caldwell's.

29. Caroline Preston Caldwell to Erskine Caldwell, internally dated, spring, 1953, Caldwell Collection.

30. Erskine Caldwell to Virginia Moffett Fletcher, privately held, Apr. 4, 1953.

31. Erskine Caldwell to Virginia Moffett Fletcher, privately held letters, Apr. 27, 1953; May 10, 1953; and May 24, 1953.

32. Later, after Virginia had assumed Caldwell's secretarial duties, a spilled filing cabinet required that she reassemble its contents; in the process she found and read the reporter's letters to him. The contents of those written after she thought she and Caldwell somewhat had stabilized their relationship especially gave her pause. They raised doubts greater than those she previously considered about the wisdom of her eventually marrying him—a proposal he seldom let her forget (Virginia Caldwell, telephone interview with author, June 5, 1981). What Virginia could not have realized at the time was that he might have counted her deferrals as rejections, in effect feeding an insecurity which sought comfort from other women.

33. ——— to Erskine Caldwell, June 9, 1953, June 15, 1953, Houston, Caldwell Collection.

34. ——— to Erskine Caldwell, Oct. 5, 1953, Caldwell Collection.

35. Virginia Caldwell, interview with author, Scottsdale, Ariz., Nov. 30, 1978.

36. Betty Pustarfi, interview with author, Thousand Oaks, Calif., Dec. 1, 1978.

Chapter 19

1. Foreword to *God's Little Acre* (New York: Modern Library, 1933), ix.
2. Devlin, *Erskine Caldwell*, 116.
3. Ibid.,116.
4. Cook, *Fiction of Poverty*, 170.
5. Devlin, *Erskine Caldwell*, 130.
6. Arnold, *Conversations*, 272.
7. Devlin, *Erskine Caldwell*, 39, 78.
8. Ibid., 87.
9. Ibid., 68.
10. Ibid., 55.
11. Ibid., 63.
12. June Caldwell to Erskine Caldwell, Mar. 1, 1954, Caldwell Collection.
13. Jim Brown to Erskine Caldwell, Aug. 18, 1954, Caldwell Collection.
14. Despite Caldwell's *Might* justification (229), there is no written evidence that June made this painful demand. All of her written correspondence suggested other alternatives, but not this one.
15. Alfred Morang to Erskine Caldwell, June 29, 1954, Caldwell Collection. Ironically and sadly, Morang's paintings are now highly valued and fetch prices in the thousands.
16. Jay Caldwell, interview with author, Santa Monica, Calif., June 1, 1978.
17. Caldwell's appointments for those two days, for Monday from 12:00 to 3:00 P.M. and on Tuesday from 4:30 to 8:30 had been crossed out, with "Kit" marginally bracketed for those periods. During the twelve years since their divorce, Kit had written Erskine only once. A year earlier she had forwarded a letter addressed to him which had arrived at the Darien address, enclosing with it a friendly account of her recent activities along with best wishes for his continued success. Otherwise the silence between them had remained unbroken.

    What makes the marginal "Kits" provocative is that Margaret happened to be in New York at the time, shooting a project on the Jesuits in America. Equally as suggestive is the fact that while Caldwell and Jay subsequently visited Dabney on one of his geological study sites near Millinocket, Maine, Kit had been close by, visiting her good friend, the Jesuit seismologist Daniel Linnehan, then on location for her feature (*Life*, Oct. 1, 1954, 131–48). Further, Caldwell had left Jay with Dabney one afternoon and night while he slept at the hotel.

    When asked twenty-five years later about the Kit marginalia and his and

Bourke-White's coincidental Maine visits, Caldwell looked genuinely perplexed, denying ever having seen Margaret after their divorce. Caldwell's characteristic behavior concerning his previous wives seems to support his claim. By avoiding them after the divorce and by seldom mentioning them again by name except when necessary, he appears to have forced them out of consciousness and his present experience. Moreover, Virginia's presence in New York might have argued against Caldwell's meeting with Kit.

18. Jim Brown to Erskine Caldwell, Apr. 24, 1954, Caldwell Collection.

19. Erskine Caldwell to Julius Weiss, Oct. 1, 1954, Caldwell Collection.

20. Jim Brown to Erskine Caldwell, Oct. 7, 1954, Caldwell Collection.

21. Jim Brown to Stan Salmen, Oct. 8, 1954, Caldwell Collection.

22. Jim Brown to Erskine Caldwell, Nov. 5, 1954, Caldwell Collection.

23. Stan Salmen to Erskine Caldwell, Dec. 24, 1954, Caldwell Collection.

24. Jim Brown, interview with author, Nov. 10, 1978, New York.

25. Less than six months later the American Legion was to aim its "Firing Line" salvo at Caldwell, repeating the State Department's questions and answering them with smear-tactic innuendos. It specifically devoted one-and-a-half pages of its three-page accusations to linking Caldwell directly to Maxim Lieber's supposed involvement with "the Soviet apparatus" ("Firing Line," May 15, 1955, Caldwell Collection).

26. R. B. Shipley, director, U.S. Passport Office, to Erskine Caldwell, Nov. 12, 1954, Caldwell Collection.

27. Erskine Caldwell to R. B. Shipley, Nov. 14, 1954, Caldwell Collection.

28. R. B. Shipley to Erskine Caldwell, telegram, Nov. 16, 1954, Caldwell Collection.

29. Erskine Caldwell to Mrs. I. S. Caldwell, Dec. 6(?), 1954, Phoenix, Caldwell Collection.

30. Ruth Carnall to Erskine Caldwell, Dec. 1, 1954; Sept. 22, 1955; Caldwell Collection.

31. Erskine Caldwell to June Caldwell, May 10, 1955, Caldwell Collection.

32. This citation and others supporting Pustarfi's impressions of Caldwell are gleaned from both her taped interview on December 1, 1978, in Thousand Oaks, Calif., and the copy of an undated summary forwarded to an unpublished biographer some eight years earlier. Since both are complementary and elaborate upon the same themes, they are, for economy's sake, presented as a single source from which the Pustarfi-related information has been drawn.

33. Arnold, *Conversations*, 303.

34. William Kimball to Erskine Caldwell, June 25, 1955, Caldwell Collection.
35. Jim Brown to Erskine Caldwell, Nov. 22, 1955, Caldwell Collection.
36. June Caldwell to Erskine Caldwell, internally dated, Nov. 55, Caldwell Collection.
37. ——— to Erskine Caldwell, Jan. 8, 1956, Caldwell Collection.

Chapter 20

1. Virginia Moffett Fletcher to Jay Caldwell, June,1956, Caldwell Collection.
2. Jim Brown to Erskine Caldwell, Dec. 3, 1956, Caldwell Collection.
3. Cook, *Fiction of Poverty*, 94, 95.
4. Ibid., 203, quoting from *Annette*, 5.
5. "Female Intuition, a Marital Pitfall," *San Francisco Examiner*, Aug. 19, 1963, Erskine Caldwell Scrapbook #5, Caldwell Collection.
6. Cook, *Fiction of Poverty*, 196.
7. Ibid., 202.
8. Virginia Caldwell, recorded telephone interview with author, June 5, 1981.
9. Ibid.
10. Virginia Caldwell to Caroline Preston Caldwell, July 31, 1963, San Francisco, Caldwell Collection. That Virginia seriously advanced such excuses to Mere at the same time Caldwell would have been writing his piece seems more than coincidental. Perhaps the consistency lies in Caldwell's undeviating claim that in writing, as in life, it is impossible to separate the comic from the tragic.
11. *Cavalier*, Dec. 1957.
12. *Cavalier*, Nov. 1957.
13. *Cavalier*, Dec. 1957.
14. Jim Brown to Erskine Caldwell, Oct. 7, 1957, Caldwell Collection.
15. Jim Brown to Erskine Caldwell, May 3, 1957, Caldwell Collection.
16. *Rocky Mountain News*, Denver, Mar. 15, 1957, Erskine Caldwell Scrapbook #5, Caldwell Collection.
17. By way of example, both in 1958 and 1959 the Caldwells spent more than half of each year "on the road." (Calculations figured from the daily logs Virginia maintained to record events.) Whatever writing Caldwell then accomplished had to be squeezed into those rigidly scheduled San Francisco writing days.
18. Virginia Caldwell to Caroline Preston Caldwell, June 20, 1957, Caldwell Collection.
19. Virginia Caldwell to Caroline Preston Caldwell, Nov. 5, 1957, Caldwell Collection.

20. Undated review, *San Francisco Chronicle*, Erskine Caldwell Scrapbook #5, Caldwell Collection.

21. Writing to Virginia, Mere apparently had observed that as an only child, Erskine had not had the experience of having to share. Virginia concurred: "You are right. He doesn't completely understand why you and I like to give." (Virginia Caldwell to Caroline Caldwell, Sept. 12, 1962, Caldwell Collection.)

22. *Westward Magazine*, June 1957, Erskine Caldwell Scrapbook #5.

23. Al Manuel to Victor Weybright, Apr. 16, 1958, Caldwell Collection.

24. Victor Weybright to Theodore Pratt, Dec. 8, 1958, Caldwell Collection.

25. Carvel Collins, *Atlantic Monthly*, July 1958, 57.

26. Caroline Preston Caldwell to Erskine Caldwell, May 25, 1958, Caldwell Collection.

27. Erskine Caldwell to Phil Yordan, May 21, 1958, Caldwell Collection.

28. Herb Caen, *San Francisco Chronicle*, Dec. 19, 1958, Erskine Caldwell Scrapbook #5.

29. Later in the year, as the gulf between Caldwell and Brown widened, he cautioned Caldwell against recklessly spending money on business-related ventures merely to avoid paying more money either to June or to the U.S. Treasury (Brown to Caldwell, May 5, 1959, Caldwell Collection). Possibly he likewise came to regard Caldwell's gratuitous payments as deductible ploys meant to deprive June rather than to reward loyalty and friendship.

30. Jim Brown to Erskine Caldwell, Jan. 19, 1958, Caldwell Collection.

31. Address delivered Jan. 28, 1958, undesignated clipping, Erskine Caldwell Scrapbook #5, Caldwell Collection.

32. Erskine Caldwell to Jim Brown, Feb. 17, 1958, Caldwell Collection.

33. Virginia Caldwell to Caroline Preston Caldwell, July 1, 1961, Caldwell Collection.

34. Unidentified newspaper article, Mar. 16, 1959, Erskine Caldwell Scrapbook #5, Caldwell Collection.

35. *London News Chronicle*, Mar. 15, 1959, Erskine Caldwell Scrapbook #5, Caldwell Collection.

36. Virginia Caldwell to Caroline Caldwell, Mar. 2, 1965, Caldwell Collection.

37. Erskine Caldwell, taped conversation with author, Scottsdale, Ariz., Nov. 30, 1978.

38. Virginia Caldwell to Caroline Caldwell, Apr. 2, 1959, Caldwell Collection.

39. Jim Brown to Erskine Caldwell, Apr. 9, 1960, Caldwell Collection.

40. Jim Brown to Erskine Caldwell, May 22, 1959, Caldwell Collection.

41. Erskine Caldwell to Jim Brown, May 24, 1959, Caldwell Collection.
42. The new additions, "A Visit to Mingus County," "The Story of Mahon," and "When You Think of Me," were included in that sketch collection issued as *When You Think of Me.*
43. Herb Caen, *San Francisco Chronicle*, undated clipping, Erskine Caldwell Scrapbook #5, Caldwell Collection. European critics proved no kinder. One believed that the novel read like a first draft version that twenty-five years earlier Caldwell "would have had the integrity to scrap." The Italian publisher Mondanari refused to issue it because Italian readers failed to appreciate Caldwell's later works as much as they did his earlier.
44. Jim Brown to Erskine Caldwell, May 5, 1959, Caldwell Collection.

Chapter 21

1. Virginia Caldwell to Caroline Caldwell, July 23, 1961, Caldwell Collection.
2. Virginia Caldwell to Caroline Caldwell, July 31, 1963, Caldwell Collection.
3. Virginia Caldwell to Caroline Caldwell, June 4, 1961, Rochester, Caldwell Collection.
4. Caldwell's version of the Little, Brown parting in *With All My Might* (268) is again fictionally embellished in his favor. Therein Jim Brown allegedly and impetuously severs the long-standing relationship without Caldwell's knowledge or participation. That conceit leaves him, as usual, a trusting and blameless victim of actions and forces beyond his control. This biographical account follows evidence gathered from correspondence between Caldwell and Brown and other written sources concerning the causes and consequences of the shift from Little, Brown to Farrar, Straus and Giroux.
5. *New York Herald Tribune*, Jan. 19, 1961, Erskine Caldwell Scrapbook #5, Caldwell Collection.
6. Erskine Caldwell to June Caldwell, June 20, 1961, Caldwell Collection.
7. Erskine Caldwell to Jim Brown, May 18, 1961, Caldwell Collection.
8. Virginia Caldwell to Jim Brown, May 28, 1961, Caldwell Collection.
9. Virginia Caldwell to Victor Weybright, May 11, 1962, Caldwell Collection.
10. John Farrar to Erskine Caldwell, unknown date, Caldwell Collection.
11. Roger Straus to Virginia Caldwell, June 10, 1962, NY, Caldwell Collection.
12. In one of his later letters urging Pix to practice financial expediency, Caldwell claimed that when his yearly income had dropped by 50 percent, he "got out of the high rent house at 831 Mason Street and moved to Rheem where it was 50% less." "Strictly economic and realistic," he testified (letter, Feb. 18, 1963, Orinda, Caldwell Collection). As usual Caldwell may have masked a complexity of motives behind a rational pose.

13. Quoted in Maggie Vaughn's "Through a Keyhole," *Daily American*, Nov. 14, 1963, Erskine Caldwell Scrapbook #5, Caldwell Collection.

14. Virginia Caldwell to Caroline Caldwell, May 22, 1967, Caldwell Collection.

15. Virginia Caldwell to Caroline Caldwell, May 21, 1966, Caldwell Collection.

16. Quoted in *Daily American*, Nov. 14, 1963, Erskine Caldwell Scrapbook #5, Caldwell Collection.

17. Virginia Caldwell to Caroline Caldwell, Sept. 12, 1962, Caldwell Collection.

18. Erskine Caldwell to Dabney Caldwell, Apr. 24, 1968, Caldwell Collection.

19. Virginia Caldwell to Caroline Caldwell, July 20, 1962, Caldwell Collection.

20. Virginia Caldwell to Caroline Caldwell, Sept. 8, 1961, Caldwell Collection.

21. Virginia Caldwell to Caroline Caldwell, May 23, 1961, Caldwell Collection.

22. Virginia Caldwell to Caroline Caldwell, Mar. 30, 1964, Caldwell Collection. Questioned about this scene some fifteen years later, Janet did not recall the specific incident from among the many others lost through time (Janet Gooding, taped interview with author, Beaufort, N.C., Jan. 22, 1979).

23. Virginia Caldwell to Caroline Caldwell, Feb. 15, 1965, Caldwell Collection.

24. Virginia Caldwell to Caroline Caldwell, Mar. 10, 1963, Caldwell Collection.

25. Quoted in *London Daily Express*, Oct. 18, 1962, Erskine Caldwell Scrapbook #5, Caldwell Collection. On other occasions Caldwell was to offer the same lament.

26. Jim Brown to Erskine Caldwell, letters, May 7, 1962, May 10, 1962, Caldwell Collection.

27. Roger Straus to Elizabeth Otis, Feb. 28, 1963, Caldwell Collection.

28. Roger Straus to Erskine Caldwell, telegram, Mar. 4, 1964, NY, Caldwell Collection.

29. Virginia Caldwell to Caroline Caldwell, Mar. 10, 1963, Caldwell Collection.

30. Virginia Caldwell to Caroline Caldwell, June 3, 1964, Caldwell Collection.

31. Although perpetually disdaining critics, Caldwell a few years earlier had spoken of them with bitter contempt: "[Critics] all hate me. I never get a fair deal from them. If they like my writing, I think they don't know what they are talking about. If they dislike me, they are just my enemies, that's all." (*London News Chronicle*, Apr. 15, 1959, Erskine Caldwell Scrapbook #5, Caldwell Collection).

32. Virginia Caldwell to Caroline Caldwell, June 3, 1964, Caldwell Collection.

33. Virginia Caldwell to Caroline Caldwell, June 3, 1964, Caldwell Collection.

34. If Caldwell did not purposely change place names in *Bisco*, he and Virginia may have explored some of the same places he and Margaret had visited for their *Faces* study. Photographs of people from Demopolis and Laurel, Mississippi, and Bastrop, Louisiana, had appeared there first. Almost thirty years later Caldwell used the same places as settings for the stories black people allegedly told through the vehicle of *Bisco*.

35. Virginia Caldwell to Caroline Caldwell, Mar. 30, 1964, Caldwell Collection.

36. Caldwell's total immersion in his work at that time awed Virginia: "I never cease to marvel at his remarkable self-discipline and ability to shut out everything not involved with the work of the moment. He says he will work hard until 1970 when he will have reached the retirement age of 65 and then he will take some time off, and I'm going to hold him to it." (Virginia Caldwell to Caroline Preston Caldwell, Mar. 30, 1964).

37. Virginia Caldwell to Caroline Caldwell, June 9, 1964, Caldwell Collection.

38. Virginia Caldwell to Caroline Caldwell, Oct. 17, 1964, Caldwell Collection.

39. Shirley Ann Grau, "The Southern Mind, Black/White," *Cosmopolitan*, Aug. 1964, 34–49.

40. Erskine Caldwell to Martin Luther King, Jr., Nov. 11, 1964, Caldwell Collection.

41. Caroline Caldwell to Erskine Caldwell and Virginia Caldwell, undated letter, 1964 correspondence files, Caldwell Collection.

42. In-house memo from Robert Giroux to Roger Straus, Aug. 12, 1964, Caldwell Collection.

43. C. L. Cooper, 48:39, May 1, 1965, Caldwell Collection.

44. *New Yorker*, May 22, 1965, 174–77.

45. Virginia Caldwell to Caroline Caldwell, Apr. 26, 1965, Caldwell Collection.

46. Arthur Thornhill to Erskine Caldwell, Mar. 16, 1964, Caldwell Collection.

47. Caldwell incorrectly claimed (*With All My Might*, 281) that Roger Straus "relentlessly drove" him to accept the lecture offer to help promote his books. Straus had instigated the single Missouri lecture; he had not urged this tour. Caldwell had negotiated this one through the Elizabeth Otis agency.

48. Virginia Caldwell to Caroline Caldwell, Feb. 21, 1965, Caldwell Collection.

49. Virginia Caldwell to Betty Pustarfi, July 4, 1965, Caldwell Collection.

50. Virginia Caldwell to Caroline Caldwell, Oct. 19, 1965, Caldwell Collection.
51. Roger Straus to Erskine Caldwell, Oct. 28, 1965, Caldwell Collection.
52. Erskine Caldwell to Roger Straus, Nov. 1, 1965, Caldwell Collection.
53. Roger Straus to Erskine Caldwell, Nov. 3, 1965, Caldwell Collection.
54. Elizabeth Otis to Erskine Caldwell, Nov. 15, 1965, Caldwell Collection.
55. Victor Weybright to Erskine Caldwell, Jan. 3, 1966, Caldwell Collection.
56. Erskine Caldwell to Dale Speer, May 21, 1966, Caldwell Collection.
57. Virginia Caldwell to Caroline Caldwell, Sept. 29, 1966, Caldwell Collection.

Chapter 22

1. Erskine Caldwell to Gyula Batari, July 7, 1966, Caldwell Collection.
2. Virginia Caldwell, interview with author, Hanover, N.H., Sept. 28, 1978.
3. Mary Maner, interview with author, Jan. 21, 1979, Louisville, Ga.
4. Mere had come to anticipate the visits, rides, and dinners among her few enjoyments. Stories that Mary Maner tells about her Aunt Carrie measure the limits of a few of those other pleasures which had become lifelong habits. Always one concerned about her appearance, she could touch the floor with both palms well into her eighties because she continued to maintain a regimen of exercises. But one of the less strenuous and more evident pleasures she enjoyed fixed upon her fascination with hats. Finding one she liked in the bargain basement of a store, she would return weekly until it had been reduced to its lowest price. Then her sense of frugality would overwhelm her. She would buy perhaps three or four identical hats because she "could not bear to pass up such a good bargain" (Mary Maner, interview with author, Louisville, Ga., Jan. 21, 1979).
5. Caroline Caldwell to Virginia Caldwell and Erskine Caldwell, July 15, 1964, Caldwell Collection.
6. Virginia Caldwell to Caroline Caldwell, Mar. 10, 1963, Caldwell Collection.
7. Virginia Caldwell to Caroline Caldwell, Oct. 3, 1961, Caldwell Collection.
8. Virginia Caldwell to Caroline Caldwell, Oct. 20, 1964, Caldwell Collection.
9. Ibid.
10. *Choice*, June 1970, 540.
11. Quoted in "Scene #8," an unidentified column written by one William G. Smith, Nov. 1, 1962, Erskine Caldwell Scrapbook #5, Caldwell Collection.
12. *Best Sellers*, Dec. 15, 1973, 423.
13. *Choice*, Mar. 1974, 86.

14. Erskine Caldwell to Victor Weybright, Feb. 10, 1969, Caldwell Collection.
15. Various skeptics regularly noted that such figures did not accurately reflect actual sales.They argued that paperback returns from distributors to publishers diminished the total number somewhat.Granting such nonverifiable claims, astute business practices would have allowed only a small percentage of such exceptions, certainly not enough to discredit Caldwell as much as they seemed to desire.
16. Erskine Caldwell, letters to author, May 5, 1974, and May 16, 1974. When finally the study tour did not materialize, Caldwell wrote to express disappointment but hoped that such an experience could be rearranged for future years (Erskine Caldwell, letter to author, Nov. 19, 1974).
17. The depth of Caldwell's appreciation for Korges's analysis must be inferred. After finally discovering and reading the pamphlet, Caldwell addressed two unacknowledged letters to the author in care of the University of Minnesota Press. Not until eight years later was he to learn that Korges had died in an auto accident shortly after completing his tribute to Caldwell and his writings.
18. Gilroy had expressed to Lathem a dissatisfaction with the completed work. Although he had felt his subject's depth and sensitivity, he had not been able to draw out Caldwell's character, feeling that despite all his efforts he had failed to portray the hidden, inner person (Ed Lathem to Erskine Caldwell, Jan. 11, 1972, Caldwell Collection).
19. Erskine Caldwell quoted by Virginia Caldwell, letter to author, Sept. 29, 1977.
20. *With All My Might*, 308.
21. Erskine Caldwell quoted in *The Palm Beach Post*, Section B, p. 8, Mar. 20, 1978.
22. Erskine Caldwell, interview with author, Scottsdale, Ariz., Nov. 29, 1978.
23. Virginia Caldwell, letter to author, Sept. 2, 1977.

Chapter 23
1. Virginia Caldwell, letter to author, Apr. 1, 1979, Scottsdale, Ariz.
2. Quoted in *The Palm Beach Post*, Section B, 8, Mar. 20, 1978.
3. Ibid.
4. Ibid.
5. Virginia Caldwell, letter to author, Dec. 30, 1978, Scottsdale, Ariz.
6. "Among Other Things," *San Francisco Chronicle*, Jan. 8, 1979.
7. Ibid.

8. Virginia Caldwell, letter to author, Apr. 23, 1981, Scottsdale, Ariz.

9. *The Palm Beach Post*, Section B, 8, Mar. 20, 1978.

10. *With All My Might*, 205, 239.

11. Ibid., 239

12. Virginia Caldwell, interview with author, Scottsdale, Ariz., Nov. 18, 1988.

13. Ibid.

14. Ibid.

15. Vicki Goldberg, letter to author, June 14, 1984, New York.

16. Richard Kelly and Marcia Pankake/1982, "Fifty Years Since *Tobacco Road*: An Interview with Erskine Caldwell," in Arnold, *Conversations*, 219.

17. Marilyn Dorn Staats, "Erskine Caldwell at Eighty-One: An Interview," in Arnold, *Conversations*, 263.

18. Arnold, *Conversations*, 289.

19. Ibid., 296.

20. Charles Truehart, "Erskine Caldwell: The Final Chapter," in Arnold, *Conversations*, 303.

21. Virginia Caldwell, interview with author, Nov. 18, 1988, Scottsdale, Ariz.

22. Dr. Bradley Gordon, interview with author, Nov. 19, 1988, Scottsdale, Ariz.

23. Virginia Caldwell, interview with author, Scottsdale, Ariz., Nov. 19, 1988.

24. Dr. Bradley Gordon, interview with author, Scottsdale, Ariz., Nov. 19, 1988.

25. Virginia Caldwell, interview with author, Scottsdale, Ariz., Nov. 19, 1988.

26. Ibid.

27. Ibid.

28. Ibid.

29. *With All My Might*, 330.

30. Virginia Caldwell, interview with author, Nov. 19, 1988, Scottsdale, Ariz.

Selected Bibliography

Archives

Erskine Caldwell Collection. Baker Library, Dartmouth College.

Alfred Morang Collection. Harry Elkins Widener Memorial Library, Harvard University.

Scribner's Archives. Scribner's Publishing Co., New York.

Margaret Bourke-White Collection. George Arendts Research Library, Syracuse University.

Special Collections Dept. University of Georgia Library, Athens.

C. Waller Barrett Collection. Alderman Library, University of Virginia, Charlottesville.

Works by Erskine Caldwell

Afternoons in Mid-America: Observations and Impressions. Illus. Virginia Caldwell. New York: Dodd, Mead & Co., 1976.

All Night Long. New York: Duell, Sloan & Pearce, 1942.

All-Out on the Road to Smolensk. New York: Duell, Sloan & Pearce, 1942.

American Earth. New York: Scribner's, 1931.

Annette. New York: The New American Library, 1973.

Around About America. New York: Farrar, Straus, 1964.

"The Art, Craft, and Personality of Writing," *Texas Quarterly* 7 (Spring 1964), 37–43.

The Bastard. New York: Heron Press, 1929.

Call It Experience: The Years of Learning How to Write. New York: Duell, Sloan & Pearce, 1951.

Claudelle Inglish. Boston: Little, Brown, 1958.

Close to Home. New York: Farrar, Straus & Cudahy, 1962.

Deep South: Memory and Observation. New York: Weybright & Talley, 1968.

The Earnshaw Neighborhood. New York: World Publishing Co., 1971.

Episode in Palmetto. New York: Duell, Sloan & Pearce, 1950.

Georgia Boy. New York: Duell, Sloan & Pearce, 1943.

"The Georgia Cracker." *Haldeman-Julius Monthly* 4 , no. 6 (Nov. 1926): 39–42.

God's Little Acre. New York: Viking Press, 1933.

Gretta. Boston: Little, Brown, 1955.

Gulf Coast Stories. Boston: Little, Brown, 1956.

A House in the Uplands. New York: Duell, Sloan & Pearce, 1946.

In Defense of Myself. Portland, Maine: Privately printed, 1929.

In Search of Bisco. New York: Farrar, Straus & Giroux, 1965.

Introduction to *American Earth.* New York: Duell, Sloan & Pearce, 1950. Rpt. in
    MacDonald, ed., *Critical Essays on Erskine Caldwell.*

Introduction to *God's Little Acre.* New York: The Modern Library, Inc. 1934.

Introduction to *God's Little Acre.* New York: Duell, Sloan & Pearce, 1949. Rpt. in
    MacDonald, ed., *Critical Essays on Erskine Caldwell.*

Introduction to *A House in the Uplands.* New York: Duell, Sloan & Pearce, 1949.
    Rpt. in MacDonald, ed., *Critical Essays on Erskine Caldwell.*

Introduction to *Kneel to the Rising Sun.* New York: Duell, Sloan & Pearce, 1951.
    Rpt. in MacDonald, ed., *Critical Essays on Erskine Caldwell.*

Introduction to *Tobacco Road.* New York: Duell, Sloan & Pearce, 1948. Rpt. in
    MacDonald, ed., *Critical Essays on Erskine Caldwell.*

Jackpot: The Short Stories of Erskine Caldwell. New York: Duell, Sloan & Pearce,
    1940.

Jenny by Nature. New York: Farrar, Straus & Cudahy, 1961.

Journeyman. New York: Viking Press, 1935.

Kneel to the Rising Sun and Other Stories. New York: Viking Press, 1935.

A Lamp for Nightfall. New York: Duell, Sloan & Pearce, 1952.

The Last Night of Summer. New York: Farrar, Straus, 1963.

Love and Money. New York: Duell, Sloan & Pearce, 1954.

Miss Mamma Aimee. New York: New American Library, 1967.

"Mr. Caldwell Protests." In MacDonald, ed., *Critical Essays on Erskine Cald-
    well,* 32-33.

Moscow Under Fire: A Wartime Diary. London: Hutchinson, 1942.

A Place Called Estherville. New York: Duell, Sloan & Pearce, 1949.

Poor Fool. New York: Rariora Press, 1930.

The Sacrilege of Alan Kent. Portland, Maine: Falmouth Book House, 1936.

Some American People. New York: McBride, 1935.

Southways. New York: Viking Press, 1938.

Summertime Island. New York: World Publishing Co., 1968.

The Sure Hand of God. New York: Duell, Sloan & Pearce, 1947.

This Very Earth. New York: Duell, Sloan & Pearce, 1948.

Tobacco Road. New York: Scribner's, 1932.
Tragic Ground. New York: Duell, Sloan & Pearce, 1944.
Trouble in July. New York: Duell, Sloan & Pearce, 1940.
We Are the Living. New York: Viking Press, 1933.
The Weather Shelter. New York: World Publishing Co., 1969.
With All My Might. Atlanta: Peachtree Publishers, Ltd., 1987.
Writing in America. New York: Phaedra, 1967.

With Margaret Bourke-White

North of the Danube. New York: Viking Press, 1939.
Russia at War. London: Hutchinson, 1942.
Say, Is This the U.S.A. New York: Duell, Sloan & Pearce, 1941.
You Have Seen Their Faces. New York: Viking Press, 1937.

Other Sources

Arnold, Edwin T., ed. *Conversations with Erskine Caldwell.* Jackson, Miss.:
    Univ. Press of Mississippi, 1988.
————, ed. *Erskine Caldwell Reconsidered.* Jackson: Univ. Press of Mississippi,
    1990.
————. "Interview with Virginia Caldwell." In *Erskine Caldwell Reconsidered.*
Bailey, Kenneth K. *Southern White Protestantism in the Twentieth Century.* New
    York: Harper & Row, 1964.
Bandry, Michael. "Erskine Caldwell's Civilization's Freaks." *Pembroke Maga-*
    zine 11 (1979), 76–82.
Baumbach, Jonathan. *The Landscape of Nightmare: Studies in the Contemporary*
    American Novel. New York: New York Univ. Press, 1965.
Beach, Joseph Warren. *American Fiction: 1920–1940.* New York: Macmillan &
    Co., 1941.
Benedict, Stewart H. "Gallic Light on Erskine Caldwell." In MacDonald, ed.,
    Critical Essays on Erskine Caldwell, 255–59.
Becker, Howard. "Sacred and Secular Societies Considered with Reference
    to Folk-State and Similar Classifications," *Social Forces* 28 (May 1950),
    361–78.
Bode, Carl. In MacDonald, ed., *Critical Essays on Erskine Caldwell,* 246–48.
Bourke-White, Margaret. *Portrait of Myself.* New York: Simon & Schuster, 1963.
Bowen, Robert O. "Hope vs. Despair in the New Gothic Novel." *Renascence* 13
    (Winter 1961), 47–52.

Brooks, Cleanth. "Regionalism in American Literature." *The Journal of Southern History* 26 (Feb. 1960), 35–43.

Brunner, Edmund. *Church Life in the Rural South*. New York: Negro Univ. Press, 1923.

Burke, Kenneth. "Caldwell: Maker of Grotesques." In MacDonald, ed., *Critical Essays on Erskine Caldwell*, 167–73.

Brinkmeyer, Robert H. "Is That You in the Mirror, Jeeter?: The Reader and Tobacco Road." *Pembroke Magazine* 11 (1979), 47–50.

Buck, P. H. "Poor Whites of the Old South," *American Historical Review* 25 (Oct. 1924), 541–48.

Burke, Kenneth. "Caldwell: Maker of Grotesques." In *Psychoanalysis and American Fiction*, edited by Irving Malin. New York: Dutton, 1965.

"Caldwell's Collapse." In MacDonald, ed., *Critical Essays on Erskine Caldwell*, 86–87.

Canby, Henry Seidel. Introd. to *The Pocket Book of Erskine Caldwell Stories*. Rpt. In MacDonald, ed., *Critical Essays on Erskine Caldwell*, 214–20.

Cantwell, Robert. "Caldwell's Characters: Why Don't They Leave," *Georgia Review* 11 (Spring 1957), 252–64.

Carmichael, Peter A. "Jeeter Lester, Agrarian Par Excellence," *Sewanee Review* 48 (1940), 21–29.

Cash, W. J. *The Mind of the South*. New York: A. A. Knopf, 1941.

Collins, Carvel. "Erskine Caldwell at Work: A Conversation with Carvel Collins." *Atlantic* 202 (July 1958), 21–27.

Comsa, Ioan. "Caldwell's Stories: Common Reader Response, Analysis and Appreciation at Home and Abroad." *Pembroke Magazine* 11 (1979), 51–58.

Cook, Sylvia Jenkins. "Caldwell's Fiction: Growing Towards Trash?" *Southern Quarterly* 27 (1989), 49–58.

———. *Erskine Caldwell and the Fiction of Poverty*. Baton Rouge, La.: Louisiana State Univ. Press, 1991.

———. "Erskine Caldwell and the Literary Left Wing." In MacDonald, ed., *Critical Essays on Erskine Caldwell*, 361–69.

———. *From Tobacco Road to Route 66: The Southern Poor White in Fiction*. Chapel Hill: Univ. of North Carolina Press, 1976.

"Cop Reviews *God's Little Acre* in St. Paul: Prosecutor Bans It," *Publishers' World* 149 (June 1, 1946), 2907.

Couch, William T., ed. *Culture in the South*. Chapel Hill: Univ. of North Carolina Press, 1934.

Cowley, Malcolm. *And I Worked at the Writer's Trade.* New York: Viking Press, 1978.

———. *The Dream of the Golden Mountains: Remembering the 1930's.* New York: Viking Press, 1980.

———. "Erskine Caldwell's Magic." *Pembroke Magazine* 11 (1979), 6–7.

———. "The Two Erskine Caldwells." *New Republic,* Nov. 6, 1944, 599–600.

Cross, Carlyle. *Erskine Caldwell as a Southern Writer.* Ph.D. diss., Univ. of Georgia, 1967.

Daniels, Jonathan. "Happy Birthday, Dear Erskine! . . . and Many Happy Returns, Georgia Cracker!" *Pembroke Magazine* 11 (1979), 183–85.

Davidson, Donald. "Erskine Caldwell's Picture Book." In McDonald, ed., *Critical Essays on Erskine Caldwell,* 59–67.

Devlin, James E. *Erskine Caldwell.* Boston: Twayne Publishers, 1984.

Frohock, W. M. "Erskine Caldwell: Sentimental Gentleman from Georgia." In MacDonald, ed., *Critical Essays on Erskine Caldwell,* 201–13.

———. *The Novel of Violence in America.* Dallas: Southern Methodist Univ. Press, 1950.

Godden, Richard L. "Does Anybody Live in There? Character and Representative, Type and Cartoon in Caldwell's *Trouble in July.*" *Pembroke Magazine* 11 (1979), 102–12.

Gossett, Louise Y. *Violence in Recent Southern Fiction.* Durham: Duke Univ. Press, 1965.

Goldberg, Vicki. *Margaret Bourke-White: A Biography.* New York: Harper & Row, 1986.

Gwynn, Frederick L., and Joseph L. Blotner, eds. *Faulkner in the University.* Charlottesville: Univ. of Virginia Press, 1954.

Harper, Roland M. "Distribution of Illiteracy in Georgia," *High School Quarterly* 7 (July 1919), 254–62.

Hersey, John. "Tribute to Erskine Caldwell." In Arnold, ed., *Erskine Caldwell Reconsidered.*

Hoag, Ronald Wesley. "Canonize Caldwell's *Georgia Boy*: A Case for Resurrection." In Arnold, ed., *Erskine Caldwell Reconsidered. .*

———, and Elizabeth Pell Broadwell. "Erskine Caldwell on Southern Realism." *Mississippi Quarterly* 36 (1983), 577–84.

Holman, C. Hugh. "Detached Laughter in the South." In *Comic Relief: Humor in Contemporary American Literature.* Edited by Sarah Blacher Cohen. Urbana: Univ. of Illinois Press, 1978.

Howard, William L. "Caldwell on Stage and Screen." In Arnold, ed., *Erskine Caldwell Reconsidered.*

Iosifescu, Silvian. "The Comic and the Tragic (in Caldwell)." *Pembroke Magazine* 11 (1979), 178–80.

Klevar, Harvey L. "Caldwell's Women." In Arnold, ed., *Erskine Caldwell Reconsidered.*

———. "Interview with Helen Caldwell Cushman." In Arnold, ed., *Erskine Caldwell Reconsidered.*

———. "Some Things Holy in a Godforsaken Land." *Pembroke Magazine* 11 (1979), 65–76.

Kitajima, Fujisato. "Caldwell in Japan." In Arnold, ed., *Erskine Caldwell Reconsidered.*

Korges, James. *Erskine Caldwell.* Univ. of Minnesota Pamphlet Series. Minneapolis: Univ. of Minnesota Press, 1969.

Kubie, Laurence S., M.D. *"God's Little Acre:* An Analysis." *Saturday Review of Literature* 11 (Nov. 24, 1934), 305–6.

Krutch, Joseph Wood. "The Case of Erskine Caldwell." *The Nation,* Feb. 12, 1938, 190.

Lelchuk, Alan, and Robin White. "An Interview With Erskine Caldwell," *Per/Se* 2 (Spring 1967), 11–20.

"Life Visits the Erskine Caldwells." *Life,* Oct. 1, 1945, 134–37.

MacDonald, Scott. "An Evaluative Check-List of Erskine Caldwell's Short Fiction." In MacDonald, ed., *Critical Essays on Erskine Caldwell,* 342–60.

———. "Enough Good Reasons for Reading, Studying and Teaching Erskine Caldwell." *Pembroke Magazine* 11 (1979), 7–18.

———. "Repetition as Technique in the Short Stories of Erskine Caldwell." In MacDonald, ed., *Critical Essays on Erskine Caldwell,* 330–41.

———, ed. *Critical Essays on Erskine Caldwell.* Boston: G. K. Hall & Co., 1981.

McIlwaine, Shields. *The Southern Poor White: From Lubberland to Tobacco Road.* Norman: Univ. of Oklahoma Press, 1939.

McKinney, John C., and Edgar T. Thompson, eds. *The South in Continuity and Change.* Durham, N.C.: Duke Univ. Press, 1965.

Maclachen, John M. "Folk and Culture in the Novels of Erskine Caldwell." *Southern Folklore Quarterly* 11 (Jan. 1945), 93–101.

Marshall, Margaret. "Caldwell Comes a Cropper." *The Nation,* Dec. 26, 1942, 720–22.

Martin, Jay. "Erskine Caldwell's Singular Devotions." In *A Question of Quality:*

Popularity and Value in Modern Creative Writing. Edited by Louis Filler. Bowling Green, Ohio: Bowling Green Univ., Popular Press, 1976.

Noble, Donald R. "Erskine Caldwell: A Biographical Sketch." *Pembroke Magazine* 11 (1979), 165–78.

Owen, Guy. *"The Bogus Ones*: A Lost Erskine Caldwell Novel." *Southern Literary Journal* 11 (1978), 32–39.

————. "Erskine Caldwell and D. H. Lawrence." *Pembroke Magazine* 11 (1979), 18–21.

————. "Erskine Caldwell's Unpublished Poems." *South Atlantic Bulletin* 43 (1978), 53–57.

Owsley, Frank L. *Plain Folk of the Old South.* Baton Rouge: Louisiana State Univ. Press, 1949.

Peden, William. "Caldwell Country Revisited: Some Rambling Comments." *Pembroke Magazine* 11 (1979), 99–102.

Pugh, David. "Reading Caldwell Today: Perceiving Craft and Culture." *Pembroke Magazine* 11 (1979), 122–130.

Ransom, John Crowe, et al. *I'll Take My Stand.* New York: Harper, 1930.

Rascoe, Burton. "Caldwell Lynches Two Negroes." In MacDonald, ed., *Critical Essays on Erskine Caldwell,* 74–78.

Rubin, Louis D., Jr. *The Curious Death of the Novel: Essays in American Literature.* Baton Rouge: Louisiana State Univ. Press, 1967.

————. *The Faraway Country: Writers of the Modern South.* Seattle: Univ. of Washington Press, 1963.

————. "The Historical Image in Modern Southern Writing." *Journal of Southern History,* 22 (May 1956), 147–66.

————, ed. *Southern Renascence: The Literature of the Modern South.* Baltimore: Johns Hopkins Univ. Press, 1953.

Rundus, R.J. "A 'World Indispensable'?—Caldwell, the Critics, and the Shaping of One Man's Literary History." *Pembroke Magazine* 11 (1979), 140–54.

Sale, Richard B. "An Interview in Florida with Erskine Caldwell." In MacDonald, ed., *Critical Essays on Erskine Caldwell,* 279–93.

Schwartz, Edward P. "Caldwell 'On-the-Road' and Censorship Interlude." *Pembroke Magazine* 11 (1979), 85–86.

Simkins, Francis B. *The Everlasting South.* Baton Rouge: Louisiana State Univ. Press, 1963.

Smoller, Sanford. "Erskine Caldwell—A Recaptured Past." *Pembroke Magazine* 11 (1979), 155–63.

Staats, Marilyn Dorn. "Erskine Caldwell at Eighty-One: An Interview." *Arizona Quarterly* 41 (1985), 247–57.

Sutton, William A. *Black Like It Is/Was: Erskine Caldwell's Treatment of Racial Themes.* Metuchen, N.J.: Scarecrow Press, 1974.

Terrie, Henry. "Caldwell at Dartmouth." In Arnold, *Erskine Caldwell Reconsidered.*

———. "Erskine Caldwell's *Journeyman:* Comedy as Redemption." *Pembroke Magazine* 11(1979), 21–30.

Tharpe, Jac. L. *Interview with Mr. Erskine Caldwell.* vol. 13, Mississippi Oral History Program of the Univ. of Southern Mississippi, Hattiesburg, 1973.

Tindall, George. *The Emergence of the New South, 1913–1945.* Baton Rouge: Louisiana State Univ. Press, 1967.

Van Doren, Carl. "Made in America: Erskine Caldwell." In MacDonald, ed., *Critical Essays on Erskine Caldwell,* 155–58.

Wade, Donald. "Sweet Are the Uses of Degeneracy." *Southern Review* 1 (1935–36), 449–66.

Wagenknecht, Edward. *Cavalcade of the American Novel.* New York: Holt, 1952.

Walls, Dwayne E. "Caldwell's Realism." *Pembroke Magazine* 11 (1979), 130–32.

Weybright, Victor. "Georgia Boy—A Recollection from the Inner Sanctum." *Pembroke Magazine* 11 (1979), 115–20.

Woodward, C. Vann. *The Burden of Southern History.* Baton Rouge: Louisiana State Univ. Press, 1960.

———. *Origins of the New South, 1877–1913.* Baton Rouge: Louisiana State Univ., 1951.

Index

Hibbs, Ralph, 416
Hibbs, Virginia Caldwell. *See* Caldwell, Virginia
Hollywood, Calif., 97–98, 129–41
Home Town (Anderson), 232
Hound and Horn, 96
A House in the Uplands (Caldwell), 262, 268
Houston Post, 69
Howard, Amplus, 32
Howe, Irving, 284–85
Hull, Henry, 146, 150, 156–57, 161, 250
Hungary, Caldwell in, 210
Hutchinson and Company, 239

In Search of Bisco (Caldwell), 13, 76, 376, 378–79
In the Shadow of the Steeple (Deep South) (Caldwell), 381–82, 384
Indian Rocks, Fla., 124
"Indian Summer" (Caldwell), 27
"Inspiration for Greatness" (Caldwell), 87
Italy, Caldwell in, 287

Jackpot compendium, 232, 399; reviews of, 235–36
Jagger, Dean, 147, 150
Jefferson Reporter, 34
Jenny by Nature (Caldwell), 364, 365
"Joe Craddock's Old Woman" (Caldwell), 83
John Reed Club, 135
"John the Indian and George Hopkins" (Caldwell), 87, 96
Johns, Richard, 87, 88, 103, 106
Johnson, June. *See* Caldwell, June Johnson
Journeyman (Caldwell), 127, 142, 157–58, 260, 433n.4; decision to

publish, 142–44, 146–47 150, 152–53; dramatization of, 203, 205; reviews of, 157
Joyce, James, 280

Kansas Writer's Conference, 278, 279–80
Kearney, Patrick, 128
Kelly, Edward J., 161
Keysville, Ga., 177
King, Martin Luther, Jr., 377, 385
Kirkland, Jack, 113, 127, 128, 142, 144, 146
Kneel to the Rising Sun (Caldwell collection),157, 158–59
"Kneel to the Rising Sun" (Caldwell short story), 145, 273
Knowlton, Isabel, 197, 198
Korges, James, xv, 392, 461n.17
Kresge's, 56, 424n.9
Kreymborg, Alfred, 83
Kronenberger, Louis, 124–25
Krutch, Joseph Wood, 145, 205, 214

A Lamp for Nightfall (Autumn Hill) (Caldwell), 306–7, 430n.35
Landon, Michael, 345
Lane, Rose Wilder, 135
Lange, Dorothea, 399
Lannigan, Helen. *See* Caldwell, Helen Lannigan
Lannigan, "Pop," 59–61
The Last Night of Summer (Caldwell), 374
Lathem, Edward Connery, 392, 393, 395, 406, 461n.18
Lawrence, D. H., 75, 95, 280
Lehigh University, 56
Let the Hurricane Roar (Lane), 135
Lewin, David, 366
Lewis, Eddie, 278, 279, 351, 365